JACK KEROUAC

JACK KEROUAC

COLLECTED POEMS

Marilène Phipps-Kettlewell, *editor*

THE LIBRARY OF AMERICA

Contents

Jack Kerouac, in His Own Words

by Marilène Phipps-Kettlewell

"America is a permissible dream . . ."[1]

"Merrily we roll along / Dee de lee dee doo doo doo / Merrily merrily all the day . . . Yes, life woulda been / a mistake without music . . ."[2]

"I love jazz, I / love North Carolina, I / love Socialism. I'm sel- / fish, I'm irresponsible, / I'm weak, I'm afraid. I'm / Jack Kerouac the poet, the / seaman, the scholar, the / laborer, the newspaperman, / the lover, the athlete, / the flyer, the Lowellian?"[3]

"I am a poet / & / here is my poem / Watch how fancy I write / Skeletons of Compassion . . ."[4]

"Inside, Inside Me, / I'se free / Free as the bee / Inside he. / Lord have a mercy . . ."[5]

"I am a hoodlum and a saint."[6]

2—Do You Want to Play?

"Ling the long Chinese peeswallower, / a lad like ye, / Laid his hand on Garty's knee / and paid the pree— / Shong the mong of anisfore, / Maharajah / Dusty, kinked the from of Jaidphur / from the Konk mirror free / So all Bojangles Banghard / had to do / Was roil his rolly tooty / mot the polyong, / And if you knew what I meant / you would say / You disgust me—"[7]

3—With a Poet

"When I was born in Tathagatas / Assembled from all universes / And chanted in my ear . . . And I Void Listened / To the Eternal Return . . ."[8]

"The songs that erupt / Are gist of the poesy, / Come by themselves, hark, / Stark as prisoners in a cave / Let out to sunlight, ragged / And beautiful when you look close / And see underneath the beards . . ."[9]

"Well roofed pleasant little hut, / screened from winds: / That's all I need. Foursquare / The image of the Buddha in my brain, / Drawing from the countryside . . ."[10]

"I'm an idealist / who has outgrown / my idealism / I have nothing to do / the rest of my life / but do it / and the rest of my life / to do it."[11]

"I believe in order, tenderness and piety."[12]

"I'd better be a poet / or lay down dead."[13]

4—Who Had a Mission

"We've all been sent / On a mission / to conquer the desert . . ."[14]

"Emancipate the human masses / Of this world from slavery to life / And death, by abolishing death / and exterminating birth—"[15]

"How often! how many million times I came into the world, and was befouled on / earth, until I was finally justified in heaven . . . and went to my Nirvana, but made the Vow / to return . . . in order to spread the Dharma and each time a / little closer to perfection as my Karma was worked out . . ."[16]

"Every one of us Roman Circus / sacrifices, every one, / Returned for payment / In America Madhouse."[17]

5—A Lonesome, Generous Heart

"O live quietly; live to love / Everybody. / Be devout under trees / At midnight on the ground. / No hope in a room / of dispelling the gloom / that's assembled / Since Moses / . . . Forgive everyone for yr own sins / And be sure to tell them / You love them which you do."[18]

"All the houses of Richmond Hill in the still night—a great camp of ignorance, / each family inside thinking itself different from the others—their hatreds, dark . . ."[19]

"So the Living Loathe the Dead, / themselves— / So forgive, reassure, pat, protect, / and purify them / whatever way is best."[20]

"It's the only thing you got free, / the Mind."[21]

"Importunate fool that I was, / I raved to fight Saviors."[22]

6—A Dialogue With Death

"I caught a cold / From the sun / When they tore my heart out / At the top of the pyramid."[23]

"Dead and dont know it . . . The idea of living is the same / as the idea of death."[24]

They let the zombies out—the Haitian vodou priest, Rose-En-Fer, had died. This was Haiti in the seventies. His wife, a mambo, put a notice in the paper. She asked that all the bourgeois of Pétion-Ville who kept zombies at her husband's, come and claim them. Nobody came. She let the zombies out.

The zombies' odd beauty was suddenly exposed—the dead not dead, the undead, held outside of life, like poetry unread, poems in books kept shut.

Tall and short, slow and uncomprehending, but gathering speed, they walked down the Montroui road by the ocean whose internal rhythm had accompanied their grave-like existence up to now. They were people left for dead—they had been made to swallow the herb potion that induces a deathlike state, the ancestral secret mixture used to turn a man into a zombie.

One wonders, what are the visions of the undead? What are the emotions of Baudelaire's albatross, this great poet-like bird, majestic in his flight, but awkward on the ground—his large, large wings hindering his steps? What are the dreams of the poet left in an open tomb of the spirit near the sea?

". . . I would work my way on tramp steamers, I would drink with the crew in every port, I would moil amid the reeking masses of the Orient, poking my nose into mysterious doorways and antique shops; I'd mush to the Arctic, I'd tramp though the jungles of Brazil and Africa, I'd have women in Capetown, in Singapore, in Port Said, in Istanbul, in St. Petersburg, in San Francisco, in Havana, in Liverpool, in Shanghai, in Morocco, in Sydney, in Sumatra . . . I'd lope along on strawberry roans through the stifling dried wastes of Arizona, I'd stride along little roads in France, in England, and especially in Scotland . . . I'd lie lolling among the green hills of Ireland; I'd yawn whole afternoons away along the Mississippi, in New Orleans; I'd . . . but Oh this could go on all night."[25]

Zombies slipped out of their long-suffering darkness to redis-cover sunlight, people-poems, once standing tall, once loved, but imperfectly, then betrayed, forgotten. Zombies walked, having endured. Curiosity brought out crowds. People drove slowly, a near crawl really, along the road under the vast open sky of Montrouis to espy the unearthed and newly exposed.

It is a vulnerable, lonely moment when one is brought to

bear the scrutiny of strangers, when one lays bare features long ignored, beauty long devalued, in a bold attempt to be properly seen, read, understood, explained, argued for, as if the extraordinary and the disquieting could truly delight, be comfortable and be treasured, as if immortality could be correctly apprehended, deservedly granted, especially when Death himself is here like the active trickster in indigenous religions, involved in mock-defiant, sacrilegious dances of profanity within a theater that combines the tragic with the absurd.

Poets are made to contain, not carry. Yet they endure their fate as sacrificial zombies or lambs of God, taking on the pain of the world: "And when they saw me / Rowin my sailin canoe / Across the lake of dreams / In the Lotus Valley Swamp, / And arrested me / For the size / Of my heart, / T's' then I decided / 'Don't Come Back' / They'll eat your heart alive / Every time."[26]

7—Yet Was Gripped by a Fear of Death

"I saw my father die, / I saw my brother die, / I saw my mother die / my mother my mother my mother / inside me— / Saw the pear trees die, / the grapes, pearls, penny trees—"[27]

"The critical mass collapses / And like a tumbled Sand castle / When the tide of disintegration / And its conception rise, / Flops into the sea softmaw . . ."[28]

"My father in downtown red / Walked around like a shadow / Of ink black, with hat, nodding, / In the immemorial lights of my dreams . . . Is the image of Ignorant Man / Hurrying to his destiny which is Death / Even though he knows it."[29]

". . . in 1946, the year when my father died I was insane and played cardgame baseball games in my room, till thanksgiving. At Thanksgiving I went mad and began trembling all over and leaned out the window anxiously waiting for a friend to arrive. He never came . . ."[30]

". . . they slide / From Europe to Ukraine / And down the Belgian Rivers, / And blankly in the void / Swim back to spawn / And die with longfaced pouts / —poor fish."[31]

". . . the gray / Immense morning I was conceived i the womb, / And the red gory afternoon delivered therefrom. / Wow. I could sing you hounds / make you bell howl packs, / Zounds, I'd-a lived & lived laughing / as a child / If somebody coulda told me / it was unreal: / I was scared. The dark / was full of phantoms / come from the other side of death / to claim the hearts / Of Sacrificial little children . . ."[32]

"Then what am I to do / Beyond writing this instructing / Poesy, ride a magic carpet / Of self ecstasy, or wait / For death like the children/ In the Funeral Street after / The black bus has departed— / Or—what?"[33]

". . . suffer and die, / Gritting my teeth awhile / Till it's all over."[34]

8—Struggled with the Meaning of Life

"Merde and misery, / I'm completely in pain / Waiting without mercy / For the worst to happen. / I'm completely at a loss . . ."[35]

"If you only could hold / what you know / As you know it forever, / instead-a / Moving from griefy to griefy, / lament to lament, / Groan, and have to come out / and smile . . ."[36]

"How solid our ignorance— / how empty our substance / and the conscience / keeps bleeding . . ."[37]

"*Poor!* I wish I was free / of that slaving meat wheel / and safe in heaven dead."[38]

"Why was I born with a body, / Why do I have this painful hive / Of hope-of-honey-milk yet bane / Of bitterest reward, as if, to wish / for flesh was sin alone itself—?"[39]

"I'm no apprentice / When it comes to remembering / The eternity of suffering . . ."[40]

"Love's multitudinous boneyard / of decay . . ."[41]

"Ah I wish I could fight out / Of this net of mistakes / And anxieties among others / Who wait in my silence / Till I end up my work / Which never began and / Never will end—"[42]

"I keep falling in love / with my mother, / I don't want to hurt her / —Of all people to hurt. / . . . the Doll she is, / The doll-like way / she stands / Bowlegged in my dreams, / Waiting to serve me . . ."[43]

"A Baby in Pain: / tell the proud seminal mother / how many more of that she wants / to satisfy her fertile ego / and how many more babies / crying in the night, angry screech, / knowing that their flesh is on the block / of death the hungry butcher."[44]

"Myself, the dharma is slipping away from my consciousness

and I cant think of anything to say about it any more . . . Cant see the purpose of human or terrestrial or any kinda life without heaven to reward the poor suffering fucks. The Buddhist notion that Ignorance caused the world leaves me cold now, because I feel the presence of angels."[45]

"Buddhism is a big bomb on the head / and it hurts / After which comes I know / the milky fliss, / fluff, soft AW eternities, / skyrockets, / snowflakes, hope revealed, / snow / Gerard, Pa, lamb, / Sax, / Heaven, you, me."[46]

9—*Gained Inner Quiet through a Denial of Death*

Jack Kerouac's measured, guilt-ridden, indignant, defeating dance with death started in childhood: "When I was 4 my brother Gerard was 9, at his deathbed several nuns took down his last words about Heaven and went away with the notes, which I've never seen. They said he was a little saint."[47]

Gabrielle, mother of the two boys, wished that Jack had died instead of Gerard. She would reproach him throughout his life for being alive instead of Gerard.

Jack was twenty-one when his best friend Sebastian Sampas, also twenty-one, died at war.

Jack was twenty-four when Leon, his father, died in his arms of stomach cancer at fifty-six.

Jack was forty-two when his sister Caroline died of a heart attack at forty-four—her husband had just called her to say he was leaving her for another woman.

Jack was forty-seven when he died of alcoholism in 1969. March 12th, 1922 had been his date of birth.

Gabrielle survived her husband and her three children.

Stella Sampas, Jack's wife, had taken care of him with great selflessness until the end. She continued to take care of Jack's mother who died of a series of strokes in 1973, four years after Jack. Stella stayed on in their St. Petersburg house, Florida, until she died in 1990, twenty-one years after Jack.

The ghost of Gerard turned curse and muse for Jack. Both were overwhelming. He sought relief in a spirituality that denies death. The ardent poet-son, filled with a will to live, sought his freedom in a language that defies.

He was inhabited by an indigenous god of death, a trickster come out of a spiritual but savage inner wilderness. This trickster was intent on whirling his fury over the earth, brandishing an overactive penis, mocking and desecrating, spouting profanity, dancing, smoking and drinking to excess, until he is finally able to quiet down, settle himself on a rickety chair, take someone's hands into his own, to look into their open palms and elaborate on the past and the future, no in-between—the present is a fog—because this poet himself is moved, as are these trickster god-poets, shamanic poets, by visionary creativity, one that propels them, impels them, to find, and articulate, the significance of life:

> The Saha-Tripleness is a dream
> The chemical solidity is a dream
> Smells are a dream
> Bonfires are a dream
> Pain is a dream
> Defecation is a dream
> My gray page Legend is a dream
> All my various pencils were dreams
> All erections were dreams
> Pa, Gerard were a dream
> Ma, Nin, Paul are dreams
> Allen is a dream
> I am a dream
> This moment is a dream
> This couch is a dream
> I am glad it's only a dream
> God is a dream
> Buddha is a dream
> Mind is the dreamer.[48]

If nothing really exists—life is a dream—we cannot die if we never lived— death is not real—Gerard is not dead—sorrows resulting from death are not real—if there is no real sorrow for man to feel, there is nothing for man to fear—guilt, grief and loss are unnecessary: "Got up and dressed up / and went out & got laid / Then died and got buried / in a coffin in the grave, / Man— / Yet everything is perfect, / Because it is empty, /

Because it is perfect / with emptiness, / Because it's not even happening.[49] One never dies, / One's never born / So sing the optimists / Of holy old religion, / trying to assuage—[50] I was never born, will not die; we only thought we existed."[51]

Yet the hundreds of pages of philosophical prose and poetry found in *Some of the Dharma* and in *The Scriptures of the Golden Eternity* that Kerouac devoted to explaining the illusion and non-existence of the Mind attest, not to the unreality of Mind, Life, or Death, but to the incontestable presence and power of the poet's own unique Mind, and the uncontrollable, exuberant, delightful manifestation of his and all spirit on earth, his own being one of the most fiery.

It is true that this poet can be said, as all of us, to have been part of "figures in a dream that will be no more."[52] Yet all the writing the poet did to explain or prove that he did not exist only leaves us grateful that Jack Kerouac did in fact exist, and that his essence, in his writings, forever remains with us: "When your body vanishes and everything / that belongs to self, such as its ego- / personality, vanishes with it, there re- / mains what does not belong to self but / only was 'loaned' to it, universal mind, / which, when shedding off a body, is not / changed nor added to nor subtracted from."[53]

10—Felt the Faith and Wound of a Catholic

"Oh god how I rejoice in sorrows now, as though I had asked You for them . . . I rejoice in these sorrows. Like steel I will be, God, growing harder in the forge-fires, grimmer, harder, better: as you direct . . ."[54]

"Saints, I give myself up to thee. / Thou hast me. What mayest thou do? / What hast thou? Hast nothing? / Hast illusion. Hast rage, regret, / Hast pain. Pain wont be found / Outside the Monastery only—"[55]

"And all my own sins / Have been forgiven somewhere— / I don't even remember them, / I remember the sins of others. / Let me meditate on my sins. / (Judgment Gate, somebody / stuck a spear / through the heart / of the Judgment Gate) . . . Archangels have true eyes— / They look sideways at you / And make you excise / The end from the tax bit / of your doubts— / 'S all about angels' sins."[56]

"'No—Bible.' / Every chapter & phase / Historical,

anthropological, / Archaeological, Logical, / Magical, /
There's not after they / Get thru with the Bible / Much of it
Left."[57]

"Religion is thy sad heart."[58]

Jack Kerouac was like a man observing his river, sitting in the
rain, letting it soak through his clothes, his skin, his being, his
self; a man weighed down, feeling the cold, his tears as opaque
as his heart. He was a Catholic man, "I'm a Catholic all along.
I was really kidding Gary Snyder. Boy, they're so gullible;"[59] he
was a man imbued with service and sacrifice; he was a lover of
God invested in the purification of the soul to be made ready
for the resurrection of the dead; yet he was a creature confused
by the conflicting pulls between loving and dying, willful indi-
vidualism and martyrdom.

Still, he was a Catholic poet—his cross was not a plain cross,
not a Protestant cross, stripped of the body of the sacrificed
man-God. His cross bore Christ on it, and Christ was his own
heart that bled like an iron rose, a *Rose-En-Fer*: "Wealth was
neither a power / nor a consolation; he could only exist
through love, through / religion, and through his faith in the
future. Love made him / understand eternity. His heart and the
gospels marked out / two worlds awaiting him. Night and day
he was plunged in / the depths of infinite thoughts, which for
him perhaps merged / into one."[60]

II—Suffered from Alcoholism and the Defeat of the Spirit

Jack Kerouac suffered from alcoholism and was eventually de-
stroyed by it. In fact, his father had encouraged him to drink
beer during meals since his high school days. Yet Jack knew
better. He tried hard to stop all drinking at the time of his initial
involvement with Buddhism:

"Drinking heavily, you abandon people—and they abandon
you—and you abandon yourself—It's a form of partial self
murder but too sad to go all the way . . ."[61]

"Shun drink; make no man drink; / Sanction no drinking.
Mark / how drink to madness leads . . ."[62]

But the family history weighed heavily:

"This is a very important story because it deals with a man who was also named Jack Kerouac . . . This strong personage died when my father was fifteen years old, and in a very tragic manner. He died melodramatically, indicating perhaps that someday a poet would stem from his blood. And I'll be dammed if it didn't happen that way. This is a very important story. I must treat it carefully, reverently, and tragically. Honest Jack they called him in his home town . . . the best carpenter in town, and the father of eight children; Honest Jack, who like the poet of his posterity, stood about five feet ten inches tall and was built like an oak, and whose foot-steps my father can still hear, coming down the streets of Nashua . . . a firm powerful step of a firm powerful man. Honest Jack was a staunch Catholic . . . Honest Jack was a Breton . . . The hardy Celts of France, blue eyes and black hair, the sea, women standing on the shore waving at departing ships . . . Whenever there was a thunderstorm, he would stand on the large porch of his home and roar at the heavens, waving his bony fist at the lashing tempest . . . At other times, Honest and Fearless Jack would take an oil lamp and juggle it, all the time daring God to blow him up right then and there. His wife . . . used to stand by in fear, watching her magnificent husband do the strong things that he did, wondering why he wasn't weak like other men, not knowing that only real men are considered mentally amiss . . . One day, he suddenly grew tired of life. He began to drink each night, rising early in the morning to go to his work, always on time, but every night he would get drunk again, and come back home early in the morning, muttering. On Sundays, he would not drink, but would stalk around the kitchen humming church hymns. After a year of this, his son (my father's brother) denounced him for his actions, and he died that night . . . It was tragic . . ."[63]

"As it's now Dec. 19, the end of this pivotal year is near—and I am at / the lowest beatest ebb of my life, trapped by the police, 'retained in dismal / places,' scorned and 'cheated' by my friends (plagiarists), misunderstood by my / family, meanwhile mutilating myself (burning hands, Benzedrine, smoking, goof-balls), / also full of alcoholic sorrow and dragged down by the obligations of others, con- / sidered a criminal and insane and a sinner and an imbecile, myself self-disappointed / & endlessly sad because I am not doing what I knew should be done . . . a year's delay, a deepening / of the sea of troubles, sickness, old age creeping around my tired eyes, decrepitude / and dismay, loss. . ."[64]

"What to do? Buddhism has killed all my feelings, I have no feelings, no inclinations to go anywhere, yet I stay here in this house a sitting duck for the police who want me for penury & non-support, listless, bored, world weary at 32, no longer interested in love, tired, unutterably sad as the Chinese autumn-man . . ."[65]

12—Involved in a Writer's Brotherhood

The unbelievably prolific outpouring found in *Some of the Dharma* and in the numerous volumes of prose and of poetry written by Jack Kerouac testify to the poet's intense, constant grappling, weighing and balancing of the impenetrable complexities, engulfing vulnerabilities, and insoluble demands that life made on his heart and mind.

How to withstand and also find use for loneliness and unrest, when all that Kerouac wanted was "to be a quiet saint living in a shack in solitary meditation of universal mind?"[66] To stand and remain alive in the midst of it all was a daily act of generosity and bravado from his part. Writing was part of that gesture.

The medley of words used by this poet were like an army he organized to help him think, argue, debate, judge, ponder, deliberate, meditate, contemplate, consider, ruminate, brood, recollect, visualize, dream, fantasize, and give, give, give all of himself away. But it was all too much for one man alone to keep.

So, because of this, Jack Kerouac's friendships had the same necessity, intensity and meaning that they once had between men of ancient Greece. As men did in ancient Greece, Jack and his friends valued more the friendships, the goals and bonds they had with each other than their relationships with women. The men of ancient Greece did not focus on women to find emotional fulfillment, the sharing of dreams, ideals, and common journey. Women were only a traditional accessory required for the creation of family. Carmela Ciuraru wrote that "the Beats, and those affiliated with that core group, were mostly men, and the work they produced was almost entirely male-focused . . . Women were usually idealized (or demonized) as maternal figures, or else honored for their skills in bed . . ."[67]

And so Jack Kerouac, this most modern of poets, yet imbued with classical ideals and vision, cried, "this is clear . . . surprising it is, that the 'Friends' are harder to part with than food & wine & lust. . ."[68]

Allen Ginsberg's name may come first when we now recall the significant friends of Jack Kerouac's life. However, had he not died so very young during the war, Sebastian Sampas's might be the name that we first think of in relation to Jack Kerouac. He still was, years later, in the late '50s, the inspiration for the book *Old Angel Midnight*, originally called "Sebastian Midnight." In *Lonesome Traveler*, Kerouac wrote, "Decided to become a writer at age 17 under influence of Sebastian Sampas, local young poet who later died on Anzio beach head."

Together they created the Piomcthcans, a group of youths involved in literature and theater. It is significant that they looked to Greece and chose Prometheus as their emblem—a demigod, one of the Titans, who stole fire from Zeus's heavens to give it back to earth, and thus to man.

It is indeed a poet's fate and emotional struggle to have to suffer daily for sharing in the gods' fire, living the fate of Prometheus who was punished by the gods for his daring. Prometheus was condemned to have his liver torn and eaten each day by an eagle, a torment that was each day renewed since the liver grew back each night. It is worth noticing here that Jack Kerouac grew up speaking Joual, a Canadian-French language in which the words for "faith" and "liver" are the same, pronounced the same way, even though their spelling differs from one single letter "e" placed at the end of one—liver—a letter called an *e-muet*, a dumb-e, because it is neither pronounced nor heard. We are then strangely able to surmise that Jack-Kerouac-the-poet, himself a demigod like Prometheus-the-fire-giver, had his faith torn from his entrails each day, and that it was renewed and grew back each night.

Is it possible to propose that, without the death of his brother Gerard, and the complex scar this death left on his four-year-old mind, this poet's sensibility, struggles, attractions, and literary choices would have been different? It is only after his brother's death that Jack started to enjoy friendships and share in sports games outside of the family. Considering the freshness and surprise these new friendships must have represented, and the intense need and void they must have filled for the bereft boy, is it possible to suggest here that the theme of brotherhood might never have been so central in Kerouac's life if Gerard had not died and left him with a wound of brotherhood, and that the novel *On the Road* might never have been written, a book whose subject and center is friendship?

While Jack Kerouac's friendships were central to his writing, one must also point out that these were friendships with writers. They were men on the same team. But while dialogues with his friends were a constant, live feed for him, the friendships and dialogues he entertained with dead writers were also foremost to who he became, and what use he made of his life—Thoreau, Blake, Whitman, Thomas Wolfe, Dostoyevsky are the ancestors Jack Kerouac chose for himself. With their minds and thoughts always accessible to him, in a way that his own are to us now, Jack Kerouac was never alone and could always find direction. With them as friends, he was not abandoned, not lost, but lifted from the fog of indiscriminate life-forms. With them, he belonged in the "permissible dream" that he called America, a dream in which he hoped to blossom, because Jack thought of himself foremost as an American boy.

13—*Taught Playfulness, Rhythm and Easy Flow in Writing*

"Honest jack was fearless. He dared God to strike him with a thunderbolt . . . He would use his enormous language against the storm . . . the language called Canadian-French . . . it is one of the most languagey languages in the world. It is unwritten . . . it is a terrific, a huge language."[69]

"I believe that form has been stressed too / much . . . my system / has more vitality, what with the dialogue, the comments, / and the dramatic action . . . So long and take it easy, because if you start / taking things seriously, it is the end of you . . ."[70]

"I am one of the world's / Great Bullshitters . . .[71] Sooladat smarty pines came prappin down / My line of least regard last

Prapopooty / And whattaya think Old Father Time / made him? a western sponnet / Without no false on bonnet, / Trap in the cock adus time of the Nigh, / Slight the leak of recompense being hermasodized / By finey wild traphoods in all / their estapular / glories."[72]

"Remember above all things, Kid, that to write is not / difficult, not painful, that it comes out of you / with ease . . . don't mind critics, don't / mind the stuffy academic theses of scholars, they / don't know what they're talking about, they're way / off the track, they're cold . . ."[73]

"You'll never know what you wanted to say about something till you're scribbling furiously into it, reaching the center, then scribbling out again. This is BLOWING . . ."[74]

"Dreams and daydreams happen in the present tense, show the scene and go. This is your chapter. Chapters should be Blowing Sessions, like the Jazz Musician his chorus before it's begun is done forever. Why Jazz is Great. / But writers go on changing words and halting and erasing and rearranging chapters and fouling up their crystal . . . For if you want to write about Things, write *like* Things, spontaneously & purely . . ."[75]

"There is chaos, but not in / you, not way down deep in your heart, no chaos, / only ease, grace, beauty, love, greatness . . . please Kid, do not forget yourself; save / that, save that, preserve yourself; turn out those / mean little old tales by the dozens, it is easy, / it is grace, do it American-wise, drive it home."[76]

14—Handed Us a Writer's Legacy

Kerouac's work has prompted a rich array of responses. Here are some of the voices:

Carmela Ciuraru: "Like punk, grunge, and most other countercultural trends, the avant-garde Beat movement . . . was soon snapped up by mainstream America . . . Their language was dizzying, drunken, irreverent, tender, scatological, elegiac, and often hilarious. They were the Beats. Strictly speaking, the group comprised Allen Ginsberg, Jack Kerouac, William Burroughs, Neal Cassady, and Herbert Huncke, but the term also extended to intersecting groups of post–World War II American writers—among them poets of the San Francisco Renaissance, the Black Mountain School, and the New York School. Additionally, there were various hangers-on, wannabe bohemians, and so-called second-generation Beats—all disillusioned (but not cynical) young people struggling to redefine themselves, to discover sexual and political liberation and perhaps a new kind of faith. 'Beat' was not just about common aesthetic. It was also a lifestyle, a state of mind . . . overturning convention is partly what the spirit of that movement was about . . . their utter refusal to be tamed by anyone . . ."[77]

Regina Weinreich: "Among the literati who knew him best, Jack Kerouac was a poet supreme who worked in several poetry traditions, including sonnets, odes, psalms, and blues (which he based on blues and jazz idioms). He also successfully adapted haiku into English . . . As with all of Kerouac's work in prose and poetry, process is key to his search for more refined language . . . What Kerouac 'got' more than any other Beat poet working in this genre was the rendering of a subject's essence, and the shimmering, ephemeral nature of its fleeting existence. This sensitivity to impermanence appears again and again in his work . . .

"Contemporary poets such as Cor van den Heuvel became interested in haiku after reading *The Dharma Bums*. A flourishing American haiku tradition is much admired by poets worldwide, and many cite Kerouac's efforts as an early influence . . . Even in this tight poetic expression, he will always be revered as a daring literary artist."[78]

Robert Creeley: "Jack was a genius at the register of the speaking voice, a human voice talking. Its effect on my poetry? He gave an absolute measure of what the range of that kind of writing was.

"Before that, the standards ranged from Cummings to Prévert, but with Kerouac we had a human voice, not as imitation, but as fact of that voice talking. That he could do it in both poetry and prose interested me . . . He was classified as a novelist despite the evidence . . . that the distinction between the two forms was in certain writers artificial—they are inseparable.

Kerouac's simultaneous ability in prose and poetry, like Hardy, like Lawrence, like Joyce, like Jean Genet, like Burroughs, proposes questions that are more fruitful to contemplate than to dismiss . . ."[79]

Lawrence Ferlinghetti: "I was influenced by Kerouac . . . I stole quite a few images from him . . . I picked up on how you can blend the French and English . . . He's a hero to French Canadian writers, not only to prose writers but also brother to Québecois poets . . ."[80]

Allen Ginsberg: "[Kerouac's] influence is worldwide, not only in spirit, with beat planetary Youth Culture, but poetic, technical. It woke Bob Dylan to world minstrelry . . . He said it was the first poetry that spoke his own language . . . My own poetry's always been modeled on Kerouac's practice of tracing his mind's thoughts and sounds directly on the page . . .

"Reading *Mexico City Blues* . . . had given [the Ven. Chögyam Trungpa] a new idea of American poetry, for his own poetry— thus Trungpa Rinpoche's last decade's open-form international spontaneous style *First Thought Best Thought* poetry collection. Thus two years later the 'Jack Kerouac School of Disembodied Poetics' was founded with Naropa Institute, certainly a center for meeting of classical Eastern wisdom meditative practice with Western alert spontaneous candid thought . . .

"Gary Snyder preparing to go to Japan was impressed by Kerouac's intuitive familiarity with Dharma sutra and its manifestation in *Blues* . . .

"Michael McClure was inspired to the later ditties of *September Blackberries* . . . [He said] 'I was illuminated, thrilled, deeply moved by seeing the natural unplanned growth of them, poem after poem, each with a life of its own' . . .

"All San Francisco Renaissance poets were curious, interested, impressed, sometimes inspired by Kerouac's solitary autochthonous strength, ear, Kerouac's sound, his unobstructed grasp of American idiom . . .

"The second generation of New York school, well-versed in the spontaneous sophistications of O'Hara and Ashbery, recognized Kerouac's genius and were influenced by this American spontaneity—Ted Berrigan and Aram Saroyan notably, who interviewed him for *Paris Review*; Tom Clark and Anne Waldman, themselves powers at St. Mark's Poetry Project, inherited some of Kerouac's energy and intelligence in U.S. ordinary mind—sacred mind, pop art mind, Bop mind. And Leroi Jones (Amiri Baraka), who liberated a world of African-American verse, also caught some of Jack Kerouac's mind and musical vibration and publicly praised Kerouac's theoretic rationale of authentic oral spontaneity . . .

"Certainly a colossus . . . Kerouac is a major, perhaps seminal, poet of the latter half of U.S. XX Century . . . a poetic influence over the entire planet. Jack Kerouac was above all a poet's poet, as well as a people's poet and an Ivory Tower poet. . ."[81]

To be a poet's poet is to hurt. To hurt singularly, to hurt incomprehensibly, to suffer a wound that never heals, a wound not meant to heal because bleeding is the very nature of this wound—it is a divine gift—it is the wound of a savior.

Yet how wondrous that a "poet's poet," a man of flesh manifesting a continuously wounded sensibility, can also be called a "colossus"—whole, enduring, indestructible, larger than life—he supports and guards the temple of the gods.

Compassion is such a weight, because the pain of the world is endless, the array of emotions to feel through compassion is dizzying, forever renewed and multiplied. And to be a people's poet is to suffer compassion—compassion as a mission—compassion so shrill within one's heart that it overflows and reaches out in abundance to teach and elevate the hearts of others. And thus, despite the burdens it carries, compassion reveals itself as a Grace, one that Jack Kerouac accepted, endured, and shared generously, courageously, as if a mission.

And it is a painful irony that a people's poet can also be an "Ivory Tower poet"—a man standing alone within the crowd to whom he feeds himself; a man feeling encased within himself—a man very alone, a being stretched so thin at times as to feel like he is only a single, silken thread sensing God within the solitude of eternity; a brave, exalted voice who, however far and deep he traveled, never tired of sending out jewels of the mind, and of sharing his peculiar humanity and wisdom:

"Walking on water wasn't / built in a day."[82]
"When rock becomes air / I will be there."[83]
"Believe in the holy contour of life."[84]

———

The works cited have been identified by the following abbreviations: JKCP: *Jack Kerouac: Collected Poems*. All page numbers refer to this Library of America edition except for the following: AU: *Atop an Underwood*, ed. Paul Marion (New York: Penguin Books, 1999); BH: *Book of Haikus*, ed. Regina Weinreich (New York: Penguin Poets, 2003); BP: *Beat Poets*, ed. Carmela Ciuraru (New York: Everyman's Library Pocket Poets, 2002); HOP: *Heaven and Other Poems*, ed. Donald Allen (San Francisco: Grey Fox Press, 1993); JKSL: *Jack Kerouac: Selected Letters 1957–1969*, ed. Ann Charters (New York: Penguin, 1999); PASCL: *Pomes All Sizes* (San Francisco: City Lights Books, 1992); SD: *Some of the Dharma* (New York: Penguin, 1999); SGECL: *The Scripture of the Golden Eternity* (San Francisco: City Lights Books, 1994); SHD: *Safe in Heaven Dead*, ed. Michael White (New York: Hanuman Press, 1990); WW: *Windblown World: The Journals of Jack Kerouac 1947–1954*, (New York: Viking Penguin, 2004).

1. JKCP, p. 40; 2. JKCP, p. 41; 3. JKCP, p. 580; 4. JKCP, p. 519; 5. JKCP, p. 138; 6. WW, p. 155; 7. JKCP, p. 150; 8. JKCP, p. 101; 9. JKCP, p. 137; 10. JKCP, p. 152; 11. JKCP, p. 27; 12. SHD, p. 40; 13. JKCP, p. 220; 14. JKCP, p. 94; 15. JKCP, p. 152; 16. SD, p. 169; 17. JKCP, p. 41; 18. JKCP, p. 90–91; 19. SD, p. 172; 20. JKCP, p. 119–20; 21. JKCP, p. 15; 22. JKCP, p. 18; 23. JKCP, p. 11; 24. JKCP, p. 164; 25. AU, p.79; 26. JKCP, 12; 27. JKCP, p. 70; 28. JKCP, p. 118; 29. JKCP, p. 75; 30. SD, p. 116; 31. JKCP, p. 123; 32. JKCP, p. 65–66; 33. JKCP, p. 160; 34. JKCP, p. 67; 35. JKCP, p. 161; 36. JKCP, p. 137–38; 37. JKCP, p. 94; 38. JKCP, p. 148; 39. JKCP, p. 148; 40. JKCP, p. 80; 41. JKCP, p. 163; 42. JKCP, p. 35; 43. JKCP, p. 106–107; 44. JKCP, p. 152; 45. JKSL, p. 237; 46. JKCP, p. 132; 47. HOP, p. 39; 48. SD, p. 49–50; 49. JKCP, p. 83; 50. JKCP, p. 74; 51. SD, p. 63; 52. SD, p. 63; 53. SD, p. 68; 54. JKCP, p. 584; 55. JKCP, p. 155; 56. JKCP, p. 47; 57. JKCP, p. 55; 58. JKCP, p. 184; 59. SGECL, p. 11; 60. SD, p. 68; 61. SD, p. 112; 62. SD, p. 156; 63. AU, p. 151–52; 64. SD, p. 185; 65. SD, p. 103; 66. SD, p. 63; 67. BP, p. 14; 68. SD, p. 130; 69. AU, p. 151; 70. AU, p. 160; 71. JKCP, p. 56; 72. JKCP, p. 153; 73. AU, p. 153; 74. SD, p. 119; 75. SD, p. 106; 76. AU, p. 54; 77. BP, p. 13–15; 78. BH, p. x–xxxvii; 79. PASCL, p. iv; 80. PASCL, p. ii–vi; 81. PASCL, p. vii; 82. JKCP, p. 687; 83. JKCP, p. 165; 84. HOP, p. 47.

MEXICO CITY BLUES

NOTE
I want to be considered a jazz poet
blowing a long blues in an afternoon jam
session on Sunday. I take 242 choruses;
my ideas vary and sometimes roll from
chorus to chorus or from halfway through
a chorus to halfway into the next.

1st Chorus

Butte Magic of Ignorance
Butte Magic
Is the same as no-Butte
        All one light
        Old Rough Roads
        One High Iron
        Mainway

    Denver is the same

"The guy I was with his uncle was
the governor of Wyoming"
  "Course he paid me back"
  Ten Days
    Two Weeks
      Stock and Joint

"Was an old crook anyway"

The same voice on the same ship
The Supreme Vehicle
        S.S. Excalibur
        Maynard
        Mainline
        Mountain
        Merudvhaga
         Mersion of Missy

2nd Chorus

Man is not worried in the middle

Man in the Middle
Is not Worried
He knows his Karma
Is not buried

3

But his Karma,
Unknown to him,
May end—

Which is Nirvana

Wild men
Who kill
Have Karmas
Of ill

Good men
Who love
Have Karmas
Of dove

Snakes are Poor Denizens of Hell
Have come surreptitioning
Through the tall grass
To face the pool of clear frogs

3rd Chorus

Describe fires in riverbottom
sand, and the cooking;
the cooking of hot dogs
spitted in whittled sticks
over flames of woodfire
with grease dropping in smoke
to brown and blacken
   the salty hotdogs,
   and the wine,
   and the work on the railroad.

$275,000,000,000.00 in debt
   says the Government
Two hundred and seventy five billion
   dollars in debt
Like Unending
   Heaven

And Unnumbered Sentient Beings
Who will be admitted—
Not-Numerable—
To the new Pair of Shoes
Of White Guru Fleece
O j o !
The Purple Paradise

4th Chorus

Roosevelt was worth 6, 7 million dollars
He was Tight

Frog waits
Till poor fly
Flies by
And then they got him

The pool of clear rocks
Covered with vegetable scum
Covered the rocks
Clear the pool
Covered the warm surface
Covered the lotus
Dusted the watermelon flower
Aerial the Pad
Clean queer the clear
blue water

AND THEN THEY GOT HIM

The Oil of the Olive
Bittersweet taffies
Bittersweet cabbage
Cabbage soup made right
A hunk a grass
Sauerkraut let work
in a big barrel
Stunk but Good

5th Chorus

I am not Gregory Corso
The Italian Minnesinger—
Of the Song of Corsica—
Subioso Gregorio Corso—
The Haunted Versemaker
        King
Of Brattle Street.
In streets of snow
He wove the show
And worried in tunnels
And mad dog barked

KIND KING MIND
Allen Ginsberg called me

William Burroughs
Is William Lee

Samuel Johnson
Is Under the sea

Rothridge Cole parter
Of Peppers
Is Numbro
Elabora

If you know what I
        p a l a b r a

6th Chorus

This Thinking is Stopped.

Buddha's Secret Moonlight:—is
the Ancient Virtue of laying up
and thinking happy & comfortable
thoughts—This, which modern
Society has branded "Loafing," is

made available to people now
apparently only by junk.

Self depends on existence of other
self, and so no Solo Universal Self
exists—no self, no other self,
no innumerable selves, no
Universal self and no ideas
relating to existence or non-
existence thereof—

The Greatest, Who Has Undertaken
to Comfort Innumberable Beings

The Kind One
The Art-of-Kindness Master
The Master of Wisdom
The Great Ferryman
The Great Vehicle Being

7th Chorus

He Who is Free From Arbitrary Conceptions
of Being or Non-Being

The Genius of the Elephant

The Destroyer of Elephant-Trainers
    by Death

The Destroyer of Elephants by Death
The Destroyer of Death
The Destroyer and Exterminator
    of Death

Exterminator of Being and Non-Being
Tathagata
The Essence Master
The Womb

The Manifestor
Man's Made Essence
Essence's Made Man
The Maker of Light
The Destroyer of Light

8th Chorus

Mysterious Red Rivers of the North—
Obi Ubang African Montanas
    of the Gulchy Peary
    Earth—
Lakes of Light—Old Seas—
Mississippi River, Chicago,
    the Great Lakes—
The Small Rivers like Indiana,
    the Big Ones
Like Amazon.
Joliet flew.
    Alma, the River of Snowy Love
    —Amida, of Brightest
        Perfect
        Compassion

The Tamiyani Trail across
    the Everglades—

Ai la ra la
    la rai la ra—

Singing breasts of women
    of earth receiving
Juicy Rivers—red earth

9th Chorus

We're all taking short cut
Through Death Valley
  The Volcanic Mountains
  And the Lizard Ice
  And the Lice of Sand
  —Lhasas of Weedblack
    Cock Rock Philtrite—
Redwoods so Huge
They climb passes by God—
  The Giant Angels
  In the Washington D C Blue Sky
  — —The Heroines of Cathedral
    Fellaheen Mexico—
Commenting on the Great Cities
    of the World,
The Blue Marvel of New Orleans
    (land a swamps)

Ingers had done windows
    with penal Australia
too—pear Attantisatasa
  the Central Essential
    Indy Portuga
      c o i t

10th Chorus

The great hanging weak teat of India
    on the map
The Fingernail of Malaya
  The Wall of China
  The Korea Ti-Pousse Thumb
  The Salamander Japan
    the Okinawa Moon Spot
  The Pacific
  The Back of Hawaiian Mountains
    coconuts
Kines, balconies, Ah Tarzan—

And D W Griffith
the great American Director
   Strolling down disgruntled
   Hollywood Lane
   —to toot Nebraska,
     Indian Village New York,
     Atlantis, Rome,
     Peleus and Melisander,
     And

         swans of Balls

Spots of foam on the ocean

11th Chorus

Brown wrote a book called
The White and the Black

     Narcotic City
      switchin on

     Anger Falls—

      (musician stops,
     brooding on bandstand)

12th Chorus

Indian songs in Mexico
 (the Folk Chanties of Children
at dusk jumprope—
at Saturday Night power failure—)
are like the little French Canuckian
     songs my mother sings—
Indian Roundelays—
Row Canoe—
          Ma ta wacka
          Johnny Picotee
          Wish-tee
          Wish-tee

Negwayable

Tamayara
     Para ya
     Aztec squeaks

(ONLY THE MOTHERS ARE HAPPY)

13th Chorus

I caught a cold
From the sun
When they tore my heart out
At the top of the pyramid

          O the ruttle tooty blooty
          windowpoopies
               of Fellah Ack Ack
               Town that russet noon
               when priests dared
               to lick their lips
               over my thumping meat
                    heart—
               the Sacrilegious beasts
               Ate me 10,000 million

Times & I came back
Spitting Pulque
    in Borracho
    Ork
    Saloons
       of old Sour Azteca

Askin for more
I popped outa Popocatapetl's
Hungry mouth

14th Chorus

And when they saw me
    Rowin my sailin canoe
    Across the lake of dreams
    In the Lotus Valley Swamp,
    And arrested me
    For the size
    Of my heart,
    T's' then I decided
    'Don't Come Back'
    They'll eat your heart alive
    Every time.
       But there's more blood
       I shed
       Outa my pumpin heart
       At Teotihuacan
       And everywhere else
       Including Turban Block,
       Lookout, Ork—
       I got more water
       Pissed in the Ocean
       As a sailor of the several
          seas
       Than Sallow's
          Aphorism
       will allow

15th Chorus

Meaning—
        I'm just an old calvert
    cross
                dead of die pork

I believe in the sweetness
            of Jesus
And Buddha—
            I believe
In St. Francis,
            Avaloki
Tesvara,
            the Saints
Of First Century
            India A D
And Scholars
            Santivedan
And Otherwise
            Santayanan
            Everywhere

16th Chorus

Santayana meaning,
        holy vehicle,
Uno—
            One Cross
            One Way
            One Cave inward
                    down
                    to
                    moon

        Shining essences
    of universes of stars
    disseminated into powder
    and dust—

blazing
in the dynamo
of our thoughts
in the forge
of the moon

In the June
of black bugs
in your bed
of hair earth

17th Chorus

Starspangled Kingdoms bedecked
in dewy joint—
DON'T IGNORE OTHER PARTS
OF YOUR MIND, I think,
And my clever brain sends
ripples of amusement
Through my leg nerve halls

And I remember the Zigzag
Original
Mind

of Babyhood
when you'd let the faces
crack & mock
& yak & change
& go mad utterly
in your night
firstmind
reveries

talking about the mind

The endless Not Invisible
Madness Rioting
Everywhere

18th Chorus

The bottom of the repository
    human mind

The Kingdom of the Mind,
    The Kingdom has come.

It's the only thing you got free,
    the Mind

Per Se Williams, the critic
    and author,

Slept in a rainbow
When he discovered
the perfect accommodation
of Universal Mind
in its active aspect

    You'll have a Period of Golden Age
        Restitution of Loss
I've had all I can Eat
Revisiting Russet towns
Of long ago
On carpets of bloody sawdust

19th Chorus

    Christ had a dove on his shoulder
    —My brother Gerard
      Had 2 Doves
      And 2 Lambs
      Pulling his Milky Chariot.

    Immersed in fragrant old
        spittoon water
    He was Baptized by Iron
      Priest Saint Jacques

De Fournier in Lowell
    Massachusetts
In the Gray Rain Year,
    1919
When Chaplin had Spats
    and Dempsey
Drank no whisky by the track.

My mother saw him in heaven
Riding away, prophesying
Everything will be alright
Which I have learned now
By Trial & Conviction
In the Court of Awful Glots

20th Chorus

The Art of Kindness   A Limping Sonnet
How the art of kindness doth excite,
The ressure and the intervening tear,
What horizons have they fled,
What old time's blearest dream!
But atta pressure of the Two Team,
Finding nothing to surfeit the bloated corpse,
Rabbed the Whole She bo be bang
And rounded them a Team.
Beam! Bleam! So no one cared.
Except the High Financier.
       Ah, but wine was never Made
        That sorely tongues gave grace & aid.

Because I cant write a sonnet
Does that make me Shakespeare?

There's a sonnet of the lotus
A rubicund rose
Death in a rose
Is prouder than satin
Esmerald Isles

Blest
In the Archipelagoan
    Shore—
Ferry's arrived.

21st Chorus

Not very musical, the Western ear
    —No lyres in the pines
        compare with the palms

Western Sorcery is Sad Science—
        Mechanics go mad
        In Nirvanas of hair
        and black oil
        and rags of dust
            and lint of flint

Hard iron fools raging in the gloom

But here's East, Cambodian
        Saloons of Air
        And Clouds Blest.
        Blakean Angel Town.
        Grove of Beardy Trees
            & Bearded Emptily—
        Expressing Patriarchal
            Authority
        To us listeners
            Of the Holy See

    Saw,
        said,
            Saved

Saved my Bhikkucitas

22nd Chorus

Saved my bhikkucitos
        for the holy hair

that was found wanting
        in merde air—

Ninety devils jokin with me
And I'm running on the catwalk
At Margaritee
Jumping from car to car
In a 60 mile freight
Runnin up the pass maw
Tunnel Gore waited Ore
The fantastic steelsmoke
In choke mad tunnels
    of Timbercountry Calif.
where if I'd-a fell,
   I'd-a fell on peb pebbles
of sore iron grit,
      of hard put to it

Importunate fool that I was,
I raved to fight Saviors
Instead of listening in
To the Light—still a fool

23rd Chorus

CHORUS NO. 1 of
    Blues in Bill's Pad

CHORUS NO. 23 of
    San Francisco Blues

FOURTEEN CHORUSES
    of Blue City Blues

Fifteen O Choruses
      of Genu wine blues

Sing you a blues song
      sing you a tune
Sing you eight bars
      of Strike Up the Band

Eight of Indiana, eight
      of Israel,
Eight of Chubby's Chubby,
      eight of old Wardell

Yes baby, Count Blue
      Basie's fat old Chock
      Wallopin Fat Rushing
      Was a wow old saloon man

24th Chorus

All great statements ever made
    abide in death
All the magnificent & witty
    rewards of French Lettrism
Abide in death

All the Roman Sculptor
    of Heroes, all Picassos
    and Micassos and
          Macayos
          and
          Machados
and K e r o u a c o ' s —

even Asvaghosha's Glorious Statement
and Asanga's and Holy Sayadaw
and all the good and kind saints
and the divine unabstractable ones
the holy and perfect ones

All Buddhas and Dharmas
All Jesuses and Jerusalems
And Jordans and How are You's
—Nil, none, a dream,

A bubble pop, a foam snit
        in the immensities of the sea
        at midnight in the dark

25th Chorus

Dont worry about death
Once you're there
Because it is trackless

Having no track to follow
You will rest where you are
In inside of the essence

But the moment I say essence
I draw that word back
And that remark—essence's
Unspoken, you cant say a word,
essence is the word for the finger
that shows us bright blankness

When we look into the God face
We see radiant irradiation
From middleless center
Of Objectless fire roe-ing
In a fieldstar all its own

Is my own, is your own,
Is not Owned by Self-Owner
but found by Self-Loser—
Old Ancient Teaching

26th Chorus

Knew all along
That when chicken is eaten
Rooster aint worried
And when Rooster is eaten
Chicken aint worried

Because what's there to worry
What's there to grow teeth
To eat rebirth's beginningless
Meat of Eternal Comeback?

For Christ Sake stop saying
And saving your lives,
It's only one more hour
Beyond your pale light

There's no end on all sides
The saylessness, the sayless ork
          awk ah of child
          on afternoon sidewalk

Or of Hurubela Elephant Cow
          of Ant Colonies
          M'e'r y o cking
          in a moment
          of the Landscape day
          in Vast Acadian
               PureLand—
     Buddha loved all sentient beings

27th Chorus

Krissake Wakeup
Nuts like Carl Solomon
A sharp Jew I know,
Say that all's already ended,
A dream a long time done.
Sit in the Bedlam high

Inside Mind listening dreaming
To the music of the time
Coming through the Aura Hole
Of Old Father Time
   Mustache on a Jimmy the Greek
                 stage

Ork, song of Nova Scotia,
   Silly, any, songs,
   Floating in the Open Blue,
   Balancing on Balloons,
     Balloons, BALLOONS,
     BALLOONS of Rosé Hope,
     balloons Balloons BALLOONS
     the Vast Integral Crap
            a
         Balloons

BALLOONS is your time
B a l l o o n s is the ending
   THAT'S THE SCENE

28th Chorus

The discriminating mind.
Discrimination is when, say,
    you're offered something
And you accept it one way
    or the other,
Not thinking of improving;
Then comes the Craft Gleam
And you look over to see
What's to be to advantage,
And find it, pouncin like a Puma,
Like a Miser Hero of Gold
             Cellars
           & Herring
           in barrels,

—And you seek to achieve
   Greater satisfaction
   Which is already impossible
   Because of Supreme Reality
     and Time
And Timelessness Entire
All conjoined & arranged & finished
By Karmas of Rue
In heavenlands remote—
You suffer & you fall,
You discriminate a ball.

29th Chorus

"Man, now, you wont let me talk"
Gripes the irreligious feline cat—

That cat has no trumpet
But bubblegum to blow on

Poor sad Bhikku of the Forest
Of poor, lost little Nino

In Calles of Forever,
Streets of Old Burma,
Be saved secret wretched
Urchin brother hero
   You are protected
   By the Guardians
      of
      the
     Alone

All is alone, you dont have to talk

One Light, One Transcendental Ecstasy

If they dont understand that
In the South, it's because
All their Baptists
Have not been to Shool

30th Chorus

Tender is the Night
Tender is the Eve Star

F. Scott Fitzgerald, the Alamoan
        Huckster Crockett Hero
        Who burned his Wife Down
        and tore up the 95 Devils
        with crashes of laughter
        and breaking of glass
        in the monocled Ibyarritz
        the Little Grey Fox
        OF NEW HAVEN CONN
        via Princeton O Sure

Tender is the marlin spike,
        Tender is the sca,
        Tender the London Fog
        That Befalls to Me

Tender is the Cat's Bath
Blue Meow
The Little Grey Fox
        That nibbled at the grapes
Tender was his foreskin,
        tender his Nape.

31st Chorus

Three Saints in Four Acts
        by Gertrude Stein
A Great Prophet
        is a Great Teacher

But he is also
    a Great Saint
And he is furthermore
    a Great Man
And more than that
    an incomparable listener
    to music and non-music
    everywhere

And a Great Sitter Under Trees,
And a Man of Trees,
And a Man of Sorrows,
And a Lemon Light
    of Angel Sounds
    and Singer of Religion
    wild singer of come-igion
    wild lover of the origin
    wild hater of hate his own

Convulsive writer of Poems
And dialog for Saints
Stomping their feet
On Pirandelloan stage

32nd Chorus

Newton's theory of relativity
    and grave gravity
Is that rocks'll fall on your head

Pluto is the Latest Star

Astronomical facts
    from under the bar.

Little cottages on hills receive
the Constellation of
the Southern Hemisphere

Where rosy doves're seen flyin
   Past Pis Cacuaqaheuro
   Monte Visto de Santo
   De Gassa—healing helium
     gas—from the substance
     on the sun star—
     gas discovered on the sun
      by spectral gazing

Sorcerers hoppity skop
      with the same familiarity
In my Buddhaland dreams—

    Monotonous monotony
      of endless grape dirigible stars

33rd Chorus

   A vast cavern, huh?
   I stop & jump to other field
   And you wander around
   Like Jap prisoners
   In Salt Lake Cities
   Under San Francisco's
   Sewage disaster.
   "An explorer of souls
and cities—"
   "A lowdown junkey"—
   "Who has discovered
   that the essence of life
   is found only in the poppy plant

   with the help of odium
   the addict explores
      the world anew
   and creates a world
      in his own image
   with the help of Madame
      Poppy

I'm an idealist
   who has outgrown
     my idealism
I have nothing to do
   the rest of my life
     but do it
     and the rest of my life
     to do it"

34th Chorus

"I have no plans
  No dates
    No appointments with anybody

So I leisurely explore
    Souls and Cities

Geographically I'm from
    and belong to that group
    called Pennsylvania Dutch

But I'm really a citizen
    of the world
      who hates Communism
      and tolerates Democracy

Of which Plato said 2000 years
    ago,
Was the best form of bad government

I'm merely exploring souls & cities
From the vantage point
Of my ivory tower built,
Built with the assistance
    of Opium

That's enough, isnt it?"

35th Chorus

It was the best show,
  the guys used to give up
  a good movie
  just to hear him talk

Now is the Time
Now is the Time
To kill an hour
  and Delaware Punch
  each

A Star is Born—
   muckle lips in the movie
   "I'd rather not"—
   "I really don't wanta go"—
   Yeah, fuck the movie.

Fuck the mambo.
Fuck is a dirty word
But it comes out clean.

  Everything (after a gasp)
  is fine, already really.
  Whatever is was.
  "Anyway it happened"
  Says Allen (Poe) Ginsberg—
  Quote from Plato right?
  Time on a Bat—growl of truck.

36th Chorus

No direction
No direction to go

Burroughs says it's a time-space
  travel ship
Connected with mystiques
  and mysteries

Of he claims transcendental
    majesties,
Pulque green crabapples
    of hypnotic dream
In hanging Ecuad vine.
Burroughs says, We have destiny,
Last of the Faustian Men.

            No direction in the void
            Is the news from the void
            In touch with the void
            Everywhere void

No direction to go
            (but)
                    (in) ward

Hm
    (ripping of paper indicates
    helplessness anyway)

37th Chorus

Mad about the Boy—
Tune—Fué—
Going along with the dance
Lester Young in eternity
    blowing his horn alone
Alone—Nobody's alone
For more than a minute.
    Growl, low, tenorman,
    Work out your tune till the day
    Is break, smooth out the rough night,
    Wail,
    Break their Beatbutton bones
    On the Bank of Broad
    England Ah Patooty
    Teaward Time
    Of Proust & bearded
        Majesty

In rooms of dun ago
        in long a lash
        alarum speakum
        mansions tennessee
        of gory william tree
        —(remember that little
            box of tacks?)

38th Chorus

(Pome beginning with parenthesis:—
God!)
Garver has an Aztec Hammer
To batter the tacks in
It's made of Pyramid Stone
    The shape of a Knot—
    Cleopatra's Knot—
    The Knotty issue Marc
    Brandelian Antonio
    Julius Marc McAnthony
    Thorny horn of hare
    Propensities and hair
    And disgusting to the bare.
        Aztec Hammer, never stop.
        Folded ripplefold over there
            nice,
            Tacks went in,
            "It's take an artist
                to do all this"

            Careful man of cellophane
                decks
                  &
                sometimes
                ceremonial
                silver foil
                but
                usually
            plain pleasant paper

39th Chorus

Comfortable Patience—
Talkin about a Hobbyman
Who draws cartoons for a livin,
Banging in tacks carefully
For King Features Syndicate
   Has got him by the balls
   And Hammerthongs
   And central Goonyak
       Worp Ward
       Orphantail—

Aztec Stick—
      ugly Spew Smoke
      Dragon Beoryen
      smitherwolf
      Wildstar
      Monster Over the Fence
      is Frankenstein

Careful, true, Nirvana,
Patient in his Comfort,
Humble in his Demands,
Weary of the Fear,
No longer fearing
The fair happy air
Permeated with Cherub
And fingers a pair
In V Victory—meaning One

40th Chorus

Did bespat and beshit himself Rabelais,
Roundelay, singing with a chocolate
               mouth

Did tangle in the gangles
   of legs' hair

And scream with the wine
    in his glut.

"What do you think?"

This cover is most excellent,
It's shiny and red,
This car will do nicely
All over the bed.

Rabelais was a mad nut
And also a doctor
And wrote of priests' jocks
  In 1492

Wha' hoppen in Oaxaca?

—gluts rained glut
    guts out of her
    brimy bottard
    and washed the old man's
    river underwear

41st Chorus

That other part of your mind
Where everything's refined
To thin hare screamers
Must be in the cavern
    Somewhere.

But was is its self-nature
    of location?
Nada, nadir, naparinirvana
    ni parinirvana
But Most Excellent & Wise,
  the Glorious Servant
  of Sentient Needs

Tathagata Akshobya,
    Brother of Merudhvhaga,
    Kin to Sariputra—
    Holy & Wise
    Like John in the Wood

No location to thin hare screamers
In the min   d's central comedy
      (ute
      and
      long   Nothing
      ago
      lament)
        of mind's central
           comedy   BALLOONS

42nd Chorus

POEM WRITTEN ON A SAILBOAT
It's a powerful sock powerful
Mock powerful breeze blowin
Across this leeward shirsh
Of fought waters thrashin
Up to spit on the deck
Of Heroing Man,
Ah, as we sail the jibboom
Upon the va va voom
And Saltpeter's her petter
Again, The Larceny Commission'll
Hear of this, fight the lawyers,
Upset the silly laws, anger
          the
          hare
          brain
          bird
          of
          wine
In his railroad tam o shanter
Commemorative termagant

Able to dissect such tycoon
Burpers outa their B Movies'
Investment in Black.
'Bop'
      Even on a sailboat
      I end up writin bop

43rd Chorus

Mexico City Bop
I got the huck bop
I got the floogle mock
I got the thiri chiribim
      bitchy bitchy bitchy
      batch batch
     Chippely bop
        Noise like that
        Like fallin off porches
        Of Tenement Petersburg
        Russia Chicago O Yay.

Like, when you see,
      the trumpet kind, horn
      shiny in his hand, raise
      it in smoke among heads
      he bespeaks, elucidates,
      explains and drops out,
      end of chorus, staring
      at the final wall
      where in Africa
      the old men petered
      out on their own account
      using their own Immemorial
      Salvation Mind
        SLIPPITY BOP

44th Chorus

Waves of cantos and choruses
And lilypads of anything
Like flying carpets that are
    nowhere
And all's bugged with the scene—
Ah I wish I could fight out
Of this net of mistakes
And anxieties among others
Who wait in my silence
Till I end up my work
Which never began and
Never will end—hah—
Bespeak thyself not, soft spot,
Aurorum's showed his Mountain
                  Top
Of Eastern be Western morning
  To Indicate by Moon Magic
    Constellative Stardom
          of
       Gazers
    in Mock Roman
    Arabian Kimonos,
   the lay of the pack
    in the sky

45th Chorus

Euphonism, a softening of sounds
Euphemism, a softened word—
  One is sonic, one is human
  Both are imaginary metaphors

Metaphysical Exception taken
   by the old euphonious
   phoney of Arkansaw
   River bridge

Excisor of taxes via tickets
       of taxes
With what Euphonic
       doesnt-matter
Really pronunciation
       price

Dolichocephalic?
Ichthyocephalic,
   Encephalotherapy.
   Dont point at your head
   The Judge says you're crazy
       Breaky cephalic
       Ouch
       Inch of Grace, sigh.

46th Chorus

I had a dream that Bill
G. here, was lying on his bed
talking to me in a room
in Mexico City on a
horrible afternoon, as
he mumbles information
about the crossroads of the world
I wander like a Giggling Ling
Chinese boy without rice
in a Fog Over Grass
Land vast and like life,
—in my thoughts—but
return to re-listen to what
he was saying, about loaning
money on interest, Christians,
Medicis, Churches, therefores,
Coats of Arms, Balls,
Bridge Post Pots, Guards,
I realize I am dreaming
In beginnings already

And ending's nowhere
To be seen
Yet forgotten—
Is all

47th Chorus

Where is Italy?
How can I find it in my mind
If my mind is endless.
   Skulls on the slavemarket,
     blacksmiths, doctors—
I end up bleakly giggling
     in gleak romany rooms
Sliced by Sardinian fiends
And shot fulla morphine
   By sadistic doctors
   That didnt dream of Japan
   With me the night I dreamed
   Of the Japanese Boy
   With black wool cap
   Sitting on a wall
   On Kamikaze Boulevard
   Near the Sea's Hurricane,
     In low gloomy dark
     Dusk of War 1943—
     What happened in Italy?

48th Chorus

Marco Polo had canals
     and Venetian genitals,
In the war between Genoa
     and Venicia,
Marco Polo's was captured
And then they wrote the book
And that's all she wrote,
Because after that

the Wandering Jesuit
Italian Monk
made his way to the wall
in the China—far
in the Indes of the
                    Saints,

far in the cave of reality
down the suicide steps
into underground caves
where worshippers
like Ignatius Loyola
and the Hearer & Answerer
of Prayer, Samantabhadra,
what's his Indian name,
preside
        (like before they were born)

49th Chorus

They got nothing on me
        at the university
Them clever poets
        of immensity
With charcoal suits
        and charcoal hair
And green armpits
        and heaven air
And cheques to balance
        my account
In Rome benighted
        by White Russians
Without care who puke
        in windows
Everywhere.

They got nothing on me
        'Cause I'm dead

They cant surpass me
'Cause I'm dead
And being dead
  I hurt my head
  And now I wait
  Without hate
  For my fate
  To estate

50th Chorus

Maybe I'm crazy, and my parts
Are scattered still—didnt gather
Em when form was passin out
The window of the giver,
So I'm looking for derangement
To bring me landward back
Through logic's cold moon air
Where water everywhere
Appears from magic gems
And Asphasiax the Nymph
  of India by the Sea
  Dances princely mincing
    churly jargots
  In the oral eloquent air
    of tents'
Canopied majesty,
  Ten thousand Buddhas
  Hiding Everywhere—
  How can I be crazy
  Even here?
      —or wait
    Maybe I'm an Agloon
    doomed to be spitted
    on the igloo stone
    of Some North mad

51st Chorus

America is a permissible dream,
Providing you remember ants
Have Americas and Russians
Like the Possessed have Americas
And little Americas are had
By baby mules in misty fields
And it is named after Americus
Vespucci of Sunny Italy,
And nobody cares how you hang
Your spaghetti wash
On the Pasta Rooftops
Of Oh Yawn Opium
Fellaheen Espagna
Olvierto Milano
   Afternoon, when men
   gamble & ramble & fuck
   and women watch the wash
   with one eye on the grocer boy
   and one eye on the loon
   and one eye
      in the universe
        is Tathagata's
          Transcendental
            orb of the balloon

52nd Chorus

I'm crazy everywhere
Like the guy sailed on that ferry
   for 3 years
Between Hong Kong & China—

The British shoulda given him
   temporary residence in Hong Kong;
   but they didnt want any part
   of him first place he didnt
     have any money

Citizen somehow
   of a country behind the Iron Curtain
   Ex-Spy from Skid Row

I'm crazy everywhere
            like Charlie Chaplin
            dancing in moral turpitude
            playing Bluebeard killer
            on Satin asskiss couches
            with itchy mustache
            so well known to dreamers
            of Choice's Century

Every one of us Roman Circus
         sacrifices, every one,
Returned for payment
      In America Madhouse

                53rd Chorus

      Merrily we roll along
      Dee de lee dee doo doo doo
      Merrily merrily all the day

      Roll along, roll along,
      O'er the deep blue sea
            "Yes, life woulda been
               a mistake without music"
         Most primitive thing we know
         About man is music, drums—
         first thing we hear—drums,
         fifes, reed instruments—
         naturals—catgut violins
         and heavenly lyres
         and along that line
         what the hell's the name
         of that instrument
            the Aeolian Lyre
            by the Sea

The Organ they made too—
Demosthenes listened by the sea
    with a rock in his teeth
And complained when he spent
    more on bread than wine—
S h h h says the Holy Sea

54th Chorus

One night in 1941 I was a kid
And ran away from college
And took a bus to the South
Where bedbugs got in my hair
In the Heatwave Night
And all I saw on the long
Avenue were Negroes

Once I went to a movie
At midnight, 1940, Mice
And Men, the name of it,
The Red Block Boxcars
Rolling by (on the Screen)
    Yessir
            life
                finally
                    gets
                        tired
                            of
                                living—

On both occasions I had wild
Face looking into lights
Of Streets where phantoms
Hastened out of sight
Into Memorial Cello Time

55th Chorus

When I was in the hospital
I had a big fat nurse
Who kept looking over my shoulder
At the book I was reading,
'The Brothers Karamazov,'
By Gambling Man Fyodor
        Dostoevsky
Of Czarist Russia, a Saint,
And in the chapters
        called Pro and Con
She kept giggling & insisting
That Pro meant Prophylactic
        and Con Contraceptive
In all her laughs & gestures.
        Of this Holy Nurse
        I learned bed wet
        comforts of hot water
        and senile satisfaction
        'I'll Take You Home Again Kathleen'
        Sang the old white Cancer man
                in the corner
        when the children guitared
                at my footbed,
        Kolya Krosotkins
                of my railroad

56th Chorus

At another hospital
I almost died
with ecstasy
Glancing at the Babylonian
Rooftops of the Bronx,
And at my fellow

Kaiser was dying of Leukemia,
Not enough thick blood,

I had too much.
I was dying of die-sadness,
Others had diabetes
        like my Uncle John;
Others had sores in the stomach,
        ulcers, worriers?—
Sexfiends I'd say.

Old Italian Fruiterer
Had Banti's Awful Disease,
        the bloating of the belly
        by undigested water
        come from food,
        everything he ate
        turned to water.

57th Chorus

Green goofballs,
Blue Heavens,
Sodium amythol,
Sleeping compound.

Thirty of em
To commit suicide—
Lethal dose is 30 to 50
Times the therapeutic dose,
The therapeutic dose is une—
Take thirty to be safe—
Or else praps forty be better—
If you take too many
You throw em up—
        You gotta let alone
        Your stomach, if you
        threw it right down
        you would throw it up
        then, in lethal powder
        form

Better to eat the capsules
Swallow about six at a time,
Take em with cold water,
Till you get about 35 in ya
And then lay down on your back

58th Chorus

All about goofballs,
        all about morphine,
        so I read all about it,
        that's what it said,
        'Lethal dose is 30 times
        the Therapeutic dose'

Very painful death, morphine
        or heroin; never
Try to kill yourself with
        heroin or morphine;
It's a very painful death.

Doctor give me a mainline shot
Of H grain—Jesus I
thought the whole building
was falling on me—
went on my knees, awake,
lines come under my eye
I looked like a madman
In 15 minutes I begin
        to straighten up a little bit
Says "Jesus Bill I thought
        you was dead
A goner, the way you
        looked
When you're standin there"

59th Chorus

Then I always manage to get
    my weekly check on Monday,
Pay my rent, get my laundry
    out, always have enough
Junk to last a coupla days

Have to buy a couple needles
    tomorrow, feels like
Shovin a nail in me

    Just like shovin a nail in me
Goddamn—(Cough)—

For the first time in my life
I pinched the skin
And pushed the needle in
And the skin pinched together
And the needle stuck right out
And I shot in and out,
Goofed half my whole shot
On the floor—
    Took another one—
    Nothin a junkey likes better
    Than sittin quietly with a new shot
    And knows tomorrow's plenty more

60th Chorus

    C i l
    Rubberbands Seventyfivedollars
    I came out of the dream
That time with mind made
Of misery and tried to remember
        the member
        of the ball
        who it did seem to me
        was the most proficient
        at devaluating the advance

of my profit & loss
company, Holmes—
Whatever that means

It means that I have been asked
To receive a brother
Who sinned against me
And I knew all the time
The Saints were for me.

The Saints are still for me,
    are Still,
C h i c o ,
    small angels,
  I am still for them
  I got eyes of Avalokitesvara

61st Chorus

And all my own sins
Have been forgiven somewhere—
I dont even remember them,
I remember the sins of others.

Let me meditate on my sins.
    (Judgment Gate, somebody
    stuck a spear
    through the heart
    of the Judgment Gate)
        (with her surl of leer)

and that's how we got in

Powerful Tea you gotta smoke
    to believe that

About the actual honey
    of women's limbs

Archangels have true eyes—
They look sideways at you
And make you excise
The end from the tax bit
        of your doubts—
'S all about angels' sins

62nd Chorus

A warrant for arrest
Is a mandate,
An order from the Court
Or from the Roayal Coart
Or from the Royal King
Or from
        the Royal Coast,
        or Coat of Arms,
        or Charms,
        Boudoirs,
        Histories by Voltaire,
        Arrested disorderly
            Louis Ferdinand Celine's
            of South Africa

        murderous intelligent

If you got a lot a money
    You're a felon
If you got not but little money
    Misdemeanor

Mal-Hishaps-Deameaning
Lost Ass-Kicked Out
        or go to jail
    Keep the door locked

63rd Chorus

Rather gemmy,
        Said the King of Literature
Sitting on a davenport
        at afternoon butler's tea.

Rather gemmy, hm,
Always thought these sonnets
Of mine, were rather gemmy,
As you say,
                pureperfect gems
                of lucid poetry

Poetry being what it is today

Rather gemmy, I concluded,
        thinking you were right—
It isnt my fault that Buddha
        gave me helmet
Of Right Thought, and indices
    of long Saints
To Cope my Lope along
        with,
Seeing I never had harm
        from anything
But a Heavenly Farm.

64th Chorus

I'd rather die than be famous,
I want to go live in the desert
With long wild hair, eating
At my campfire, full of sand,
Hard as a donut
Cooked by Sand
The Pure Land
        Moo Land
        Heavenland Righteous
        sping
        the thing

I'd rather be in the desert sand,
Sitting legs crossed, at lizard
High noon, under a wood
Board shelter, in the Dee Go
Desert, just west a L A,
Or even in Chihucha, dry
Zackatakies, High Guadalajara,
—absence of phantoms
    make me no king—

rather go in the high lone land
of plateau where you can hear
at night the zing of silence
from the halls of Assembled

65th Chorus

To understand what I'm sayin
You gotta read the Sutras,
The Sutras of the Ancients, India
Long ago, when campfires at night
Across the Rahuan River
Showed lines of assembled bo's
With bare feet bare the naked
Right shoulders of passing houris,
Sravasti late at night, tinkle
Goes the Indian Dancinggerl—
    There's One Thousand
    Two hundred and fifty
    Men
    Sitting around a grove
                of trees
Outsida town
                right now

    With Buddha
      Is their leader
        Discoursing in the middle,

Sitting lotus posture,
Hands to the sky,
Explaining the Dharma
In a Sutra so high

66th Chorus

Dharma law
    Say
  All things is made
            of the same thing
            which is a nothing

All nothings are the same
                as somethings
                the somethings
                are no-nothings,
                equally blank

Blank
    bright
            is the whole scene
            when you let your eyes
            wander beyond the mules
            and the fields and carpets
            and bottles on the floor
            and clean mahogany radios,
dont be afraid
the raid hasnt started
panic you not
            day the better
            arriveth soon
And the gist of it Nothing-ness
        SUCH-NESS

67th Chorus

Suchness
Is *Tathata*, the name,
Used,
>   to mean, Essence,
>   all things is made
>   of the same thing
>   essence

The things is pure nature,
>   not Mother Nature

The thing is to express
the very substance of your thoughts
>   as you read this
is the same as the emptiness
>   of space
>   right now

and the same as the silence you hear
>   inside the emptiness
>   that's there
>   everywhere,
>   so nothing in the way
>   but ignorant sofas
>   and phantoms & chairs,
>   nothing there but the picture
>   in the movie in your mind

68th Chorus

My disciples of the modern world.
Christ was born in a barn because
the inn was full. Egyptian,
Babylonian, African. They
met in the desert and saw
the star and God was
s'posed to have spoken to em
—picked up.

Like wild.
    A hayloft in a barn.
  All will appeal
  to Slaves
Every saint of Christ
  was the guilt of slaves
Inherit the Earth, O
  Camel thru the eye
  of a needle
Rich man full of heaven
  follow me
  Poor
Never die.

69th Chorus

Mary
Who's my mother?
  Goes back to Isis

Who *is* my mother?
  Christ said—You are
  all my mothers.
    All my brothers
    and sisters.
    Peace.

    The faith
      and belief
        in him

That
  through their faith
    eyes of God—
But the Catholic Church
  S hw vass iss?

70th Chorus

Who *is* my father?
Who is my mother?
Who is my brother?
Who is my sister?
I say you're all my father
              all my mother
              all my sister
              all my brother

    "Rather a good thing"
    —that we're all
    brothers & sisters
Men Of Good Will
is Something we Need
in the World Today

    Men of Philosophy
        that Cannot be of Good
        Will
        Are the Communists
        & Fanatical Jews

71st Chorus

Fanatical spews
Fanatical mews

It is magic
That men have anything
    to do with birth

Say the Primitives.
"I never objected to the word
    God"

The crazy sex
    the Protestant has

They're Brigham Me Young
God hid some tablets
    full of Gold Heroin
In the Mormon Bible

And flew pigeons & cocks
    W e l c o m e   H o m e

72nd Chorus

The higher criticism
If you know what I mean
  "Literary Criticism?"
  "No—Bible."
Every chapter & phase
  Historical, anthropological,
    Archaeological, Logical,
     Magical,
      There's not after they
      Get thru with the Bible
      Much of it Left

    Mo the Span
        Pure Boy

   I must n a w
    remember

Na o

73rd Chorus

The Book of Pluviums
"You want some coffee
  before I get it too good?"
  A O Kay,
  Straighten me out.
  Z a r o o o m o o o

(The Bus outdoors)
and he-hey the
     Nay Neigh
     of the Heaven
     Mule
        Nice clean Cup
        Mert o Vik lu
        Nut—upanu.
        Yes
        Sir.
        Merp.
        HOOT GIBSON

74th Chorus

"Darling!"
Red hot.
That kind of camping
I dont object to
unless it's kept
within reason.

"The coffee is delicious."

This is for Vidal

Didnt know I was
a Come-Onner, did you?
   (Come-on-er)

I am one of the world's
Great Bullshitters,
Girls

Very High Cantos

75th Chorus

But cantos oughta sing

 HE WAS AN
                    OLD CROOK

The hand of death
Wrote itself

Jumping over the moon
With a Cow and Jesus

Now Onions, chickens,
Noodle end of it

Mo

Not too many hands
        of death
In slave Arabia
        the post hot
Top town
        of
            Thieves

76th Chorus

A GUY'S ASKING A QUESTION
It's better not to wake them up
So they wont know
They're dreaming?

It's better to wake them up
        because
        they're dreaming.

It's not better to wake them up
        because they dont know
        that they're dreaming?

Who, no, who said I
        was dreaming?

You said, who said, I say
You're dreaming?

Lise is a fl dreaming
        phantasm

"Go on, you're having one big dream,
That would be my answer." (Bill)

77th Chorus

"Dreery my dear"
   The time we crossed Madrid
   in a car
    and Kelly pointed out
    the dreary Spanish
    Ar chitecture
    As they OO'ed
    And aa'ed
    In a hired
     Li mousine
     Of the Zara
   Nazarenes
        smiling to be bold
        in foretold of old
         And they stopped
         At a balcony

78th Chorus

A Porte Corrière
Of Spanish
Portugy
Blazed
By guitars
Like Spanish Cows
Ortega y gassa
   Monte de eleor
   De manta
      Moda
      Fawt
         Ta caror
         Ta fucka
         Erv old
            Men

79th Chorus

Story About What?
(Story About Babyhood)
 While walking down
               the boulevard
 Contemplating suicide
I sat down at a table
And much to my surprise
My friend was goofing
          at a table
And he was goofing out loud
And this is the result
Of what he Said.

Take your pick

Winds up in such
A predicament
You won't know
What to do with yourself
Live or die

80th Chorus

GOOFING AT THE TABLE
"You just dont know."
What dont I know?"
"How good this ham n eggs
          is
"If you had any idea
          whatsoever
How good this is
Then you would stop
          writing poetry
And dig in."

"It's been so long
   since I been hungry
   it's like a miracle."

   Ah boy but them bacon
   And them egg—
   Where the hell
      is the scissor?
SINGING:—"You'll never know
just how much I love you."

81st Chorus

Mr Beggar & Mrs Davy—
Looney and CRUNEY,
I made a pome out of it,
Havent smoked Luney
          & Cruney
In a Long Time.

   Dem eggs & dem dem
   Dere bacons, baby,
   If you only lay that
      down on a trumpet,
      'Lay that down
          solid brother

'Bout all dem
　　bacon & eggs
Ya gotta be able
　　to lay it down
　　　solid—
All that luney
　　　& fruney

82nd Chorus

Fracons, acons, & beggs,
Lay, it, all that
　　be bobby
　　be buddy
　I didnt took
　I could think
　　So
　　bepo
　　beboppy

　　Luney & Juney
　　—if—
　　that's the way
　　　they get
　　kinda hysterical

Looney & Boony
Juner and Mooner
Moon, Spoon, and June

83rd Chorus

Dont they call them

cat men

That lay it down
with the trumpet

The orgasm
Of the moon
And the June

I call em

   them cat things

"That's really cute,
   that un"

William
Carlos
Williams

84th Chorus

SINGING:—
By the light
  Of the silvery moon
  I like to spoon
  To my honey
  I'll
  Croon
     Love's Dream

By the light
  Of the silvery moon
  We'll O that's the
  part I dont remember
  ho ney moon—
    Croon—
      Love—
        June—

     O I dont know
     You can get it out of a book
     If the right words are
       important

85th Chorus

Do you really need
the right word
Do you really need
Of course it's all asinine
    Forms of asininity
        Once & for all

Mr. William Carlos
            Williams

Anyway,
        An asinine form
        which will end
        all asininity
        from now on

That's a poem
The poem
Will end
Asininity

86th Chorus

Take your pick,
If you wanta commit suicide.
So that we'll know
What it woulda been
    like without life.
Woulda been like
Peaceful and Golden.

A Crashing Movie
    The world
    Full of beet skins
    And fist stars
    And editorial
    Poon yaks.
A crashing movie

    The World
    Full of craze
      Beware
      The Share
      is Merde
      Air

87th Chorus

These things in a big structure of Confession—
And "Later"—"Later the Road"—
Or "On the Road" simply. New
Haven Railroads of the Night
Couldnt be Tighter, than Slaw,
The Riverbottom Rog Man, Screaming
In the Passaic Rocks ready to throat
And drown the sodden once-dry dog
In a multifarious Pool of Pearls
Containing Amethystine Paradises
And Worlds a Hundred Million in Number
Fit for the following Kings:
Ashapur, Parteriat, Klane,
Thor, Mordelowr, Power,
Thwatmalee, Rizottle the Bottle
The Funny King of the Aisles—
      Ah the insane—
Make it a great story & confession
Of all the crazy people you've known
Since early Nineteen Fifty One,
In the Twat and the Twaddle
Of the Lovegirl Marriage.

88th Chorus

"I wanted to marry a lovegirl,
A girl-only-interested-in-love girl,"
that would be the first sentence
    of this masterpiece
Of golden litteratur—

Brap. All the crazy people
I've known since I was 4 years old
—6 years old I saw the sun red
on windows of snowy centralville,
and wondered "Who am I?"
with truthful little eyes
turned to the skies of paradise—
no answer came.

I was the first crazy person
I'd known.

Had bundles and scarves a hundred miles
                                        long
Wrapt in my heart of the library,
I had bottles and barts, & Xmas Trees,
and every thing known to man,
including 6 year old ache pains
in the Poxy back.
            Was afraid of myself simply,
            And afraid a everyone else.

89th Chorus

Remembering my birth in infancy, the coughs,
The swallows, the tear-trees growing
From your eyeballs of shame; the gray
Immense morning I was conceived i the womb,
And the red gory afternoon delivered
                            therefrom.

Wow. I could sing you hounds
        make you bell howl packs,
Zounds, I'd-a lived & lived laughing
        as a child
If somebody coulda told me
        it was unreal:
I was scared. The dark
        was full of phantoms

Come from the other side of death
       to claim the hearts
Of Sacrificial little children
       laying up in the winter night
In cribs by howling windows
       of the cold & forlorn
Earth of Massachussetts February,
       Massachussetts March,
Wild howl Lupine Cold the Moony
       and Loony nights.

90th Chorus

I thought I was a phantom,
       me, myself,
Suffering. One night I saw
       my older brother Gerard
Standing over my crib with wild
       hair, as if he had just
       pee-visited the pail
       in the hall of snores
       and headed back for his room
       was investigatin the Grail,
       Nin & Ma's bedroom,
       Who slept in the same bed
       and in the crib alongside.
       Oily is the moment so
       that phantom was my brother
       only in the sense that cotton
                          is soft,
       Only in the sense that
          when you die
            you muffle
              in your sigh
                the thorny hard
                  regret of rocks
                    of life-belief.
I knew, I hoped, to go be saved.

91st Chorus

If that phantom was real
And wanted to hurt me, then,
All I had to do was suffer & die,
Gritting my teeth awhile
Till it's all over.
If the phantom was unreal
And was only a friendly shade
Standing commiserating compassionately
At my side as I slept and sighed
In the Shakespearean night,
Perhaps, may be, it was my brother.
And my brother didnt seek to hurt me.
        If he did, I crashed,
        I saw stars, marvels,
        My miracle hullabaloo
        Balloon Rainbow
        Turned out to be "Bone
        the Brother-Crash"—
        You get socked on the jaw
        By your best friend—
        You keep thinking
        It's going to happen
        And it never happens,
                Pow!

92nd Chorus

It was all right,
And I was the strangest creature
    of them all.
At Xmas they brought me a toy house
        in and out of which
        Caroline my sister
        played little valentine
        armies showing little sad
        people of the prime
        pip Vienna smalltoot

towns, with orchestras
of the square,
and in the brown light
of the kitchen I wondered

"What is this?—mystery of little people.
Is each one as frightening as me?
Is each one afraid as me?
Is each one got to sleep
        in the dark at night?
Did any of them lil cardboard soldiers
See the Sun of Sadness at Six
In the windows of their snow slope?"

93rd Chorus

But I knew they hadnt.
They hadnt thought such thoughts.
No—I knew.
I knew I knew I knew.
It was like the Lankavatara
                Scripture
I got to read 30 years later,
It said: "These little cardboard
Houses and people, may be real,
Considered as real, if you steal
Little reel from the wheel
Every neel till the eel
In the skeel keep the weal
Of all men intact in city
                halls
Of poop hope.
        In other words, son,
        hang on—dont tip,
        lose balance, see reality
        in images like cardboard
        —nor in the brown light
        of this very kitchen."
        I pouted in my childhood.

94th Chorus

But now I will describe
The crazy people I've known.
These things.
      My mother would take us
      To a three story tenement
      on Lakeview Avenue, still
      standing there—washlines
      of Araby hung from ropes
      on the brown porch—
      spend all day in there
      talkin & gossipin—
      lockin and rossipin
and plopperin and
dopperin and sopperin—
—it's easy to go crazy
I go crazy sometimes.
Can't get on with my story,
write it in verse.
           Worse
      Aint go no story, just verse
It was a crazy place to take us, I mean

95th Chorus

It was where I learned to say "door"
Meanwhile a thousand things
Were happening in the Maldoror wood
Of our neighborhood, Beaulieu Street
Up ahead, with rats of rat winery
And pestils and poolsharks
And pests of tenement crooners,
Looners—the dreary population
   Of the world in 1924.
   Two years old, I sat on the sidewalk
   Contemplating time in white sand,
   That was up on Burnaby Street.
         Names of Silly Streets.
         We have a meet to keep.

"Simplificus? Ridiculous?
 Immensicus? Marvailovous!"
The wild a thousand and one thousand
                things
    To do & be done
            when you're a kiddy
            of two or four
            in the bright ball
            inside your mind
            of heaven given
            joy.

96th Chorus

I tumbled down the street
On a tricycle, very fast,
I coulda kept going
And wound up in the river,
—Or across the trolley tracks
And got cobble mashed
And all smashed so that later on
I cant have grit dreams
Of Lakeview Avenue,
And see my father die,
Had I died at two—
        But I saw my father die,
        I saw my brother die,
        I saw my mother die
    my mother my mother my mother
            inside me—
Saw the pear trees die,
        the grapes, pearls, penny trees—
Saw little white collar girl
        with little black dress
And spots of rose on each cheek,
        die, in her glasses
In a coffin.
        But I raced my bicycle safely.

97th Chorus

Meanwhile there's my Pa, alone in street,
Coming for supper, under heaven bleak
The trees of March black twigs
Against the red & gory sundown
That blazed across the River
sinking in the ocean to the East
beyond Salisbury's latest & last
                    grain of sand,
Then all's wet underneath, to Eclipse
(Ivan the Heaven Sea-Ice King, Euclid,
Bloody Be Jupiter, Nucleus,
Nuclid, What's-His-Name—the sea
The sea-drang Scholar with mermaids,
Bloody blasted dadflap thorn it
— N e p p y T u n e —)
All's wet clear to Neptune's Seat.
        Sensing the aura, the news
        Of that frost, my father
        Hurries in his Woe-Street
        Conscious he is a man
        Doomed to mortal destiny.
    "And my poor lil Ti Pousse,"
        he thinks of me,
    "He'll get it too."

98th Chorus

My father loves me,
        my mother too,
            I am all safe,
                and so are you.

My father adores me
        thinks I am cute
            hates to see me
                flash sheroot

Or bespatter bedspreads
    with mule of infant
        woodsy odors—
            blash aroot

My old man's only 28 years old
And is a young insurance salesman
And is confidently clacking down the street
And chuckling to think of the boys
And the poker game and gnaws
His fingernails worried about how fat
He's getting, "no coal bill's been
Highern this 1924 coalbill
I got to watch my dollars
Pretty soon the poorhouse"—
    ("Wish I was God," he adds to think)

99th Chorus

My father, Leo Alcide Kérouac
Comes in the door of the porch
On the way out to downtown red,
 (where Neons Redly-Brownly Flash
An aura over the city center
As seen from the river where we lived)
—"Prap—prohock!" he's coughing,
    Busy, "Am," bursting to part
        the seams of his trousers with power
        of assembled intentions.
                "B-rrack—Brap?"
(as years later GJ would imitate him,
"your father, Zagg, he goes along,
 Bre-hack! Brop?" Raising
        his leg, bursting his face
            to rouge outpop huge mad eyes
            of "big burper balloons
            of the huge world")
To see if there's any mail in the box

My father shoots 2 quick glances
Into all hearts of the box,
No mail, you see the flash of his anxious
Head looking in the void for nothing.

100th Chorus

That's the porch of the Lupine house.
Afternoons I sleep upstairs,
In the sun, on the porch, in October,
        I remember the dry leaves
            in the blue sky.
I remember one day being parked in the
                            wickerbasket
Baby carriage, under huge old tree,
In family photos we've preserved it,
A great elm rising from dust
Of the little uphill road —
By dry hedges on a late afternoon
In November in the North, sun warm
But air cold, I am wrapt
And beswallered in sweet ebony
With wraps and puffcream caps
And chinkly pinkly pink baby,
Gleering at the world with little
                    wet lips,
Glad, Ah John,
—that tree is still standing
but the road has moved over.
        Such is the might of the baby
            in the seat
        He hugens to re-double
            the image, in words.

101st Chorus

We strove to go to movies
And re discover the happiness
    of the baby—
We built up towers of prayer
    in ivory and stone—
Roused denizens from their proper
    rat-warrens—
    "Simplificus the baby,
    what hast thou thought,
    should he be serried
    and should we be clobber
    the agent of the giant
    in the picture?
        or let him guess?
          I say, let's
            let him guess.

Then he'll come crying
    & sneaking thru the tent
      looking for the showing
        of proud discontent,
          the circus of mirkus,
            pile it on thick,
            —befriend—
            it's a show to go to movies
            but a blow the baby be"

102nd Chorus

"See to it that he never ends,"
    they might have added anyhow.

One never dies,
    One's never born
        So sing the optimists
Of holy old religion,
    trying to assuage—

Your shoes may look nice,
          your baby buggies neater,
               but one dies,
                    one's born.

What the Tathagata of Buddhism
                              preaches,

The Prophet of Buddhahood
          is that
          nothing
          is really
          born nor dies

But that Ignorance is its Prince,
The essence never moved
From folded magnificence.

103rd Chorus

My father in downtown red
Walked around like a shadow
Of ink black, with hat, nodding,
In the immemorial lights of my dreams.
For I have since dreamt of Lowell
And the image of my father,
Straw hat, newspaper in pocket,
Liquor on the breath, barber shopshines,
Is the image of Ignorant Man
Hurrying to his destiny which is Death
Even though he knows it.
          'S why they call Cheer,
          a bottle, a glass, a drink,
          A Cup of Courage—

Men know the mist is not their friend—
They come out of fields & put coats on
And become businessmen & die stale
The same loathsome stale death

They mighta died in countryside
     Hills of dung.
My remembrance of my father
     in downtown Lowell
     walking like cardboard cut
     across the lost lights
is the same empty material
as my father in the grave.

104th Chorus

I'd rather be thin than famous,
I dont wanta be fat,
And a woman throws me outa bed
Callin me Gordo, & everytime
          I bend
          to pickup
          my suspenders
          from the davenport
          floor I explode
          loud huge grunt-o
          and disgust
          every one
          in the familio

    I'd rather be thin than famous
    But I'm fat

Paste that in yr. Broadway Show

105th Chorus

Essence is like absence of reality,
Just like absence of non-reality
Is the same essence anyhow.

Essence is what sunlight is
At the same time that moonlight is,

Both have light, both have shape,
Both have darkness, both are late:

Both are late because empty thereof,
Empty is light, empty is dark,
    what's difference between emptiness
    of brightness and dark?

What's the difference between absence
Of reality, joy, or meaning
In middle of bubble, as being same
As middle of man, non-bubble

Man is the same as man,
The same as no-man, the same
As Anyman, Everyman, Asiman,
      (asinine man)
Man is nowhere till he knows,

      The essence of emptiness
        is essence of gold

      106th Chorus

Man is nowhere anyway
Because nowhere is here
And I am here, to testify.

Nowhere is
    what nowhere was

I know nowhere
More anywhere
Than this here
Particular everywhere

When I fell thru the eye of the needle
And became a tumbling torso
In the Univers-O,

Brother, let me
            tell you,
I thought
I was moving
from somewhere
to everywhere
but nothing moved
so I musta been
and still be
(must) no
where be
But that's all up to the Saints
I aint gonna say the Saints of Innisfree

107th Chorus

Light is Late
      yes
            because

it happens after you realize it
      You dont see light
      Until sensation of seeing light
      Is registered in Perception.

Perception notifies Discrimination,
      etc., Consciousness

Until then there was no light
So light is late

Darkness is late
      You dont conceive of darkness
      Till you've been late with light
      When you learned difference
      Between equal poles abright
      with Arbitrary i d e a s
      About somethin bein this
      Or that, abiding in this abode,

Denying in that abode—
Equal, positive, electric shock,
    coil, dacoit, tower,
oil—it's all late

108th Chorus

Neither this nor that
    means,
        no arbitrary conceptions,
        because if you say
        arbitrarily, the RAMMIS
        is the RAMMIS, !—
        and the TSORIS is the TSORIS,
        or the FLORIST,
        or the—
                arbitrary conceptions
                have sprung into existence
                that didnt have to be there
                in the first place
                when your eyes were bright
                with seeing emptiness
                in the void of holy sea
                where creatures didnt
                abound, nor crops grow,
                and nothing happened,
                    and nobody lived,
                    and nobody cared—

        You didnt need
        arbitrary concepts there
        and need them now
        you say you need them now
        I say, you say,
        Why should you need them now
        Why should you now

109th Chorus

"Was it a bright afternoon,
        bright with seeing?"
Asks the literary type
        sitting in a chair
In an afternoon's dream
And you see his buddy comin in,
Holding his coat to the hook
After closing the door,
You see it on a Thurber Cartoon,
In New Yorker, the funny
Fat figures V-cut and Z-cut
In squares, spilling cartons
of spaghetti to their orb ball
OON LINE ANOON
    POP CLOUD - WORD - HOLE
    And people thumb thru
            Reg'ally
    And up comes the laugh, the yok,
            Funny Thurber
            Cartoon there,
    "Was it a bright afternoon,
bright with seeing?"
            looking over his newspaper
            or poetry pad

110th Chorus

I know how to withstand poison
And sickness known to man,
In this void. I'm no apprentice
When it comes to remembering
The eternity of suffering
Quietly I've been through,
Without complaint, sensing inside
Pain the gloriful um mystery.
Afternoons as a kid I'd listen
to radio programs for to see
the scratch between announcements,

Knowing the invalid is glad
only because he's mad
enough to appreciate every
little thing that blazons there
in the swarmstorm of his eye
Transcendental Inner Mind
where glorious radiant Howdahs
are being carried by elephants
through groves of flowing milk
past paradises of waterfall
into the valley of bright gems
be rubying an antique ocean
floor of undiscovered splendor
in the heart of unhappiness

111th Chorus

I didnt attain nothin
When I attained Highest
                    Perfect
                        Wisdom
            Known in Sanskrit as
            Anuttara Samyak Sambodh

I attained absolutely nothing,
Nothing came over me,
        nothing was realizable—

In dropping all false conceptions
        of anything at all
I even dropped my conception
        of highest old wisdom
And turned to the world,
        a Buddha inside,
And said nothing.

People asked me questions
about tomatos robbing the vine
and rotting on the vine

and I had no idea
what I was thinking about

and abided
in blank ecstasy

112th Chorus

Dont sound reasonable,
        dont sound possible,
                when you bring it up
But if you dont bring it up,
                everything is alright.
Dont believe Mr. Believe Me?
Dont think about him
                and boy
                you'll see how he vanishes
                in morning's mist
                when the moon
                is a crescent a banana
                and birds jump
and far over the Atlantic
where Red Amida is Shining
you'll hear the Call Trumpet
of East is Alright with the West
In the Orb of the Womb
                of Tathagata
                        so round
                        so empty
                so unbelievably
                        false-lyingly
                empty of persimonny

113th Chorus

Got up and dressed up
        and went out & got laid
Then died and got buried
        in a coffin in the grave,
Man—
        Yet everything is perfect,
Because it is empty,
Because it is perfect
        with emptiness,
Because it's not even happening.

Everything
Is Ignorant of its own emptiness—
Anger
Doesnt like to be reminded of fits—

You start with the Teaching
        Inscrutable of the Diamond
And end with it, your goal
        is your startingplace,
No race was run, no walk
        of prophetic toenails
Across Arabies of hot
        meaning—you just
        numbly dont get there

114th Chorus

Everything is perfect, dear friend.
When you wrote the letter
I was writing you one,
I checked on the dates,
Just about right, and One.

You dont have to worry
        about colics & fits
From me any more
        or evermore either

You dont have to worry bout death.
Everything you do, is like your hero
The Sweetest angelic tenor of man
Wailing sweet bop
On a front afternoon
When not leading the band
And every note plaintive,
Every note Call for Loss
          of our Love and Mastery—
          just so, eternalized—

You are a great man
I've gone inside myself
And there to find you
          And little ants too

115th Chorus

LANGUID JUNKEY SPEECH WITH LIDDED EYES
So bleakly junk hit me never.
Must be something wrong with the day.
"How you feel?"—"Um—Ow"—
Green is the wainscot, wait
For the vaquero, 1, 2, 3—
     all the faces of man
     are torting on one
     neck

Lousy feeling of never-get-high,
I could swallow a bomb
And sit there a-sighing,
T's a Baudelairean day,
Nothing goes right—millions
Of dollars of letters from home
And the feeling of being,
Ordinary, sane, sight—
          Arm muscles are tense
          Nothing ever right
You cant feel right

Hung in Partiality
    For to feel the unconditional
    No-term ecstasy
    Where, of nothing,
        I mean, of nothing,
        That would be best

116th Chorus

The Jews Wrote American Music

      Niki Niki Niki- la
      Che wa miena
          Pee tee Wah

Song of Lil Mexico Children

      Kitchi Kitchi
        Kitchy val

Big fat mustachio'd businessmen
Have just to finish their commercial
And go home, saw em at five
Drinking beer at Bar's Alive
While old Canuck Pot
  Looked white & cold
  In corner, countin candles

Music

It's an Aztec Radio
    with the sounds thick & guttural
    kicking out of the teeth
The Great Jazz Singer
    was Jolson the Vaudeville Singer?
No, and not Miles, me.

117th Chorus

Me, Paraclete, you. Ye—
Me, Paraclete, Thee—
Thou Maitreya Love of the Future
—Me.
    Me Santiveda me, saint,
   Me sinner me—Me baptist
   A-traptist of Lower
         Absafactus
Me—You
Me, alone in understandin old
     void of I love you,
     feel fine

Me, you gotta love yourself,
     love, somethin,
     thass all I can say

The witchcraft Indiana girls
     that didnt sing with their hearts,
     where never in a better
     shock of hay hocks
     than the oldtime
     singer with dusty feet
     that chased death
     comes and enfolds you

118th Chorus

It's all the same to me.
The radio I dont wanta hear
And cant have to hear
Plays one thing and another
Of great Sarah Vag

        but no I stop
        and grasp
        and I forget
        that it's my own fault

See how you do it?

And having grasped
go on singing
because I wouldnt
be writing these poems
if I didnt know

That I grasp I sing

I've had times of no-singing,
they were the same

Music is noise, Poetry dirt

119th Chorus

Self be your lantern,
Self be your guide—
Thus Spake Tathagata
Warning of radios
That would come
Some day
And make people
Listen to automatic
Words of others

and the general flash of noises,
forgetting self, not-self—
Forgetting the secret . . .

Up on high in the mountains so high
the high magic priests are
swabbing in the deck
of broken rib torsos
cracked in the rack
of
Kallaquack
tryin to figure yr way

outa the calamity of dust and
eternity, buz, you better
get on back to your kind
            b o a t

120th Chorus

Junkies that get too high
Shoot up their old stock of stuff
And sit stupidly on edge
Of bed nodding over
The single sentence in the paper
    They been staring at all night—
    Six, seven hours they'll do this,
    Or get hungup on paragraphs:

"You go on the nod,
        Then you come up,
            Then you start readin
                it again
            Then you go on the nod again
            and everytime you read it
                it gets better"

    You dont remember the next
                rebirth
            but you remember
            the experience

"Took me all evening to read
3 or 4 pages, ossified,
on the nod"

121st Chorus

Everything is in the same moment
It doesnt matter how much money you have
It's happening feebly now,
    the works
I can taste the uneaten food
    I'll find
In the next city
    in this dream

I can feel the iron railroads
    like marshmallow

I cant tell the difference
    between mental and real

It's all happening
It wont end
It'll be good
The money that was to have been spent
    on the backward nations
of the world, has already been
    spent in Forward Time

Forward to the Sea,
    and the Sea Comes back to you
    and there's no escaping
    when you're a fish
    the nets of summer destiny

122nd Chorus

We cannot break
Something that doesnt exist

Derange pas ta tendresse,
Dont break your tenderness

Is advice that comes to "me"

What a poem the knowledge
    that Time
With its Pasts & Presents
    & Appurtenant
Futures, is One Thing
THE THING ONE WHOLE MASS
Getting dimmer and dimmer
       to the feel

What glorious repose knowing
What a Golden Age
    of Silent Darkness
    in my Happy Heart
    as I lay contemplating
    the fact that I shall die
   anyhow regardless of race
    regardless of grace

123rd Chorus

The essence is realizable in words
That fade as they approach.
What's to be done Bodhisattva?
O live quietly; live to love
Everybody.
  Be devout under trees
  At midnight on the ground.
      No hope in a room
      of dispelling the gloom
      that's assembled
      Since Moses

Life is the same as death
But the soul continues
In the same blinding light.

Eating is the same as Not Eating
But the stomach continues,
The thinking goes on.

You've got to stop thinking,
        stop breathing.
How can you travel from Muzzy
                        to
                    Muzzy?
        Forgive everyone for yr own sins
        And be sure to tell them
You love them which you do

124th Chorus

The tall thin rawboned fellow
Come up to Paw and me
On the misty racetrack.
"Got a good one in the fourth."
"How do YOU know"
        says my Dad
"I'm a jockey"
His hat waved over his eyes
In the rain.
I saw Arkansaw
behind him.
He looked too big to be a jockey
        to me—
"Just put 4 dollars to win
And give me half
        the winnings."
I dont remember now
        whether my father fell
And got laid by that line,
    But "too big
            man
            he too big
            to be a jockey"
            was my thought

125th Chorus

He shoulda been a football coach,
Joe McCarthy—the guy
that was a turncoat
at the assistant editor
of the Daily Worker?
—the tenement marble
sculptured Attican column
in the moonlight illuminating
my eyes—the ross
osh dewey bilbo long
scatter de crash talk
of Fascist BWAS!
—CLAP TRAP
the machinegunners of Goa
are in the Street mashing
the Saints of McCarthy
Cohn Captus & Company
and all I gotta say is,
remove my name
        from the list
    And Buddha's too
Buddha's me, in the list,
        no-name.

126th Chorus

Like running a stick thru water
The use and effect
Of tellin people that
                their house
                is burning,
And that the Buddha, an old
        And wise father
Will save them by holy
        subterfuge,

Crying: "Out, out, little ones,
The fire will burn you!

I promise to give you fine
                              carts
Three in number, different,
The deer cart, and
The cart of the bullock

Gayly bedecked—With oranges,
Flowers, holy maidens & trees,"
So the children rush out, saved,
    And he gives them
    The incomparable single Greatcart
    Of the White Bullock, all snow.

127th Chorus

    Nobody knows the other side
        of my house,
    My corner where I was born,
        dusty guitars
    Of my tired little street where
        with little feet
    I beetled and I wheedled
        with my sisters
    And waited for afternoon sunfall
        call a kids
    And ma's to bring me back
        to supper mainline
    Hum washing line tortillas
        and beans,
    That Honey Pure land,
        of Mominu,
    Where I lived a myriad
        kotis of millions
    Of incalculable
        be-aeons ago
    When white while joyous
        was also
    Center of lake of light

128th Chorus

How solid our ignorance—
how empty our substance

and the conscience
keeps bleeding

and decay is slow—
children grow.

The toothbone goes
Out of mushy pulp
And you cry
As if rocks
Had been dumped
From a truck
On your back
And whimper,
          saying
            'O Lord,
       Mercy on Mission.'

129th Chorus

We've all been sent
On a mission
To conquer the desert
So that the Shrouded
        Traveller
Behind us
Makes tracks in the dust
    that dont exist,
      He'll, or We'll,
          All end in Hell
          All end in Heaven
          For sure—
Unless my guess is wrong,
We are all in for it

And our time
Is Life,
The Penalty,
        Death.
    The Reward
    To the Victor
    Then Goes.
The Victor is Not Self

130th Chorus

And the Victor is Not Pride
And the Victor is not.
  Thus Spake Tathagata

        But I get tired
        Of waiting in pain
        In a situation
        Where I aint sure.

Where I am not sure
Where I am Wolfe
        Sorrow
    Whitman Free
    Melville dark
    Mark Twain Mark
        Twain
        where I am
        w i l d
Where I am M i l d

131st Chorus

Where I aim
And do not Miss

Dawdlers.
    Alla them are dawdlers.
Poets.

Call themselves poets
Call themselves Kings
Call themselves Free
Calls themself
Hennis free
Calls themself
Calls themself
Calls themself catshit
Calls themself mean
Calls themself me

132nd Chorus

Innumeral infinite songs.
Great suffering of the atomic
in verse
Which may or not be
controlled
By a consciousness
Of which you & the
ripples of the waves
are a part.
That's Buddhism.
That's Universal Mind

Pan Cosmodicy

Einstein believed
In the God of Spinoza

(—Two Jews
—Two Frenchmen)

133rd Chorus

"Einstein probably put a lot
of people in the bughouse by
saying that

All those pseudo intellectuals
went home & read Spinoza
then they dig in
to the subtleties
of Pantheism—
    After 10 years of research
    they wrap it up
    & sit down on a bench
    & decide to forget
    all about it.

Because Pantheism's
Too Much for Em.

    They wind up trying to
find about Plato, Aristotle,
    they end up in a
    vicious Morphine circle"

134th Chorus

"The only cure for
        morphine poisoning
Is more morphine."

This is the real morphine.

Now it's after supper
And the little kids
Are out on the street
Yelling "Mo perro,
Mo perro, mo perro"
And the sky is purple
In old hazish Mexico

of Hashisch, Shaslik
And Veal Parmezan.

Russian Spy Buses
        Tooting
        "Salud"

135th Chorus

The ants are gone asleep
By now, out on those plains
Of pulque and rice
Beyond Pascual
And the Cactus Town
    Matador pan
    Pazatza cuaro
    Mix-technique
    Poop
    Indio
        Yo yo catlepol
        Moon Yowl
        Indian
        Town & City

Vendors of Take a Giant Step
Say Hailé
In back se malleys
Selling drunks

136th Chorus

I always did say
Aunt Semonila
The Amapola Champeen
Of Yon Yucatan
will never find
    her potatoes
        Till she sticks in her hands

Potatoes of paternity
Grow deep,
  Edie.

Nut went Crazy
Fife Faces of Man
In One Cell
Ow are you?
 Fall.

137th Chorus

AZTEC BLUES
"A kek Horrac"
I hear in the Aztec Night
Of Mystery
Where the Plateau Moon
With Moon Citlapol
Over the dobe roofs
Of Heroé Mexico.
" S c r e e a a - ra - sarat"
The Scraping of Chair,
Followed by Toot & Boom.
 Punk! says Iron Pot Lid.
 Tup! says finger toilet.
 Tuck! says dime on Ice.
 Ferwutl says Beard Bird.
Howl of Moondogs in Monterrey
When dry is Riverbottom
Baseball Rock
Nothing nada like this scene
Of Apish majesty
In April's hide of hair

138th Chorus

It's really a Brooklyn Night
   the Aztec Night
   the Mix Toltec Night
   the Saragossa Night
   the Tarasco Night

   Jaqui Keracky
   Grow Opium
   In Ole Culiacan

       (BLANK, the singer
           sings nothing)

139th Chorus

I said Well
Bad time of month for me—
So last I saw or heard a
    him—
   Matter of fact, he even—
   But he never hardly
     gave me the 10 pesos

So I was figuring it was
     worthwhile to keep
     the bum outa my hair,
     ten pesos

Only one guy I ever known
He always paid me back
Angel Gabriel
Bright on High

140th Chorus

Fifty pesos

3 Cheers Forever
It's beautiful to be comfortable
Nirvana here I am

When I was born in Tathagatas
Assembled from all universes
And chanted in my ear
The gray song of Nirvana
   Saying "Dont Come Back"
     Then my Angel Gerard
     Protected & comforted me
     In the Rainy Misery
     And my mother smiled
     And my father was dark
     And my sister
     And I sat on the floor
     And I Void Listened
     To the Eternal Return
     With no Expression

141st Chorus

Zoom
S t a r
of Holy
I n d i a n
N I G H T

The Tathata
of
Eminence
is
Silence

The Clear Sight
of Varied Crystal

Shining Mountains
shifting in the Air

Exploding Snow

is Transcendental
Brilliant Shattered
Hammered Smithy
Emerald Green
Rubioso Mostofo
Be spark snaked

142nd Chorus

Muck Ruby
Crystal Set
Smithereen
Holylilypad
Bean—
A la Pieté—

Truss in dental
Pop Oly Ruby
Tobby Tun w d l
1 x t s 8 7 r e r (

Gainesville Georgia—Sleeping in the
grass on a July night—
Dream of climbing night bank
behind the Joe Louis signatures
We die with same
unconcern we live

143rd Chorus

(pause)

Junkies
Should be practical nurses
And be given permits
To get 3 to 5 grains a day
Every day,
The older addicts need more.
        Drug addicts
        Are human beings
        Less dangerous
        Than alcoholics

        And alcoholics arent so bad
Look at the speed drivers
Look at the sex fiends

144th Chorus

Look at the sex fiends
Speeding thru their suicide!
    Nembutols!
    Guns & jumps in the river!
    Lilly saved the man's life!
        Flying with legs
        out the window
            to crash the locomotive
            at the X Crossing

        X!

I been in crashes,
I been in many a bad night,
I been in Nova Scotia
Investigating the Blight.
    And Bright the Vast

Atlantic Greenland
Mountain cap
Of Old Atombomb
Atlantis

145th Chorus

A BANG OF M
A razor mountain—
An Empire State Building
        needle Hypo—
A boiling cauldron
        cucharra—
A sneeze, a wheeze—
                A Cough
A cotton sucking—
        A Bang of M
Anticommunism is an
        arbitrary distinction
Depending on Communism
        A shoot-in
        Pull out needle

James Huneker
Alfred Knopf
H L Mencken
Edgar Lee Masters

146th Chorus

The Big Engines
In the night—
The Diesel on the Pass,
The Airplane in the Pan
        American night—
Night—

The Blazing Silence in the Night,
        the Pan Canadian Night—

The Eagle on the Pass,
    the Wire on the Rail,
the High Hot Iron
    of my heart.

The blazing chickaball
    Whap-by
Extry special Super
    High Job
Ole 169 be
    floundering
Down to Kill Roy

147th Chorus

The Sock
    Wock Williby
        Balloons
In the shitfence

The Angels
    in Heaven
        I knew

The Angel in Heaven
    Gabriel Toot Boy
    Horn n All
    Blows Awful
    Blues When
    Toy Doy
    Done Bo Moy
    From China mo Moy
    To Ole Penoy,
        Oy—y—
      Y gerta
        was gordo

148th Chorus

Instrucciones
Precaucion

Whichever way you look
       you're looking East

Same with West

Whichever etc. way you look
       you're looking West

Thus Spake Tathagata

In the Eastern Heavens I knew
Blue Auroras of the new
Most of David ever knew
Find the Bible Desert,
Rock,
     Ti Jean Picotée
     Silence
        Bzzzzz
   the razor in-cut
of void meat

149th Chorus

I keep falling in love
     with my mother,
I dont want to hurt her
—Of all people to hurt.

Every time I see her
     she's grown older
But her uniform always
     amazes me
For its Dutch simplicity
And the Doll she is,
The doll-like way

she stands
Bowlegged in my dreams,
Waiting to serve me.

And I am only an Apache
Smoking Hashi
In old Cabashy
By the Lamp

150th Chorus

Appeasement is Hypnotism
When the Houri Indian
        snakecharmer gets under way
            swaying his crock toilet
            picoloette clarinoot
            at the snake's bony
            leer
                    he is leading a band
                    like Sammy Kaye
                    that could erupt
                    and kill him

The Weasels Wait

If Buddha appeased
        the Likhavi Tribesmen
It means he must have hypnotized
        and pleased
Their appeasable hearts
        with talk
Of Grand Nirvana's
Holy Paradise

151st *Chorus*

STILL LIFE
A candle dripped all its
          gysm
To the bottom of a strawberry
          designed
Mexican Beer tray—
          A single edge razorblade,
          Partially underneath
          The blade of a butter knife
          Abstracted from old
                    camp
                    packs—

And a tin cup.

This is the Matisse Story
Of a simple arrangement
Of natural objects
In a room on a Sunday
Afternoon—
          bits of dry dust,
          black ashes

152nd *Chorus*

The edge of the tray
          is bright red—
The strawberries are crimson
          dull painted
          juicy dimensional
          indefinable silver lights
          on the knife & blade
          brass dark death
          and the tragic gloom
          inside the lull
          of the tumbled wax
          Attican and Shapely

The rim sadness aluminum
    ALCO Shipwave
    cup—

Then, in real life not
    still life—comes
    the filthy dry gray
    ash tray of butts
    and matchlet tips

153rd Chorus

Sir Garver is cleaning
His Attic and Castle,
Sniffing & snappin
The Bardic Be
    Garters—
Wearing the huge shroud
    sorcerer's head
Picking up deadbeats
    Offa his bed.
Tucking the sheets in
    of no consequence;
Turning and struggling
    to kneel to a stand
Off the bed of dimensions
    & middles
And spans,
    that wont let him lie
        straight
    In the South American
    Pan

154th Chorus

Pan mattress, pan spang,
     pan bang,
Perdoneme, pardon
     me.

He's got a rich cover
Lines made of wine
To cover his bed with
And pull in the line

And unties his bow strings
Of bathrobe & gore,
His plue pajamas
     Poaping
               around all that
               gore
          His feet clean & shiny
          Like askin for more

155th Chorus

And as he keeps washing
     & blowing his poor nose
And waiting for death
     to make V-repose
Out of hands he now rubs with
     the towel of More.

Coffee cup's a-covered
     Friend does the Sneeze
Death'll overcome him
     in Some Fleece of Sleep

Nirvana is Snowing
Right down on his head
Everything's all right
In Heaven in High
Inside this blue bottle

us flies rage & wait
But outside is the Rosy
of Purple O Gate
O J O

156th Chorus

I know we're all straight
I knew from a tree
I leaned on a tree
And the tree told me

Tree told me Haby
The Maybe is Abey,
The Kapey is Correcty,
You'll be allarighty

Trees dont talk good
No they don't talk good
This tree just told me
   See Eternity
   Is the other side
   Of the other part
   Of your mind
   That you ignore
   Because you want to

157th Chorus

The Art of Kindness
Is a dream
That was foretold by prophets
Of Old, wd. be continuous
With no broken lines
Buddha after Buddha
Crashing in from Heavens
   Farther than expressioning,
Bringing the Single Teaching:
   Love Everywhere.

Bring on the single teaching,
It's all indeed in Love;
Love not of Loved Object
Cause no object exists,
Love of Objectlessness,
When nothing exists
Save yourself and your not-self
Hung in a Moon
Of Perfect O Canopy
Sorrowing Starborrowing
    Happiness Parade

158th Chorus

It wont happen is what
        it is—
It'll lose touch—
        It was the same in past
                        eternities

        It will be with the bees
        now

        the feeling of in and out
        your feeling of being alive
        is the feeling of in & out
        your feeling of being dead
        u n a l i v e

When it comes you wont
        sneeze no more, Gesundheit.

It wont happen, is what
        is—
        And
        it aint happenin now

Smile & think deeply

159th Chorus

Blook Bleak.
Bleak was Blook,
    an Onionchaser Hen
    necked Glutinous
    Huge Food monster
    that you ate
    with FLAN & Syrup
    in a sticky universe

Blook on the Mountaintop,
    Bleak;
Blake by the Mountainside,
    Baah!—
Boom went the Crasher
    Mountain Heidi
    Kerplunk Archagelan
    Swiss Funnel
    Top of Funny Ships
    Singing & sinking
    In a Glutinous Sea
    (of Lese Majesty.)

160th Chorus

Poppa told me a perfect pome.
It's simple
The smiles of hungry sexy
    brunettes
Looking to lock you in
    lock joint and all
And those eyes of Italian
    deep scenery
In Riviera's of Caviar
    Tree
And Mulberry Bee
    Lampshade
    Sun Ahmenides

Ahmenemet!
Ak!
   That's your rosy
   Figury,
           another word
                for future—
That's your come itself

161st Chorus

It's a starry disaster
Wobbling many times
Like Sick-to-my-Stomach
The All Slop of Brothers,
Every word that Pegler utters,
"So-pa-top-a-ta!"
Shout children on street—
("Luz!" is her call name)
Horn of Sunday car, yar
Of yak-pass mufflerless
Cars—"You writing that down?
"Not necessarily in agreement
With general trend against
The labor movement"—but here's
his takeoff on Eleanor
Roosevelt 'This is My Day,'
It's a funny statement—
Pegler took out My Day
And rolled into thought
Tortilla & puts it on one
           article—
           (con salsa—)

162nd Chorus

BILL'S DREAMS
Slim girls in thin kimonos
Of blue silk, thin gossamer,
Long, that you could see thru,
Lying down, half-sitting,
Smoking through long tubes
In which every once in a while
An attendant places drug,
In a central bowl,
   And as they smoke on
   An attendant sprinkles
   their eyes with talcum
      powder
And they flutter their eyes
To the joy of it.
     Then, back in the Tombs,
      He's smoking in his cell
      And the smoke became
      Singing people fading
      And coming with smoke
      and a guy passing bread
       Passes him up—

163rd Chorus

Left the Tombs to go
   and look at the
   Millions of cut glass—
—a guy clocking them,
as you look you swallow,
you get so fat
you can't leave the building,
—stand straight,
dont tip over, breathe
in such a way yr fatness
deflates, go back to

the Tombs,
ride the elevator—
            he tips over again,
gazes on the Lights,
eats them, is clocked,
    gets so fat
        he cant leave elevator,
has to stand straight
and breathe out the fat—
—hurry back to the Tombs

164th Chorus

Grand Central Station,
    side entrance
    where they unload produce

—He & friends get scraps
    of meat & cabbage,
All starving,
    on floor are iron plates
    hot, not too hot,
They all start slowly
    cooking, but keep moving up
    as men with central
    hotplate heat
    get impatient & eat
    meat half raw—
    so he keeps pushing up
    his little meat
    towards the center—
These people are all bums—
Hang around in restaurants
Where there's nothing to eat
And you sit a table
And suddenly there's a guy

165th Chorus

under the table
cooking your leg
in some kind of steam
—much quicker job
with the steam on the leg
than central radiant
wildheat of cabbage
                    plates
            in Grand C Station

And I see: "Everybody's eatin you.
You eat them,
makes no difference,
the essence does not pass
From mouth to mouth
And craw to craw,
it's ignorance does.
          ignorant form.
          the essence is not
                disturbed
                  really,
      Like the sudden thought
        of India is a dream"

166th Chorus

A home for unmarried fathers.

He said I must investigate
          some day, that—
Homefront married fathers,
—some whacky idea—
like a home for unmarried fathers
          would be.
Pegler and the Cabinet
    of Peligroso FDR
      —Firstbase, Perkins;
          Eleanor, Right field;

Pitching, Cervantes
the Cuban Newcomer
from downriver
Harlem
    riding a white
    horse riot
    Picasso
    in his helmet
    Jesus

167th Chorus

The details are all the same,
Like honey stored in beehives,
Like atomic power, so many
Atoms, the details per
Square inch are the life of it
And the death of it
    The critical mass collapses
    And like a tumbled Sand castle
    When the tide of disintegration
    And its conception rise,
        Flops into the sea softmaw
        Sand salvaging, bells
        Toll it not offshore.
        The Castle was a Dream.
            Now learn
            that the water is a dream
            For when the Tide of Disaster
            Rises water will disintegrate
            And all will be left
            Is the Successful Savior
            Abiding Everywhere in
            Beginningless Ecstatic Nobody

168th Chorus

Asking questions and listening
    is sincerity;
Asking questions and listening
    without really listening
Is a kind of sincerity; but
Talking about yourself alla
    time, is not insincere.

It's all the same thing
In the long run, the short run
    the no run

Whitman examined grass
    and concluded
It to be the genesis
    & juice, of pretty girls.

"Hair of Graves," footsteps
Of Lost Children,
Forgotten park meadows,
—Looking over your shoulder
    At the beautiful maidens—

169th Chorus

Lie down
    Rest
        Breathe slowly

Dead in Time
You're dead already
What's a little bit more time got to do
                    with it
So you're dead
So the Living Loathe the Dead,
    themselves—
So forgive, reassure, pat, protect,
    and purify them

Whatever way is best.
       Thus Spake, Tathagata.

The girls are pretty
But their cherries are itty

And if they aint got cherries
       Sleep in the Park anyway

And if you dont go near them
You dont get that sensation
Of their inexhaustible delicacy

Dead in Time—Rest in Time

170th Chorus

Rest in Delicacy
The far border of the puff lace
       clouds of Amida's Western
       Heaven of Diamond Repose
       is Delicate

And delicate is the Spanish
       language, delicate the Spanish
       they speak in Upper Bleak
       where King Sariputra
       holds forth a tablet of ice
       (I mean diamonds)
       to be read by the highest
       most delicate Bodhi papa
       in the whole confraternity
       —Old Buddha of Old
       In his Magic Selves
       Commingled as One, Maitri,
       Coos delicate songs
       To the lyres & guitars
       Of the minds of the Lapis
       Lazuli old Saints

171st *Chorus*

When I hear that serenade
    in blue—
Tell me darling are these things
    the same
That we had always known
    Well all alone
And true, it's that serenade
    O serenade,
In the blue, in the blue.

Oopli da da
Aow dee a dee e-da-ha
  You never had no chance
  Fate dealt you wrong hands

Romance never came back

Crashing interruptions
       So I'm with you
     happy once again
    and singing all my blues
  in tune with you
     with you

172nd *Chorus*

When I hear that
     serenade in bleu,

 OO dee de ree,
     —a song I could sing
     in a low new voice
     to be recorded
     on quiet microphones
     of the Roman Afternoon,
     tape, a new kind of voice,
     sung for the self
     sung for yourself

to hear in a room
where you dont
want to be
interrupt
ed

Or made to sing dirges
Of suicide & main
in the candle of the handle
of the coffin to blame

173rd Chorus

The funerals of the doornails
Gay Chocolateers with sadness
        of Marshes across
        their Germany
Hope of Eleanoras of Russia
        rising from
        the railroad
        Nevsky track
Loud upturned chocolate bedpans
        of Saturday Night
        Drugstore Windows
        showing rubber
        and the sexfiend
        watching
Oldtime childhood shoesheens
The Music of the uninhabited spheres
        being played & developed
        over ages for no one
That's the Radio to me
The Ultimo Actual Soundbody
        discriminating in the air
        by means of men tubes
        invented by the 95 devils

174th Chorus

The freshwater eels of Europe
That climb up their rivers
And presumably raid fjords
And eat up pools, curious
Proustian visitors from up the
                              mountain
Of the sea, which, when they die,
they re-cross, to Bermuda,
from whence they came, to die.

Must be that these eel
Have a yen to explore
The veins of Old Atlantis
From their sunken mountaintop
This side Canaryas
But no—they slide
From Europe to Ukraine
And down the Belgian Rivers,
And blankly in the void
Swim back to spawn
And die with longfaced pouts
—Poor fish.

175th Chorus

Cunalingus
My sister's playin piana in Vienna
The Jews are Genius Gypsies
The Moors are Poor.
Aristotle, Isabel,
Ferdinand the Bull.

Ferdinand was no Dumb-Bell—
Piano high was Vienna
When Freud interviewed
   The oversexed Rothschilds
   And Richjews of Vienna

And the Gypsies were camped
In apartments—with lamps—

All the wealth of Europe
        had poured
Into Vienna—Freud was there—
So his Psychoanalysis Sex
Chart of Mad talk
Was accepted as Gospel
By undermined golfcourses
        of the River West—
The multiple too-much of the world

176th Chorus

The reason why there are so many things
Is because the mind breaks it up,
The shapes are empty
That sprung into come
But the mind wont know this
Till a Buddha with golden
Lighted finger, hath pointed
    To the thumb, & made an aphorism
    In a robe on the street,
    That you'll know what it means
    For there to be too many things
    In a world of no-thing.

                One no-thing
                Equals
                All things

When sad sick women
Sing their sex blues
In yr ear, have no fear
        have no fear—
    the moon is true, enough,
    but, but, but, but, but,
    it keeps adding up

177th Chorus

Farewell, tendril

I dont wanta play like that
    when I find you
    as a world
    In my heart
    I dont want
    To talk it lightly
    And make jokes
    And find myself
    Paranoically
    Grunting loud huge grunt
    of Gordo Exer-
    Indian-Cise
        I'd—O Christ—
        wouldn't want to be cool
        in hot hell
        and be goofing
        when yr sweet attentions
        all me, thee,
        describe, self-descried
        in one essential
            l i g h t ,
        the holy gold so-called

178th Chorus

Put the blame on intelligence—
    the reason, no,
    not the bloody reason,
    the asskissed burned
    Chicago Putdown
    talk of time—
who was it maimed
    the rescue,
and made—the mistake—
    and held
    the loft

and lost
and got lost
and knew nothing—

What knew the blame?
Who put the blame?
Who's trying to throw me
                    out?

Who am I?
do I exist?
          (I don't even exist anyhow)

179th Chorus

Glenn Miller and I were heroes
When it was discovered
That I was the most beautiful
Boy of my generation,
They told Glenn Miller,
Whereby he got inspired
And wrote the saxophone
Wrote the reed sections—
like sautergain & finn—
and then they all did dance
and kissed me mooning stars
and I became the Yokum
of the wall-gang, flowers,
and believed in truth & loved
the snowy earth
          and had no truck
          and no responsibility

a bhikku in my heart
waiting for philosophy's
          dreadful murderer
                    B U D D H A

180th Chorus

When you work on that railroad
You gotta know what old boy's
                    sayin
In that en-gyne,
      When you head brakie
      just showin up for work
      on a cold mist dusk
      ready to roll
      to on down the line
      lettuce fields
      of Elkhorn
      & sea-marshes
      of the hobo highriding
      night, flash Salinas—

"Somebody asked me where
          I come from
I tell them it's none a their
               business,
      Cincinnatta"—

      Poetry just doesnt get there

181st Chorus

The girls go for that long red
                 tongue,
From the pimp with the long red
                 car,
They lay it in his hand
The profits' curfew
He takes it "The Yellow Kid"
—He's the Man—

She goes home and hustles,
Remembering Caroline,
The hills when little
      The raw logcabin

rotting in the piney woods
where the mule was mush
and pup-dog howled
for no owner
all one owl-hoot night
and watermelon flies
on the porch

But she love that long red tongue

And the Man
is a Sucker

"SOMEONE LOWER THAN SHE IS"

182nd Chorus

The Essence of Existence
is Buddhahood—
As a Buddha
you know
that all the sounds
that wave from a tree
and the sights
from a sea of fairies
in Isles of Blest
and all the tastes
in Nectar Soup
and all the odors
in rose arbour
—ah rose, July rose—
bee-dead rose—

and all the feelings
in the titwillow's
chuckling throat
and all the thoughts
in the raggedy mop
of the brain—
one dinner

183rd Chorus

"Only awake to Universal Mind
And realize that there is nothing
Whatever to be attained. This
Is the real Buddha."

Thus spake Hsi Yun
          to P'ei Hsiu

Names so much like each other
You know it cant be wrong
You know that sweet Hsi Yun
Had eyes to see the Karma
Wobbling in the balloon
—shiney—
          millions of dollars damage
          from rains and floods—
vast fading centers of a Kansas
          central standard time

                    buss-i-ness
                    my fron

Only awake to Universal Mind,
          accept everything,
          see everything,
          it is empty,
Accept as thus—the Truth.

184th Chorus

"Men are afraid to forget
          their own minds,
Fearing to fall thru the void
With nothing to which they can cling.

They do not know
          that the void
          is not really void

but the real realm
of the Dharma"—

Wow, I thought reading that,
    when I start falling
    in that inhuman pit
    of dizzy death
    I'll know (if
    smart enough t'remember)
    that all the black
    tunnels of hate
    or love I'm falling
    through, are
       really radiant
    right eternities
            for me

185th Chorus

Farewell, pistil—
    "as old as space"
    "without the faintest tendency
    towards rebirth"

No-self, no-self, no-self,
Dass iss the order of the day,
Virya, Zeal, Wednesday,
When I can turn this old
    patayo Matago dun's
    nest of hornet toad
    shoot bewallopers
    worrying in Finnegan's
    Whorehouse about nothing,
    into a Pagoda of Bright
       Jesus Lace Snow
       Japana dreams,
       with showers of aura
       arras flower rose
       bepetalling pet by pet

from the holy dispenser
of dogs—
    Farewell, puppy

186th Chorus

It's all happening in snow
But I shudder.
    Now there's no reason for that.
    Now argue the sky saints.
    And down below, I mourn
        and low like a old cow
        in a rastro slaughterhouse
        in the I-Dont-Know
        district of Hellavides'
        Devil Dang—
        No, hmf, damn, boy,
        boom—hell's clutters
        that meated dante
        when he virgilized
        his poign—
            bom—
                om, atva,
                svaha, snatva,
        Holy Old Howl Who'll
            Ya
            Is Okay

187th Chorus

Do not Seek,
        and Eliminate nothing,
        concluded the Chinese
        Master of 840 B.C.

"Observe the Void which lies
    before your eyes
    How can you set about
      eliminating it?"

Buddhism is a big bomb on the head
   and it hurts

After which comes I know
    the milky fliss,
fluff, soft AW eternities,
    skyrockets,
snowflakes, hope revealed,
    snow
Gerard, Pa, lamb,
    Sax,
Heaven, you, me.

188th Chorus

And tonight I'll pray
    And O I'll call Fugen
    and Kwannon to my aid
    and ask them to let me
    hear their transcendental
    silence sound,
           learning
           thereby
           Fugen
           Avaloki-
           tesvara'an
           mostafokas
           fakirs, makers,
        sing sound silence
        of my sound

O bless me, make me safe,
    say, 'No-Yo' but save
   'Me no?' save
      No-me—I beseech
      save no-me

189th Chorus

Petronic, Satiricon—
The Black Mass is the Christian
Devil Mass
            "A guy in there
            gives a supper
            and has his funeral oration
            spoken, & coffin bared
            in which he is to lie,
            all dishes are black,
            all food black & white
             (that which can be)
            —they have world-food
            at this banquet of death,
            the wealthy man celebrant
            says he'll die early
            and violently"
                    and Does he?

Petronius Arbitum—
        elegant queer,
            my dear

190th Chorus

What I have attained in Buddhism
        is nothing.
What I wish to attain,
        is nothing.

Let me explain.
In perceiving the Dharma
        I achieved nothing—
What worries me is not
        nothing
But everything, the trouble is
        number,
But since everything is nothing
        then I am worried nil.

In seeking to attain the Dharma
    I failed, attaining nothing,
And so I succeeded the goal,
Which was, pure happy
    nothing.
No matter how you cut it
    it's empty delightful boloney

191st Chorus

My startingplace and my goal
are right here in this simple
             space hole

Sings Shinran:—
"All that have obstructions
Are not impeded
By the Clouds of Light."

It is like the Iddhi Magic
Mentioned in Surangama Sutra,
Where say, The Bhikshu
Who delights in Transcendental
Solitude and Brilliant Silence
And Rhinoceros Sorrow
Shall be saved, & transported
   Magically in the air
   To his Blessed Pure Land
   Diamond Irradiation
   Form the Crown of Buddha.
   Wild—I wait by candlelight
      for confirmation
   (And I see waving whitenesses)

192nd Chorus

"O thou who holdest the seal
  of power, raise thy diamond
  hand, bring to naught, destroy,
  exterminate.

O thou sustainer, sustain
  all who are in extremity.

O thou purifier, purify all
  who are in bondage to self.

May the ender of suffering
  be victorious. Om!

Om! Oh! Thou perfectly enlightened,
  enlighten all sentient beings.
O thou who are perfect in wisdom
  and compassion,
Emancipate all beings, & bring
  them to Buddhahood. Om!

Adoration to Tathagata (Attainer
  to Actual Isness), Sugata
  (Attainer to Actual Goodness),
  Buddha (Who is Awake), Perfect
  in Pity and Intelligence

193rd Chorus

Who has accomplished,
And is accomplishing,
And will accomplish,
All these words
Of mystery,
Svaha,
So be it,
Amen."

Numberless roses arranged,
The milk of merriment
        without the curds,
The Pleased Milk
        of Humankindness
The Frowns of worried saints,
The Helpless Hands of Buddha
        burning,
The Crown Prince of the Lotus
        Blossom Sky,
Lover of all the mental phantoms
        in the mind—
Wordmaker, curdmaker
        Kingmaker, Ding
Dong, the Buddha's Gong

194th Chorus

Being in selfless one-ness
With the such-ness
That is Tathagatahood,
So is everybody else
Lost with you
In that bright sea
Of non-personality.

In teaching the Paramitas
Of Virtue and Sweetness,
The Wu-Weis of Love,
The Tehs of Sensibility,
And all the Tibetan Arhat
Secrets of the Buddha Mountain
World up & down of which
We race in celestial racingcars
On imaginary hills seeking
Salvation at the goal,
    Flagged by Dominos of Bodhi
    And Oil men Ragged Hero
        Mechanic Sariputran
    Minnesinging Gurus, on we rave.

195th Chorus

The songs that erupt
Are gist of the poesy,
Come by themselves, hark,
Stark as prisoners in a cave
Let out to sunlight, ragged
And beautiful when you look close
And see underneath the beards
the holy blue eyes of humanity
And brown.

The stars on high sing
songs of their own, in motion
that doesnt move, real,
Unreal, singsong, spheres:—

But human poetries
    With God as their design
        Sing with another law
            Of spheres & ensigns
                    And rip me a blues,
                    Son, blow me a bop,
                    Let me hear 'bout heaven
                    In Brass Fluglemop

196th Chorus

So I write about heaven,
Smoke for the scene,
Wanta bring everyone
Straight to the dream.

If you only could hold
        what you know
As you know it forever,
        instead-a
Moving from griefy to griefy,
        lament to lament,
Groan, and have to come out

and smile once again,
—S teada all that,
A hospital for the sick,
Lying high in crystal,
In heaven of pure
    adamantine
Consanguine
Partiality devoid
Of conditions, free—
    Here I go rowin
    Thru Lake Innifree
    Looking for Nirvana
      Inside me

197th Chorus

Inside, Inside Me,
I'se free
Free as the bee
Inside he.
    Lord have a mercy
    on Hallelujah Town
I got to stomp my foot,
And say, whee,
    hey dad, now oan,
    from now oan,
    I dont wanta
    cant wanta
    wont wanta
      hear about it
not in my Oakland
    Saloon, not in my bar
    Not in my brokenglass
    Not in my jar

Blue, black, race, grace,
      face,
    I love ye.

198th Chorus

Nirvana aint inside me
    cause there aint no me.

Nirvana's everywhere
    'xceptin' what's everywhere
And so all is nowhere.

  Swimmin free, in the lake free,
  Rowing to the other beachy.

  Tall guards you say? tall
    saloons? maloons?
  Tall goons? Tall tunes?

      Tall stately heroes
      Tall calm saints
      Tall long tendrils
        of cloud-air
      Tall unobstructed
        ghost whitenesses
      Imagining on the edge
        of the pier—
      Just not there.

199th Chorus

Empty balloons of gorgeous?
Wild upskies bedazzling radiant?
Immense arcades of secret joy?
Caves of light, Ya-Vingo,
    dream-material palaces
    high in the texture
      of the high thought?

Nirvana? Heaven?
    X? Whatyoucallit?

S w e a r

Huge milky areas of silence
Permeated by rose petals
crushed in diamond vats—
Great baths of glory?—
Singing quiet humsound?
White light of black eternity?
    Golden Secret Figures
    Of Unimaginable
    Inexpressible Flowers
    Blooming in the One Own
      Mind
      Essence

200th Chorus

White figures throughout
    made of light,
Like a truck becomes a square
    mass of shining light bars,
Empty Apparitional secret
    figure of the mind.
More than that. Face
    is mass of swarm-roe
    starlight, insanity
    itself personified
    & taking up space
    & penetrable throughout.

Secret parleys with saviour
Angels outside brown rooms
Where phantoms converge
In light, black and white,
Dazzling in the middle
With one Insane Bar Light—
    One Shiningness
  And you know darkness nullifies
    the color
    Into Nirvana No

201st *Chorus*

When the girls start puttin
    Nirvana-No on their lips
Nobody'll see them.
    Poor girls, did they always
Want attention? Did they
    always disturb
The sitting saint in the woods
    and make him feel
Cheap by sayin: "Those
    guys think they
can sit down & be God."
—"They think they dont
    have to work
    because they are God
    and they sit down
    and think they are God"
    —Those Guys . . .
Over their heads is the unbelievable
                  unending
                  emptiness
                  the enormous
                  nothingness
                  of the skies
    And they claim

202nd *Chorus*

A white poem, a white pure
    spotless poem
    A bright poem
    A nothing poem
    A no-poem non poem
      nondream clean
      silverdawn clear
      silent of birds
      pool-burble-bark
          clear
        the lark of trees

the needle pines
the rock the pool
the sandy shore
the cleanness of dogs
the
frogs
the
pure white
spotless
Honen
Honey Land
Blues

203rd Chorus

Heaven's inside you but there's no you.
What does that mean?
said the teacher,
The Great Holy the All Holy
Old Teacher:—

All you've got to do
Everytime you feel sick
Is stop (this madhouse
shot of yours
is not exactly
the immemorial miel)

stop—and stare
through the things
before your eyes
with eyes unfocused
and as soon as they move
you will have seen
that they move
to illusion.

Seeing that all's illusion
You lose your mind

In meditation
And heal yourself well
   (AND WHAT'S BEEN HEALED?)

204th Chorus

What's been buried in the grave?
      Dust.
Perfect dust?
      Perfect dust in time.
   Time.
      Time is dust.
      Time's not dust
      Time's already happened
            immemorially
      The pearl of the gods
      the agonizer of Wests
      the ball in the bubble
            void

      Time—
            Dont worry bout time.

What's been buried inside me
      for sure?
The substance of my own father's
      empty light
Derived from time working
      on dirt
And clay bones.
            Buddha's River.

205th Chorus

Enter the Holy Stream.
March with the Saints.
Follow along the emptiness.
Follow bright the ferrymen
And follow the All Star

And sing with the others
In praise of the light
In praise of the emptiness
    so bright
In praise of the OO-LA-LA'S
Of Parisian Women.

In praise of the singsong
    mingsong
    brokesong
    lostsong
      Ah Time
          Ah Perturbable

      Me, Sir,
Dis-beturbable Ameget
      Me

206th Chorus

Maaaaaah! said the sheep
And opened its foxtail soft
Mouth to say something empty,
To express its reverentation,

And M n a a a came
    the bull cry something-cry
Because you cant sing
    open yr mouth with poems
    without you make sound
    and sound is wrong
      sound is noise
    But only human speech
      and also all sentient
      communication
      pointing to the finger
      that points at sound
      saying 'Sound is Noise'—
      Otherwise

sound itself
un-self-enlightenable
would go on blatting
& blaring unrecognized
as emptiness and silence

207th Chorus

Aztec Blues—Imitation of Pound
A God called "Drink the Flood
     Water"—HUETEOTL—
Is a very old God.
What older God could you get
   GLED-ZAL-WAD-LE,
   The Sound of the Feathered Serpent,
   cause of the flood.
   He came from:
   "Destroyed-Over-Flooded-Land-
      Exiled-Him-Water-Pour,"
   Which means: He is Water.
            He is the Flood.
            He is the Ocean that Floods

Serpent as the Sign of Flood, Ah
                         Sax—

Bird-feather is a sign of escape,
flight, exile—
      The Feathered Serpent
      Snakes that Fly
      Nail Eternity
      To bye/
      TONA TI UH:- "Of the Sunken Your Ear"

208th Chorus

Anciently in cities
 men have been sitting
 in waiting rooms
 in the night bloated
 with food and alcohol
 waiting waiting waiting
 as though the city existed not.
They are so old.
 They think all alike.
  I've seen them die in chairs
  Quietly in cities they never planned.
  Seen them sing in saloons
  For muffled uproars.
  Seen men in coffee houses
  Shoot the opium cup
  With Greeks of Brotherhood.
  Aztec Pulque Distributors
  Rembrandtian city committees
  And unions of Masons—
Shoot the sperm cup to me, Jim,
These partitioned Anglo Spanese
Singing sneerers perturbing
You in the background
Are your father's kindly
  buriers

209th Chorus

Well, that about does me in.
I've packed my bags and time
Has come to start to heaven.
Afraid of the trip. Always
Thought it was short & snappy
And I wouldnt worry. Or
Always thought I'd be glad to go.
 But who's glad to go? I want gold.
 I want rich safety in my legs
 And good bones made of empty milk

Of God-Kindness—I want
I need I cry like baby
I want my Partotooty
Sweety backpie back
And dong strang bang bong
Dont scrounge my yoll-scrolls
And try to fool with me
One more time & I report you
To the pimp, whore God—
       I got the woozes
       Said the wrong thing
       Want gold want gold
       Gold of eternity

210th Chorus

Impressionism. The drowned afternoon
    along the sunny carnival—
Trees waving over rock walls
    of drowned scummers—
Glutted bloatbellies blue as the bay
    scummed in tangle raft—
Shit on a leaf, by the pier,
    shit used as leaf paper
Piled by flooded Ack Merrimoil
    the Plantaneous River
    of Fra Devilico Mojostico
    the Funny Folly Phoney balloon
    of Polateira Mia OOLA
    the Crap' in-ping, Caing,
    and mutter of imbecile
    boys in jungle beehive fish.
      Blop.
    Centurions. Potalishakions.
    Prerts. F. Funks. P.l.u.p.s.
    Frains Trails Moss.
       Scum. Sing my lil yella
       basket. A tisket. Tasket.
       Athabasket. Ma the basket.

211th Chorus

The wheel of the quivering meat
                              conception
Turns in the void expelling human beings,
Pigs, turtles, frogs, insects, nits,
Mice, lice, lizards, rats, roan
Racinghorses, poxy bucolic pigtics,
Horrible unnameable lice of vultures,
Murderous attacking dog-armies
Of Africa, Rhinos roaming in the
                              jungle,
Vast boars and huge gigantic bull
Elephants, rams, eagles, condors,
Pones and Porcupines and Pills—
All the endless conception of living
                              beings
Gnashing everywhere in Consciousness
Throughout the ten directions of space
Occupying all the quarters in & out,
From supermicroscopic no-bug
To huge Galaxy Lightyear Bowell
Illuminating the sky of one Mind—
        Poor! I wish I was free
        of that slaving meat wheel
        and safe in heaven dead

212th Chorus

All of this meat is in dreadful pain
Anytime circumstances attain
To its attention like a servant
And pricking goads invest the flesh,
And it quivers, meat, & owner cries
And wishes "Why was I born with a body,
Why do I have this painful hive
        Of hope-of-honey-milk yet bane
        Of bitterest reward, as if, to wish
        For flesh was sin alone itself—?"

And now you gotta pay, rhinoceros
                          and you,
   Tho his hide's toughern ten young men
Armed with picks against the Grim
                          Reaper
Whose scythe is preceded by pitchforks
Of temptation & hell, the Horror:
   "Think of pain, you're being hurt,
   Hurry, hurry, think of pain
   Before they make a fool of you
   And discover that you don't feel
   It's the best possible privilege
   To be alive just to die
   And die in denizen of misery"

213th Chorus

Poem dedicated to Allen Ginsberg
—prap—rot—rort—
mort—port—lort—snort
—pell mell—rhine wine—
roll royce—ring ming—
mock my lot—roll my doll—
pull my hairline—smell my kell—
wail my siren—pile my ane—
loose my shoetongue—sing my aim—
loll my wildmoll—roll my
                          luck—
lay my cashier gone amuk—
suck my lamppole, raise the bane,
          hang the traitor
          inside my brain
     Fill my pail well,
ding my bell, smile for the ladies,
          come from hell

214th Chorus

Ling the long Chinese peeswallower,
    a lad like ye,
Laid his hand on Garty's knee
    and paid the pree—

Shong the mong of anisfore,
    Maharajah
Dusty, kinked the from of Jaidphur
    from the Konk mirror free
So all Bojangles Banghard
    had to do
Was roil his rolly tooty
    mot the polyong,
And if you knew what I meant
    you would say
You disgust me—

Aright, ring the devil free—
    Bong—Ring the devil free
    Prong—ring the devil free,
    Song, ring the devil free,
Ong, ring the biney free

215th Chorus

Moll the mingling, mixup
    All your mixupery,
And mail it in one envelopey:
      Propey, Slopey, Kree.
      Motey, slottey, notty,
      Potty, shotty, rotty, wotty,
      Salty, grainy, wavey,
      Takey, Carey, Andy
        Sari Pari Avi Ava
      Gava lava mava dava
      Sava wava ga-ha-va
      Graharva pharva
        Dharma rikey rokkkk

Tokkkk sokkkk
M r o c k k , the Org
Of Old Pootatolato
England Ireland
O
Sail to Sea

216th-A Chorus

Fuck, I'm tired of this imagery
—I wanta quit this horseshit
go home
and go to bed

But I got no home,
sickabed,
suckatootle,
wanta led
bonda londa
rolla molla
sick to my
bella bella
donna donna
I'm a goner
Soner, loner,
moaner,
Poan, cornbelly,
No loan,
Ai, ack,
C r a c k /

I'm sick of this
misery poesy/ flap Jean
Louis
Miseree

216th-B Chorus

Filling the air with an arbitrary dream—
When no desire arises, that is the original
Feeling of peace in Actual Nature—
It is not moot to question how a dream
                                        ends
Whenaslong as it ends—
A Baby in Pain:
        tell the proud seminal mother
        how many more of that she wants
        to satisfy her fertile ego
        and how many more babies
        crying in the night, angry screech,
        knowing that their flesh is on the block
        of death the hungry butcher.
        —how many pigs hung upsidedown
            and slowly bled to death
            by reverent ritual fools
            with no noses and no eyes

Emancipate the human masses
Of this world from slavery to life
And death, by abolishing death
And exterminating birth—
        O Samson me that—
The Venerable Kerouac, friend of Cows
DEPEND ON VAST MOTIONLESS THOUGHT

216th-C Chorus

Well roofed pleasant little hut,
        screened from winds:
That's all I need. Foursquare
The image of the Buddha in my brain,
Drawing from the countryside the verdant
Fantasm of conception, saying:
"We green imageries of bush & tree,
Like you, have risen from a mystery,
And the mystery is fantastic,

Unreal, illusion, and sane,
And strange—It is: When ye
Are not born, thou never showest:
When thou art born thou showest,
Thou showest emeralds and pine trees
And thou showest, and if not born
Thou showest naught in white
Dazzling buried in mindless obscure sea
That strange eternity devises to befool,
Befoul and play unfair with Mag
The worshipper and worrier, Man,
Mag, Mad,
          it's all green trees, men
          And dogs of toothbone:
          All shine in the dust,
          All the same Novice Scotia"

217th Chorus

Sooladat smarty pines came prappin down
My line of least regard last Prapopooty
And whattaya think Old Father Time
made him? a western sponnet
Without no false on bonnet,
Trap in the cock adus time of the Nigh,
Slight the leak of recompense being
                    hermasodized
By finey wild traphoods in all
               their estapular
               glories
Gleaming their shining-rising spears
      against the High Thap All Thup—
So I aim my gazoota always
      to the God, remembering the origin
Of all beasts and cod, Bostonian
By nature, with no minda my own,
Could write about railroads, quietus
These blues, hurt my hand more,
   Rack my hand with labor of nada

—Run 100 yard dash
in Ole Ensanada—
S what'll have to do,
this gin & tonics
Perss o monnix
twab
twab
twabble
all day

218th Chorus

Sight the saver having from the coast
put further items down—what? you
wish to talk to me, hear me scratch
at the mean little door, hiding in my bonnet—
O come off it, the vast canopial
Assemblies wait for yr honest spontaneous reply.
What shall it be?
I promise to reject pain when next
My turn comes back again
I promise not to steal, nor go to hell
For stealing
I promise to say Na
When Tathagata's Angels
Ride for me. Na—
I wanta go to Inside-Me,
Is there such a place? No is.
Flap the wack I smack the hydrant
of desire, sip sop the twill—
(hiding all them guys—'twere
as I told you, old dreams
of young brides'll do you no more good)
Wake up Scribe! Pharisee!
The a x x a b a t a
fl O R I A N I O L A
S P R I N G   T I M E
OW OH ALL
OFFICIAL SEMINARY

219th Chorus

Saints, I give myself up to thee.
Thou hast me. What mayest thou do?
What has thou? Hast nothing?
Hast illusion. Hast rage, regret,
Hast pain. Pain wont be found
Outside the Monastery only—
    Hast decaying saints like Purushka
    Magnificent Russian-booted bird loving
    Father Zossima under the cross
    In his father cell in Holy Russia
    And Alyosha falls to the ground
    And Weeps, as Rakitin smears.
    Grushenka sits him on her lap
    And lacky daisies him to lull
    And love and loll with her
    And wild he runs home in the night
    Over Charade Chagall fences
        snow-white
    To the pink cow of his father's ear,
    Which he slits, presenting to Ivan
    As an intellectual courtesy, Dmitri
    Burps, Smerdyakov smirks.
    The Devil giggles in his poorclothes.
Saints, accept me to the drama
of thy faithful desire.
No me? No drama to desire?
No Alyosha, no Russia, no tears?
Good good good good, my saints.
No saints? No no no my saints.
No no? No such thing as no.

220th Chorus

Pieces of precious emerald and jade
Come from igneous rock once on fire,
Erupted through a volcano, sandstone,
Came out oozing in crevices
Pieces of light long buried in the earth

Are diamonds and floods of them.
"Amen the Jewel in the Lotus!"
Prays the Tibetan Saint with Prayerwheel,
"Om Mani Padhme Hum,"
He wants to pile up credit
Like the jewel in the rock
So that when he's found
The doves will have laid aground
Eggs of bright amethystine
Wallowing splendorous decay,
Kings of Ore, art of fathers
Handed to sons, fire and air.
Kingdoms have been founded on diamonds,
Emeralds and pearls, and walkways
Of padded lily milky meshed
And crushed in holy feet, Maha
Graha Sattva, Being of Great Power,
Fortunes in Wisdom, Stores of Love.
     Mountains rise high, diamonds shine,
     Men ride high the alumpshine
          The lump sunshine
               Delicious is the taste of Porcupine

221st *Chorus*

Old Man Mose
Early American Jazz pianist
Had a grandson
Called Deadbelly.
Old Man Mose walloped
     the rollickin keyport
     Wahoo wildhouse Piany
     with monkies in his hair
     drooling spaghetti, beer
     and beans, with a cigar
     mashed in his countenance
     of gleaming happiness
     the furtive madman
     of old sane times.

Deadbelly dont hide it—
    Lead killed Leadbelly—
Deadbelly admit
    Deadbelly modern cat
Cool—Deadbelly, Man,
Craziest.
        Old Man Mose is Dead
        But Deadbelly get Ahead
        Ha ha ha

222nd Chorus

Mexico Camera
I'm walking down Orizaba Street
looking everywhere. Ahead of me I
see a mansion, with wall, big
lawn, Spanish interiors, fancy
windows very impressive

Further bloated copulated bloats

Silent separative furniture
    The Story of No-Mad, silent
        separative corpses;
      Ignorino the Indian General
        He Chief, wow,
          Of Southern Sonora,
            You know the Bum,
            what was his name?
      Asserfelter Shnard Marade,
    the Marauding Hightailer
        of Southern Slopetawvia,
          krum, full of kerrs and kierke
                    gaard/
        and bash bah
         the P l a p

223rd Chorus

Pineys hursaphies,
        Finally allawies,
                Fonally finalles.
Hookies from OO-SKOOL,
        Polls for Who Hook Fish,
                Fowl for Fair Weather.
Wu! cries the Indian Boy
        in the South Sampan Night,
"Esta que ferro," you be of iron,
I'll be a damn tootely wow
        wot Rot Moongut Rise Shine
        Hogwater Wheel—
                Juice a the eel—
        In Old Lake Miel—
                Honey wheel–
Sound
        E Terpt T A pt T E rt W—
        Song of I Snug Our Song
                Sang of Asia High Gang
                Clang of Iron O Hell Pot—
                Spert of Ole Watson Ville
                Gert—
                Smert—
                Noise of old sad so
                Such Is
Sing a little ditty of the moon inside the loony
boon of snow white blooms in Parkadystan
                I S T A M H O W   H U C K

224th Chorus

Great God Amighty
        What's to be done?
        O what's to be done?
Sings the majestical keener
        and moaner
At the Mexican Funeral home—
And from a clap in the upclouds

Comes a clap of clouts,
"All has been done."
As Theravada say "Nothing"
Nada moonshine number, whats been done?
All been done—all singly blessed—
     All has been done? The mansion's
     been built and Damema
     grown old & died
         in burning house within?
     And Seventeen Sutras & Lotuses
     Transmitted by Perfumed Hand
     From Jingle to Jiggle
     The Hip Hou Parade
         of Togas & Mowrdogrogas
     Of Maharajah India—
         'All's been done'
          'so rest'
         Repose yourself

225 Chorus

The void that's highly embraceable
     during sleep
Has no location and no fret;
Yet I keep restless mental searching
And geographical meandering
To find the Holy Inside Milk
Damema gave to all.

Damema, Mother of Buddhas,
     Mother of Milk

In the dark I wryly remonstrate
With my sillier self
For feigning to believe
In the reality of anything
Especially the so-called reality
Of giving the Discipline
The full desert-hut workout

And superman solitude
And continual enlightened trance
With no cares in the open
And no walls closing in
The Bright Internal Heaven
Of the Starry Night
Of the Cloud Mopped afternoon—
          Oh, Ah, Gold, Honey,
          I've lost my way.

226th Chorus

There is no Way to lose.
If there was a way,
     then,
          when sun is shining on pond
          and I go West, thou East,
          which one does the true sun
          follow?
          which one does the true one
          borrow?
          since neither one is the true one,
          there is no true one way.
          And the sun is the delusion
          Of a way multiplied by two
          And multiplied millionfold.
Since there is no Way, no Buddhas,
No Dharmas, no Conceptions,
Only One Ecstasy—
          And Right Mindfulness
          Is mindfulness that the way is No-Way—
               Anyhow Sameway—
Then what am I to do
          Beyond writing this instructing
          Poesy, ride a magic carpet
          Of self ecstasy, or wait
          For death like the children
          In the Funeral Street after
          The black bus has departed—
          Or—what?

227th Chorus

Merde and misery,
I'm completely in pain
Waiting without mercy
For the worst to happen.
I'm completely at a loss,
      There is no hope
Though I know the arbitrary conception
    of suffering is racking
    my metaphysical
    handicapped ribs,
    and I dont even exist less sing,
    and I been paid
    for work I done
    when I was young
    and work was fun
    and I dont know name from mercy,
    aint got no blues
    no shoes no eyes
    no shoetongues, lungs,
    no happiness, no art,
    nothing to do, nothin to part,
    no hairs to split,
    sidewalks to spit,
    words to make flit
    in the fun-of make-it,
        horror & makeshift poetry
        covering the fact I'm afraid
        to work at a steady job
    jungles of hair on my wrists
    magnified 1000 times
        in Hells of Eternity

228th Chorus

Praised be man, he is existing in milk
    and living in lillies—
And his violin music takes place in milk
    and creamy emptiness—
Praised be the unfolded inside petal
    flesh of tend'rest thought—
    (petrels on the follying
    wave-valleys idly
    sing themselves asleep)—
Praised be delusion, the ripple—
Praised the Holy Ocean of Eternity—
Praised be I, writing, dead already &
    dead again—
  Dipped in ancid inkl
      the flamd
      of T i m
  the Anglo Oglo Saxon Maneuvers
  of Old Poet-o's—
     Praised be wood, it is milk—
     Praised be Honey at the Source—
Praised be the embrace of soft sleep
—the valor of angels in valleys
  of hell on earth below—
Praised be the Non ending—
Praised be the lights of earth-man—
Praised be the watchers—
    Praised be my fellow man
    For dwelling in milk

229th Chorus

In the ocean there's a very sad turtle
(Even tho the *SS Mainline* Fishin Ship
    is reeling in the merit like mad)
Swims longmouthed & sad, looking
    for the Impossible Except Once
    afternoon when the Yoke, Oh,

the old Buddha Yoke set a-floatin
is in the water where the turtle raises
his be-watery snop to the sea
and the Yoke yokes the Turtle
 a Eternity—
"Tell me O Bhikkus,
 what are the chances,
  of such a happening,
   for the turtle is old
    and the yoke free,
    and the 7 oceans bigger
     than any we see
     in this tiny party."
Chances are slender—
 In a million million billion kotis
 of Aeons and Incalculables, Yes,
 the Turtle will set that Yoke free,
 but till then, harder yet
 are the chances, for a man
 to be reborn a man
 in this Karma earth

230th Chorus

Love's multitudinous boneyard
 of decay,
The spilled milk of heroes,
Destruction of silk kerchiefs
 by dust storm,
Caress of heroes blindfolded to posts,
Murder victims admitted to this life,
Skeletons bartering fingers and joints,
The quivering meat of the elephants of kindness
 being torn apart by vultures,
Conceptions of delicate kneecaps,
Fear of rats dripping with bacteria,
Golgotha Cold Hope for Gold Hope,
Damp leaves of Autumn against
 the wood of boats,

Seahorse's delicate imagery of glue,
Sentimental "I Love You" no more,
Death by long exposure to defilement,
Frightening ravishing mysterious beings
    concealing their sex,
Pieces of the Buddha-material frozen
    and sliced microscopically
In Morgues of the North,
Penis apples going to seed,
The severed gullets more numerous than sands—
      Like kissing my kitten in the belly
      The softness of our reward

231st *Chorus*

Dead and dont know it,
    Living and do.

The living have a dead idea.

A person is a living idea;
    after death, a dead idea.

The idea of living is the same
    as the idea of death.

The dead have a living idea—
Dead, it aint my fault
    I was only an idea—

Respected penitence in a shack
    dedicated to the study of Origin—

The good Buddha-material
    is not a sin-cloth—
Cloth of Light—
Beings alive indicate death
    by their jaunty work

Just as the dead indicate the living
    by their silence
        When rock becomes air
    I will be there

232nd Chorus

Buddhists are the only people who dont lie,
In the Sacred Diamond Sutra
Mention is made that God will die—
    "There are no Buddhas
    and no Dharmas"—means—
    There is no Universal Salvation Self,
    The Tathagata of Thusness has understood
    His own Luvaic Emanations
    As being empty, himself and his womb
    Included—No Self God Heaven
    Where we all meet and make it,
    But the Meltingplace of the Bone Entire
    In One Light of Mahayana Gold,
    Asvhaghosha's singing in your ear,
    And Jesus at your feet, washing them,
    And St. Francis whistling for the birds—
    All conjoined though and melted
    And all be-forgotten, pas't on,
    Come into Change's Lightless Domain
    And beyond all Conception,
    Waiting in anticipatory halls
    Of Bar-Light, ranging, searchlights
    Of the Eye, Maitreya and his love,
    The dazzling obscure parade
    of elemental diamond phantoms
    And dominos of chance,
    Skeletons painted on Negresses
    Standing by unimportant-to-you
    Doorways, into Sleep-With-Me
    The alley way behind.

233rd Chorus

There is no selfhood that can begin the practice
Of seeking to attain Anuttara Samyak Sambodhi
Highest Perfect Wisdom
    Yet
  "Faithfully and earnestly observe and study
  and explain this Scripture to others"
      is the gory reminder of bone.
      Others. "Listen, Subhuti! Wherever
      This Scripture shall be observed and studied
      and explained, that place
      will become sacred ground
      to which countless devas and angels
      will bring offerings. Such
      places, however humble they may be,
      will be reverenced as though
      they were famous temples & pagodas,
      to which countless pilgrims will come
      to offer worship and incense.
      And over them the devas & angels
      Will hover like a cloud & will sprinkle
      offerings of celestial flowers
      upon them."

      The Pilgrims are happy.

The Pilgrim of the Holy Grail, the Snail,
The Pilgrim of the Fine Pagoda,
The Pilgrim of the Five Tendencies
      to Hear and Support Prayer—

No selfhood that can begin the practice
      of seeking to attain

234th Chorus

Holy poetry.
>"All things are empty of self-marks."
>"If it is space
>>that is perception of sight
>You ought to know,
>>and if we were to substitute
>One for the other, who'd win?"
>>Santiveda, St. Francis, A Kempis
>>Hara

A sinner may go to Heaven
>by serving God as a sinner

235th Chorus

Dont camp,
You know very well
>What'll happen to you
When you die
>and claim
>>you dont know you're dead
>>when you die and you know
>>"I know dont know that I'm dead"

Dont camp. Death, the no-buzz,
>no-voices, is, must be, the same,
>as life, the tzirripirrit of thupsounds
>in this crazy world that horrifies my mornings
>and makes me mad wildhaired in a room
>like old metaphysical ogrish poets
>in rooms of macabre mysteries.

But it's hard to pretend you don't know
That when you die you wont know.

I know that I'm dead.
I wont camp. I'm dead now.
What am I waiting for to vanish?

The dead dont vanish?
Go up in dirt?
How do I know that I'm dead.
Because I'm alive
and I got work to do
Oh me, Oh my,
Hello–Come in—

236th Chorus

The Buddhist Saints are the incomparable saints
Mooing continue of lovemilk, mewling
And purling with lovely voices for love,
For perfect compassionate pity
Without making one false move
of action,
Perfectly accommodating commiserations
For all sentient belaboring things.
Passive Sweetsaints
Waiting for yr Holyhood,
Hoping your eventual join
In their bright confraternity.

Perfect Divines. I can name some.
What's in a name. They were saints
Of the Religion of the Awakening
From the Dream of Existence
And non-existence.
They know that life and death,
The knowing of life, muteness of death,
Are mutual dual twin opposites
Conceptioning on each side of the Truth
Which is the pivot in the Center
And which says: "Neither life
nor death—neither existence
nor non-existence—but the central
lapse and absence of them both
(in Love's Holy Void Abode)"

237th Chorus

"Ma mère, tu est la terre."
What does that mean?
For one thing, Damema was the mother of Buddhas,
     in Ancient India and Modern Asia
     you put up a Virgin Mary very weird
     in your altars and ikons, Damema,
     with crowns of light coming out of her head
     and lotuses and incense sticks
     and big sad blue eyes inside Flowers.

People light perpetual candles to her name,
Wax in glass with wick, fire,
For 30 days the pale Mystic Face
Of Damema flickers in the ceiling corner
And the dogs bark outside.
          They get water from the moon,
          Send boys out of sight in baskets,
          Sleep in the streets of night,
          Playing flutes & having curbstone nightclubs
          And the curbstone put there by the British—
          They honor and beseech and pray to
                    Damema.

To me Damema is like Virgin Mary,
Mother Maya of Siddhartha Buddha
Died at his childbirth,
Like all mothers should be,
Going to heaven on their impulse
     Pure and free and champion of birth.
          Damema the Milky Mother
          Damema the Secret Hero

238th Chorus

Who was it wrote "Money is the root of all evil?"
Was it Oscar Wilde in one of his witties?
Was it Celine—nah.
Was it Alexander Pope, Benjamin Franklin
    or William Shakespeare—
Was it Pope in one of his many
    clever lines?
Benjamin in his Almanac of Peers
    has Richard the Chicken Liver
    Express a private pear.

Or is Shakespeare blowing wild
Confucius-Polonius witticismical
Paternity-type advice—
"Money is the root of all evil"
For I will
Write
In my will
"I regret that I was not able
To love money more."
For which reason I go into retreat
And monastery—all monastic in a cell
With devotions and hellpellmell
And Yumas Arctic Gizoto Almanac
Priotho Consumas Konas
    In the Corner, & Mother Damema

239th Chorus

Charley Parker Looked like Buddha
Charley Parker, who recently died
Laughing at a juggler on the TV
after weeks of strain and sickness,
was called the Perfect Musician.
And his expression on his face
Was as calm, beautiful, and profound
As the image of the Buddha
Represented in the East, the lidded eyes,

The expression that says "All is Well"
—This was what Charley Parker
Said when he played, All is Well.
You had the feeling of early-in-the-morning
Like a hermit's joy, or like
                the perfect cry
Of some wild gang at a jam session
"Wail, Wop"—Charley burst
His lungs to reach the speed
Of what the speedsters wanted
And what they wanted
Was his Eternal Slowdown.
A great musician and a great
                creator of forms
That ultimately find expression
In mores and what have you.

240th Chorus

Musically as important as Beethoven,
Yet not regarded as such at all,
A genteel conductor of string
                orchestras
In front of which he stood,
Proud and calm, like a leader
                of music
In the Great Historic World Night,
And wailed his little saxophone,
The alto, with piercing clear
                lament
In perfect tune & shining harmony,
Toot—as listeners reacted
Without showing it, and began talking
And soon the whole joint is rocking
And everybody talking and Charley
                Parker
Whistling them on to the brink of eternity
With his Irish St Patrick
              patootle stick,

And like the holy piss we blop
And we plop in the waters of
                         slaughter
And white meat, and die
One after one, in time.

241st Chorus

And how sweet a story it is
When you hear Charley Parker
                    tell it,
Either on records or at sessions,
Or at official bits in clubs,
Shots in the arm for the wallet,
Gleefully he Whistled the
                    perfect
                    horn

Anyhow, made no difference.

Charley Parker, forgive me—
Forgive me for not answering your eyes—
For not having made an indication
Of that which you can devise—
Charley Parker, pray for me—
Pray for me and everybody
In the Nirvanas of your brain
Where you hide, indulgent and huge,
No longer Charley Parker
But the secret unsayable name
That carries with it merit
Not to be measured from here
To up, down, east, or west—
—Charley Parker, lay the bane,
   off me, and every body

242nd Chorus

The sound in your mind
    is the first sound
        that you could sing

If you were singing
    at a cash register
        with nothing on yr mind—

But when that grim reper
    comes to lay you
        look out my lady

He will steal all you got
    while you dingle with the dangle
    and having robbed you

Vanish.
    Which will be your best reward,
    T'were better to get rid o
    John O' Twill, then sit a-mortying
    In this Half Eternity with nobody
    To save the old man being hanged
    In my closet for nothing
    And everybody watches
    When the act is done—

Stop the murder and the suicide!
    All's well!
        I am the Guard

THE SCRIPTURE OF THE
GOLDEN ETERNITY

1 Did I create that sky? Yes, for, if it was
anything other than a conception in my mind
I wouldnt have said "Sky"—That is why I am the
golden eternity. There are not two of us here,
reader and writer, but one, one golden eternity,
One-Which-It-Is, That-Which-Everything-Is.

2 The awakened Buddha to show the way, the
chosen Messiah to die in the degradation
of sentience, is the golden eternity. One that
is what is, the golden eternity, or, God, or,
Tathagata—the *name*. The Named One.
The human God. Sentient Godhood.
Animate Divine. The Deified One.
The Verified One. The Free One.
The Liberator. The Still One.
The Settled One. The Established One.
Golden Eternity. All is Well.
The Empty One. The Ready One.
The Quitter. The Sitter.
The Justified One. The Happy One.

3 That sky, if it was anything other than an
illusion of my mortal mind I wouldnt have
said "that sky." Thus I made that sky, I am the
golden eternity. I am Mortal Golden Eternity.

4 I was awakened to show the way, chosen to die
in the degradation of life, because I am
Mortal Golden Eternity.

5 I am the golden eternity in mortal animate form.

6 Strictly speaking, there is no me, because all
is emptiness. I am empty, I am non-existent.
All is bliss.

7 This truth law has no more reality than the
world.

177

8   You are the golden eternity because there is
     no me and no you, only one golden eternity.

9   The Realizer. Entertain no imaginations whatever,
     for the thing is a no-thing. Knowing this then
is Human Godhood.

10   This world is the movie of what everything
     is, it is one movie, made of the same stuff
throughout, belonging to nobody, which is what
everything is.

11   If we were not all the golden eternity we
     wouldnt be here. Because we are here we
cant help being pure. To tell man to be pure on
account of the punishing angel that punishes the
bad and the rewarding angel that rewards the good
would be like telling the water "Be Wet"—Never
the less, all things depend on supreme reality,
which is already established as the record of
Karma earned-fate.

12   God is not outside us but is just us, the
     living and the dead, the never-lived and
never-died. That we should learn it only now, is
supreme reality, it was written a long time ago
in the archives of universal mind, it is already
done, there's no more to do.

13   This is the knowledge that sees the golden
     eternity in all things, which is us, you,
me, and which is no longer us, you, me.

14   What name shall we give it which hath no
     name, the common eternal matter of the mind?
If we were to call it essence, some might think it
meant perfume, or gold, or honey. It is not even
mind. It is not even discussable, groupable into
words; it is not even endless, in fact it is not

even mysterious or inscrutably inexplicable; it is
what is; it is that; it is this. We could easily
call the golden eternity "This." But "what's in
a name?" asked Shakespeare. The golden eternity
by another name would be as sweet. A Tathagata,
a God, a Buddha by another name, an Allah, a Sri
Krishna, a Coyote, a Brahma, a Mazda, a Messiah,
an Amida, an Aremedeia, a Maitreya, a Palalakonuh,
1 2 3 4 5 6 7 8 would be as sweet. The golden
eternity is X, the golden eternity is A, the
golden eternity is △, the golden eternity is ○,
the golden eternity is □, the golden eternity is
t-h-e g-o-l-d-e-n e-t-e-r-n-i-t-y. In the
beginning was the word; before the beginning, in
the beginningless infinite neverendingness, was
the essence. Both the word "God" and the essence
of the word, are emptiness. The form of emptiness
which is emptiness having taken the form of form,
is what you see and hear and feel right now, and
what you taste and smell and think as you read
this. Wait awhile, close your eyes, let your
breathing stop three seconds or so, listen to
the inside silence in the womb of the world, let
your hands and nerve-ends drop, re-recognize
the bliss you forgot, the emptiness and
essence and ecstasy of ever having been and
ever to be the golden eternity. This is
the lesson you forgot.

15 The lesson was taught long ago in the
other world systems that have naturally
changed into the empty and awake, and are here
now smiling in our smile and scowling in our
scowl. It is only like the golden eternity
pretending to be smiling and scowling to
itself; like a ripple on the smooth ocean of
knowing. The fate of humanity is to vanish
into the golden eternity, return pouring into
its hands which are not hands. The navel shall

receive, invert, and take back what'd issued
forth; the ring of flesh shall close; the
personalities of long dead heroes are blank
dirt.

16   The point is we're waiting, not how
comfortable we are while waiting.
Paleolithic man waited by caves for the
realization of why he was there, and hunted;
modern men wait in beautified homes and try
to forget death and birth. We're waiting for
the realization that this is the golden eternity.

17   It came on time.

18   There is a blessedness surely to be
believed, and that is that everything
abides in eternal ecstasy, now and forever.

19   Mother Kali eats herself back. All things
but come to go. All these holy forms,
unmanifest, not even forms, truebodies of blank
bright ecstasy, abiding in a trance, "in emptiness
and silence" as it is pointed out in the Diamond-
cutter, asked to be only what they are: *Glad*.

20   The secret God-grin in the trees and in
the teapot, in ashes and fronds, fire
and brick, flesh and mental human hope. All
things, far from yearning to be re-united with
God, had never left themselves and here they are,
Dharmakaya, the body of the truth law, the
universal Thisness.

21   "Beyond the reach of change and fear,
beyond all praise and blame," the
Lankavatara Scripture knows to say, is he who
is what he is in time and in time-less-ness,
in ego and in ego-less-ness, in self and in
self-less-ness.

22 Stare deep into the world before you
as if it were the void: innumerable
holy ghosts, buddhies, and savior gods there hide,
smiling. All the atoms emitting light inside
wavehood, there is no personal separation of
any of it. A hummingbird can come into a
house and a hawk will not: so rest and be assured.
While looking for the light, you may suddenly be
devoured by the darkness and find the true light.

23 Things dont tire of going and coming. The
flies end up with the delicate viands.

24 The cause of the world's woe is birth,
the cure of the world's woe is a bent
stick.

25 Though it is everything, strictly speaking
there is no golden eternity because everything
is nothing: there are no things and no goings and
comings: for all is emptiness, and emptiness is
these forms, emptiness is this one formhood.

26 All these selfnesses have already vanished.
Einstein measured that this present universe
is an expanding bubble, and you know what that means.

27 Discard such definite imaginations of
phenomena as your own self, thou human
being, thou'rt a numberless mass of sun-motes:
each mote a shrine. The same as to your shyness
of other selves, selfness as divided into infinite
numbers of beings, or selfness as identified as
one self existing eternally. Be obliging and noble,
be generous with your time and help and possessions,
and be kind, because the emptiness of this little
place of flesh you carry around and call your soul,
your entity, is the same emptiness in every direction
of space unmeasurably emptiness, the same, one, and
holy emptiness everywhere: why be selfly and unfree,

Man God, in your dream? Wake up, thou'rt selfless
and free. "Even and upright your mind abides nowhere,"
states Hui Neng of China. We're all in Heaven now.

28   Roaring dreams take place in a perfectly silent
mind. Now that we know this, throw the raft
away.

29   Are you tightwad and are you mean, those
are the true sins, and sin is only a
conception of ours, due to long habit. Are
you generous and are you kind, those are
the true virtues, and they're only conceptions.
The golden eternity rests beyond sin and virtue,
is attached to neither, is attached to nothing,
is unattached, because the golden eternity is
Alone. The mold has rills but it is one mold.
The field has curves but it is one field. All
things are different forms of the same thing.
I call it the golden eternity—what do you
call it, brother? For the blessing and merit
of virtue, and the punishment and bad fate of
sin, are alike just so many words.

30   Sociability is a big smile, and a big
smile is nothing but teeth. Rest
and be kind.

31   There's no need to deny that evil thing
called GOOGOO, which doesnt exist, just
as there's no need to deny that evil thing
called Sex and Rebirth, which also doesnt exist,
as it is only a form of emptiness. The bead
of semen comes from a long line of awakened
natures that were your parent, a holy flow,
a succession of saviors pouring from the womb
of the dark void and back into it, fantastic
magic imagination of the lightning, flash, plays,
dreams, not even plays, dreams.

32   "The womb of exuberant fertility,"
      Ashvhaghosha called it, radiating forms
out of its womb of exuberant emptiness. In
emptiness there is no Why, no knowledge of Why,
no ignorance of Why, no asking and no answering
of Why, and no significance attached to this.

33   A disturbed and frightened man is like
      the golden eternity experimentally pretending
at feeling the disturbed-and-frightened mood; a
calm and joyous man, is like the golden eternity
pretending at experimenting with that experience;
a man experiencing his Sentient Being, is like
the golden eternity pretending at trying that out
too; a man who has no thoughts, is like the golden
eternity pretending at being itself; because
the emptiness of everything has no beginning and
no end and at present it is infinite.

34   "Love is all in all," said Sainte Thérèse, choosing
      Love for her vocation and pouring out
her happiness, from her garden by the gate, with
a gentle smile, pouring roses on the earth,
so that the beggar in the thunderbolt received
of the endless offering of her dark void.
Man goes a-beggaring into nothingness.
"Ignorance is the father, Habit-Energy is
the Mother." Opposites are not the same
for the same reason they are the same.

35   The words "atoms of dust" and "the great
      universes" are only words. The idea
that they imply is only an idea. The belief
that we live here in this existence, divided
into various beings, passing food in and out
of ourselves, and casting off husks of bodies
one after another with no cessation and no
definite or particular discrimination, is
only an idea. The seat of our Immortal Intelligence

can be seen in that beating light between the eyes
the Wisdom Eye of the ancients: we know what
we're doing: we're not disturbed: because
we're like the golden eternity pretending at
playing the magic cardgame and making believe
it's real, it's a big dream, a joyous ecstasy
of words and ideas and flesh, an ethereal flower
unfolding and folding back, a movie, an
exuberant bunch of lines bounding emptiness,
the womb of Avalokitesvara, a vast secret
silence, springtime in the Void, happy young
gods talking and drinking on a cloud. Our
32,000 chillicosms bear all the marks of
excellence. Blind milky light fills our night;
and the morning is a crystal.

36   Give a gift to your brother, but there's
no gift to compare with the giving of
assurance that he is the golden eternity. The
true understanding of this would bring tears to
your eyes. The other shore is right here, forgive
and forget, protect and reassure. Your tormentors
will be purified. Raise thy diamond hand. Have
faith and wait. The course of your days is a
river rumbling over your rocky back. You're
sitting at the bottom of the world with a head
of iron. Religion is thy sad heart. You're the
golden eternity and it must be done by you. And
means one thing: Nothing-Ever-Happened.
This is the golden eternity.

37   When the Prince of Kalinga severed
the flesh from the limbs and body of Buddha,
even then Buddha was free from any such ideas as
his own self, other self, living beings
divided into many selves, or living beings
united and identified into one eternal self.
The golden eternity isnt "me." Before you
can know that you're dreaming you'll wake up,
Atman. Had the Buddha, the Awakened One,

· cherished any of these imaginary judgments
of and about things, he would have fallen
into impatience and hatred in his suffering.
Instead, like Jesus on the Cross he saw
the light and died kind, loving all living
things.

38   The world was spun out of a blade of
grass: the world was spun out of a mind.
Heaven was spun out of a blade of grass: heaven
was spun out of a mind. Neither will do you
much good, neither will do you much harm.
The Oriental imperturbed, is the golden eternity.

39   He is called a Yogi, he is called a
Priest, a Minister, a Brahmin, a
Parson, a Chaplain, a Rôshi, a Laoshih,
a Master, a Patriarch, a Pope, a Spiritual
Commissar, a Counselor, an Adviser, a
Bodhisattva-Mahasattva, an Old Man, a Saint,
a Shaman, a Leader, who thinks nothing of
himself as separate from another self, not
higher nor lower, no stages and no definite
attainments, no mysterious stigmata or secret
holyhood, no wild dark knowledge and no
venerable authoritativeness, nay a giggling sage
sweeping out the kitchen with a broom. After
supper, a silent smoke. Because there is no
definite teaching: the world is undisciplined
Nature endlessly in every direction inward
to your body and outward into space.

40   Meditate outdoors. The dark trees at
night are not really the dark trees at night,
it's only the golden eternity.

41   A mosquito as big as Mount Everest is
much bigger than you think; a horse's hoof
is more delicate than it looks. An altar
consecrated to the golden eternity, filled with

roses and lotuses and diamonds, is the cell of
the humble prisoner, the cell so cold and dreary.
Boethius kissed the Robe of the Mother Truth in
a Roman dungeon.

42 Do you think the emptiness of the sky
will ever crumble away? Every little child
knows that everybody will go to heaven. Knowing
that nothing ever happened is not really knowing
that nothing ever happened, it's the golden eternity.
In other words, nothing can compare with telling
your brother and your sister that what happened,
what is happening, and what will happen, never
really happened, is not really happening and never will
happen, it is only the golden eternity. Nothing was
ever born, nothing will ever die. Indeed, it didnt
even happen that you heard about golden eternity
through the accidental reading of this scripture.
The thing is easily false. There are no
warnings whatever issuing from the golden eternity:
do what you want.

43 Even in dreams be kind, because anyway there
is no time, no space, no mind. "It's all
not-born," said Bankei of Japan, whose mother
heard this from her son and did what we call
"died happy." And even if she had died unhappy,
dying unhappy is not really dying unhappy, it's
the golden eternity. It's impossible to exist,
it's impossible to be persecuted, it's impossible
to miss your reward.

44 Eight hundred and four thousand myriads
of Awakened Ones throughout numberless
swirls of epochs appeared to work hard to save
a grain of sand, and it was only the golden eternity.
And their combined reward will be no greater and
no lesser than what will be won by a piece of
dried turd. It's a reward beyond thought.

45 When you've understood this scripture,
throw it away. If you cant understand
this scripture, throw it away. I insist on
your freedom.

46 O Everlasting Eternity, all things and
all truth laws are no-things, in three ways,
which is the same way: AS THINGS OF TIME they dont
exist and never came, because they're already gone
and there is no time. AS THINGS OF SPACE they dont
exist because there is no furthest atom than can
be found or weighed or grasped, it is emptiness
through and through, matter and empty space too.
AS THINGS OF MIND they dont exist, because the mind
that conceives and makes them out does so by seeing,
hearing, touching, smelling, tasting, and mentally-noticing
and without this mind they would not be seen or
heard or felt or smelled or tasted or mentally-noticed,
they are discriminated that which they're not
necessarily by imaginary judgments of the mind,
they are actually dependent on the mind that makes
them out, by themselves they are no-things, they
are really mental, seen only of the mind, they
are really empty visions of the mind, heaven is
a vision, everything is a vision. What does it
mean that I am in this endless universe thinking
I'm a man sitting under the stars on the terrace
of earth, but actually empty and awake throughout
the emptiness and awakedness of everything? It
means that I am empty and awake, knowing that I
am empty and awake, and that there's no difference
between me and anything else. It means that I
have attained to that which everything is.

47 The-Attainer-To-That-Which-Everything-Is,
the Sanskrit Tathagata, has no ideas
whatever but abides in essence identically with
the essence of all things, which is what it is,
in emptiness and silence. Imaginary meaning

stretched to make mountains and as far as the
germ is concerned it stretched even further to
make molehills. A million souls dropped through
hell but nobody saw them or counted them. A lot
of large people isnt really a lot of large people,
it's only the golden eternity. When St. Francis
went to heaven he did not add to heaven nor
detract from earth. Locate silence, possess
space, spot me the ego. "From the beginning,"
said the Sixth Patriarch of the China School,
"not a thing is."

48   He who loves all life with his pity
      and intelligence isnt really he who
loves all life with his pity and intelligence,
it's only natural. The universe is fully
known because it is ignored. Enlightenment
comes when you dont care. This is a good
tree stump I'm sitting on. You cant even
grasp your own pain let alone your eternal
reward. I love you because you're me.
I love you because there's nothing else to do.
It's just the natural golden eternity.

49   What does it mean that those trees
      and mountains are magic and unreal?—
It means that those trees and mountains are
magic and unreal. What does it mean that those
trees and moutains are not magic but real?—
it means that those trees and mountains are not
magic but real. Men are just making imaginary
judgments both ways, and all the time it's
just the same natural golden eternity.

50   If the golden eternity was anything other
      than mere words, you could not have said
"golden eternity." This means that the words
are used to point at the endless nothingness
of reality. If the endless nothingness of
reality was anything other than mere words, you

could not have said "endless nothingness of
reality," you could not have said it. This
means that the golden eternity is out of our
word-reach, it refuses steadfastly to be
described, it runs away from us and leads us
in. The name is not really the name. The
same way, you could not have said "this world"
if this world was anything other than mere words.
There's nothing there but just that. They've
long known that there's nothing to life but just
the living of it. It Is What It Is and That's
All It Is.

51   There's no system of teaching and no
reward for teaching the golden eternity,
because nothing has happened. In the golden eternity
teaching and reward havent even vanished let alone
appeared. The golden eternity doesnt even have to
be perfect. It is very silly of me to talk about
it. I talk about it because there's no command or
warning of any kind, and also no blessing and no
reward. I talk about it simply because here I am
dreaming that I talk about it in a dream already
ended, ages ago, from which I'm already awake, and
it was only an empty dreaming, in fact nothing
whatever, in fact nothing ever happened at all.
The beauty of attaining the golden eternity is
that nothing will be acquired, at last.

52   Kindness and sympathy, understanding and
encouragement, these give: they are better
than just presents and gifts: no reason in the
world why not. Anyhow, be nice. Remember the
golden eternity is yourself. "If someone will
simply practice kindness," said Gotama to
Subhuti, "he will soon attain highest perfect
wisdom." Then he added: "Kindness after all
is only a word and it should be done on the spot
without thought of kindness." By practicing
kindness all over with everyone you will soon

come into the holy trance, definite distinctions
of personalities will become what they really
mysteriously are, our common and eternal blissstuff,
the pureness of everything forever, the great bright
essence of mind, even and one thing everywhere the
holy eternal milky love, the white light everywhere
everything, emptybliss, svaha, shining, ready, and
awake, the compassion in the sound of silence, the
swarming myriad trillionaire you are.

53 Everything's alright, form is emptiness
and emptiness is form, and we're here
forever, in one form or another, which is empty.
Everything's alright, we're not here, there, or
anywhere. Everything's alright, cats sleep.

54 The everlasting and tranquil essence, look
around and see the smiling essence everywhere.
How wily was the world made, Maya, not-even-made.

55 There's the world in the daylight. If it
was completely dark you wouldnt see it but
it would still be there. If you close your eyes
you really see what it's like: mysterious
particle-swarming emptiness. On the moon
big mosquitos of straw know this in the kindness
of their hearts. Truly speaking, unrecognizably
sweet it all is. Dont worry about nothing.

56 Imaginary judgments about things, in this
Nothing-Ever-Happened wonderful Void,
you dont even have to reject them, let alone
accept them. "That looks like a tree, let's
call it a tree," said Coyote to Earthmaker at
the beginning, and they walked around the
rootdrinker patting their bellies.

57 Perfectly selfless, the beauty of it,
the butterfly doesnt take it as a personal
achievement, he just disappears through the trees.

You too, kind and humble and not-even-here,
it wasnt in a greedy mood that you saw the light
that belongs to everybody.

58 Look at your little finger, the emptiness
of it is no different than the emptiness
of infinity.

59 Cats yawn because they realize that
there's nothing to do.

60 Up in heaven you wont remember all these
tricks of yours. You wont even sigh "Why?"
Whether as atomic dust or as great cities, what's
the difference in all this stuff. A tree is
still only a rootdrinker. The puma's twisted face
continues to look at the blue sky with sightless
eyes, Ah sweet divine and indescribable verdurous
paradise planted in mid-air! Caitanya, it's only
consciousness. Not with thoughts of your mind,
but in the believing sweetness of your heart,
you snap the link and open the golden door
and disappear into the bright room, the
everlasting ecstasy, eternal Now. Soldier,
follow me!—there never was a war. Arjuna,
dont fight!—why fight over nothing?
Bless and sit down.

61 I remember that I'm supposed to be a man
and consciousness and I focus my eyes and the
print reappears and the words of the poor book
are saying, "The world, as God has made it"
and there are no words in my pitying heart
to express the knowless loveliness of the
trance there was before I read those words,
I had no such idea that there was a world.

62 This world has no marks, signs, or evidence
of existence, nor the noises in it, like
accident of wind or voices or heehawing animals,

yet listen closely the eternal hush of silence
goes on and on throughout all this, and has been
going on, and will go on and on. This is because
the world is nothing but a dream and is just thought
of and the everlasting eternity pays no attention
to it. At night under the moon, or in a quiet
room, hush now, the secret music of the Unborn
goes on and on, beyond conception, awake beyond
existence. Properly speaking, awake is not really
awake because the golden eternity never went to
sleep: you can tell by the constant sound of
Silence which cuts through this world like a
magic diamond through the trick of your not
realizing that your mind caused the world.

63 The God of the American Plateau Indian
was Coyote. He says: "Earth! those beings
living on your surface, none of them disappearing,
will all be transformed. When I have spoken to
them, when they have spoken to me, from that
moment on, their words and their bodies which
they usually use to move about with, will all
change. I will not have heard them."

64 I was smelling flowers in the yard, and
when I stood up I took a deep breath and
the blood all rushed to my brain and I woke up
dead on my back in the grass. I had apparently
fainted, or died, for about sixty seconds. My
neighbor saw me but he thought I had just
suddenly thrown myself on the grass to enjoy
the sun. During that timeless moment of
unconsciousness I saw the golden eternity. I saw
heaven. In it nothing had ever happened, the
events of a million years ago were just as phantom
and ungraspable as the events of now or of a
million years from now, or the events of the next
ten minutes. It was perfect, the golden solitude,
the golden emptiness, Something-Or-Other, something
surely humble. There was a rapturous ring of

silence abiding perfectly. There was no question
of being alive or not being alive, of likes and
dislikes, of near or far, no question of giving
or gratitude, no question of mercy or judgment,
or of suffering or its opposite or anything.
It was the womb itself, aloneness, alaya vijnana
the universal store, the Great Free Treasure, the
Great Victory, infinite completion, the joyful
mysterious essence of Arrangement. It seemed
like one smiling smile, one adorable adoration,
one gracious and adorable charity, everlasting
safety, refreshing afternoon, roses, infinite
brilliant immaterial golden ash, the Golden Age.
The "golden" came from the sun in my eyelids,
and the "eternity" from my sudden instant
realization as I woke up that I had just
been where it all came from and where it
was all returning, the everlasting So, and
so never coming or going; therefore I call it
the golden eternity but you can call it
anything you want. As I regained
consciousness I felt so sorry I had
a body and a mind suddenly realizing I
didnt even have a body and a mind and nothing
had ever happened and everything is alright
forever and forever and forever, O thank you
thank you thank you.

65   This is the first teaching from the
      golden eternity.

66   The second teaching from the golden eternity
      is that there never was a first teaching
from the golden eternity. So be sure.

BOOK OF BLUES

In my system, the form of blues choruses is limited by the small
page of the breastpocket notebook in which they are written,
like the form of a set number of bars in a jazz blues chorus, and
so sometimes the word-meaning can carry from one chorus
into another, or not, just like the phrase-meaning can carry
harmonically from one chorus to the other, or not, in jazz, so
that, in these blues as in jazz, the form is determined by time,
and by the musician's spontaneous phrasing & harmonizing
with the beat of the time as it waves & waves on by in mea-
sured choruses.

    It's all gotta be non stop ad libbing within each chorus, or
the gig is shot.

San Francisco Blues

1st Chorus

I see the backs
Of old Men rolling
Slowly into black
Stores.

2nd Chorus

Line faced mustached
Black men with turned back
Army weathered brownhats
Stomp on by with bags
Of burlap & rue
Talking to secret
Companions with long hair
In the sidewalk
On 3rd Street
San Francisco
With the rain of exhaust
    Plicking in the mist
    You see in black
    Store doors—
    Petting trucks farting—
    Vastly city.

3rd Chorus

3rd St Market to Lease
Has a washed down tile
Tile entrance once white
 Now caked with gum
Of a thousand hundred feet
Feet of passers who
 Did not go straight on
Bending to flap the time
Pap page on back

With smoke emanating
From their noses
But slowly like old
  Lantern jawed junkmen
  Hurrying with the lump
  Wondrous potato bag
     To the avenues of sunshine
     Came, bending to spit,
  & Shuffled awhile there.

4th Chorus

The rooftop of the beatup
  tenement
     On 3rd & Harrison
     Has Belfast painted
     Black on yellow
      On the side
     the old Frisco wood is
     shown with weatherbeaten
  rainboards & a
  washed out blue bottle
  once painted for wild
   commercial reasons by
   an excited seltzerite
    as firemen came last
  afternoon & raised the
  ladder to a fruitless
   fire that was not there,
    so, is Belfast singin
       in this time

5th Chorus

  when brand's forgotten
    taste washed in
    rain the gullies broadened
    & every body gone
  the acrobats of the

tenement
  who dug bel fast
  divers all
and the divers all dove

ah
  little girls make
  shadows on the
  sidewalk shorter
than the shadow
  of death
    in this town—

6th Chorus

Fat girls
In red coats
With flap white out shoes

  Monstrous soldiers
  Stalk at dawn
Looking for whores
  And burning to eat up

Harried Mexican Laborers
  Become respectable
  In San Francisco
Carrying newspapers
Of culture burden
And packages of need
Walk sadly reluctant
  To work in dawn
Stalking with not cat
In the feel of their stride
  Touching to hide the sidewalk,
  Blackshiny lastnight parlor
  Shoes hitting the slippery
With hard slicky heels
  To slide & Fall:
    Breboac! Karrak!

7th Chorus

Dumb kids with thick lips
And black skin
Carry paper bags
Meaninglessly:
"Stop bothering the cat!"
His mother yelled at him
Yesterday and now
He goes to work
Down Third Street
In the milky dawn
Piano rolling over the hill
To the tune of the English
Fifers in some whiter mine,
'Brick a brack,
  Pliers on your back;
  Mick mack
  Kidneys in your back;
    Bald Boo!
  Oranges and you!
    Lick lock
    The redfaced cock'

8th Chorus

Oi yal!
She yawns to lall
  La la—
  Me Loom—
    The weary gray hat
    Peacoat ex sailor
    Marining meekly
    Hands a poop a pocket
    Face
    Lips
Oh   Mo   Sea!
  The long fat yellow
  Eternity cream
  Of the Third St Bus

Roof swimming like
A monosyllable
Armored Mososaur
Swimming in my Primordial
Windowpane
    Of pain

9th Chorus

Alas! Youth is worried,
Pa's astray.
What so say
    To well dressed ambassadors
    From death's truth
    Pimplike, rich,
    In the morning slick;
    Or sad white caps
    Of snowy sea men
    In San Francisco
Gray streets
    Arm waving to walk
    The Harrison cross
        And earn later sunset
        purple

10th Chorus

    Dig the sad old bum
No money
    Presuming to hit the store
And buy his cube of oleo
    For 8 cents
    So in cheap rooms
    At A M   3 30
    He can cough & groan
    In a white tile sink
     By his bed
    Which is used
    To run water in

And stagger to
In the reel of wake up
Middle of the night
   Flophouse Nightmares—
   His death no blackern
   Mine, his Toast's
   Just as well buttered
   And on the one side.

11th Chorus

There's no telling
What's on the mind
Of the bony
   Character in plaid
Workcoat & glasses
   Carrying lunch
   Stalking & bouncing
   Slowly to his job

Or the beauteous Indian
Girl hurrying stately
   Into Marathon Grocery
Run by Greeks
   To buy bananas
    For her love night,
   What's she thinking?
     Her lips are like cherries,
   Her cheeks just purse them out
   All the more to kiss them
   And suck their juices out.

12th Chorus

A young woman flees an old man,
Mohammedan Prophecy:
And she got avocados
Anyhow.

The furtive whore
Looks over her shoulder
While unlocking the door
  Of the tenement
  Of her pimp
Who with big Negro Arkansas
Or East Texas Oilfields
Harry Truman hat's
  Been standin on the street
    All day
    Waiting for the cold girl
    Bending in thincoat in the wind
    And Sunday afternoon drizzle
    To step on it & get some bread
      For Papa's gotta sleep tonite
      And the Chinaman's coming back

13th Chorus

  "No hunger & no wittles
    neither deary"
    Said the crone
    To Edwin Drood

Okay.
  There'll be an answer.
  Forthcoming
When the morning wind
  Ceases shaking
    The man's collar
    When there's no starch in't
    And Acme Beer
      Runs flowing
      Into dry gray hats.
        When
          Dearie
          The pennies in the
          palm multiply
          as you watch

14th Chorus

When whistlers stop scowling
Smokers stop sighing
Watchers stop looking
And women stop walking

When gray beards
Grow no more
And pain dont
Take you by surprise
  And bedposts creak
  In rhythm not at morn
  And dry men's bones
  Are not pushed
  By angry meaning pelvic
    Propelled legs of reason
    To a place you hate,
    Then I'll go lay my crown
Body on the heads of 3 men
    Hurrying & laughing
      In the wrong direction,
        my Idol

15th Chorus

Sex is an automaton
Sounding like a machine
Thru the stopped up keyhole
—Young men go fastern
  Old men
  Old men are passionately
    breathless
  Young men breathe inwardly
  Young women & old women
  Wait

There was a sound of slapping
When the angel stole come

And the angel that had lost
    Lay back satisfied

Hungry addled red face
With tight clutch
    Traditional Time
    Brief case in his paw
Prowls placking the pavement
    To his office girl's
        Rumped skirt at 5's
            Five O Clock Shadows

16th Chorus

    Angrily I must insist—
    The phoney Negro
    Sea captain
With the battered coat
Who looks like
Charley Chaplin in a
movie about now filmed
    in the air by crews
    of raving rabid
    angels drooling happi
    ly
        among the funny fat
        Cherubim
Leading that serious
    Hardjawed sincere
    Negro stud
    In at morn
        For a round of crimes
        Is Lucifer the Fraud

17th Chorus

Little girls worry too much
For no one will hurt them
Except the beast
Whom they'd knife
In another life
In the as well East
As West of Bethlehem
And do of it much

   Rhetorical Third Street
Grasping at racket
   Groans & stinky
    I've no time
    To dally hassel
    In your heart's house,
    It's too gray
    I'm too cold—
    I wanta go to Golden,
    That's my home.

18th Chorus

I came a wearyin
 From eastern hills;
Yonder Nabathacaque recessit
The eastward to Aurora rolls,
Somewhere West of Idalia
Or east of Klamath Falls,
One—Lost a blackhaired
   Woman with thin feet
   And red bag hangin
   Who usta walk
    Down Arapahoe Street
   In Denver
    And made all the
     cabbies cry
    And drugstore ponies
    Eating pool in Remsac's

Sob, to See so Lovely
All the Time
    And all so Tight
    And young.

19th Chorus

Pshaw! Paw's Ford
Got Lost in the Depression
He driv over the Divide
    And forgot to cleave the road
Instead put atomic energy
 In the ass of his machine
And flew to find
    The gory clouds
Of rocky torment
    Far away
    And they fished him
    Outa Miner's Creek
    More dead n Henry
    And whole lot fonder,
    Podner—
        Clack of the wheel's
        My freight train blues

Third Street I seed

20th Chorus

And knowed
  And under ramps I writ
    The poems of the punk
  Who met the Fagin
    Who told him 'Punk
  When walkin with me
    To roll a Sleepin drunk
  Dont wish ya was back
    Home in yr mother's parlor
    And when the cops

Come ablastin
With loaded 45's
  Dont ask for gold
Or silver from my purse,
  Its milken hassel
  Will be strewn
    And scattered
    In the sand
    By an old bean can
      And dried up kegs
        We'd a sat & jawed on—

21st Chorus

Roll my bones
In the Mortiary
 My terms
    And deeds of mortgagry
  And death & taxes
    All wrapt up.

Little anger Japan
  Strides holding bombs
To blow the West
  To Fuyukama's
Shrouded Mountain Top
  So the Lotus Bubble
Blossoms in Buddha's
  Temple Dharma Eye
May unfold from
    Pacific Center
    Inward Out & Over
      The Essence Center World

22nd Chorus

For the world's an Eye
And the universe is Seeing
Liquid
Rare
Radiant.

Eccentrics from out of town
    Better not fill in
        This blank
        For a job on my gray boat
        And Monkeysuits I furnish.

        Batteries of ad men
        Marching arm in arm
            Thru the pages
            Of Time & Life

23rd Chorus

The halls of M C A

Singing Deans
In the college morning
Preferable to dry cereal
When no corn mush

Cops & triggers
Magazine pricks
    Dastardly Shadows
And Phantom Hero ines.

Swing yr umbrella
    At the sidewalk
    As you pass
    Or tap a boy

On the shoulder
Saying "I say
Where is Threadneedle
            Street?"

24th Chorus

San Francisco is too sad
Time, I cant understand
Fog, shrouds the hills in
Makes unshod feet so cold
Fills black rooms with day
  Dayblack in the white windows
  And gloom in the pain of pianos:
Shadows in the jazz age
  Filing by; ladders of flappers
  Painters' white bucket
  Funny 3 Stooge Comedies
    And fuzzy headed Hero
    Moofle Lip suckt it all up
    And wondered why
    The milk & cream of heaven
      Was writ in gold leaf
      On a book—big eyes
      For the world
        The better to see—

25th Chorus

And big lips for the word
And Buddhahood
And death.
  Touch the cup to these sad lips
Let the purple grape foam
In my gullet deep
 Spread saccharine
  And crimson carnadine
  In my vine of veins
And shoot power

To my hand
  Belly heart & head—
    This Magic Carpet
    Arabian World
    Will take us
      Easeful Zinging
    Cross the Sky
    Singing Madrigals

26th Chorus

  To horizons of golden
  Moment emptiness
Whither whence uncaring
    Dizzy ride in space
      To red fires
      Beyond the pale,
      Rosy gory outlooks
      Everywhere.

San Francisco is too old
  Her chimnies lean
    And look sooty
After all this time
    Of waiting for something
    To happen
    Betwixt hill & house—
    Heart & heaven.

27th Chorus

  San Francisco
  San Francisco
  You're a muttering bum
    In a brown beat suit
    Cant make a woman
    On a rainy corner

Your corners open out
San Francisco
To arc racks
Of the Seals
  Lost in vapors
  Cold and bleak.

28th Chorus

You're as useless
As a soda truck
Parked in the rain
With cases of pretty red
   Orange green & Coca Cola
      Brown receiving rain
   Drops like the sea
      Receiveth driving spikes
Welling in the navel void.

I also have loud poems:
Broken plastic coverlets
   Flapping in the rain
    To cover newspapers
    All printed up
      And plain.

29th Chorus

Guys with big pockets
In heavy topcoats
 And slit scar
 Head bands down
 The middle of their hair
 All Bruce Barton combed
   Stand surveying Harrison
   Folsom & the Ramp
    And the redbrick clock
   Wishin they had a woman
   Or some money, honey

Westinghouse Elevators
Are full of pretty girls
With classy cans
   And cute pans
   And long slim legs
   And eyes for the boss
   At quarter of four.

30th Chorus

Old Age is an Indian
With gray hair
And a cane
In an old coat
  Tapping along
  The rainy street
   To see the pretty oranges
  And the stores
   On his big day
When the dog's let out.

Somewhere in this snow
I see little children raped
By maniacal sex fiends
Eager to make a break
But the F B I
In the form of Ted
  Stands waiting
   Hand on gun
  In the Paranoiac
   Summer time
   To come.

31st Chorus

I knew an angel
 In Mexico City
Call'd La Negra
Who the Same eyes
   Had as Sebastian
   And was reincarnated
     To suffer in the poker
     House rain
     Who had the same eyes
       As Sebastian
     When his Nirvana came

Sambati was his name.

Must have had one leg once
And expensive armpit canes
 And traveled in this rain
 With youthful hidden pain

32nd Chorus

Beautiful girls
 Just primp
  But beautiful boys
  Do suffer.

White wash rain stain
Gravel roof glass black
 Red wood blue neon
 Green elevators
 Birds that change color
 And white ants
   Climbing to your knee
     Earnest for deliverance.

33rd Chorus

It was a mournful day
The B O Bay was gray
Old man angry-necks
Stomped to escape sex
And find his Television
In the uptown vision
  Of the milk & secret
    Blossom curtain
    Creak it.

Cheese it the cops!
Ram down the lamb!
  700 Camels
  In Pakistan!

Milk will curdle, honey,
If you sit on stony penises
Three times moving up & down
And 7 times around

34th Chorus

While young boys peek
  In the Hindu temple window
  To grow
    And come
  To A-mer-ri-kay
    And be long silent types
    In the night clerk cage
  Waiting for railroad calls
    And hints from Pakistan
    Beluchistan and Mien Mo
    That Mahatmas
    Havent left the field
      And tinkle bells
      And cobra flutes

Still haunt our campfires
In the calm & peaceful
Night—
   Stars of India

35th Chorus

And speak bashfully
   Thru strong brown eyes
Of olden strengths
   And bad boy episodes
   And a father
      With sacred cows
   A wandering in his field.
"Rain on, O cloud!"

   The taste of worms
   Is soft & salty
   Like the sea,
   Or tears.

   And raindrops
   That dont know
You've been deceived
Slide on iron
   Raggedly gloomy

36th Chorus

Falling off in wind.

I got the San Francisco
   blues
Bluer than misery
I got the San Francisco blues
Bluer than Eternity
      I gotta go on home

Fine me
Another
Sanity

I got the San Francisco
    blues
Bluer than heaven's gate,
    mate,
  I got the San Francisco blues
Bluer than blue paint,
    Saint,—
      I better move on home
     Sleep in
      My golden
      Dream again

37th Chorus

I got the San Acisca blues
Singin in the street all day
    I got
    The San Acisca
    Blues
Wailin in the street all day
    I better move on, podner,
    Make my West
    The Eastern Way—

San
  Fran
Cis
  Co—
San
  Fran
Cis
   Co
     Oh—
        ba
         by

38th Chorus

Ever see a tired
   ba by
Cryin to sleep
   in its mother's arms
Wailin all night long
   while the locomotive
Wails on back
A cry for a cry
In the smoke and the lamp
Of the hard ass night

  That's how I
    fee-
      eel—
   That's how
    I fee-eel!
  That's *how*
      I feel—
What a deal!
Yes I'm goin ho
      o
       ome

39th Chorus

Yes I'm goin
    on
      home
       today

Tonight I'll be ridin
The 80 mile Zipper
And flyin down the Coast
Wrapt in a blanket

Cryin
And cold

So brother
Pour me a drink
  I got lots of friends
  From coast to coast
  And ocean to ocean
       girls
    But when I see
    A bottle a wine
    And see that it's full
    I like to open it
     And take of it my fill

40th Chorus

And when my head gets dizzy
And friends all laugh
And money pours
      from my pocket
And gold from my ears
And silver flies out
     and rubies explode
I'll up & eat
And sing another song
And drop another grape
  In my belly down

Cause you know
What Omar Khayyam said
   Better be happy
   With the happy grape
   As make long faces
     And groan all night
       In search of fruit
        That dont exist

41st *Chorus*

So Mister Engineer
And Mister Hoghead
Conductor Jones
And you head brakeman
And you, tagman
    on this run
Give me a hiball
Boomer's or any kind
    Start that Diesel
    All 3 Units
        Less roll on down that rail
        See Kansas City by dawn
        Or grass of Amarilla
    Or rooftops of Old New York
        Or banksides green with grass
        In April
            Anywhere

42nd *Chorus*

I'd better be a poet
Or lay down dead.

Little boys are angels
Crying in the street
Wear funny hats
Wait for green lights
    Carry bust out tubes
        Around their necks
        And roam the railyards
        Of the great cities
            Looking for locomotives
        Full of shit
            Run down to the waterfront
            And dream of Cathay
            Hook spars with Gulls
                Of athavoid thought.

43rd Chorus

Little Cody Deaver
A San Francisco boy
    Hung by hair of heroes
Growing green & thin
    And soft as sin
    From the tie piles
Of the railer road
    Track where Tokay
    Bottles rust in dust
    Waiting for the term
    Of partiality
To end up there
    In heaven high
    So's loco can
    Come home
    Con poco coco.

44th Chorus

Little heroes of the dead
Found a nickle instead
And bought a Borden half & half
    Orange Sherbert & vanil milk
    Trod the pavements
    Of unfall Frisco
    Waiting for its earthquake
To waver houses men
    And streets to spindle
    Drift to fall at Third
    Street Number 6–15
Where Bank now stands
Jack London was born
And saw gray rigging
At the 'barcadero
    Pier, His bier
    commemorated in marble
    To advertise the stone
    Of vaults where money rots.

45th Chorus

Inquisitive plaidshirt
Pops look at trucks
In the afternoon
While Mulligan's
Stewing on the stove
And Calico spreads
  Her milk & creamy legs
  For advertising salesman
    Passing thru from Largo
  Oregon where water
      Runs the Willamette down
      By blasted to-the-North
        Volcanic ashes seft.

46th Chorus

Babies born screaming
    in this town
Are miserable examples
    of what happens
Everywhere.

  Bein Crazy is
  The least of my worries.

Now the sun's goin down
In old San Fran
  The hills are in a haze
  Of Shroudy afternoon—
  Bent withered Burroughsian
  Greeks pass
    In gray felt hats
    Expensively pearly
    On bony suffer heads

47th Chorus

And old Indian bo's
With no stockings on
  Just Chinese Shuffle
  Opium shoes
Take the snaily constitutional
  Down 3rd St gray & lost
  & Hard to see.

  Tragic burpers
  With scars of snow
  Bound bigly
  Huge to find it
  To the train
    Of time & pain
  Waiting at the terminal.

Young punk mankind
  Three abreast
    Go thriving downwards
    In the hellish street.

48th Chorus

  Red shoes of the limpin whore
Who drags her blues
  From shore to shore
    Along the stores
    Lookin for a millionaire
      For her time's up
      And she got no guts
      And the man aint comin
    And I'm no where.

He aint done nothin
  But change hats
And go to work
And light a new cigar

And stands in doorway
Swingin the 8 inch
Stogie all around
  Arc ing to see
Mankind's vast

49th Chorus

Sea restless crown
Come rolling bit by bit
  From offices of gloom
  To homes of mortuary
  Hidden Television
  Behind the horse's
    Clock in Hopalong
    The Burper's bestfriend
      Ten gat waving
      Far from children
      Sadly waving
      From the balcony
      Above this street
    Where Acme Paper
          Torn & Tattered
  S'down the parade
  Thrown to clebrate
  McParity's return:

50th Chorus

All ties in
Like anacin.

Well
      So unlock the door
      And go to supper
And let the women cook it,
  Light's on the hill

The guitar's a-started
  Playing by itself
  The shower of heaven notes
  Plucked by a gypsy woman
  In some old dream
   Will bless it all
     I see furling out
     Below—

51st Chorus

The laundress has bangs
  And pursy lips
  And thin hips
  And sexy walk
And goes much faster
 When she knows
   The booty in her
   laundry bag
   Is undiscovered
     And unknown
     And so no cops watching
           she steps on it
           t'escape the Feds
           of Wannadelancipit
           Here in the Standard
               Building
           Flying High
               the
           Riding Horse
       A Red—

52nd Chorus

None of this means
anything
  For krissakes speak up
          & be true
      Or shut up
      & Go to bed

Dead

    The wash is waving goodbye
    Towards Oakland's russet

I know there are huge clouds
Ballooning beyond the bay

    And out Potato Patch,
    The snowy sea away,
    The milk is furling
      Huge and roly
        Poly burly puffy

53rd Chorus

Pulsing push
To come on in
Inundate Frisco
 Fill the rills
And ride the ravines
And sneak on in
With Whippoorwill
    To-hoo— To-wa!
      The Chinese call it woo
      The French les brumes
      The British
            Fog
L A
      Smog
Heaven
      Cellar door

54th Chorus

Communities of houses
Caparisoned by sunlight
On the last & fading hill
Of American a-rollin
    Rollin
To the Western Chill

And delicacies of statues
Hewn by working men
Neoned, tacked on,
Pressed against the sign
    Mincin
    Mincin
To sell the swellest coupon

Understand?

Light on the fronts
    of old buildings
Like in New York
In December dusks
When hats point to sea

55th Chorus

This means
    that everything
        has some home
        to come to
Light has windows
    balconies of iron
        like New Orleans

It also has all space
    And I have windows
    balconies of iron
        like New Orleans

I also have all space

And St Louis too

Light follows rivers
I do too

Light fades, I pass

56th Chorus

Light illuminates
The intense cough
Of young girls in love
Hurrying to sell their
future husband
On the Market St
Parade

Light makes his face
reddern
Her white mask

She sucks to bone him dry
And make him happy
Make him cry
Make him baby
Stay by me.

57th Chorus

Crooks of Montreal
Tossing up their lighters
To a cigarette of snow
Intending to plot evil
And break the pool machine
Tonight off Toohey's head
And the Frisco fire team
Come howling round
The corner of the dream

58th Chorus

Immense the rivets
In the broadsides
Of battleships
    Fired upon head on
    In face to face combat
    In the Philippines
    Anchored Alameda
    Overtime for toilets
    On Labor Day

59th Chorus

IL
 W
 U
    Has tough white seamen
    Scrapping snow white hats
    In favor of iron clubs
    To wave in inky newsreels
    When Frisco was a drizzle
        And Curran all sincere,
        Bryson just a baby,
    Reuther bloodied up,
    —When publications
Of Union pamphleteers
    Featured human rock jaws
    Jutting Editorialese
  Composed by angry funny
        redhead editors
    Walking with their heads down
        To catch the evening fleet
        And wave goodbye to sailors
        passing rosely dreams
        Into a sparkling cannon
        Gray & spicked & span
        To shine the Admiral
        In his South Pacific pan—

60th Chorus

No such luck
   For Potter McMuck
Who broke his fist
On angry mitts
In fist fights
Falling everywhere
From down Commercial
   To odd or even
All the piers
   Blang! Bang!
   I L W U had a hard time
   And so did N A M
   And S P A M
   And as did A M

61st Chorus

YOU INULT ME EVERY NIME, MALN BWANO
Ladies and Gentle-man
  The phoney woiker
  You here see
   Got can one time
  In Toonisfreu
   Ger ma nyeee
   Becau he had
      no dime
  To give the con duck teur
    Yo see he stiffled
      For his miffle
  And couldnt cough a little
    Bill de juice ran
       down his Sfam.

62nd Chorus

JULIEN LOVE'S SOUND
"All
       right!
Here we are
   with all the little lambs.
Has anyone disposed
      of my old man
Last night?
       Mortuary deeds,
       Dead,
   Drink, me down
   Table or two,
   Wher'd you put it
              Kerouac?
   The bottoms in your bag
Of cellar heaven doors
And hellish consistencies
   Gelatinous & composed
   Will bang & break
Apon the time clock
   Beat prow stone bong
   Boy
   Before I give YOU
   An idgit of the
      Kind Love Legend"

63rd Chorus

JULIEN LOVE'S JUDGMENT
"Seriously boy
 This San Francisco
       Blues of yours
  Like shark fins
      the summer before
  And was it Sarie
  Sauter Finnegan
    Some gal before—

It's a farce
  For funny you
                you know?
I dont think I'll buy it"

Slit in the ear
  By a bolo knife
Savannah Kid just nodded
At the beast that
  Hides.

Secret
Poetry
Deceives
Simply

64th Chorus

California evening is like Mexico
The windows get golden oranges
The tattered awnings flap
Like dresses of old Perdido
  Great Peruvian Princesses
    In the form of Negro Whores
    Go parading down the sidewalk
    Wearing earrings, sweet perfume
    Old Weazel Warret

  tradesmen
   sick of selling
   out their stores stand in
      the evening lineup
      before identifying cops
      they cannot understand
      in the clouds of can
      and iron moosing
      marshly morse
      of over head

65th Chorus

Daughters of Jerusalem
Prowling like angry felines
Statuesque & youthful
  From the well
  Embarrassed but implacable
  And watched by hungry worriers
    Filling out the whitewall
        Car with 1000 pounds
        Of "Annergy!
            Thats what I got!
        An-nergy!"
        To burn up Popocatepetl's
        Torch of ecstasy.

The neons redly twangle
  Twinkle cute & clean
  Like Millbrae cherry
    Nipptious tostle
        Flowers tattled
        Petal for the joss stick
        Stuck in neon twaddles
        To advertise a bar
  —All over SanFranPisco
  The better is the pain

66th Chorus

—"Switch to Calvert"
  Runs an arrow eating
    Bulb by bulb
    Across the bulbous
        Whisky bottle
And under the Calvert clock

  Tastes better!   Everyone
        Tastes better
        All the time

And fieldhands
  That aint got aznos
    But the same south Mexican
    Evening soft shoe
      walk
Slow in dusts of soft
in Ac to pan
Here in Frisco City
        American
 The same way walk
    To buy some vegetables

67th Chorus

For the bedsprings on the roof
  Not keep the rain on out
Or bombed out huts
  In dumpland—Blue
Workjacket, shino pants,
   It's like Mexico all violet
    At ruby rose & velvet
     Sun on down
       On down
     Sun on down
       Sundown

Red blood bon neon
  Bon runs   don   blon

By Barrett
        Wimpole
            Trackmeet

68th Chorus

And like Mexico the deep
Gigantic scorpic haze
Of shady curtain night
  Bein drawn on civilized

And Fellaheen will howl
Where the cows of mush
Rush to hide their sad
Tan hides in the stonecrump
Mumps bump top of hill
Out Mission Way
Holy Cows of Cross
And Lick Monastery

Velvet for our meat
Hamburgers

And doom of pained nuns
Or painted
One
Mexico is like Universe

69th Chorus

And Third Street a Sun
Showing just how's done
The light the life the action
The limp of worried reachers
Crawling up the Cuba street
In almost dark
To find the soften bell
Creaming Meek on corner
One by one, Tem, Tim,
Click, gra, rattapisp,
Ting, Tang—

Blink!   Off
Run!   Arrow!
Cut!   Winkle!   Twinkle!
Fill
Piss!   Pot!
The lights of coldmilk
supper hill streets
make me davenport
and cancel Ship.

70th Chorus

3rd St is like Moody St
Lowell Massachusetts
It has Bagdad blue
  Dusk down sky
  And hills with lights
And pale the hazel
  Gentle blue in the
      burned windows
Of wooden tenements,
  And lights of bars,
      music brawl,
  "Hoap!" "Hap!" & "Hi"
In the street of blood
And bells billygoating
  Boom by at the ache
    of day
The break of personalities
  Crossing just once
  In the wrong door

71st Chorus

Nevermore to remain
  Nevermore to return
  —The same hot hungry
    harried hotel
    wild Charlies dozzling
      to fold the
    Food papers in the
      mahogany talk
Of television reading room
Balls are walled
  and withered
  and long fergit.

Moody Lowell Third Street
  Sick & tired bedsprings

Silhouettes of brownlace
eve night dowse—
All that—
And outsida town
The aching snake
Pronging underground
To come eat up
Us the innocent
And insincere in here

72nd Chorus

And Budapest Counts
Driving lonely mtn. cars
On the hem of the grade
Of the lip curve hill
Where Rockly meets
Out Market & More—
The last shore—
View of the sea
Seal

Only Lowell has for sea
The imitative Merrimac

And Frisco has for
snake
The crowdy earthquake
cataract
And Hydrogen Bombs
of Hope
Lost in the blue
Pacific
Empty sea

73rd Chorus

Bakeries gladly bright
Filled with dour girls
Buying golden pies
For sullen brooding boys

On 3rd St in the night

But by day
  The Greek Armenian
    Milk of honey
  Bee baclava maker
  Puts his sugars
  On the counter
    For bums with avid jaws
  And hollow eyes
    Eager to eat
    Their last dainty.

74th Chorus

Marchesa Casati
Is a living doll
Pinned on my Frisco
Skid row wall

Her eyes are vast
Her skin is shiny
  Blue veins
  And wild red hair
  Shoulders sweet & tiny

Love her
Love her
    Sings the sea
    Bluely
  Moaning

In the Augustus John
    de John
    back ground.

75th Chorus

Her eyes are living dangers
'll Leap you
  From a page
Wearing the same insanity
   The sweet unconcernedly
   Italian humanity
    Glaring from black eyebrows
     To ask
      Of Renaissance:
     "What have you done now
     After 3 hundred years
     But create the glary witness
     Which out this window
     Shows a pale green
      Friscan hill
      The last green hill
      Of America
        With a cut   a band

76th Chorus

Of brown red road
   Coint round
   By architects of hiways
    To show the view
       To ledge travellers
   Of Frisco, City, Bay
    And Sea
       As all you do is drive around
   —By Groves of lonesome
      Redwood trees

Isolated
In physical isolation
On the bare lump
Hill like people
  Of this country
Who walk alone
  In streets all day
    Forbidden
    To contact physically
      Anybody
    So desirable—

77th Chorus

They kill'd all painters
Drown'd—Made wash
The smothering crone
Of Cathay,
  Flower of Malaya,
  And Dharma saws,
  Gat it all in,
    Like wash,
    Call'd it Renascence
    And then wearied
      From the globe—
      Hill, last hill
      Of Western World
        Is cut around
        Like half attempted
        Half castrated
        Protrudient breast
          Of milk
        From wild staring earth

78th Chorus

—The last scar
America was able
   To create
   The uttermost hill
   Beyond which is just
            Pacific
   And no more sc-cuts
   And Alamos neither
   But that can be rolled
   In satisfying sea
   Absolved of suicide—
      Except that now
      They're blasting fishermen
         Apart?"

79th Chorus

"Beyond that fruitless sea"
—So speaks Marchesa
Mourning the Renaissance
And still the breeze
Is sweet & soft
  And cool as breasts
  And wild as sweet dark eyes.

Sits in her spirit
Like she wont be long
And bright about it
   All the time, like short
         star

      An angry proud beauty
      Of Italy

80th Chorus

San Francisco Blues
Written in a rocking chair
   In the Cameo Hotel
      San Francisco Skid row
      Nineteen Fifty Four.

This pretty white city
On the other side of the country
   Will no longer be
   Available to me
   I saw heaven move
      Said "This is the End"
      Because I was tired
      of all that portend.

   And any time you need
         me
Call
      I'll be at the other
      end
   Waiting
         at the final hall

Richmond Hill Blues

DULUOZ
Name derived from early
    morning sources
In a newspaper office
Long Ago in Lowell Mass
When birds were shitting
On the canal
And Sperm was Floating
    among the Redbrick Walls
Of a Morn that had Smoke
Pouring from a Christian Hill
        Chimney—
Ah Sire, Duluoz,
  King of my Thoughts,
        Salute!
(Kick another can of beer)

THAT'S WHAT I SAID
Not what I thot I meant
O Sin-of-a-Bitch
But what I out loud said
Not—again—what in
    retrospect
And banalizing sedeora ing
    of my garage
Made it
Say what you mean
  A poem is a lark
  A pie

SCHLITZ (A drunken vision of a can of beer)
Beaded melt hotwave waters
Of outside hydrated juices
Flowing down Made in USA
& Brooklyn New York
Genuine, holed triangular.

243

WIFE & 3
Little Cathy gladdy
    with sun cheeks
    beeted
Jamie hiding hugging
    her knees
Mother Earwicker solemn,
        lovely, flesh legs
        white
King John Fartitures
    of Hop Top Heap
    Cassadee-ing in
    his Kingdom
Jamie of mother's sweetly
    sweet goodheart breast
Showing oldlady teeth
        of littlegirl glee
    And pudgy arms locked

Tristesse in the little
    hopeless Fingers,
Faisse in the shot,
        the radiant sun,
The shine of San Jose
O
    Grass
            Peotés of time!

    Steps, lost davenports,
        eternities,
Hot Night Birds,
    Billy Holiday!
—Make the quaker
    give his cream

ANY TIME
Any time you want
A write a fucken poem
Ope this book

& Scream no more
But Cream
Cry
Fret not
  Flow
  Flay
  Fray the edge of Froy
Make Frogs Alliterate
    Bekkek! Bekkek!
      Koak! Koak!
      Carra Quax!
      Carra qualquus
          Kerouacainius!

EVEN JOYCE
Even he, Joyce,
    had love—
Even blind poets

AUDEN HAD NO ASS
Auden had no ass
Butler had no balls
Carew had no crash
Dyck had no dick
Egrets had no erse
Fart had no fuck
George had no Gyzm
His honou had no H
I J Fox had no wife
J Fox had no Joke
Kerou had no Ka
Ling Woe had no Rice
M & N had no Moola
    (a lot!)
Novales had no Nodes
O vum had no Ollie
    (O'Neill Mc Shanahan)
P-ew had no Push

Quasi Quean had no Queasy
  feelings
R had no heart
Studentio
 had
   no
     Stok
To
 v
  e
   l
    e
     n
     l
      s
h had
  no

   T
    u
     p

Uvalde had no Upstarts
Vedichad no Velda
Velda had no Vim

Vish had no Rush
  her
   Vim
     hid
      his
 Or pit his ass
 gainst my pen

U had no V
V had no Victory
U V W had no
 Pesco
  X no Y or Z

THE POET
So many times since
I've seen the poet
Of Greenwich Village
Cutting to work in the gray dawn
With a lunchpail &
    bleak haircut
  Eyes to the Hudson
    Nostril to the street
    To winter, work, beneficence,
Meals, fare of folly
So many times since
I've seen the poet
Who wrote rhythms & rhymes
To be mad in Minetta's
And Minetta Lane
  Go hurrying to Work
  Sex hung, sexed, psycho-
    analyzed?
To work in the unpoetic dawn

Mornings after I'd got drunk
with Lucien & Allen
    & Allied Angels
In the Vast Manhattan
        Fish—
O America!
  Songs!
  Poems!
    Altos!   Tenors!
        Blow!
(Poet is Dead)

THUNDER
Thunder makes a booming
    noise like windows
  Being hysterically quietly
    closed—
So Papa fell down the stairs

of time
In spite of holy water
 And all yr mixed drinks
      in
 Eternity

EMILY DICKINSON
Ere so sober Emily
  Did New England sow
  With brooms of activity
  I'd the tree-rock spoken to.
But it only said to me
"This sleet's crack
  You hear cracking my hide
  Is the voice of olden poets
  Not far from rocks of here
  Did their olden eyes
  On nature bestow blue
  —" I said
"Ah Oh How So Sad."

I said—"And graves?"
And I said "Darling
Supposing it should
  To nature
  Suddenly occur
  To make unending poets
  Unendingly Blow"

Nature Said: "Mean,
  I dont know what you
Mean"—
"Ah Nature, Ah Rock,"
I cried, "Nobody's Bone
 Has so suffusèd been,
 No burden of boredom
 Greater
 No love colder

No love life less
No grave nearer
Always
Than Ye Bard"

ROSE
"Ah Rose," I cried,
"Shine in the Phosphorescent
Night."

BUG
And to the little bug which am myself
            I said
"Bug, lip, tip, tit of time,
  Try, take, take, flake, fly,
  Love is passing yr. cheekbones
  On the phosphorescent transparent
            wing
Of Kafka's cheese consuming
    Metamorphosed Bug"

HORROR
So then I saw horror,
And I cried,
"Horrer, leave me er lone."
  Horrer-horror laid me bone
  By bone in a bag of dirt,
  I was broiled in the oven
  Of heaven in the silver foil
  Of Devil Jesus God
  Which is Yr Holy Trinity

SMILES
Smiles pull flesh from the cheek
Over pearls of bone
   And make the watcher see
   The quake of cream
   In eyes of stone

ON TEARS
Tears is the break of my brow,
The moony tempestuous
      sitting down
In dark railyards
When to see my mother's face
Recalling from the waking vision
I wept to understand
The trap mortality
And personal blood of earth
Which saw me in—
   Father father
   Why hast thou forsaken me?
Mortality & unpleasure
Roam this city—
Unhappiness my middle name
   I want to be saved,—
   Sunk—can't be
   Won't be
   Never was made to—
   So retch!

WHEN OLD
When I began to grow old
   And could feel my left arm
         numben
   And brain resisted hope,
   Will sat sleeping
   Energy thubbd exhausted
      in my eye

And love fled me—
When the worst news
   Was brought to me
   And I exulted to be alone
   Go die
    I had a vision of
     the saint
    Misunderstood & too tired
     to explain why
    And sweet intentioned
     in another day—
Even Stanley Gould'll
    go to heaven

BOP
Sweet little dop a la pee—
Bit bit piano tip
   tinkle plips
 And smash prop brushes
In the little numb moment
   um

I KNOW
I know that I cannot write
   verse
But this is my beercan short
   line
Book so bear with me
   invisible
Reader and let me goof
   even
When I'm sick & have no
   ideas

GOD
Sitting over our meanings
Egomaniac God,
Lonely slick & rain glint
Also uses irritating us
In the Real.

HOPES
Poetry doesnt know:
The air conditioner
Not in use in winter
Is like my hopes—
Half in, half out,
  Green on a whitewall,
  S'only good to cast
A long shadow
  In the bleak street light

TREE
But a tree has
    a living suffering shape
Is spread in half
    by 2 limbed fate
Rises from gray rain
    pavements
To traffic in the bleak
    brown air
Of cities radar television
    nameless dumb &
    numb mis connicumb
  Throwing twigs the
      color of ink
  To white souled
      heaven, with
A reality of its own uses

TENORMAN
Sweet sad young tenor
Horn slumped around neck
Bearded full of junk
Slouches waiting
For Apocalypse,
Listens to the new
Negro raw trumpet kid
Tell him the wooden news;
And the beat of the bass
The bass—drives in
Drummer drops a bomb
Piano tinkle tackles
Sweet tenor lifting
All American sorrows
Raises mouthpiece to mouth
And blows to finger
  The iron sounds

Bowery Blues

For I
Prophesy
That the night
Will be bright
With the gold
Of old
In the inn
Within.

Cooper Union Cafeteria—late cold March afternoon, the street (Third Avenue) is cobbled, cold, desolate with trolley tracks—Some man on the corner is waving his hand down No-ing somebody emphatically and out of sight behind a black and white pillar, cold clowns in the moment horror of the world—A Porto Rican kid with a green stick, stooping to bat the sidewalk but changing his mind and halting on—Two new small trucks parked—The withery grey rose stone building across the street with its rime heights in the quiet winter sky, inside are quiet workers by neon entablatures practicing fanning lessons with the murderous Marbo—A yakking blonde with awful wide smile is makking her mouth lip talk to an old Bodhisattva papa on the sidewalk, the tense quickness of her hard working words—Meanwhile a funny bum with no sense trys to panhandle them and is waved away stumbling, he doesnt care about society women embarrassed with paper bags on sidewalks—Unutterably sad the broken winter shattered face of a man passing in the bleak ripple—Followed by a Russian boxer with an expression of Baltic lostness, something grim and Slavic and so helplessly beyond my conditional ken or ability to evaluate and believe that I shudder as at the touch of cold stone to think of him, the sickened old awfulness of it like slats of wood wall in an old brewery truck

> Shin Mc Ontario with
> no money, no bets, no
> health, pauls on by
> pawing his inside coat

no hope of ever
seeing Miami again
since he lost his pickles
on Orchard Street
and his father
S t u h t e l f e d e h r e d
him to hospitals
Of gray
bleak
bone
drying
in the moon
that mortifies his coat
and words sing
what mind
brings

Bleeding bloody seamen
Of Indian England
Battering in coats
Of Third Ave noo
With no sense and their brows
Streaked with wine sop
Blood of ogligit
Sad adventurers
Far from the pipe
Of Liverpool
The bean of bone
Bottle Liffey brown
Far   hung   unseen
Top   tippers
Of   o cean wave.

God bless & sing for them
As I   can not

*

Cooper Union Blues,
The Musak is too Sod.

The gayety of grave
Candidates makes
My gut weep
And my brains
Are awash
Down the side of the
          blue orange table
As little sneery snirfling
Porto Rican hero
Ba t ts by booming
His coat pocket
Fisting to the Vicinity
Where Mortuary
Waits for bait.
(What kind of service
Do broken barrels give?)
     O have pity
        Bodhisattva
        Of Intellectual
        Ra   diance!

Save the world from her eyebrows
Of beautiful illusion
Hope, O hope,
O Nope, O pope

————————

Crowded coat ers
In a front seat
Car, gray & grim,
Push on thru
To the basketball

*

Various absurd parades—
The strict in tact
Intent man with
Broken back

Balling his suitcase
Down from Washington
Building in the night
Passing little scaggly
Childreyn with Ma's
Of mopey hope.

Too sad, too sad
The well kept
Clean cut
Ferret man.

*

And the old blue Irishman
With untenable dignity
Beer bellying home
To drowsy dowdy TV
Suppers of gravy
And bile—
Wearing old new coats
Meant to be smooth on youths
Wrinkled on his barrel
Like sea wind
Infatuating sea eyes
To thinkin
Ripples & old age
Are real.

*

Poor young husbandry
    With coat of tan
Digging change in palms
    For bleaker coffees
Than afternoon gloom
    Where work of stone
Was endowed

With tired hope.
Hope   O hope
Cooper Union Hope
O Bowery of Hopes!
O absence!
O blittering real
Non staring redfaced
Wild reality!
Hiding in the night
Like my dead father
I see the crystal
Shavings shifting
Out of sight
Dropping pigeons of light
To the Turd World
Enought, sad ones—
False petals
Of pure lotus
In drugstore windows
Where cups of O
Are smoked

Paddy Mc Gilligan
Muttering in the street
Just hit town
From C a l c i   bleak

Ole Mop Polock Pat
Angry as a cat
About to stumble
Into the movie
Of the night
Through which he sees
M   oo   da   lands
Un seen
Like waking in the night
To transcendental Milk
In the room

Sad Jewish respectable
rag men with trucks
And watchers
Shaking cloth
Into the gutter
Saying   I dunno, no, no,
As gray green hat
Sits on their heads
Protecting them
From Infinity above
Which shines with white
Wide & brown black clouds
As Liberty Sun
Honks over the Sea
Sending Ships
From inner sea
Free
To de rool york
Pock Town of Part
Shelf High Hawk
Man   Dung   Town.
     Rinkidink Charley is Crazy.

*

Ugly pig
Burping
In the sidewalk
As surrealistic
  Typewriters
  Swim exploding by
  And bigger marines
  Lizard thru the side
  Of the gloom
  Like water
    For this
is the Sea
Of
Reality.

*

The story of man
Makes me sick
Inside, outside,
I dont know why
Something so conditional
And all talk
Should hurt me so.

I am hurt
I am scared
I want to live
I want to die
I dont know
Where to turn
In the Void
And when
To cut
Out

———————

For no Church told me
No Guru holds me
No advice
Just stone
Of New York
And on the cafeteria
We hear
The saxophone
Of dead Ruby
Died of Shot
In Thirty Two,
Sounding like old times
And de bombed
Empty decapitated
Murder by the clock.
And I see Shadows

Dancing into Doom
In love, holding
Tight the lovely asses
Of the little girls
In love with sex
Showing themselves
In white undergarments
At elevated windows
Hoping for the Worst.

I cant take it
Anymore
If I cant hold
My little behind
To me in my room
Then it's goodbye
Sangsara
For me
Besides
Girls arent as good
As they look
And Samadhi
Is better
Than you think
When it stars in
Hitting your head
In with Buzz
Of glittergold
Heaven's Angels
Wailing
Saying
We ve been waiting for you
    Since Morning, Jack
—Why were you so long
    Dallying in the sooty room?
    This Transcendental Brilliance
    Is the better part
    (Of Nothingness
    I sing)

Okay.
Quit.
Mad.
Stop.

———

MacDougal Street Blues

IN THE FORM OF 3 CANTOS

*

Canto Uno

The goofy foolish
   human parade
Passing on Sunday
   art streets
Of Greenwich Village

Pitiful drawings of
  images on an
  iron fence
  ranged there
   by selfbelieving
   artists
   with no hair
   and black berets
   showing green seas
   eating at rock
   and Pleiades
   of Time

Pestiferating at moon squid
  Salt flat tip fly toe
    tat   sand traps
   With cigar smoking interesteds
      puffing at the
        stroll

I mean sincerely
  naive sailors buying prints
Women with red banjos
  On their handbags
  And arts handicrafty

Slow shuffling
art-ers of Washington Sq
   Passing in what they think
   Is a happy June afternoon
Good God the Sorrow
   They dont even listen to me when
   I try to tell them they will die

They say "Of course I know
I'll die, why should you mention
It now—Why should I worry
About it—it'll happen
   It'll happen—Now
   I want a good time—
   Excuse me—
   It's a beautiful happy June
   Afternoon I want to walk in—

Why are you so tragic & gloomy?"
And on the corner at the
      Pony Stables
Of Sixth Ave & 4th
Sits Bodhisattva Meditating
In Hobo Rags
 Praying at Joe Gould's chair
For the Emancipation

Of the shufflers passing by,
Immovable in Meditation
He offers his hand & feet
   To the passers by
And nobody believes
That there's nothing to believe in.
Listen to Me.
There is no sidewalk artshow
   No strollers are there

No poem here, no June
      afternoon of Oh
But only   Imagelessness

Unrepresented on the iron fence
Of bald artists
  With black berets
  Passing by
  One moment less than this
Is future Nothingness Already

The Chess men are silent, assembling
Ready for funny war—
Voices of Washington Sq Blues
  Rise to my Bodhisattva Poem
      Window
 I will describe them:
  E y t   k e y   e e
    S a   l a   o s o
      F r   u p   t   u r t

Etc.
No need, no words to
     describe
The sound of Ignorance—
They are strolling to
    their death
Watching the Pictures of Hell
Eating Ice Cream
    of Ignorance
On wood sticks

That were once sincere
    in trees—
  But I cant write, poetry,
    just prose

I mean
 This is prose
   Not poetry
    But I want
      To be sincere

Canto Dos

While overhead is the perfect blue
    emptiness of the sky
With its imaginary balloons
    of false sight
Flying around in it
      like Tathagata Flying Saucers
These poor ignorant things
    mill on sidewalks
Looking at pitiful pictures
    of what they think

Is reality
And one
    a Negro with curls
Even has a camera
    to photograph
The pictures
And Jelly Roll Man
Pops his Billy Bell
  Good Humor for Sale—
W Somerset Maugham
      is on my bed

An ignorant storyteller
    millionaire queer
But Ezra Pound
    he crazy—
As the perfect sky
    beginninglessly pure
Thinglessly perfect
    waits already
They pass in multiplicity

Parading among Images
Images   Images   Looking
    Looking—
And everybody's turning around
    & pointing—

Nobody looks up
and In
Nor listens to Samantabhadra's
Unceasing Compassion

No Sound Still
S s s s t t
Seethe
Of Sea Blue Moon
Holy X-Jack
Miracle
Night—
Instead, yank & yucker
For pits & pops

Look for crashes
Pictures
Squares
Explosions
Birth
Death
Legs
I know, sweet hero,
Enlightenment has Come
Rest in Still

In the Sun Think
Think Not
Think no more Lines—
Straw hat, hands aback
Classed
He exam in a tein distinct
Rome prints—
Trees prurp
and saw—

The Chessplayers Wont End
Still they sit
Millions of hats

In underwater foliage
Over marble games
The Greeks of Chess
Plot the Pop
of Mate
King Queen

—I know their game,
their elephant with the pillar
With the pearl in it,
their gory bishops
And Vital Pawns—
Their devout frontline
Sacrificial pawn shops
Their Stately king

Who is so tall
Their Virgin Queen
Pree ing to Knave
the Night Knot
—Their Bhagavad Gitas
of Ignorance,
Krishna's advice,

Comma,
The game begins—
But hidden Buddha
Nowhere to be seen
But everywhere
In air atoms
In balloon atoms
In imaginary sight atoms
In people atoms

In people atoms
Again
In image atoms
In me & you atoms
In atom bone atoms
Like the sky

Already waits
For us eyes open to
—Pawn fell

Horse reared
  Mate Kiked Cattle
And Boom! Cop
      shot Bates—
Cru put Two—
    Out—I cried—
    Pound Pomed—
    Jean-Louis,
        Go home, Man.

I mean.—
  As solid as anything
  Is this reality of images
  In the imageless essence,
  Neither of em'll quit
  —So tho I am wise
  I have to wait like
  anyotherfool

Canto Tres

Lets forget the strollers
  Forget the scene
Lets close our eyes
  Let me Instruct Thee
      Here is dark milk
      Here is our Sweet Mahameru
        Who will Coo
        To You Too

As he did to me
One night at three
When I w k e l t
      P l e e
  knelt to See

Realit ee
   And I said
'Wilt thou protect me
      for ' ver ?'

And he in his throatless
      deep mother hole
   Replied 'H   o   m'
   (Pauvre Ange)
   Mahameru
      Tathagata of Mercy
See
  He
      Now
         in dark escrow

   In the middleless dark
of eyelids' lash obliviso
   so
   Among rains of Transcendent
            Pity
            Abides since Ever
                  Before Evermore ness
            of Thusness Imagined
            O Maha   Meru

O Mountain Sumeru
   O Mountain of Gold
      O Holy Gold
         O Room of Gold
         O Sweet peace
               rememberance
         O Navalit Yuku

Of sweet cactus
   Thorn of No Time
—Ply me onward
   like boat
   thru this Sea
   Safe to Shore

Ulysses never Sore
—Bless me Gerard
Bless thee, Living

I shall pray for all
  sentient human
 & otherwise sentient
 beings here & everywhere
 now—

No names
  Not even faces
  One Pity
    One Milk
      One Lovelight
        s a v e

*

Desolation Blues

1st Chorus

I stand on my head on Desolation Peak
And see that the world is hanging
Into an ocean of endless space
The mountains dripping rock by rock
Like bubbles in the void
And tending where they want—
That at night the shooting stars
Are swimming up to meet us
Yearning from the bottom black
  But never make it, alas—
  That we walk around clung
  To earth
  Like beetles with big brains
Ignorant of where we are, how,
What, & upsidedown like fools,
    Talking of governments & history,
—But Mount Hozomeen
The most beautiful mountain I ever seen,
Does nothing but sit & be a mountain,
A mess of double pointed rock
Hanging pouring into space
  O frightful silent endless space
—Everything goes to the head
  Of the hanging bubble, with men
  The juice is in the head—
  So mountain peaks are points
  Of rocky liquid yearning

2nd Chorus

Mountains have skin, said Peter
      Orlovsky of San Francisco—
And gorges shoot up clouds of mist
  That look like planet smoke—

Dead trees, artistic as a cottage
   on Truro,
  Look like goat horns off a rock,
—Alpine firs turn evergreen browns
By August First when summer's dead
At high elevations—the creeks roar
  And cataracts tumble pouring
  But it's all upsidedown & strange
—Why do I sit here crosslegged
On this steaming rocky surface
Of a planet called earth
Scribbling with a pencil
Unmusical songs called songs
And why worry my juicy head
And rail my bony hand at words
  And look around for more
    And nothing means nothing
      as of yore?—
T   s the primordial essence
Manifesting forms, of happy
And unhappy, stuff & no-stuff,
  Matter & space, phenomena
  Front & noumena behind,
  Out of exuberant nothingness

3rd Chorus

Yet birds mumble in the morning,
And raccoons tumble down the draws,
  I saw one hit by his own rock
  In a lil raccoon avalankey—
  And firs point as ever
        to infinity,
Their fine points top points too,
—Birds squeak like mice,
  and moonlight bucks & does
Graze in my yard like cows
With big shootable flanks,
  And hooves of eternity, clatter

        on the rocks,
    Run away when I open the door,
    Down the hill, like silly frightened
        schoolteachers—
Chipmunks are well named—
Bears & abominable snowmen
I have not yet seen—
      Proud a that line—
Rock slides take generations to form,
    I try to rush it along—
    No rain in a month, nor yet
        a month, within a month—
    The beaked furthereal pine
        points at a crazy
    Upsidedown mid morning moon
        as delicate
    As a slide, like snow

4th Chorus

All the worries that've plagued
    everybody since Moses, Homer,
Sappho, Uparli, Cannibals and
    Patawatamkonalokunopuh
Are worrin and playin me
    on this mount of mystery—
I've T S Elioted all the fogs,
    Faulknered all the stone,
Balanced nothing gainst something,
    played solitaire, smoked,
Brought bashing sticks to midnight
    frightful long tailed rats
    And ranted at mosquitos,
    And remembered my mother
        her sweet labors of home
    And the cold eyed sister
        who made a bum outa me,
    And friends, & goodtimes,
        & prayed & gave up prayer,

And pondered history, myths,
   stories, artistic plans, plays,
French movies, phalanxes
   of disordered human crazy
    Thought, & still it's upsidedown—
    Silent—stiff—wont yield—
    Wont tell—A big empty
      Puppet stage, with rock

5th Chorus

Distant valleys in Canada
   look like they'd beckon
   but I know better,—
I yearn for the flatlands again,
   the gentle hill,—
At 4 PM the clouds of hope
Are horizon salmon floaters
Full of strange promise
   abstracted from the golden age
   in my breast—
Patches of snow dont do anything
   but be
Patches of snow, till they melt,
And then water, it's nothing
   but water
Till sun evaporates, then mist,
It's (as I look) nothing but mist
As it rises ululatory responding
   to every shift of wind,
  And will be mist, and will be
  Mist,
    And ants are nothing but just
    ants,
      And rocks'll sit where they are
      forever
Lessn I move em, throw em
   down the gorge,
And then they spit a minute

6th Chorus

I just dont understand—
tho mist'll be mist till
Heavens obdure, tho man'll
Be man till heavens obdure
Or hells obscure   I just
dont
I just dont
Dont
Understand
          I dont—
    I want to know—soon's a do
I dont understand—if I said:
"I dont care" I understand—
I understand that
              it doesnt matter.
Still the birdy clings, to earth,
He dont go silent on me,
I dont stop writing,
    I dont stop living,
What a fool,—bust the bird.
    The only thing that ever happens
          to Hozomeen
    Is that he'll get a wreath
      of clouds
    Every now & then
        & breed to revel
    Without moving a mighty shoulder
—I envy him his rock

7th Chorus

But I want to live, I want
    to get down
Off this Chinese Han Shan hill
    and make it
To the city & walk the streets
And drink good wine
    (Christian Brothers Port)

Or whiskey (Early Times
    or Old Grand Dad)
And go to Chinese Movies
     on Saturday Afternoon
And buy presents in the window
and watch the dust gather
On little stationary toys
In celluloid windows of children
And go to the vast markets
    And eat tortillas beans
      ice cream
    And crime—and banana splits
      and tea
    And benzedrine & broads—
      and waterfronts
    And plays & play marquees
      and Square Times
    And you—I'd like to celebrate
      upside
    Down in cities

8th Chorus

Once I saw a giant
     in a building

He's here now, bending
   over me,
Giant diamond gone insane.
Ta, the Golden Eternity,
    Ta Ta Ta Ta,
  Tathata, trumpet, Ta Ta,
  This giant diamond might
  Here is got some name'r other
  But *I dont know*
     I dont care
     and it makes no difference
  And now I'm wise.
  When the whole wide world

                    is fast asleep I cry.
        Let me offer you
            my reassuring profile
        Saying, "It's okay, girl, we'll
            make it
        Till the sun goes down forever
        And until then what you got
                to lose
        But the losing?   We're fallen
            angels
        Who didnt believe
        That nothing means nothing."

                    9th Chorus

    We're hanging into the abyss
        of blue—
    In it is nothing but innumerable
        and endless worlds
    More numerous even (& the number
        of beings!)
    Than all the rocks that cracked
        And became little rocks
            In all that rib of rock
            That extends from Alaska,
            Nay the Aleutian tips,
            Down through these High Cascades,
                Through to California & Ensenada,
                Down, through High Tepic, down
            To Tehuantepec, down,
            The rib, to Guatemala & on,
            Colombia, Andes, till the High
            Bottom Chilean & Tierra
                    del Fuego
            O yoi   yoi
            And on around to Siberia—
    In other words, & all the grains
        of sand that comprise
        A rock, and all the grains

of atomstuff therein,
More worlds than that
    in the empty blue sea
We hang in, upsidedown,
—Too much to be real

                10th Chorus

But it's real
    it's as real as the squares
    on this page
And as real as my sore ass
    sitting on a rock
And as real as hand, sun,
    pencil, knee,
Ant, breezed, stick,
    water, tree, color,
    peeop, birdfeather,
    snag, smoke,
    haze, goat,
    appearance
    and low crazed cloud
And dream of the Far Northwest
  And the little mounted policeman
Of my dreams on a ridge—
        Not an Indian in sight—
Real, real as fog in London town
    and croissants in Paris
    and swchernepetchzels
    in Prienna
  And Praha Maha Fuckit
  —Real, real,
    unreal,
    deal,
    Zeal,
I say, dont care if it's real
        or unreal, I'se

11th Chorus

And if you dont like the tone
      of my poems
You can go jump in the lake.
I have been empowered
      to lay my hand
On your shoulder
      and remind you
That you are utterly free,
Free as empty space.
You dont have to be famous,
      dont have to be perfect,
 Dont have to work,
         dont have to marry,
Dont have to carry burdens,
      dont have to gnaw & kneel,

      the taste
         of rain—
      Why kneel?

Dont even have to sit,
         Hozomeen,
Like an endless rock camp
      go ahead & blow,

Explode & go,
      I wont say nothin,
      neither this rock,
 And my outhouse doesnt care,
 And I got no body

12th Chorus

Little weird flower,
      why did you grow?
Who planted you
      on this god damned hill?
Who asked you to grow?

Why dont you go?
What's wrong with yr. orange tips?
I was under the impression
    that you were sposed to be
    some kind of perfect nature.
Oh, you are?
      Just jiggle in the wind. I see.
  At yr feet I see a nosegay
     bou kay
  Of seven little purple apes
    who dint grow so high
And a sister of yours
    further down the precipice—
    and your whole family
    to the left—
I thot last week
    you were funeral bouquets
    for me
    that never askt
    to be born
    or die
  But now I guess
     I'm just talkin
     thru my
      empty head

Orizaba 210 Blues

1st Chorus

Ah monstrous
sweet monsters,
who spawned
thee chalk?
 God? Who
 Godded me?
 Who me'd
 God, chalk'd
 Thought, &
 Me sank
 Down
 To
 Fall

A tché tché tcha
    hoot ee
Wheet wha you—

Sweet monstranot love
By momma dears

Hey

Call God the Mother
To stop this fight

2nd Chorus

Someday you'll be lying
there in a nice trance
and suddenly a hot
soapy brush will be
applied to your face
—it'll be unwelcome
—someday the
undertaker'll shave you

*

I almost called these poems
Pickpocket Blues
because they are the repetition
                            by memory
              of earlier poems
                            stolen from me
          b y   t w e l v e   t h i e v e s

3rd Chorus

Ah monster sweet monster
Who spawned all this God
A Marva Ah Marvaila
Ah Marva Marvay
Ah marve   Ah Me
Ah John O Ah John
Oka John—
Where do you worka
John—Ah John,
How do you William the
Conqueror this morning

With your height old otay
—Nay, sight less worse,
Urp, the spur that did nape
At the wick the whack
Of the horse's piniard, urt,
So up heaved Pegasus
To rape the Sirens

And Black Bastards Hold Out their Arms

4th Chorus

One was called Boston Kitty—
He was a one-whack artist
Hold down the rope & the boy
And slip his villons i the store
—Oy—

This turp then, he was smart,
His wife was bloomer-hiding
Dress-thief, best, New York,
—Oir—

Ay
May the Wild Queen that Whanged
All the men with pipes
And ironingboard trays, i the
Movie bout paird?—
Waird!
Haird all about it in Dawson
Lass night, boys was tellin
The stove of the night
Hair—Robert Olson
Me that, Mrs Blake

5th Chorus

Pollyanna me that, Matt
Baker me Mary me Eddy
somethin bout life,—
Feed me T bone steaks
Off cows was allowed
Was allowed to be et
By men and maids
And Pomfranet

Poignardi me that,
hurt,—slip me the knife
in the chest, het—
they'll cut off my arms
and my losen legs
And my Peter Orlovsky
Clasel soul shall say:
Oido me no mo

6th Chorus

Ah moidnous two movies
Was railroad and et

Ah turpitude & turpentine
And serpentine & pine

Ah me star-veil
that I see
Majesticking mightily
on the rail
Of heaven-hailward
high's moitang

Montana, me mountain,
Me Madonna, me high
Me most marvelous marvel
That held over the pie

Me sky of the Denver
Platte alley below

Me that me, me that me,
Me that me no more

7th Chorus

Brang!—blong!—trucks
Break glass i the dog barking
Street—dwang, wur,
Ta ta ta
  ta ta
Me that was weaned in the
   heaven's machine
Me that was wailed
  in the wild bar
called fence
Me that repeated & petered
The meter & lost 2 cents
Me that was fined
To be hined
And refined
    Ay
      Me that was
      Whoo ee
      The owl
      On the fence

8th Chorus

Me that was eyed
And betied by the eyes
In the glasses, In the Place,
In the night, brown beer,
Me that was maitled
And draitled and dragged
Me that was xarmined
By Murder Machree

Me that was blarnied
By Mary Carney
Me that was loved
Me that was hay
Me that the sunshine
Burned out every day
Me that was spotted
And beshatted
   By Marcus Magee

9th Chorus

Hey listen you poetry audiences
If you dont shut up
And listen to the potry,
See, we'll get a guy at the gate
To bar all potry haters
Forevermore

Then, if you dont like the subject
Of the poem that the poit
Is readin, geen, why dont
You try Marlon Brando
Who'll open your eyes
With his cry

James Dean is dead?—
Aint we all?
   Who aint dead—

John Barrymore is dead

Naw, San Francisco is dead
—San Francisco is bleat
   With the fog
(And the fences are cold)

10th Chorus

Old, San Francisco so old,
Shining garden on the end of the gate
Great plastic garden
Full of poets and hate

Fine wild bar place with high
Flootin dandies, Portugese,
Philippino, and just plain
Ole Dandy, Mandy tendin
The bar in the Brothers McCoy
On Sixth Street near Mission,
And Old Whitecap Sailor
Goes lonely the road
And Market Street on Sunday
There's no body broad
And O I see cliffside
With electrical magic
Message it me gives out
And sending Einstein
Me n McCorkle sit there
Eating in the Dharma

11th Chorus

We booted and we brained
Every seedy wet cold hill
And walked by rubber gardens
Behind telephones of shame
And came out mid the flowers
Of Heaven's O Gate

We treed every boner
Kited and committed
Longtailed and selffloored
And worked 78 to Del Monte
And back

Crashed Lux Perpetua
And tied up the mate
And dumped him down
In Chinatown
To Vegetate
So's cooks could clew garbage
And discover entrails
of babies made by Negresses
Against fences of taxis

12th Chorus

Soft!—the mysteries lie
In Eglantine

And Tathagata Nous Dit
Toujours, pas d secour,
    Pas d secour

Soft—pie-tailed bird-dog
Sing Song Charley the Poet
From High Masquerade
Is about to shake the rain
From his empty head
And deliver a blurbery statement
About bubbles and balloons

Balloons   O balloons
BALLOONS   BALLOONS
BALLOONS   O   BALLOONS
BAL
LOONS
B A L L O O N S

13th Chorus

When the rain falls on the Concord
And grapes are growing in New Hampshire
Mud hides wine bottles of green
And gay delight—When it rains
In Mexico, Oi Oi Oi, the swish
And plump and drenching Zapoteca
Big fat lump cacti growing in the night
Slipslop the sleeps of cats by the fence
And "Alms my youth!" cry women
To the passing Americano Oi—

Hate and oido, Old San Francisco's
Going to go—

Red, white and black, and blue
The pistil was tender when vines
Hund and daundered explosives
Of surrealistic pensioners

Dishrags have faces
Flashlights have hate
Pine trees are sweetest
To sit and meditate
The Holy Virgin of Heaven
Saw us in the rainy first morning

14th Chorus

Lost me Juju beads in the woods
And stood on dry stumps
      and looked around
And Lightning Creek morely roared
And wow the wild Jack Mountain
Abominable Snowman rooted
      in a stump
Even throwing football shadow
When games is ranging in the sky
Ah Gary,—would sweet Japan

Her gardens allay me
And make end sweet perfidy
—Full belly make you say
              nice things—
When rice bowl filled, Buddha frown
I' the West, because Wall of China
Has no holds

Holdfast to temple mountain chain
Throw away the halfdollars
Big and round, & wad of gum,
And flashlight lamp—& paint—
Go be shaved head monster
In a cave—No, tea ceremony
Beneath a sweet pine tree
          (Oi?)

15th Chorus

The little birds that live on the tree
In South America
Under clouds that make faces at me
Last night beautiful faces
Mad Dog McGoy of Heaven's
White Office, was sheening
His ocean spray at me
With holes for eyes
And every kind majesty—
Mocking at faces at me,
O me,—gingerale we drank
In Montreal when Errgang was young
And Wagner bleeded on the dump
And the dust of defeat perfidy
Was as fine as it is now
In the skies of untouchable dust
  And Klings of the rooftop
  Church variety—
  My moity

16th Chorus

Auro Boralis Shomoheen
In the ancient blue Buick
Machine that cankers the highway
With Alice fat Queens, cards
Indexes burning, mapping machines,
Partings sweet sorrow
But O my patine

O my patinat pinkplat Mexican
   Canvas for oil in boil
Marrico—hash marsh m draw
The greenhouse bong eater from
fence N'awrleans, that—

Bat and be ready, Jesus is steady,
Score's eight to one, none,
Bone was the batter for McGoy
Poy—
       Used as this ditties
       for mopping the kitties
       in dream's afternoon
       when nap was a drape

17th Chorus

"Jamac!   Jamac!
De bambi   de bambi
Jamac   jamac!"

And elegant old quorums
    of fortified priests
  sighed

De bambi de bambi jamac
Jamac, and eldertwine
old tweedies fighted the prize

"Parrac!   Motak!
Pastamak   arrac!
   Arrash!
   Crrash!"

Part art tee
   tea symphony
ceremonious old bonious
   me love you
   me

18th Chorus

Henry Regalado, l'hero de la
Bataille de Patenaud

God and all the other little people

Esmack, esmack, I esmacka
You on the kisser you too
I thrun nobody oud dis joint
Since Roosevelt had all his joints

And Buddy I knowed
That old Patenaude
Was a fraude from the start,
Tonio me Kruger you that,
Hat—
Pat was the rat that had the hat

Mash patinaud
Crash toutes les shows
Grange toutes les villes
   les jilles
Mange toutes les filles

19th Chorus

The diamond that cuts through
To the other view
That I painted all white for you
I edited your rough stone,
Produced a diamond show,
Elephantine was the mine
Eglantine adamant and mad
  And madly adamantine
  My Allah you mine,
  The diamond of Dipankar
  The prime ripe wreak havoc
  Buddha pra-teeth torn
  Mouth Ya-Hoi-Ya-Hai
  Pastumintapaling porpitoi
  Turnpot of biled pata taters
  Smater Gater the Mater
  O'Shay, rife was the weather
  Was singin was gay,
  Rape were the weathers
  In heaven's O Shay

20th Chorus

Old buddy aint you gonna stay by me?
Didnt we say I'd die by a lonesome tree
And you come and dont cut me down
But I'm lying as I be
Under a deathsome tree
Under a headache cross
Under a powerful boss
Under a hoss
        (my kingdom for a hoss
            a hoss
          fork a hoss and head
          for ole Mexico)
Joe, aint you my buddy thee?
And stay by me, when I fall & die
In the apricot field

And you, blue moon, what you doon
　　Shining in the sky
　　With a glass of port wine
　　In your eye
—Ladies, let fall your drapes
and we'll have an evening
of interesting rapes
　　　　　inneresting rapes

21st Chorus

Let fall the interesting fall
And I lie and be as I be

He stayed up in my case
　　for quite awhile

Tremendous pace—He was
A petty thief or he'd sell junk
One or the other

I did my best to keep him from
　　selling junk

French fag from Montreal
Hid the capsules up his ass
And took em out in a restaurant
On Broadway and Ninety Sixth

And I went to Eighty Sixth
　　Those girls hit up on me
　　"Man is here!"
And I bought four more caps

And the fag went home with a girl
　　What a beautiful shape
　　that woman had

22nd Chorus

Ha well dear and Ah Men
The wee girl that was comin again
She was for the books
  The Ursula plea
  That I could not take

O you better baike
  O you better bake
  A better cake than this
O you better Miss
Yes you better miss
When the thing never will kwiss

O sweetheart and okay
Here's hopin we'll all be away
  It was great fun
But it was just one a
    those tings

23rd Chorus

Dom dum dom domry
Dom—dom—hahem—
Sum—(creeeeee!)—Hnf—
Shh—Hnf—Shh—Haf
Shhh—Shhh—Hiffff—
—Ma—
Snffff—(bing bring, se ting)
—"Yo conee na nache"—
D ding—d ding—d-ding—
Cramp!—O ya ta dee
—ker blum—kheum—
Hnffff—drrrrrrrr—drosh—
Pepock—Shiffle—t bda—
Want a piece a bread
    No

Jack?   Hnff—Ta ra ta ra fuee
—Te wa ta ra teur—
Grrr—he na pa powa shetaw—
    Tck tick tick   Today is Sunday

24th Chorus

Eternally the lightning runs
Through form after form formless
In positive and negative repose

It makes no difference that your uncle
Was black with sufferance & bile,
The whild childscriming skies will
Always be the muchacho same

Much words been written about it
The message from infinite
That will be was brought to us
Is one
But because it has no name
We can only call it Bibit
        "It was Liebernaut who had
           the dream of uncovering Carthage"
The snow in the sea mountains

25th Chorus

In Egypt under rosebushes
Fifi's fruits & sweets

My Egyptian connection's
Gonna be late, the conductor
Wouldnt take my change

The Egyptian conductor
Wouldnt nod

Sandalwood and piss and pulque
Burning in every door,
Mighty Marabuda River
Flows along

Sampans and river thieves
And woodsplitters and blind
Thieves' Markets & imbeciles
"See Milan and see the world"

Heppatity the twat kid
Hatted by the racetrack
Horses' moon barns
spun on a gibbee
For lying alone

26th Chorus

My poems were stolen
    by Fellaheen Thieves
In the city of the midnight

The title was "Fellaheen Blues"
And justice is done to Rome

I'll never see them again
Learn what sweet development
I'd harbored up to meditate
All's left now
    is these hateful
    New Fallaheen Blues
    which mean nothing
    and I hate them
In the other book I cried
Ah-da   Ah-da
  the parturient spinsters
  that prate i the dining hill
  Are having blue venison
  To goose their old hyms
    Og

27th Chorus

But I'll tell you—electricity
Runs through all these forms
And we call it electricity
And notice the forms
But what's hoppen in nothin
Is wha hoppen in nothin
  See?
  The butchers a de Bronx
  Ourter now dat

—the late night tweed diners
Italian restaurants on Bleecker
that sing in the staring blue street
with cigarettes of legs
  Ourter know dat
The wild outflow wow open
O gate of golden honey
Hopin hill up above
And below & within
The kin, aye, my,
What a roseate balloon
For lovers of kin

28th Chorus

Part of the morning stars
  The moon and the mail
The ravenous X, the raving ache,
—the moon Sittle La
Pottle, teh, teh, teh,—
The tatata of thusness
Twatting everywhere—

  The poets in owlish old rooms
  who write bent over words
  know that words were invented
  Because nothing was nothing

In use of words, use words,
the X and the blank
And the Emperor's white page
And the last of the Bulls
Before spring operates
Are all lotsa nothin
   which we got anyway
So we'll deal in the night
   in the market of words

29th Chorus

And he sits embrowned
   in a brown chest
Before the palish priests

And he points delicately
   at the sky
With palm and forefinger

And's got a halo
   of gate black

And's got a hawknosed
   watcher who loves to hate

But has learned to meditate
   It do no good to hate

So watches, roseate laurel
   on head
In back of Prince Avolokitesvar
   Who moos with snow hand
And laces with pearls
   the sea's majesty

30th Chorus

The little bug thrasheth
        on the table
Hungry to burn in the candle
   of flames
Jerks at the gate-bottoms
   of wax cold hide
Albions and Albans
    to his little sight
Leaps to be browned
    in the roast rite
Soars & tries to reach
    dizzy height
Falls in the temples
    and quivers & slaps
Playin like a schoolboy
    in the valleys
Of silver & ivory hate

ELEVEN VERSES OF GARVER

31st Chorus

I

I had a slouch hat too one time
The old slouch hat
I just keep walkin around
And he keeps walkin around with me
Around and round that necktie
   counter we went
When it rained I wore my old
    slouch hat

It was a good felt that
   I had to carry through many
   rainy day, late fall
   and the early spring

Perhaps it was a rainy day
And the house dick mighta saw
My hat
     Each tie on that ring
     Worth six bucks, Brooks Brothers,
     Sixty bucks wortha ties
Slacks with peculiarities
I couldnt even find a pair of slacks
I thought it was suitable to wear

32nd Chorus

II

Wrapped one pair around me
And pinned it with a safety pin
And pulled up my trousers and
  Went out looked at myself in the mirror
     'O no, those wont do'
     And I walked out

Wrap the slacks around my waist

Took two other pair
   went to the mirror
  threw them at the salesman
'No those wont do—good
    afternoon' and walked out

The slouch hat I got at Harvard
    Club, Yale Club, Princeton Club
    one or the other
    Dartmouth Club
    University Club

Always barred the Yatch Club
    because it was a little over
    my kin

33rd Chorus

III

The doorman knew that only
    Mr Astor   Mr Vanderbilt
    Mr Whitney belonged

He couldnt say 'Good morning
    Mister Astor' because
    he knew I wasnt Mister
    Astor

I always figured a way to heel
    into those other clubs

Not only a member of Who's
    Who but a Who's Who
    also have to be a member
    of Who's Who in New York
    in the special clique of Who's

Hoo—slouch hat!

    I get in the Athletic Club
    many time

34th Chorus

IV

And I'd go up in the Billiard Room
And I would wander back around
The room, hands in back,
And every coat rack I backed
Up against feel for the wallet
    One day I walked
    Outa there with ten wallets

Bellboy lookin me over
Pretty soon a very dignified looking
    gentleman came up and buzzed
    the bell boy

He says "Who?" and I says
"Man told me his name, while
  We're drinkin at the bar,
  And told me to meet him
  In the billiard-room
   of the Athletic Club
I dont see him—so I best I
  better go"

35th Chorus

V

"Tell me about the old slouch
    hat"

One of my numerous trips
    to one of the numerous clubs
    in New York City

The hat finally was left
    in the hotel
    which I had to leave
    rather hurriedly one night
    never to return
    so the hat was given
    to the castoffs of the hotel
    which they collect
    and rummage sells

May now be worn by one
Of the members of Skid Row

New York City—the Bowery

"I seen that hat
by moonlight"

36th Chorus

VI

I had a pointed mustache
    and I mean pointed
    half inch from here

Double breasted vest
        and a Derby hat
        and striped trousers
        English shoes, black,
        very pointed, they were
        Hannah Shoes

People on Broadway'd turn
        and look at me

The worst is yet to come
        I had a pince nez
        with a long black ribbon
        to my buttonhole

And I wore a carnation
        white or red

    Boy did I look like somethin

37th Chorus

VII

A year later I got caught
I was dressed differently
    and everything
But boy that mustache
    and that pince nez
      was really out of this world

I used that outfit six months
I finally had to pack it in
  because it was too well-worn

Pince nez was in a coat
  I stole
Mustache I grew in the
    sanitarium
While takin one of my
    numerous drug cures

My mother'd come to see me
    She says "Oh No!
   Cut it off!"
"I'm just havin a little fun, mother"

38th Chorus

VIII

Took it on the lam
And went to Canada

late at night I'm fulla
    morphine and I come down
    fulla goofballs too

This guy had ventriloquist doll
And he gave out this Texas Guinan
Routine "Hello Sucker, we

like your money as well
as anybody else's—s matter
of fact the bigger your roll
the more we take ya"

He used to get everybody
        interested with the doll
        and cutout silhouettes
        put stripes in your tie

Wound up in his room
        gave him a shot of morphine

39th Chorus

IX

Out on the highway I thumbed a ride
into Buffalo and I put the bum
on the guy for something to eat
—'Eat in my drugstore'—
So we went in the back
And he had corn on the cob
And boiled potatoes, 'Say fellow
I always hear people talk
about morphine, what's it look
like?'—he shows me—he
had a key a cabinet and
he had bottles of hundreds
quartergrains halfgrains
pantapon delauddit everything
and soon as he tended
the customers I emptied the
bottles—got outa there pretty
quick, bought a safety pin
in Buffalo and took a shot
in the toilet

40th Chorus

X

Come out and saw a fellow
shaving, his coat hanging there,
hung my own coat and gave
his coat a brush of my hand,
felt his wallet, washed my hands,
and went out and took off
with the wallet

So I started out on a shoplifting
campaign in Buffalo
    wasnt very experienced at it

Started out with a topcoat
and I sold it in a taxicab stand

Next day I decided to get myself
some suits
    and I went up
    I had a suitbox
I walked about & put the suitbox
in one of the dressingrooms
    Looked & fooled in the mirror
    Went out, I hocked those two

41st Chorus

XI

Next day like a damn fool
go out to the same store
but I got a newspaper
instead of a suitbox
    thought I'd try
    a new routine

Two guys kinda watchin me
I went in wrapped myself up

two suits
    went in the elevator
    bottom gentleman
    tapped me on the arm
    'Will you come with me
                please?'

And the County Jail they ate
breakfast and got oatmeal
with one spoonful of molasses,
for lunch stew, mostly bones,
Graveyard Stew, and for supper
    dinner at night
Beans—and you couldnt smoke

    ► • ◄

42nd Chorus

Kayo Mullins is always yelling
and stealing old men's shoes
Moon comes home drunk, kerplunk,
Somebody hit him with a pisspot
Major Hoople's always harrumfing
Egad kaff kaff all that
Showing little kids fly kites right
And breaking windows of fame

Blemish me Lil Abner is gone
His brother is okay, Daisy Mae
and the Wolf-Gal

    Ah who cares?
    Subjects make me sick
    all I want is C'est Foi
    Hope one time
    bullshit in the tree

Hmmmmmmmmmmmmmmmm
I've had enough of foolin me
And making silly imagery
    Harrumph me katt
    I think I'll take off
    For Cat and fish

43rd Chorus

Well & well well, so that's
The ancient fainter, the painter
Who tied up blue balloons
—Globas azul—and threw
Them asunder in the thunder
Of the ul—Ur—Obi—Ob-
Fuscate me no more travails,
Pardy hard, this rock mine
We're workin'll yield up diamond
                  hard

And then we'll cut thru conceptions
And come with answer pard

And what twill it be, sorry pard,
Aint never no mystery
Was imparted to me
Lessn you wanta try Roy McGoon
Who learned it in Innisfree

Or old Yow O Yeats, Blake,

We havent got the diamond tho
That freed Dipankara Buddha
In the Palaeolithic morning
And made him make faces
In Samapattis at me
    Let's free

44th Chorus

High Cascades or Mexico—
 headaches
Travel everywhere

Forms and costumes and noses
All this changing literature
Cyrano de Bergerac, King
of the French underworld
King for a day, Henry V,
Falstaff his father, Henry IV,
Warlike stools frowning in
'We have no more use
For your caisson iron,
It's too fat
  and the water too vile,
  I'll vouch for the master
  but water your while
  had better be bile
  to judge from the green
  of the innocent liquid'
Reading, naught, words, styles
  The only thing matter is otay

45th Chorus

English Literature
 a School of Writing

French Literature
 was closed off

How tight the lips of Zola the
       Master

Wont tell how he grips his pen
To consorts of learners

English, Old Shakespeare gathered
    bout him minor figures
    like Ben Jonson
    Maurie O'Tay
    Henry Fenelon
    And Molly O'Day

Irish Literature—that was
   where the brabac originated
   from
     Wood cracking in the sea

46th Chorus

And what is God?
The unspeakable, the untellable,
—

Rejoice in the Lamb, sang
   Christopher Smart, who
   drives me crazy, because
   he's so smart, and I'm
   so smart, and both of us
   are crazy

No,—what is God?
The impossible, the impeachable
Unimpeachable Prezi-dent
of the Pepsodent Universe
but with no body & no brain
no business and no tie
no candle and no high
no wise and no smart guy
no nothing, no no nothing,
no anything, no-word, yes-word,
everything, anything, God,
the guy that aint a guy,
the thing that cant be
and can
and is
and isnt

47th Chorus

Beverly Dickinson, wasnt it,
the distraught perfect poetess
who lived in New Hampshire
and wrote about roots & roses

Sweet old Beverly I remember her well
and her attic was fragrant,
her Attican divine
her storm bird
her fence story
her bee inside
her butterfly
her broom
her Majesty
the Queen

Said, "Emily Dickinson is as great
as Shakespeare sometimes,"
said T. S. Eliot's editor
Robert Giroux, swell fellow—
Her Attic divine, her antic,
—her

Sang in the blue hill
      her larks and mimes
And died all a silent
      in her prophecy tomb

48th Chorus

Dans son tombeau
Elle a gagnée
Toutes les lignes noires
D'Eternité

Que' s' trouve dans la terre
Quand qu'l mouille dans l'Hiver

Salonge!—Mompress!
Traboune!—Partance!

Elle a trouvée dejas
L'ange d'Archanciel
Couchez dans la mer
D'été d'nuée

Aye, oui, mes Anges toutes Francais
Mes tours d'ircanciel

Ma miel, mon or,
Mes ames deshonorées,
Mes troublages, mes lignes,
Mon vin sur la table
Ou sur le plancher

49th Chorus

Book of Dreams
(Written in dream language)
Old Hosapho we wont let up
And hear me sing the
    hm—Ole Hosapho
    he wont let me record
    me dream language

Ooogh!   he upped & come back
      Old Hosapho
But now he's down's
Gone down boy again

Hay Hosapho, say sumptin!
Hoy Hosapho, Roil!
  Nope Hosapho stay lead down
—A mani a Gloria—
    Tinkle tinkle laughter
    Dingle little pretties
      everything's happening everywhere

50th Chorus

My real choice was to go
to Princeton—I wanted
to be orange and black
on the football field

and orange Varsity letters
on black wool jackets
with buttons, and elm trees
and Sunday afternoon
the swish of the snow
and Einstein in his yard
and All's Well with
the Emily Dickinson world

And drive to New Hope
      for a drink
      or lobster

And take the sad train
on the platform of night
And ride into riot New York
On a Saturday Night
To go see Count Basie
Baying at the Lincoln
With Lester Otay Young
On Tenor Saxophone

51st Chorus

Boy, sa den du coeur, sa, le bon
vin—Mama, c'est'l'port
si fort, le vin divin—

Aye, oui, mais écoute—dans
les milieus de les nuits,
tu wé, sa den du coeur,
sa den du coeur

Ca fa du bien au beson

Besoigne?—Di mué pas la
besogne maudit, la bédenne,
maudit, la bédenne,
    sa fa du bien a bédenne
        pauvr' bédenne

A, y parle tu aussi bien
      q'ca
        a Milan
      les Italiens a gueules
Nous autres aussi on a une
belle lagne qui clacke

52nd Chorus

Dog with mouths, in Navajoa,
bent down to the mud
and slippered shining entrails
in the morning Sinaloa sun
of a dead rabbit

Then the bus come and run
    it over, the rabbit, sullen
    dog skimpered off a minute,
    came back to repeat his
        refection

Oh well, shiney priests
      eat goodies
        in every store they see

Old Navajoa shit dog, you,
your goodies are the goodiest
goodies I ever did see, how
dog you shore look mad
when yer bayin

Hoo Hound-dog!
    dont eat that dead rabbit
    in front of my face raw
    —cook it a lil bit

53rd Chorus

I had a scrap with a doctor
    one night
We were both drunk
I said "Just because you're
    a doctor you think you're
    so smart, if you're
    going to report me go
    ahead you prick"

And I fell off the stool
I was fulla goofballs

He went to the other doctor
"You better look this guy
up, he must be some kind
of a phoney"

Pony the pony the pony
the pra
Pony the pony the pony
the pra

54th Chorus

I got a grass jaw, boys,
I say, and knock out Ray
Robinson in the first minute
of the first round

Then they bring in Tiger Jones
because I made no bones

about how I was out to
Kayo Robinson, moonbless him

Tiger Jones comes on me all
fists, hard puncher, I got
nothing to do but retreat
or turn into grass, so
  I dance
  right in
  to his arms
    reach
and plow him all over
with crazy little punches
some of which are hard
    and we wake up

55th Chorus

Someday they'll have monuments
set up to reverend the mad
people of today in madhouses

As early pioneers in the knowing
that when you lose your reason
you attain highest perfect knowing

Which is devoid of predicates
such as: "I am, I will, I reason—"
—devoid of saying:-"I will do it"
—devoid

Devoid of insanity as well by virtue
    of no contact

But meanwhile these deterministic
doctors really do believe that mad
is mad—

And have erected a billion-dollar
religion to it, called, Psycho-medicine,
and ah—

Well we'll know the sanity
    of Ard Bar

In the morning, some time, alone

56th Chorus

Some'll go mad with numbers
Some'll go mad with words

Some'll pretend to lose reason
And lose reason anyway

Some wont, some'll be secret,
Some'll screw in long black
                rooms
With the fantastic short-haired
Beauty who lies on the bed
                listening

To Sinatra—some'll be candleflame
jiggling gently in the night

Some'll be racetrack operators,
some'll have soap in their pockets

Some'll sing in the Bronx Jail
and some wont sing in Riker's

Some'll come out of it
    with iron heads

Some'll wear coats
    and hard of it

57th Chorus

The monstrous jailer, he wouldnt let me
   outa that jailhouse—
      till I had smoked all the tea
      I could smoke, 'Finish up!'
      he said, & prodded me

And I gotta take big long hikes
   of draw on that cigarette tree

How'd I get outa that jail?
   By forgetting all about me

Which was the best rasperry tree
They ever ternevented in ole
Donnesfree
Cause I figure there's no difference
twixt me and dead dog mud
Made of bones and take your pick,
      sulphur or Innisfree

How'd they ever get that tap
    outa me?
Wasnt I tired givin?
    hard tap
Family tree.
I wasnt sweet givin.

58th Chorus

Las ombras vengadora
they say in little taco joints
when the shadows are coming
at about dusk-time, in Azteca,
modern Fellaheena Mexico,
Las ombras vengadora
Lass ombras venga dora
Most beautiful sound in the world
    hep!

Swing up the team, bring up
      the gangs, say, didnt I yell
      at you a minute ago?

Hoy!
      Las ombras vengadora
      in little taco sad joints
      on Sunday Afternoon
      and fathers are home
      honoring their sons

59th Chorus

Fantasm crazam crazam
Joe Kennedy stops me on
   the sidewalk of the Immemorial
University—ack hook
You got your prick out.

I look down, no such thing

What are your two balls
doing hanging on the sidewalk?

I think I'll squat & shit—
We both squat facing each
      other on the campus
If ya know what I mean,
   cream, we squat
practice 'mitate Aristophanes
and sit there too laughing
and talking, Kennedy,
one of my first mature
      Irishmen

Face each other with feet
partly out, like in Esquire
the phonies showing their shoes
      Squat n Shit!

60th Chorus

I purified language early in my
young days, I purified & squatted
& beshitted on pages, sophomore,
on my typewriter, all the dirty
words I could think of
          squrify & squat & shit
And slit—and finally I'm
in history class & the professor
says 'Kerouac—what you
dreamin about?'
And I shhoudda said Ack—
Pack—Squrify and squat
and shit, who wants to hear
about the aniards and breast
plates of warriors of the
          Medieval Ages
I wanta know about the people
on the street, what they doin?
And what the high art
hark squambling in his quiet
   temple moonlit gambymoon
writing jingles & jongles
     for the pretties on the square

61st Chorus

Orizaba Rooftop blues
Listenin to the street news
Saturday night down there
Pleep! went the new little bike
     horn
As the cat pleeped it with his
Foot zinging the bike across
the fantastic bus-driven corners
Barging everywhere, he just angles
     and amples
       like Stan Getz on tenor

And swings around right around
　　the fender okay

Orizaba rooftop, Orizaba Rooftop,
Blue, blue, blue
Blue's made of shiny everyway

Orizaba honk-honk, bus motors
Riding high for the clutch, tired,
Faces green on the benches,
Ikons in the corner
　　　　Tails of little fenelet
　　　　serpents hanging from the fender

Aik, motorcycle of no-cops,
Hotrods & Deans of Mexico,
Aik, aik, aik Mexico
　　　BORRACHO GUAPO BANJO

62nd Chorus

Pipestoon the Ribber & wobbed
old ladies of shame. the same.
party twan twit Twittenden
Charley, 'Awfully good fuck!'
　he yells out the train window,
　to his waving host of the weekend,
'I say old chap, really!!'
and then Commando Poltroon
　comes platooning up in mudsplash,
　Monty, examining every commando
　standing naked in the rain,
　'That hurt?' whacking
　a guy on the rib, 'No
sir,' 'Why not?'
　　'Commando, sir'
Finally he comes to a man
with a long hardon, & whacks
it with his military crop

—with his baton—
'That hurt?'   'No sir'
      "Why not?"
"Man behind me sir."

63rd Chorus

The star is reflected in the puddle
      and the star dont care
      and the puddle dont care
Nothing is thinking
      not even the puddle poet

That's why "This Thinking Has Stopped"
Is the best way I know to imitate
      this starry state of affairs
      in puddles

Plass!   plash!—wait a minute!—
   wait a second buddy while I
   hock up old Desroches three
   sacrifices

      For each sacrifice you're reborn
      and you're only reborn once
      because there is only One
            Sin

Slatter me pet Charley, T-rod,
pettle pole and all, believes,
and goes rosing in the woods

Purt!   Foley!   Words!   Names!
      Ahab, Starbuck & Pip
      Iago and Poltroon
      and Pipestaff the Ribber
—pain, pain, the no-name retoin

64th Chorus

On the street I seen three guys
standing talking quietly in the sun
and suddenly one guy leaps in pain
and whacks his fingers in the air
as he's burned his hand
        with a match
        lighting a butt

The other two guys dont even
        know this,
they go right on talking
        gesticulating with hands

I seen it, it was on San Jose
        Boulevard in St Joseph
        Missouri, nineteen thirty
        two

Them guys didnt even realize
pain is one thing, everywhere?

    Whai? Every golden
    sweetgirl come & befawdle
    her pillow in my hair
        and I dont care?
            Wha?

65th Chorus

JEWISH GOY IN N.Y.

Wha?   Whaddayou mean,
        there are ten thousands mysteries
        of me by the millions standing
        with hand-molded shows
        and sports jacket
        and no hair

bouncing along in one long corridor
of images in a mirror
    into infinity
    eternity
    call it what you will!

I know that!—You dont have
    pull that Buddha-stuff
    on me, Jack, I dont care

I've seen me in the picture
    stretched out everywhere
    it dont matter?
    Who cares!

I go to Lefty's & eat pastrami
    on Sunday afternoon,
    with mustard—I go hear
    some music at Carnegie Hall
    —I lay my wife—
    I sit on the bed, work

Who cares?   Wha?
    What's the moon got?

66th Chorus

What's the moon got but tunes?
Wha?   I dont care I'll talk
I'll stand right here talk
till doomsday, nobody care,
nobody say, who knows?   who
wants?   What's gonna free
what from what?   Shit!
    Gold! Girl! Honey! Call!
    What you will, call it,
    shit, I'll sit, I'll talk,
    I'll hang all day, because,
    it doesnt matter, you talk

about it doesnt matter
but you dont realize how
doesnt-matter
it really doesnt-matters,

    Wow man, I mean,

Sure, shoes, Shows, Hand
painted molds form azimuth
shoes, azipeth azipor
azinine blues, you got,
who cares, tsawright, eat,
pickles in the barrel—
    ——hail a cab—
      do what you want

67th Chorus

"It all goes down the same hole"
said Allen, eating cake & food
in a restaurant, with milk
in his coffee, no milk in the can,
no sense in the sour bottom
of that can

All goes up the same sky,
    all sucks on same air,
all plops drops impregnates
    and saves anywhere
The same limitation gentiles
    the crave for a show
on notwithstanding lost bibles
    dedicating the mystery
to a vain empty show,
'Vanity of Vanities,
    All is Vanity'
"Behold her breasts are like
    fawns"
    in the summer air,

Her eyes are like doves,
    skin like the tents
—Skin like the rents
in the heavenly air

68th Chorus

A murder   stern gird
A million dollar ba by
Ack
    Rowers of galleys,
    Candle lights,
    Hearners of yorn,
    Parturient ones,
    Poo,
    Patch art part tea
    Gart and band thee
    Harden thy garkle
    And get ye no purple kirtles
    Ere aye mice Burns
    Hands Mc Caedmon let loose
    His last tired crazy pom
            'Hung la terre,
            hang the twarrie,
            part de twaklockleme,
        gockle somackle magee'

    Down with the back rooms
    Of Dublin

69th Chorus

PRAYER

God, protect me!
   See that I dont defecate
    on the Holy See

See that I dont
   murder the bee

God! be kind!
   Free all your dedicate
    angels, for me

Or if not for me
   for anybody

God!   Hold fast!
   I'm dying in your arms
    delicately

Ah God be merciful
    to Princeton me

Ah God, alack a God,
   nobody farms
    amnesty

70th Chorus

I

There'll be no more ginger ale
for me
goodbye ginger ale
when I die
in Innisfree

That's where I'll go to die
to look and die
I'll never go there now

Because I've already told the boys
at the paper
the sound is crashing me

And they ate paper
And it was a paper party

But when they bell bonged toll,
And we all had to pay,
"Die in my arms, lamb,"
sang Rudy Vallee
from here to eternity

Die in my that's a beautiful arms,
    lad,
Die in my that's a beautiful arms,
    said God
To me

71st *Chorus*

II

That's just something
that isnt written
in Wells' history

That's something, Window Knock,
when you can make me
pray me

That'll do the reading
in London Library

And in Dublin I is free
To read
Old Innisfree

And then I'll read Finn
Again, and meet Magee
In a back alley

And get to know
    Donnelly
And the brothers Donnelly

That's where I'll be,
    My Arma Carney,
I'll be dyin
  down in Innisfree
Waiting for ye
Mary Carney

Orlanda Blues

1st Chorus

Le corp de la verité
pourre dans la terre

The body of truth
rots in the earth

nourriture dans la terre

Sanchez fourwinds bigtown,
dont wail that at me
  Fraserville Quebec
    comes back to me

  In the night sun sleep
  warm, store it in tanks

Blues of Old Virginia tree
    moonbottles over kiss time
   listener appeal
   Kissland
      Kissimee Florida
These are Orlanda Blues

2nd Chorus

O Cross on my wall
  O body of Christ

When I was awright
  Saturday night

Little in your arms
  your thousands of years

In electric resist I wanted
   to soul the liking I saw
—*words*

(musician pauses)

3rd Chorus

This book is too nice for me
They made Clay Felker editor
of Esquire
Or Rust Hills one
and what ever happened to glass
and the joke about the Lord.

The Lord is my Agent.

My message is blah blah blah

My yort tackalitwingingly
   pasta vala tt, yea, p,
   my reurnent gollagigle
   dil plat most-rat, my
    erneealieing cralmaa
    tooth, ant, mop, sh,
   my devoid less 2 immensity
   secret muzning midnight,
   my whatzit
            you wanta
              know
                   Whatzit!
      Joy   Look out!

4th Chorus

Joy look in,
   look in,
      the pretty
         sin

     Loy, t   a tt ct b
   I fooled with the long
   overload
     (wrong over road?)
   wronk

What a moistious wronk
we're in fair words,
   or is it wairds
   in your part
   of the
    Kelp,
  Laird

In Scotland we just throw
  the bones to the dogs
     & toast at the
        fireplace

5th Chorus

Well then let's have a toast
I wonder if I can write
 poems just like Gregory
 Corso:—let's see:—
   The dead are dead,
    I'll resurrect them with
   this song,   O fall
   you fair held
    cities—
   (wood wood wood)
 O held the fair held
  in the skinny bar!

(the skinny bar held Indian
    sonofabitch)
So North Mood wrote:—
C o l t i n g—The Gregory
   says "Eels & gripplings
        in
        my
      eaves"

6th Chorus

Finally I was in Stockholm at last
Cold night
  Dark in Swedenborg

Zeldipeldi my junkey friend
  from N.Y. and Maldo
  Saldo the hot trumpeter
    from Nigeria, turned on
    in the cold room overlooking
    black rooftops of winter,
      Sweden night skies February,
      Ommani pahdme hom

I wanted to catch a train
    to the Capital

I was on a seacoast town,
  the name of it was Fidel
  or Fido
      wow, mominu,
      You dont know how far
        that sky
          go

7th Chorus

Message from Orlanda:—
　You guys cant explore
　all of outer space, unless
　you want to spend
　　a million million million
　　million million million
　　　billion billion bullion
　　　bullion years at it
　　—and when you gets
　　　there, and you cant
　　　even get there, give my
　　　　regards to Captain Bligh

And lissen, before you leave,
　how bringin my money
　with you to preserve
　in eternity, see, I
　can cash in when
　I get there & spend it
　on
　　　space
　　　　　travel

8th Chorus

Thats awright, space'll carry
us maybe like little eggs,
the buggy children work
　their way out
　to the surface
　of the egg,
　　to the shell,
　　　they swim soft,
　　　& they get there
　　　& meet God
　　　The Shell
　　　The Shell

hard & cold
against the cold
gray sun
blood
in
your
Father's
Long Winter
Underwear

So sleep

9th Chorus

Me, I'm worried I'm a secret sinner
and God
Ole Tangerine
I call   Him
because one day I was settin
under trees
in
a
chair

And deciding what name
to give to God, is it
a personal God? & blam
the little tangerine
landed
squarely
on my
head
like Newton's
underwear,

& so I saw it personal
And I say the moral is simple

10th Chorus

But it landed right on the
tippy tiptop
of the sconce,
Jazz,
dazz,
and that's why I believe
(since it's all grinning
in there)
it was a little
tap reminder

I don't *need* thunderclouds!

"Maybe Eden aint so
lonesome as New England
used to be," said Emily
Dickinson sitting with
a tangerine in her hand

(They shipped it from Cuba)
It was a great show
Gasser!

11th Chorus

I guess God is alright
He'll take care of us

But there are perturbing roots
in these trees,
that claw in earth
& outa fingernails
as long as Malaya
eat up thru sucktubes
the juice of the mother
Terra Firma
Mona Leisure

        & these roots remind you
           of the roots in your grave
        I wish I could be cremated
        & sprung
                    (to the wave),
        but Ah, hell, I donno
        I think I'll go to
              Sapplewhile
           & idle away the
           unfinished poem

                12th Chorus

The evening silencius
Poetry
        is so pretty
   When you silence it like that

It's nice to pop pearl pages
the candlelight, you know,
      is dedicated to poets

Okay—dreaming fields—Blake
wants to hear the latest development
in the man the way the bleat
lambs bleakly blake it now
and that is soft,
           Ah William,
      I guess as soft as Spanish
      dreams, what was it Trappist
        said:— "Goats
                    as
                    soft
                    as
                    sleep"
Something like that
        Farewell

13th Chorus

Jack Micheline
"Feet of children playing by
  the mill"—he didnt say
  hill—When tongue gets
  caught inside the lapels
  of the mouth, that's what
    I wanta hear—Like Fred
    Katz the cellist—or is
    it chellist?

"Tongue crucified, seven stitched"
      is pretty weird

Make it down to New Orleans
      one of these days
      says Moonlight Martin

"Maniac massacred" on account
        of "blinded on stone"
Wow, whatze mean?
Like Wolfe's Underground, mad dog
      choking in tunnels of hate
    "Spring has come
        yellow teeth & black hair"

14th Chorus

  is exactly like the magnificent
  haiku mailed to President
  Eisenhower by Manosuke
  Kambe
          "They have succeeded
              in shooting up a star
          And Spring is near"

        Yeah, where down yonder
        in you now Where

Now I'm getting to sound
　　like a drearisome
　　　tangerine

Folks, read Jack Micheline,
　　　n doubt about it
He's a great poeit
And see?—read Gregory Corso
　　　too all about "bookies
　　　　& chickenpluckers"
& Read Competition Ginsberg
　　　the maddest brain
　　　in poetry

　　　　15th Chorus

Ginsberg has a poet who
has a "great precise
　practical benevolence
　　& new understanding,"
　and I have Jack
　　Micheline, Steve Tropp,
　　Steve White, and
　many other naked heads
　What I wrote first I kept,
　　　because I figure
　　　　　　　God moves
　　　　　　　the body hand
　　　　　　　because
　　　　　　　the body of the truth
　　　　　　　is a body
　　　　　　　 corruptible
　　　　　　　 in graves
　　　　　　　though
　　　　　　　nourishing,
　　　　　　　　　　　O Schweitzer
　　　　　　　Africa Trumpet!

16th Chorus

(And George Jones blows too!)

"Kneeling in the sun beside
the bright red mad beauties
of Street!" sings Corso

"I drag him into
myricolorous St Chapelle
Stained Glass marvel,"
sings Ginsberg

      Dont discourage
         the poets!

Sings Jack Micheline:
"And kiss the strangers
& plant the seeds of life among the dead"

  Because it's a distant
  hightone rail
"Flower of cities"

17th Chorus

    And these sweet lines revive
    the open poetry of hope
    in old America
        long fish

    And this sweet moth revised
      the entelechy
      in my endebechy
      in old pardodechy
      where Croo-Ba
      made it working
      boy girls in

He was hanged in the closet
   The King ate sliced sage
      John the Baptist had no head
      Jesus had nails in his skin
      The Neon's nailed to me
      I wish I were dead
      Or King of Ronald Colman
      country, or Kin to Sariputra
         Shakespeare, one

18th Chorus

Well, s'long as barrel womps we'll
   womp em on in, Used to write
   poems about Princeton boy rose

Also Baltimore bleedings
   & think rabbit plate
shit
  I wish I had
      a way
         to make
            Tuesday Sarah
            come by
               any day

With China throwup
      hadnt Puttered
      men with me

   but bile was free,
      & girl long blonde
         taffy pull

I guess best thing to do
   is to write to
   Blues Bessie

19th Chorus

I wonder what Emily's thinkin
in that groomus earth of
coral snakes & alligators
on the sidewalk, is she got down
  by Sunday in the Tomb, or
does time matter no blow out
bulbs of shame, Jesus, what
  shame in eyelid war life
  no shame at all in eyelid
  ant eat

  allied ant eat
What wars Bismarck plotted
   on accounta ambitious
   bishops, I dont know,
   what Colbert built
    for Mazarin slurp,
    or why French Blond
     Hero bombs black
      Arab dream in sand
     of Berber Ya ke
      Silhouette Blue men
    veil, kill me, I'se
    free

20th Chorus

Jazz killed itself
 But dont let poetry kill itself
Dont be afraid
 of the cold night air

Dont listen to institutions
When you return manuscripts to
      brownstone
dont bow & scuffle
    for Edith Wharton pioneers
or ursula major nebraska prose

just hang in your own backyard
& laugh play pretty
cake trombone
& if somebody gives you beads
juju, jew, or otherwise,
sleep with em around your neck
Your dreams'll maybe better

There's no rain,
there's no me,
I'm telling ya man
sure as shit

21st Chorus

That cat's in paradise
The noise of automobile sigh
dont interfere with the knowing
of me or any paper party
but's what smat smeldied
on hey-now,   Zulch!

Truth is, cry

Because the radar never was invented
could find paradise sound
or cat lost in the night
radarless
radar-less
rad-arless
radarle-ss

rrrrt
branged suitcases as a kid
& sang to Glenn Miller's
Moonlight Serenade
& Laid
But O, Lord above,
have pity on my
missin kitty

22nd Chorus

Usta smear ma lips with whiskey
　Fred and open up the doors
　to make a joke—while
　women waited
　and Bert Lahr waited
　playing what he waited
　like Duke Ellington

used to sit staring at Seymour
who implied to me the swing
　of the music by his
　　　low crash
　　　high abidin
　　　　　　shoulders,
　　　　　P a p,
　and what wow hoo?

T h o t l a t n a p e
　　Compose Vehicle
　　　Special
　　　Banana
　　　Nine

23rd Chorus

Bat bow
lack Jack
swing Bing
that's right!
Yes
backwards—wail—
You're gut okay man
swing on along
I don't care
I can do it
　too
Orlak + +
　　see

24th Chorus

If you once
 for all good
  times
Man's fine,
 know
YOU KNOW

25th Chorus

My mind! even harder than
  my path, my freedom
  is in piano
O, wow, wild wow
  NBC OOO
    piano
Like Lee Konitz
  sky,
Yay, wow?
  Sluke!
Slow! Swing? THEN
  YOU GO—
That new tenor cat
made me drop my pencil,
  Elvin Jones

26th Chorus

Zoot Sims
 and his
  Johnny Williams
"This Happy Leaping Thing"
Kitty Drum Barry
Gray, you like cemetary
  swing?
"Big Xmas Seal"
Hockey teams—?
Al? —shape

lay, & the Elington
Good high school
    sex orgy
        girls
    in the woods
        of
        rape,
        nun dear

27th Chorus

The New Orleans New York
        Club
wishes to announce
        the opening
        of
        new sessions,
    & new fields, Daddio,

        Dave Brubeck's
            the swingingest

And I wish to say
Farewell
            to
                    Al
                    Smith

    Hello Dave

28th Chorus

For Minors Only
is the name of a new record
all about trumpet
& trimban

Zlap
    Peter Orlovsky
  is the cat to play to

You see dont you dig
    on all sides
     the wild sounds?
  and o the conceptions
    you made
      on
   Thursday
   afternoon

  trumpet man, dont blow
      that thing at me,
     blow it to
       banana

29th Chorus

Timmy got back,
  soft Blakey lamb

Timmy got back
   & wrote rhymes

And we sat purring on the bed
  with Tammy

And made it 5 percent
  thousand

Times a day, swinging,
  we had sand,
  We had Gothic top
   Cathedral girls

But O in Euniceburg
   they footballed
Stupid me from Edgar
   Lear's interior
Majesty

30th Chorus

No, this lamby bit
Is what I mean

O Orlando, O sweet

No Orlander phonecalls
   Georgia Flowerbranch

Lamby mean, William,
  Lamb dust?   Nnaaa!
  Softy uglu flutey?
    Almost—

Pan flute Erdic
  Shook spear
  that Venusian cunt
  was neat when
    I'se a Nigger
      was
        a
        baby

31st Chorus

O Gary Snyder
  we work in many ways

In Montreal I suffered tile
  and rain

In Additional Christmas
    waylayed babes

In old crow Hotels
    full of blue babes
    in pink dressinggowns
            down

    But O Gary Snyder,
        where'd you go,
    What I meant was
        there you go

In Montreal I worked a manied-way

And, better than Old Post,
    I learned t'appreciate
    in many ways
    Montreal, Soulsville,
        and Drain

        32nd Chorus

    Listening to a guy play
    tenor saxophone &
    keep the tune inside
    chords & structures,
    as sweetly as this,
        you'll experience
        the same
            fitly thrill
                you got from Mozart

    It is pure musical beauty,
        like a musicale
        among wigs

People who dont understand
jazz are tone-deaf
 & dont understand
what tone-deaf &
 simply deaf
 meant to Ludwig

33rd Chorus

van
Beethoven

*

Goats as soft as break
of day
In swamp
Mexico

*

Can diamond cut iron?
Diamond cuts glass
 glass links

But can it cut
An iron link?

Nirvana means Cut-Link

If diamond dont cut glass
or iron dont count,
  hey?
  maybe the Wisdom Vow
  o the Diamondcutter
  may have made it

34th Chorus

The only responsibility to a child
  is to feed, the rest is
   interference

   Can you just see
    a man arrested
     for letting his daughter
      fuck
        around the block
        anyway
        anywhere
       just so long as she got
       home to eat her
       dinner, he's telling
         the cops
         absolutely that

And the girl gets married?
  I have a bunch of stray cats
   in my yard

I wouldnt *have* a daughter

35th Chorus

Whattayouwanta have er for
  You wanta sling sperm
   over her?
  Avin her now, ey you
   old reprobate

Lissen, just keep that daughter
   away from my knees
   after she's thirteen

And between ten & that
   tell her to lay off
   the rough stuff

With boys you can play
    as rough as you want,
    but once ye spank em
    they hate you forever

Oi Karamazov!

36th Chorus

O Apollo

  Men

   are the beautiful

The women miss cats

      Cads & rogues
        of Montreal all,

  or blue diers in deep pars
    asking for golfscore

But in any Case
    tsa united press

37th Chorus

Old dotin old fuck

There's this old man,
he come down this road
just a walking with some
 a whatyamaycallit
  in a big bottle

& I dont know what was in it
& it come night

& I was in my house
& here come this old man
        down the road
    drinking outa that bottle
        And there was Allen Wayne
    in his house

38th Chorus

& he had to hang this sheet
    on the clothesline

& that old man dropped
    that bottle in his
    yard

& that shu old man
    dropped that bottle
    down that road

    And that's all
        Uncle Fred

39th Chorus

Maybe it's resting in the arms
        of Jesus,
    or just a cloudy windy day
In the trees

                    *

But since there's an infinite
        amount of angels,
        and Infinite ends in no 's,'
        it must be
        one angel

Infinite Angels?

Maybe that bird that floats
hill belly on the wind up there,
  and that cat
    that pats
    in this grass
  is the same
    Infinite
    Worldwide
      Angel

40th Chorus

A hard hearted old farmer
hidin his wine in the cellar

When he goes out he wears
earmuffs

He has a doublebitted axe
sharp enough
to shave shit

His people are all buried
  in the same cemetery,
  which is located
  under the doorstep
  where the boy
  couldnt get through
    from the tomb

41st Chorus

If we do battle,
    Monsieur,
And you lose,
    I gain nothing,

And if I lose,
   you gain
Satisfaction

This is what the peasant said
   when the aristocrat
   challenged him to a duel

Women move slowly
   but they dont stop

Europe, weep in your gloomy
      rain

I brought it to him
   so I could get you
      in Paradise

42nd Chorus

Abraham, drinking water by the tents

Pacing up & down the soft sand
   under the stars

Worrying about Villages

Wondering if your vision was real
or just a foolish importunity
in your mind.
 Yet moving on in the morning anyway
   with the rattle of pack asses.

Abraham, the dew is in your beard
Abraham my eyes are open
 You are weird

   Abraham they've brought you
   Your rooftops are mended

Your women bend no more
   their heads under the sleepy
   tentflap, & goats dont yew
   & cry nomo in the singsong
   tentvillage night

43rd *Chorus*

Abraham I didnt write this right

44th *Chorus*

Dont ever come to Florida

A man was gettin up for work
   & reached under his bed
   in Kissimee
   and a coral snake
   bit him, February Florida
   (lookin for his shoes)

A little boy playin in his yard
was et by a alligator
   (true)

And an old lady dyin in her bed
   was et up by fire ants
   which found her
   clean from the yard

And my mother saw a lizard
   one foot long
   on the garbage pail
    that had big red eyes
(The fire ants went in
    thru the mouth, man)

45th Chorus

There's a middlewestern prurience
about Greeks.—

Your little earth-nut, O potato
war, riots mama dears around
    papap's paternal root

    S i l k y b o o

 (o o !)

    Found the Sound

46th Chorus

Hollywood boy sing dog song
Dont be fooled by gun car
Or shine in hat of Sheriff
Cochise,
      or turn that dial,
      boy, you know whats happen
      to you when yard dog
      bit your fame

Yair, & dont sweep any leaves,
    Watch me play basketball
        I guess—

        In Inverness, where I'sa
        played hogball since
            your pappy skinned
                —Okay, old
                    suit, see
                    ya more

47th Chorus

Airplanes dropping barrels
   of shit on the White House
   On Roosevelt's very head
What do the women know
   of the wood?

All they gotta do is get drunk,
   Honorary Mayor

Up sprang the butcher boy
with the spring old man!

Why'st the fool play thou?

Because fools always follow.

   Followest what?

Because fooly are always follying?

      Nay, Sire, it was forgotten
   in the body's balconeer

48th Chorus

God ushered me into my house
What a batting champeen
      honorable American Navy
Sweetheart God is to us
      Japanese Rigour Girls

Buy that, Moke!

   Dazz, I'ze innerested
      in drape fall circus
      and yo, yo got childrees
      pleak okomiko bonny

sugar, ah, sweet,
dont let Robert Burns
burn that cigar of yours
Or mice lay men
to diamondshine
your kittlepee poopoo
Grace,
Otherwise purd
Hurt
New Year

49th Chorus

Way out
But not too way out

Barefaced wretch—
you're a pretty nice
barefaced wretch—
as bare faced wretches

go

T r u e   T o y !

Great day in the morning,

Ugh-y!

50th Chorus

Hollywood, if you want
little girls raped by sex
fiends, dont hint with
symbols, give it to me
S   t r a i g h t

Otto was pretty miserable
He chased little girls
    to rape in sawdust
    apartments yet unbuilt

He was a ugly big Otto
    but O when I was
        a little girl I loved
        all that

The lovely maniac
makes me smile

51st Chorus

Who is going to get rid
of his discriminating mind,
    which is the way to
    heaven, when he is being
    eaten by crocodiles?

By means of his extremely
    slow metabolism he was
    enabled to keep far
        on the father light,
            far from the energy
            particle of the mother

Ah, it's a depressing situation:
    we imagine that
        we live and imagine
            that we die, too bad,
            too bad

Manly manly manly friend
    says the faggot on T V

Cerrada Medellin Blues

(FIRST SOLO)

1st Chorus

Even when I was a little boy
I was always alone
        with my guardian angel

Playing Tarzan
An icicle fell on me
     & cut my arm
I had a rope around my neck
I was hanged in Innifree
Had my hand cut off in Perfidee
Never had my fill
        of Thee

ST MICHAEL IN THE CORNER,
NINE FEET TALL

2nd Chorus

The Only One
    said Christ to me
When you're alone in Heaven
  with God
Who is my Father
     and Thine
You'll know that your self
   you
  And your guardian angel,
    One,
  And the self of any
Is
  The Only One—
  Sad Bent Head
    In "Cant-Get-Away
     From-That-Innisfree"

3rd Chorus

I wonder what's hiding
   in the Cross?
Did Jesus free the world?
Before him there were murders
   officially.
From body to effigy
   went history.
Emily Dickinson me that,
   Thomas Hardy.
Roll me a pearl me
   that, O Big Sur Sea.
And you, Ferlinghetti,
    how do you like that
  For rhyming free
  Free of a doctor's degree.
   Jean Louee.

4th Chorus

When I drink Bénédictine
I drink what the Holy
       Father
       Blessed
  I drink the blood of Christ?
   Naw!
   I drink Christ hisself—
   I say "Thank ye, God"
   and drink—
And kiss the bottle
With the Cross on it
And D.O.M.
   the director of drinkers—
   The Heavenly Daiquiri?
   The troublesome Innisfree.

5th Chorus

What's all this Innisfree
    Running straight thru me?
Was Yeats invented it?
  Or O'Shawn the Yurner?
  Repetitive old rolling
      smoke balloons?
  Paul Newman's mouth
    with Spanish ladies
        arguing?
What?——Some truck?
Some cigaree?   Halles
  Market onions are free?
  My Guardian Angel's
    About to tell me—

6th Chorus

Alone with my Guardian Angel
  Alone in Innisfree
Alone in Mexico
          City
Alone with Benedict,
  Cave is free,
      alone is alone,
      Thou Only One—
  Alone and Alone
    The song of the pree
(Pree means prayer
  in English & Frenchie)
Choose yr words lightly,
      shit on the world,
    Merton'll die
      when he reads
          this from me

7th Chorus

I love Lax
 A regular Pax
  I love Lax
   not Ex Lax
  but
    you see
       Now Lax
  But's teeth ne'er held
 The comedian so grand
As them Lax horse teeth
 Held prayer
    to ground
Lax is a singer
 Lax is a goner
Lax is a gonna
 get mad onner

8th Chorus

My hand is moved
   by holy angels
 The life we are in
   is invisible
   Holy Ghost

If you could see me,
  hoodlum,
You'd be Saint
  Cant slash
   at a loser
 For Oy Yai O Paint
—Those lies are for liars
And me I'm a liar,
So liars forget
  the handsome beget
The ugliest pricks
  The angel beset

9th Chorus

But I stopped to think
  The angel dont care
  Nine feet tall
  Beside the wall
  Wants me cut out
  To do the rub out
But I got fathers to care for
Father Shoyer is one
Father Gioscia is two
  That's enough for you
      —Ah Lucien
 Al Jalisco
   Ah I'm drunk
   borracho

10th Chorus

Too drunk to write
Cant see the light

It's a strange thing when nuts
  get together
 To form one cock—
  Young girls should shudder
   in that empty light—
  The holy of angels,
    I wonder what's he think?
  Shd push pencils
    for agers, masagers,
Masseurs and all?
  Oll?   Lovely bedoodlers
   in Time's Holy All
Holiest Ghostliest
  ramified Hall

11th Chorus

And, said I to the Angel,
that *shall* certainly do,
And the Angel said:
  D you remember Gregory?
Corso, the Way of Poetry?
    Orlovsky too?
      And Ginsberg O Shay?
      And Burroughs the Master
        speaks thru his teeth?
        And the writer of story
          the generous Honkey?
And   Lafcadio the Holy
    Innocent of Russia,
the Patriarch, & Sebastian?
And Lucien?
    And Neal Cassady?

12th Chorus

Move my hand Lord
    move my hand
    Tell Ray Bremser
      something calm him
        down
    Tell Leroi Jones
      & Diane di Prima
        tooo
      They dont know
        that Heaven
      which is waiting for them
    In the land of OO

(SECOND SOLO)

1st Chorus

"You can think by yourself"
        says God from Heaven
Talking to all 70 thousand
    Billion Four Thousand
    Eighty Two Trillions
    of Creatures in his Movie
called "Creation"

(pause)

2nd Chorus

He means that all
    those sentient beings
are free to think unimpeded
—Only God is the Only One
who knows that all the thinking
            going on
    is what the thinking going on

        is thinking

And none of it ever happened

SHTMIMK!

Shtmimk?

3rd Chorus

But like any other movie
  the thinking is gray
    but also big romances
    like Latin Love You music
    & all of it seems so golden
    steada gray.
  That's because it's a very strange
  movie
It is strange as dulcet gray.

Hey looka me Ma
  I'm writing like Yorkshire
    Pudding De-Headed Gray
The proof is in the pudding
    they Bray
Just like any other old Canaday

4th Chorus

The brain is a pudding
  with raisins in't
Hey looka me Ma I'm thinking
  like Otay—
    Okay, Mémo,
    Está bien, Mémo,
    Parandero.

(That's what they mean Espanish
    'Hey kiddy, dont hit
      the bars too much,
      chico.'

Hey Baby dont yup at me
  in Azmetec!)

Yair, Pard old Hoopard
Hoomingway blew his head

over Old I-day-o

5th Chorus

Hemingway Blues, is called.
Me too Blues—You Blues
—Thinkin Blues—Paris
Blues and Blacks—
Hurshy, move the tack!
Dont bring me no le-mon
    chiffin, pie, man,
      I'll break yore head in

Head already broken in
  No chin
    Yes chin
      Soft Chin
        Northport Autumn
        falling leaves blues
      And winter white
      sailboat philosopher
      blues, on sand,
Lois and Victor by name.

6th Chorus

All kindsa fine blues
  even this minute
    in Vera Cruz,
    Terre Haute,
    Montana,
      Golgotha,
        Heaven Door.

All kindsa information rattlin
  back & forth

Crazy old angel midnight
world   talkin   singin
rubbin   antennaes
High on antenni
        and go Mondadori'n
in Italy for to see sweep
of Gary Venice Door's
    Venetian oar

7th Chorus

Or go Atyastapafi'n
in other planets?
Goo, what a gaw!
And does wet boulders think?

I see the face of Christ
 in the door
 after it has been the face
 of the Dog, the Owl,
 the Lamb, the Lion,
 Christ, the Dog again,
 the Collie then suddenly
my God the Colleen!
 Her soft brown eyes,
        esperanza morena,
Then it's Christ again,
 this time in profile
—This I just saw.

8th Chorus

I'm now going into a deep trance
 where I see visions—
Mwee hee hee ha ha.
    Johnny Holmes is just about
    the funniest man I know!

He laughs in cemeteries
in the woods of Connecticutt

(Connect ton cul, we used
                    to call
                    it
                    in little
                    Canada.)

Connect your arse.
   Some come on John, connect
   your arse to a Grave,
   pal, almost lover, and
   I'll bring ye sweet
        daydrids
      in the morning
   of the 2 thieves & Me

      & You

           9th Chorus

(Written before I knew about Pascal —1965)

   But John's like Pascal,
   or like Frank O'hara even,
   He wont let his head
   Believe his heart
                    & all that
So he skeptically adjusts
his glasses, leans forward eagerly,
   almost hugely,
            & roars

      Qui à poignez
         ton cul dans
            terre!

And 2 days later he looks it up
in a French Dictionary,
wondering what I'm thinking
about, and what I think
about him thinking.
Wow Very Strange

10th Chorus

It's dillier than that
they daisies they pud
in puddinhead blues.

To Earl of Shockshire:
"Sire, in this my Inscribe
May't you'll fee."
The Earl of Shrockshire
shires & showers & shh's
on back a batch
of Tanguipore
Tangled
Telegrams
Mistaken by Saint Peter
as Hair of the Gate

POMES ALL SIZES

Bus East

Poem written on a bus April 1954
from S.F. to New York

BUS EAST

Society has good intentions
Bureaucracy is like a friend

5 years ago—other furies
  other losses—

America's trying
to control the
  uncontrollable
Forest fires,
  Vice

The essential smile
In the essential sleep
Of the children
Of the essential mind

I'm all thru playing
  the American
Now I'm going to
  live a good quiet life

The world should be
built for foot walkers

Oily rivers
Of spiney   Nevady

I am Jake Cake
            Rake
Write like Blake

The horse is not
  pleased
  Sight of his
gorgeous finery
  in the dust
Its silken nostrils
  did disgust

Cats arent kind
Kiddies arent sweet

April in Nevada—
Investigatin Dismal Cheyenne
Where the war parties
In fields of straw
Aimed over oxen
  At Indian Chiefs
In wild headdress
Pouring thru the gap
In Wyoming plain
To make the settlers
Eat more dust
  than dust was eaten
In the States
  From East at Seacoast
Where wagons made up
  To dreadful Plains
Of clazer vup

Saltry settlers
Anxious to masturbate
  The Mongol Sea
    (I'm too tired
      in Cheyenne—No
    sleep in 4 nights now, &
    2 to go)

NEBRASKA

April doesnt hurt here
Like it does in New England
The ground
Vast and brown
Surrounds dry towns
Located in the dust
Of the coming locust
Live for survival, not for "kicks"

Be a bangtail describer,
like of shrouded traveler
in Textile tenement &
  the birds fighting in yr
  ears—like Burroughs
  exact to describe &
  gettin $

The Angry Hunger
(hunger is anger
  who fears
  the hungry
  feareth
  the angry)

And so I came home
To Golden far away
Twas on the horizon
Every blessed day
As we rolled
And we rolled
From Donner tragic Pass
Thru April in Nevada
And out Salt City Way
Into the dry Nebraskas

And sad Wyomings
Where young girls
And pretty lover boys
With Mickey Mantle eyes
Wander under moons
Sawing in lost cradle
And Judge O Fastera
Passes whiggling by
To ask of young love:
"Was it the same wind
Of April Plains eve
that ruffled the dress
  Of my lost love
  Louanna
  In the Western
  Far off night
    Lost as the whistle
    Of the passing Train
    Everywhere West
    Roams moaning
  The deep basso
—Vom! Vom!
—Was it the same love
Notified my bones
As mortify yrs now
Children of the soft
Wyoming April night?
  Couldna been!
  But was! But was!"

And on the prairie
The wildflower blows
In the night
For bees & birds
And sleeping hidden
Animals of life.

Then Chicago
Spitters in the spotty street
Cheap beans, loop,
Girls made eyes at me
And I had 35
Cents in my jeans—

Then Toledo
Springtime starry
Lover night
Of hot rod boys
And cool girls
A wandering
A wandering
In search of April pain
A plash of rain
Will not dispel
This fumigatin hell
Of lover lane
This park of roses
Blue as bees
In former airy poses
In aerial O Way hoses
No tamarand
And figancine
Can the musterand
Be less kind
     Sol—
     Sol—
  Bring forth yr
  Ah Sunflower—
  Ah me Montana
  Phosphorescent Rose
  And bridge in
     fairly land
I'd understand it all—

Hitchhiker

"Tryna get to sunny Californy"—
     Boom. It's the awful raincoat
making me look like a selfdefeated self-
murdering imaginary gangster, an idiot in
a rueful coat, how can they understand
my damp packs—my mud packs—
      "Look John, a hitchhiker"
      "He looks like he's got a gun underneath
that I.R.A. coat"
      "Look Fred, that man by the road"
      "Some sexfiend got in print in 1938
in Sex Magazine"—
      "You found his blue corpse in a
greenshade edition, with axe blots"

Neal in Court

All Neal's life has been hard
And harsh
People dont believe him
And he's all alone
Look at his bones
In courthouse scenes
And look at the pictures
Of his railroad track
And judge
And have secret witnesses
Against his misery

Raven, Craven,
Nobody cares—
Hate to lose their jobs
Put old Cassady in jail

But he sits bong Buddha
Hands Catholic crossed
In the witness chair

And the afternoon wears on
In the schoolhouse kiddy court
Of old black velvet angels
With white hair
And tassels in their caps

He did make the joint;
Facts of Coupling;
"You give a sign
 To the engineer"

He's got them beat
With his young composure

Exhibit No. 4
Shows the long ladder
And the brake
Platform
Where he fell & cracked his ankle

He nods & listens patiently
To the prosecutor's counsel
Smiling speaking civilly
For the society of ladies
And respect of settlements
And has an aging chin.
The Jewish stenographess
 Writes unconcerned

In silent machine shorthand
And watches sexily
 The lips of speaking men

And frowns to catch the last word
Spoken in Eternity
Eyes gazed on suit lapel
And burping to look down—

Papers rustle, people cough
  Ivan's not here to turn
        all pale
Nor Dmitri but to shout
"You all tried to kill
        yr fathers
The Immemorial Lout!"
So have another beer
        Neal
Your money
        big or small'll
Come
And when come
  You only have a few more
        years
Like Raven
        more or less
To hang on—

For you've done it all before
In Millbrae & in Burlingame
In Samarkand, Chandrapore,
Jamie, Cathy, Johnny
All were there—
Redwood, Belmont, & Nameless
        too—
  Harsh harbors, duties,—
  Flower cars—& bums—
  Dont let the punk
  In smart brown suit
  Who cant lick you
  In street fight

Screw you out of thousands
In this million years
Of strife, the Moose
of heaven's looking down.

East end of the rail
West end of the Ram
The stars are looking down
On all yr pain & tears
  And Allen Ginsberg loves you
  And Carolyn too
  Let old Raven lie
  We'll hang him in the sea

Fog will kiss him
Make him shiver
Bones'll belie
His coral deficiency
Insincere & sad
The world's a farce
To stand and sneer at
On the corner of
        Snark & Phnark

March 30, 1954,
San Francisco City Hall

On Waking from a Dream of Robert Fournier
Long Poem In Canuckian Child Patoi Probably Medieval

Robert, Robert, ta belle grosse mere
enterez dan l'beurre—
La j me rapele
La j me rapele

Robert, t'eta tit
Mais tu waite encore plus gros
Que tu l'est deja—
C'est toute un reve qu'arretera
Avant quon l'finisse—
Quand on laisse la Divinite
    le finir
    Robert, Robert—
Ou est ton arbre?
Quosse qu'on y faite avec tes
    Indes especialles?
A tu tombez dans un trou
    de tristesse avec moi
Dans la nuit commune
    et sale et pire que mal?
Robert, ou est ton beau
    frere? Tes tite ridresse,
    laughage, riendresse, malheur'se
    aise—ou est ton son?
    Ou sont les neiges?
    les etoiles eloignez?
    Les Reves?

Ya des faces dans l'arbre
    qu'il nous moque pas.
Robert, tes fleurs, tes femmes,
    tes folles,—
    tes friandises de bines
    en cuisines.
    Es tu mort ton gros pere
    enterrez dans ma mer?
    "Dread drizzle mere, Robert.

And this is an English Blues

Robert, Robert, yr beautiful big mother
buried in butter—
Now I remember
Now I remember

Robert, you were small
But you'll be yet bigger
Than you are already—
It's all a dream that'll end
Before we finish it—
When we let Divinity
    end it
    Robert, Robert—
Where is your grass?
What'd they do with your
    special nothingness?
Did you fall in a hole
    of sadness with me
In the common night
    and dirty and worse than bad?
Robert, where is yr beautiful
    brother? Yr little laughs,
    "laughage," nothingness, unhappy
    ease—where is your sound?
    Where are the snows?
    the wandered stars?
    The Dreams?

There are faces in the tree
    that do not mock us.
Robert, your flowers, your women,
    your madwomen,—
    your delicacies of beans
    in kitchens.
    Is he dead your big father
    buried in my sea?
    "Dread drizzle mere, Robert,

dread drizzle mere"
Je vue les armes de face
   vegetables, comme des
   picottes dans ma
   noirceur d yeux—
J'attend les ti fou
chantez leur musique
idiotique et tendre
et charmant comme
comediens de Vienne,
Chante dans sa cabane,
attend—
   les rats mange sa granche
   tandis qu'il chante!
Robert, Robert, les rats
   mange son coeur, son
   nom y'est Alain—
   Alain nee Fournier
La chanson de Dieu ma
rentrez la oreilles assoir,
mon coeur, Robert, je veux
t'expliquer—
   Fa pu de face souffrante
dans les bars brunes
Laisse plus les chiens t'mordre,
Offre leux plus ta patte
de pauvre brume, viens
avec moi au ciel pur,
   ecoute
   Je voue de coupures
   de chair dan mon aise—
Mais c'est toute pardu
dans la meme luisante
ocean de l'amour de Dieu
L'amor de Dios—
   Love of God—
J'ai ta mere par les mains,
Marie Louise, je la sord,
J'l a ma dan mon
l'eglise, j'y allume des

dread drizzle mere"
I see the armies of faces
vegetable, like
pockmarks in my
darkness of eyes—
I hear the little nuts
singing their music
idiotic and tender
and charming like
comedians of Vienne,
sings in his shack,
waits—
The rats eat his barn
while he sings!
Robert, Robert, the rats
eat his heart, his
name is Allen—
Allen born Fournier
The song of God
came in my ears tonight,
my heart, Robert, I want
to explain to you—
Make no more suffering grimaces
in the brown bars
Don't let the dogs bite you any more,
Offer them no more your leg
Of poor mist, come
with me to the pure heaven,
listen
I see scars
of flesh in my ease—
But it's all lost
in the same shining
ocean of the Love of God
L'amor de Dios—
Love of God—
I have your mother by the hands,
Marie Louise, I bring her out,
I put her in my
church, I light her

fleur, j'la fa travaillez
pour le Bon Seigneur—
   est pas peur Robert,
   ame tendre et tranquil—
Ah c'est un reve pour
   cossez les chose bati,
   quoi d'autre?
   Vien avec moi
   Robert, assoir,
braille plus,—
   Rente avec moi dans
   les Indes—
Fini l'reve,—
Instruit ta mere, ton pere,
ton pauvre grand frere,
tes vieux freres du matin—
   Sort!—
   Monte!
   Ascend!
   Vas entour!
    Ou tu peu!
Sur la terre comme tu peu tu pu,
   pi c'est fini,—
Reve—inveiglez,
   emorfouillez, fou,
   candrassez,
   impossiblement vife
   et toignant—
Marde pour les chailles
   moronique du diable—
La Vie n'est Pas

Robert, Robert,
   je tu perdu
   dans la mer omnisce
   pour toujours
    dejas
     helas—!
Les vignes montres les potos,
Les hommes souffres—
   Les Bouddhes

flowers, I make her work
for the Good Lord—
    have no fear Robert,
    soul tender and tranquil—
Ah it's a dream to
    break things built,
    what else?
    Come with me
    Robert, tonight,
cry no more,—
    Come in with me
    into the Nothingnessess—
Finish the dream,—
Instruct your mother, your father,
your poor tall brother,
your old brothers of morning—
    Go out!
    Go up!
    Ascend!
    Go below!
      Where you can!
On earth as you may you stink,
    then it's finished—
Dream—inveigled,
    mortified, crazy,
    broken-up,
    impossibly quick
    and tugging—
Shit for the whores
    moronical of the devil—
Life is Not

Robert, Robert,
    I've lost you
    in the ocean of omniscience
    for ever
      already
        alas—!
The vines climb the posts,
Men suffer—
    The Buddhas

chante tranquilement
   entre tous—
La tristesse et la mort
   et l'amour false
   de jambes et larmes—
Sort!—Rentre!
Monte!   Cour!
    Dor!
Ecoute, Robert la priere
   du Seigneur—pour tue—
"O Robert—qui a la
   clef du pouvoire
Leuve ta grosse main
   diamante
Rende a rien les choses
   idiotique deboute,
   Detrui—
   Extermine—
O Robert, donneur du
   courage, donne courage
   tous qu'ils sont
   en extremite de souffrance—
O Robert, qui Purifie,
   purifie tous qu'ils sont
   escalve d'l'ego
Que le victor de
   la souffrance, gagne—
   encore et encore—
O Robert, parfaitement
   en connaissance de
   la lumiere saint,
   amene toute les
   pauvres vivants de
   l'existence a ta
   connaissance.
O Robert, parfait en
   sagesse et amour
   tendre, sort toutes
   les pauvres vivants de
   leur prison d'existence

sing tranquilly
throughout all—
The sadness and the death
and the false love
of legs and tears—
Go out!—Come in!
Go up!   Run!
    Sleep!
Listen, Robert, the prayer
of the Lord—for you—
"O Robert—who has the
key of power
Raise your big hand
of diamond.
Bring to naught the things
idiotically standing,
Destroy—
Exterminate—
O Robert, giver of
courage, give courage
to all those who are
in extremity of suffering—
O Robert, who Purifies,
purify all who are
slaves of the ego
May the victor of
suffering, win—
again and again—
O Robert, perfectly
in consciousness
of the holy light,
bring all the
poor living beings of
existence to your
consciousness.
O Robert, perfect in
sageness and love
tender, bring out all
the poor living beings out of
their prison of existence

et amene la a
    les Indes Sacrees
Om!   Amen!
Adoration a Tathagata
  le connaisseur de
  l'essence universelle
  de toutes les choses
  du reve et en dehors
  du reve. A Sugata
  le connaisseur de bonnesse
  sans fin toupartout,
  A Buddha, qui est
  reveillez pour toujours
  et a ete reveillez
  pour toujours et sera
  reveillez pour toujours,
  parfait en pitie
  et intelligence, qui
  a accompli,
  et accompli maintenant,
  et accomplira, dans
  toutes le directions vers
  dedant et vers dehors,
  toutes les mots de mystere."

Tire la manivelle
Amen
Par semaine.
A Dieu.
Bon Soir.
Un Bec.
Un nuee.
Adieu.
Autre foi.
Ma main.
Adieu.
Au Seigneur
Bon Soir.
Dormez vous.

and bring them to
    the Sacred Nothingnesses
Om!   Amen!
Adoration to Tathagata
   the knower of
   the Universal Essence
   of all things
   of the dream and outside
   the dream. To Sugata
   the knower of goodness
   unlimited everywhere,
   to Buddha, who is
   awake for always
   and has been awake
   for always and will be
   awake for always,
   perfect in pity
   and intelligence, who
   has accomplished,
   and accomplishes now,
   and will accomplish, in
   all directions in and out,
   all the words of mystery."

Turn the handle.
Amen
By the week.
To God.
Goodnight.
A Kiss.
A cloud.
Farewell.
Next time.
My hand.
Farewell.
To the Lord.
Goodnight.
Sleep you all.

October 10, 1955, Berkeley

God

In his jests serious, in his murders victim,
      or which, is God? Who began
      before non-existence's dependence
      on existence, Who came before
      the chicken and the egg

Who started out
                        enormous Light
      the dark brilliance of the Mystery
      for all good hearts to shroud inside
      and keep their understanding sympathy
      intact as Beethoven's courageous
                  slow sigh.

In his atrocities victim?
   In his jests damned?
   In his damnation damnation?
Or is God just the golden hover
      light manifesting Mayakaya
      the illusion of the moon, branches
      across the face of the moon?

O perturbing swttlontaggek
      montiana godio
   Thou high suffermaker!
   Tell me now, in Your Poem!

Haiku Berkeley

Haiku Snyder
      I hurt the black ink
      on your kind book
   the only inconsistency sin
   I done yet to you
   sweet heart

And John Wino anyway
   was to blame

Dont kick me out
   of your tea
     house
   great man

Still a boy
Noble Youth
And when I meet you
Smash Mountain Man
A Million Ones from now
And offer you 5 Giant
          Flowers
And you predict me
      Tree Lover
  the Coming Lover
      Buddha
    of All the Worlds
   With no body
    & nothing distinguishable
   from other bodies & yours
 By which time you'll be
(you see) 6,000,000,000
      years old
I'll still call you Noble Youth,
  O Ever Weeping

             *

Learned!   Learned!

This is the end
   of my enlightenment!

             *

And you Whalen
   world slinger (like I said)
   Kelt—
    You started it all
   And yr ideal eyes
   Blue love shining
   Everywhere
   Leave me never alone
    For I whine
    When otherwise
     Tryna be human

With no Buddha guts
& cant bend tendons
—O how collapsed
the tendon beam!—
Worms, a million years long
—Phillipi, shield,
  sun-star, wailer,
  Whalen, alright,
  excuse me for popping
        off

To hear the desert sigh

           *

And you sweet Allen
  Ah Allen   Ah Me
   You know
    About me
     What I'd say
    Let it be
     We know
     We're old friends
& Never die

Lamantia Finally
Brilliant & Beautiful
What did you do?

(If I may ask a question)
With the golden rosary beads
I gave you 1955 years
              ago

                    *

I say "I'd like to see
The poems Li Po
Distributed in the Yellow River"
And Whalen says "Alright
We'll go down and dive
And see."

Poim

Walking on Water
   Nothing Ever Happened
   Not Ever Happening
        True Story
        Old Story
        New Story
        Old & New
      HOLY BOLONEY
        Holy Cow
        Holy Cats
          Wow
        Whatever
   To The Feast
     Story Book
        Book
        Story Words
   "Anyway, It Happened"
     Nothing Happened
   Everybody Invited

Various Little Pomes

The ants go roaming
in the mirror of
　the mind,
　over sand
　which I see
　　falsely

*

I know this to be
an empty state,
that is to say,
a state of form

My dream of a
horrible city is
individual discrimination
—the actual
city is universal
mind

*

I stop dreaming
And the ripples
Disappear from
　universal mind's
　actual face
and what's left
　is I'm not here
any more

"Bodhisattva-Heroes have no separated individuality"

The reality is
nothingness—
We think
we strive

*

Primordially Undifferentiated

Sravasti, City of
Wonders, is now Village
of Sahet-Mahet,
River Rapti

*

Alone-one-All,
  I meditate Alone,
imitating Brahma
  God   Allah

Two Dharma Notes

"The Buddha-Teaching
must be relinquished:
how much more so
misteaching."

(Price's *Diamond Sutra*)

Mind Essence
(Tathagata-garbha)
is Non-Assertion
(Wu-Wei-Fa)

The
essence
is not
disturbed

"Unformulated
        Principle"

                        *

7 treasures: gold,
silver, lapis lazuli,
cornelian, red pearls,
crystal, agate.

Gatha

Sitting in the chair
In the morning ground
Is no sitting in no
chair in no morning ground

No returning, no
    non-returning
No Karma, no
    non-Karma

"Happiness, abiding
in peace, in seclusion
in the midst of the
forest"
            is
        abiding nowhere

UnHappiness, abiding
  in anxiety in society
  in the midst of the
    city

is
abiding nowhere

Not-two,
means,

no abider in his
abode

No realizer in his
realizing

"Develop a pure
lucid mind"

*

All things in the
River of Extinction
already dead &
extinct—
rocks, people,
flowers—
even empty space
is extinct, since
it will have, has,
nothing to divide,
nothing to fill its
empty form

The simplest fact
is that all things
die off—the
least fact faced
anywhere—
"All living beings
are not, in
fact, living beings"
because they're
dead in time—
time's a minute,
a pop—

No
time—Time is
extinct since it
will have, has, nothing
to change, nothing to fill
its empty form

*

At present, the
100,000,000th
myriad of multimillionth
Buddha is
    myself
  my-not-self

Thus　如口

       (Tathagata,
       Arriver-at-Actual-Isness)

Come　來

This is my VYAKARANA Prediction
In the ages of the
future you will come to
be a Buddha called Smash
Mountain Man
(Gary Snyder)
In the ages of the future
I will come to be a
Buddha called Tree Lover
"Why predict the predictable?"

                    *

The white eyes of the criminals of Alcatraz thinking
thoughts of Love on their little Island Blest
while San Francisco crawls with hatred in the streets

And in rolls the Holy Fog from Jesus ballooning
Shrouds of puff over Gold's Gate—the mysterious
Source East of Western Torment, Western Me

                    *

Humility
  is
      Beatitude
      THE BEATIfiC GENERATION

                              *

Beginning to see the light, outside the church—
The Negro boy and the White boy
Hand in hand—Sunday morning with Philip Lamantia

                              *

There is the delusion of existence
because of my failure to realize
not-two-ness, i.e., deluded
and the deluding is the double
                trick

Failure
          which is not really a failure
          really—
                      Ripple of delusion is
                        that it is

Con the train

                              *

There is gladness which the Saint feels;
there is mating, which the bitter husband feels;
but when gladness of mating is, is Love

                              *

BATH TUB THOUGHT
                          A rock is like space
                          because it doesnt move;
                          And space is like a rock
                          Because it is empty.
                          Words are Buddhas.

*

Nothing's wrong
Something's right

W.C.Fields' Bathrobe

*

If I dont leave San Francisco
Soon—I'll be weeping cruds.
Wandering fair blossoms
        of false ethereality
        is what I see now.
Pretty soon I'll be down
On the Battered Internationale
Listening to devoured little girls
Who dance before the devout
And hungry men who devour
Her limb by limb, that
She's an artist
    Though clumsy
    Her big limbs move
    But she caint cackle
    Nor kick
        And nobody knows
        what to do
        with my woodshed
        blues.
    Goodbye, Rexroth
      until another time.

Beginning with a Few Haikus
Some of Them Addresses in the Book

Lee Crawford
1126 San Benito
  Burri Burri,
    So. San Francisco
      Calif.

  F train
    to University
    & Shattuck
  One block to left
    (Ginsberg)

      Snow Love

"Charming little bedraggled
  princes"—Allen

  1 HAIKU?

Disappointed in the
waning moon—
Pleiades, vine,
    wine bottle.

    2
    The waters see
    The waters saw
    So this is eternity

3

Can time crack rock?
    Marble'll chip,
    Diamond die.

4

Soup wont burn—
Spiders cant get
outa sinks—
Brew more tea

5

Mist in the window
Flower, weed,
Birds at dawn

6

Juju beads on
    Zen Manual—
My knees are cold

7

Morning, hot sun,
empty hard ground,
invisible voidness

8

Leaves dry Autumn
  yard,
Bed of white posies,
Spice bush sprouting

9

Flowers waiting,
Phantoms,
Phantasmal surface
of earth under
blue old space

10

NOT EVEN WORD FETTERED!
  NOT EVEN WAITING!
  NOT EVEN!

11 WALTER LEHRMAN'S HAIKU

One Friday when we were all dead
He said 'I didnt think it would
be so good.'

12

Dry old bigleaf,
  twisted young vine,
    pot with rag,
      million grasses
        shining

13 GARY SNYDER'S HAIKU *(Spoken on the Mountain)*

"Talking about the literary
life—the yellow
aspens."

14 GARY SNYDER'S SECOND HAIKU

"I get a hardon from here
to Connecticut, Goodness,
3,000 miles."

15 GARY SNYDER AGAIN

"I was thirteen
before I started skiing
during the war."

16 GARY AGAIN

"Just mad waiting for these
cocksucking letters—And
I go out to Central Park"

17 GARY AGAIN

"And there she is just an elegant—
And I'm wearing an old
pair of jeans"

18 GARY ONCE MORE

"There she is—I'm wearing
an old pair of jeans—
I say 'I've got to'"

19

Listen to the birds
sing!   All the little birds
will die!

20

Dusk: the bird on the fence
a contemporary
of mine

21

Nightfall: too dark
to read the page,
too cold.

22

Useless, useless,
heavy rain driving
into the sea!

23 GARY SNYDER

"Goofballs in the wine—
truck
goes by."

24

Drunk in the early morn
"Oooh" says my good
Buddha friend

25 Haiku-Koan

Does a dog have
the Buddha-nature?
Water is water.

26

You're bored.
Why?   I'm getting
to be old

27

First we buy the meat
and then we buy
the pot

28

There is no sin—
I know perfectly well
where I am

29

The Tathagata doesnt exist
in honor of which I will go
and climb mountains

30 GATHA

When I said to you
in Washington Square Park
"Am I my brother's keeper?"
it was Autumn

31 NATALIE'S HAIKU

"Remember that poet—
the girls are
talking now"

32 GARY

"Hundreds of comedies
about
aldultery"

33 HAIKU FROM A CARDBOARD BOX

Giant Tide
Gamble Made
in America

34 GATHA

The world is old
   and wise
And I am tired
   of my eyes

35 GATHA

All kinds of young love
for sale
I cant get my black hands
on it

36

Decorated for the re-emergence
of the great
Virgin Fuck

37 PHILLIP WHALEN'S HAIKU

"Walked 5 miles with wine
then brought me
geranium"

"When you become enlightened"

When you become enlightened
you will know that you've
been enlightened all along

*

Alright, I'm sick of this
enlightenment—now I'm
dumb again—the
delicate blue morning
sky thru the tree.

*

Dont worry about food,
Little John, there's some
   e v e r y w h e r e

*

Allen says "When people get
religious they start feeding
   e v e r y b o d y"

*

—The morning of
the end of my enlightenment

*

Enlightenment is: do what
      you want
   eat what there is

*

The soul burns out the eyes

World, it's about time you
realized there's too much food
for everybody to eat

*

The secret shape of the sun
Is a shield—flying to the right
To the West presumably
Just like the Roman Ear
Of Ezra Pound
In the Surrealist drawing
Just like Charioteer

*

The monument in the park
For the institute of the blind
Because it is not seen
Is truly a great monument

Would to God I could make one
So artistically fabulous
As that with my hands

*

Flowers aim crookedly
For the straight death

*

On Ether

Jordan Belson: "Everything is reduced
to its absolute meaning"

The Heel of Eloheim

Ether brings them out

*

Let slide sweetly
the transformations
of the thinking

*

The liberation
from Jack Kerouac

*

With Mike long ago
Under the little
dawn clouds—
waiting for the
work-car—Sebastian
was phenomenally
alive, is now
noumenally dead,
          just
             as
                pure
                   as I

Letter to Allen 1955

I dont wanta see
   no Señora
De Hueva from Chappy
   Chi-a-pas—
Wot I got to do
   mit jungles?
And boogs? Malaria—
   Frogs, bulls, volcanoes,
   —

      hammocks of no rest
      hung in trees
      of antiquity
      full of moss
      and bacterii

Wanta go, I do,
   to sweet Watsonville,
   sleep in the river
   of Cairi

However, Garver and I
   do hereby formally
   request for Robert
   Lavigne's Mazatlan Address

Mexico Rooftop

It's blue—with a pink movie neon
   E-changing in the jungle sky
   where rats havent chanced to swamp
   the mudstilt builders, but Who climbed,
   the builders, and made it the High Plateau

So's on October Fullmoon Nights, a palm
   hairs in the scene, and Aztec Temple
   apartment house arches stare

with a premeditated ogling glare
with light-holes & pool-puddles

And the dog barks at Stars—they
are pretty quiet—Tho all kinds
drams and whistlers hongkong the noise
of the street the stars are as faint
and as happy as they glow

In Sweet Canada or Carthage below,
in Rome and in Sisyphus bosom
—Urk, the brown strange glare
of modernized Mexican architecture
housingprojects cant be deAztecfied

It's blue—with day yellows night lemon
and daywhites nightpale
the color of chalk at a chalk quarry
or gravel in hell—the walls
of Jugurtha never as grim

I guess, as the walls of that side
of the building—but music reforms
the scene, atch or tortay, poor leetles
Mexican lovers boys draining
out their *corazon* for love of the sun

Awright, this poem's a failure—
Throw it in a drawer

Mexican Loneliness

And I am an unhappy stranger
grooking in the streets of Mexico—
My friends have died on me, my
lovers disappeared, my whores banned,
my bed rocked and heaved by
earthquake—and no holy weed

to get high by candlelight
and dream—only fumes of buses,
dust storms, and maids peeking at me
  thru a hole in the door
  secretly drilled to watch
  masturbators fuck pillows—
I am the Gargoyle
of Our Lady
    dreaming in space
    gray mist dreams—
My face is pointed towards Napoleon
——I have no form——
My address book is full of RIP's
  I have no value in the void,
        at home without honor,—
My only friend is an old fag
        without a typewriter
Who, if he's my friend,
        I'll be buggered.
I have some mayonnaise left,
a whole unwanted bottle of oil,
peasants washing my sky light,
  a nut clearing his throat
  in the bathroom next to mine
  a hundred times a day
  sharing my common ceiling—
If I get drunk I get thirsty
—if I walk my foot breaks down
—if I smile my mask's a farce
—if I cry I'm just a child—
—if I remember I'm a liar
—if I write the writing's done—
—if I die the dying's over—
—if I live the dying's just begun—
—if I wait the waiting's longer
—if I go the going's gone—
if I sleep the bliss is heavy—
the bliss is heavy on my lids—
—if I go to cheap movies
        the bedbugs get me—

Expensive movies I cant afford
—If I do nothing
nothing does

The Last Hotel

The last hotel
I can see the black wall
I can see the silhouette in the window
He's talking
I'm not interested in what he's talking about
I'm only interested in the fact that it's the last hotel

The last hotel
Ghosts in my bed
The goats I bled
The last hotel

Berkeley Song in F Major

FAREWELL TO MY BABIES

Walt Whitman is striding
  Down the mountain of Berkeley
  Where with one step
  He abominates & destroys
  The whole atomic laboratory
  Wherein it becomes a jewel
  In his heel, O Eloheim!

With one quick look
  His belly golden bull
  He turns Mrs Matchyot
  To butter, one quick look
  Eats up the fairies & robbers
In Robbies coffee saloon,

On he goes—wild hat
Big white beard
Fifteen feet tall
—No more lung stew
 "Why—Isnt he hungry?"
 "He eateth no more
 This is the final end—
He bears the 32 marks of perfection
He's on his way to Oakland
The cesspool of the Coast
Where beyond the dumps
I see telephone pole
A hundred miles high
With invisible wires
Of Transcendency—
Walt!   Jack!
Then across the Blue Bay
Gold step the Isle
Of Alcatraz, white eyes
Of lovely criminals,
Hatred Beaches, cops,
Pails, pockets, buckets,
Stores, sleeping bags,
Gold Gates & the Fog
Which Jesus Sendeth
from Up by Japan
the Alaskan Seal
Rock Territory
Known/ as Potato

(it all adds up to roil,
   or royal, one)
Walt Bluebeard Handsome
 Whitman, farewell
—For he also strides
 to East & gobbles
 Up Burma & Tits
 the Mock Top Peaks
 of T h i b e t a —
 Returning, like sun

the shield
Around the other side
Where first we thought
We saw him visioning
Down the shuddering mount
Of Berkeley's Atomic
Test Laboratory
Full of mice & men

—And it's snowing
This sunny morning

And the grass blade
    (so celebrate)
jostles slowly
        like a woman's
                beautiful
                breast
        side to side
    In the Peep Show
        of Eternality
        & Salvation
            &
            and

S'nuf,—this parsimonious
pwap pwap tiddle
        all all day
We'll have no more jots & tittles
We'll have no more leaves
    broken off at the base
    of the Stem
    That means
        we'll have more jots & tittles
        more leaves like that
More
More gold
            & snow
            & show
But dont be fooled, kiddies—

The white screen is still
A White Screen
And the movie 'bout monkies
You see there
in the Vines & Berkelies
is projected by the spectral
  Honogrank Machine
  known as: Chaplin

Another name for film—
  T'all come from ether
  And t's'ether
  Either that or—What?
    Whop What But
      Bot Go On
        Bop Wallower?
Nay—
      Jack the middle
      Mass everything

                        *

There's a tomato plant
In this mad garden of yrs
Allen Ginsberg
That grew six foot tall
And ran around along the
                        high
                        weed
With its empty-reed middle
The nature of which is as
                        empty
                        as
The sun that follows two guys
Walking away from the same
                        poor
                        pond
  And I seen the secret of the ant:
Which is:
  To them sand is boulders

And the boulders are pure
                        empty
                        gold
Essence aint the ants
Essence aint Jack Whatyrcallit
Essence
Essence isnt a butter bee
                on a white petal
                dreaming of far
                pure lands learned
                long ago
    Essence
    Essence, it means,
      Essence is the ants
      Is the Jack W i t t t
      Is the essence
      Is the long bee
            I told about

  Is is
  Is

A Sudden Sketch Poem

Gary's sink has a shroudy burlap
  the rub brush tinware plout
      leans on right side
      like a red woman's hair
  the faucet leaks little lovedrops
The teacup's upsidedown with visions
    of green mountains and brown lousy
    Chinese mysterious up heights
  The frying pan's still wet
  The spoon's by 2 petals of flower
  The washrag's hung on edge like bloomers
  I dont know what to say
        about the dishpan, the soap
    The sink itself inside or what

is hidden underneath the bomb burlap
Shroudflap except two onions
  And an orange and old wheat germ.
Wheat meal. The hoodlatch heliograph
With the cross that makes the devil
Hiss, ah, the upper coral sensen soups
  And fast condiments, curries, rices,
Roaches, reels, tin, tip, plastickets,
  Toothbrushes and armies, and armies
Of insulated schiller, squozen gumbrop
  Peste pans, light of marin, pirshyar,
Magic dancing lights of gray and white
And all for verse I wrote it

April 1956, McCorkle's Shack

Poem Written in the Zoco Chico

He walks
  without thinking about the sea
His older brother
  shows his gold tooth
    trying to prove something on Sunday afternoon
One boy has a green fez
    that gives him permission from the sea
He's the *jamal* in the sea
that restores him harmlessly
He has any kinda claim
    to a gold chain
Some Burgher Berbers have false teeth
Then comes and overruns the great mock wave

Some bulldogs have rubber teeth
The submarines are there to gyp the Egyptians
I see nothing there but a bird
The history of the world is lost in silence.

Three Tangier Poems

Vapors mere
Shapes so dear?
Bell rung,
What's sung?

*

I strike at that snake-heart that hurt my family

*

Ah but Ah but Ah
    Where ocean water kisses beach sand
Lonely living blue balloon

The boys are kicking the ball
        far across the field—
The lonely goalie waits

What the Buddhas are saying
    in the "upper air":
Fish-film facing lost life-sea

My sweet spring sex loins
        joined to yours
Beneath the molten moon

Tangier Poem

Your father spurted you out in perfect ghost-form

All you gotta do is die
All you gotta do is fly.
If your father's name is Dedalus
how can you be Icarus?

Poem

Anyway the time has come to explain
      the Golden Eternity
and how the iridescent paraphernalia of radiating candles
      ceases
      when mentation ceases
because I know what it's like to die,
      to cease mentating, one day I died,
I fainted actually, I was stooping smelling
strapping flowers in the cosmos yard
of my mother's cozy flower house
in Auffinsham Shire, in Queens,
and stood up fast taking deep breath,
   blood rushed from head, next thing I knew
   woke up flat on my back in the grassy sun
   and had been out fine minutes.

And I had seen the Golden Eternity.
   The Lamb was alone with the Lamb.
   The Babe was alone with the Baby Lamb.
   The Shroud was alone with the Golden Shroud.

I was alone with God, who
   is God, who was Me,
   who was All,
      he stood high on a hill
   overlooking Mexico City
      radiating messages
      out of a white Tiot

Flies

And wasnt there ever a time when flies
  didnt seek the sun through forbidden
windowpanes?

And when men didnt pray for God
  to deliver them from mistake,
  Gesundheit?

Or when football players didnt huddle
  and plot the fall of opposing team
On chalkmark?

Who cares? God loves us all, his Own
  thought & Images in His dream,
Gesundheit.

No Jew of Torah or incantatory
  Koran was ever smarter
  than God.

Loved God—all love God, themselves
—why worry about the queer in Room 3?
God bless you.

Drink whisky sours in the Ritz
  at 3 pm Sunday talk of Tolstoy,
quien care?

    All I want outa this persephone
    is poems instructing lovemilk thru
anemone—

Poem

I could become a great grinning host
like a skeleton

Hung Up In Heaven

How to Meditate

—lights out—
fall, hands a-clasped, into instantaneous
ecstasy like a shot of heroin or morphine,
the gland inside of my brain discharging
the good glad fluid (Holy Fluid) as
I hap-down and hold all my body parts
down to a deadstop trance—Healing
all my sicknesses—erasing all—not
even the shred of a "I-hope-you" or a
Loony Balloon left in it, but the mind
blank, serene, thoughtless. When a thought
comes a-springing from afar with its held-
forth figure of image, you spoof it out,
you spuff it off, you fake it, and
it fades, and thought never comes—and
with joy you realize for the first time
"Thinking's just like not thinking—
So I dont have to think
      any
    more"

Buddha

I used to sit under trees and meditate
on the diamond bright silence of darkness
and the bright look of diamonds in space
and space that was stiff with lights
and diamonds shot through, and silence

And when a dog barked I took it for soundwaves
and cars passing too, and once I heard
a jet-plane which I thought was a mosquito
in my heart, and once I saw salmon walls
of pink and roses, moving and ululating
with the drapish

Once I forgave dogs, and pitied men, sat
in the rain countin Juju beads, raindrops
are ecstasy, ecstasy is raindrops—birds
sleep when the trees are giving out light
in the night, rabbits sleep too, and dogs

I had a path that I followed thru piney woods
and a phosphorescent white hound-dog named Bob
who led me the way when the clouds covered
the stars, and then communicated to me
the sleepings of a loving dog enamoured
of God

On Saturday mornings I was there, in the sun,
contemplating the blue-bright air, as eyes
of Lone Rangers penetrated the dust
of my canyon thoughts, and Indians
and children, and movie shows

Or Saturday Morning in China when all is so fair
crystal imaginings of pristine lakes, talk
with rocks, walks with a Chi-pack across
Mongolias and silent temple rocks in valleys
of boulder and tarn-washed clay,—shh—
sit and otay

And if men were dyin or sleepin in rooftops
beyond, or frogs croaked once or thrice
to indicate supreme mystical majesty, what's
the diff? and I saw blue sky no different
from dead cat—and love and marriage

No different than mud—that's blood—
and lighted clay too—illuminated intelligent
faces of angels everywhere, with Dostoevsky's
unease praying in their X-brow faces,
twisted and great,

And many a time the Buddha played a leaf
on me at midnight thinkin-time, to
remind me 'This Thinking Has Stopped,'
which it had, because no thinking was there
but wasnt liquidly mysteriously brainly there

And finally I turned into a diamond stone
and sat rigid and golden, gold too—didnt dare
breathe, to break up the diamond that cant
even cut into butter anyway, how brittle
the diamond, how quick returned thought,—
Impossible to exist
          Buddha say:
       'All's possible'

Poem

I am God

Haiku

Came down from my
       ivory tower
And found no world

My Views on Religion

Heaven has everything to do with healing
and healing has nothing to do with heaven

If Jesus Christ is the son of God so am I

If suffering has anything to do
—if cake wont do, or cookies—
Heaven has everything to do with the way I feel
and I say *Heaven*! what you doin
down there, making like youse out
to beat hell—*Heaven*! How come

How come you got sixteen-year-old beauties
with lips parted open, in the moonlight
Italian balcony of me heart! *Heaven!*
Ope up them crazy open portal gates
and let the people pass, people pass

Revoke the Harrison Act! It is a Barbaric
act—It will cause desperate criminals
and gunmen to arise from our midst,
for evidential reasons—Ope nope—
It's like Prohibition, it wont, work,
—If the people want alcohol and dope
let em have alcohol and dope and all
the poison they can get if poison they want
—you cant tell the people what
to take in themselves—you cant stop
the people—I say this in the name of Peace
and I am not a Communist I'm a Dove

O ope them gordol golden gates

Buddha was not a medicine man,
he was a beyond-partition man,—
nor did he "limp for duty

and crawl
for charity"
—*Chuangtse*

Buddha is God, the Father of Jesus Christ
A N D   G O D   I S   G O D

Lady

The universe is a lady
Holding within her the unborn light—
Our Lady, Nostre Dame.
It is fitting that Nostradamus could predict the future.
That is a function of our lady,
We the tealeaves.

Caritas

Ah charity,—a little boy of eight or
seven, came up to sell little basket
flower candies in the teenage jukebox
soda saloon—nope, nobody buy—
and he walked barefoot in the rain

'Pas'd' Zapatas?' I think, No Shoes?
and I think 'I'll take out ten pesos
and give him for the shoes, say,
'Por usted, por tu zapatas'
and even show him how to hide the money

A sad song is playing, a harmonica,
as I first see his sad feet padding by
in the puddles of the sidewalk, O
the world is full of marvels—

Nostalgia, and I go after him to give
him his money, he goes into a huge
apartment house and there's the man
standing reading the floor-numbers
quietly, as little boy waits, both facing me

that's across the street with money in hand,
both stare, movingless, wait, the drape falls,
Aztec shrouds her mystery, & up they go
as grawmim elevator door closes
on both their heavenly chagrins

I think "Is he gone up there, he lives
up there with his folks and sells bonbons
barefoot, or is just hitting the joint
door to door to sell among the government
employee families of Childe Mexico"

And think "And it was said in the
Diamond Sutra so holy and so high,
practice generosity without entertaining
in mind any limited conceptions of the
reality of the feeling of generosity, or

what'll it accomplish for you, pard,
this is the word from old Buddha-hard
and he's spoken by a diamond tree,
and thousands-a people go barefoot,
it's written in every hemisphere

                    song of every sphere

Song of every sphere from every Child Revere
—Song of any morning waters blue with dream
by the broken Coney Island Staten statue
with no Medusa Snakehead arms and
no stone afoot, O Marva my foot

And we drive along in an insane dream
with our mouths distorted and eyes gleaming
crookedly every way, driving by iron rusty
steerages belonging to Babylonian Old
Zapoteca Arabian Neolithic
apathetic

old somervance, prance, hand me the foot,
we come di-vowing down the planks
and hit the water's admirable edge
and there's a tent and Side-Show
that I go to, to see girls

Poem

Old hornet me
Would woo thee
Fair, soft Sara
Of the flowers;
But bee's not kind
That seeks to find,
Peers too deep
Shares no sleep;
And anyway,
Who woos bees?

Lil Poem on Louis Ferdinand Céline

Where the madman plays with his fertilizers,
Where the mad priest comes in the window covered with mud,
Where the submarine knocks down the walls of the publisher,
Céline, Céline, Céline.

Skid Row Wine

I coulda done a lot worse than sit
in Skid Row drinkin wine

To know that nothing matters after all
To know there's no real difference
between the rich and the poor
To know that eternity is neither drunk
nor sober, to know it young
and be a poet

Coulda gone into business and ranted
And believed that God was concerned

Instead I squatted in lonesome alleys
And nobody saw me, just my bottle
and what they saw of it was empty

And I did it in cornfields & graveyards

To know that the dead dont make noise
To know that the cornstalks talk (among
one another with raspy old arms)

Sittin in alleys diggin the neons
And watching cathedral custodians
Wring out their rags neath the church steps

Sittin and drinkin wine
And in railyards being divine

To be a millionaire & yet to prefer
Curlin up with a poorboy of tokay
In a warehouse door, facing long sunsets
On railroad fields of grass

To know that the sleepers in the river
are dreaming vain dreams, to squat
in the night and know it well

To be dark solitary eye-nerve watcher
of the world's whirling diamond

The Moon

The moon her magic be, big sad face
Of infinity   An illuminated clay ball
Manifesting many gentlemanly remarks

She kicks a star, clouds foregather
In Scimitar shape, to round her
Cradle out, upsidedown any old time

You can also let the moon fool you
With imaginary orange-balls
Of blazing imaginary light in fright

As eyeballs, hurt & foregathered,
Wink to the wince of the seeing
Of a little sprightly otay

Which projects spikes of light
Out the round smooth blue balloon
Ball full of mountains and moons

Deep as the ocean, high as the moon,
Low as the lowliest river lagoon
Fish in the Tar and pull in the Spar

Billy de Bud and Hanshan Emperor
And all wall moongazers since
Daniel Machree, Yeats see

Gaze at the moon ocean marking
the face—

    In some cases
    The moon is you

    In any case
    The moon

Poem

Told him all about Minoan Civilization
    in front of Father Duffy's statue
      Told him all about
        Minoan Civilization
In Father Duffy's statue
Told him all about portals
Gotta be holy high

The Thrashing Doves

In the back of the dark Chinese store
    in a wooden jailhouse bibbet box,
    with dust of hay on the floor, rice
    where the rice bags are leaned,
    beyond the doomed peekokoos in the box
    cage

All the little doves'll die.
    As well as the Peekotoos—eels
    —they'll bend chickens' necks back
    oer barrels and slice at Samsara
    the world of eternal suffering with silver
    blades as thin as the ice in Peking

As thick & penetrable as the Wall of China
    the rice darkness of that store, beans,
    tea, boxes of dried fish, doodlebones,

pieces of sea-weed, dry, pieces of eight,
all the balloon of the shroud on the floor

And the lights from little tinkly Washington St.
Behung, dim, opium pipes and gong wars,
Tong, the rice and the card game—and
Tibbet de tibbet the tink tink tink
them Chinese cooks do in the kitchen
Jazz

The thrashing doves in the dark, white fear,
my eyes reflect that liquidly
and I no understand Buddha-fear?
awakener's fear? So I give warnings
'bout midnight round about midnight

And tell all the children the little otay
story of magic, multiple madness, maya
otay, magic tree-sitters and little girl
bitters, and littlest lil brothers
in crib made of clay (blue in the moon).

For the doves.

The Sea-Shroud

The Sea-Shroud comes out of a slip
of water in Brooklyn Harbor, night,
it emerges from a submerged tug
right from the enamel underwear
of the pilot's cabin

Right through up comes the shroud head,
a draining drape of wet weedy
watery sea net spray, ephemeral,
climbing to knock knees against the bow
and make the bit on the dock

And come on vanishing instead
    reappearing as a Man
    with a briefcase, on Borough Hall,
    saying nothing with a watery face
    saying nothing with an ogoo mouth

Saying nothing with a listening nose,
    saying nothing with a questionmark mouth,
    saying nothing, the briefcase full
    of seaweed—what happens to floating
    bonds when they get in the hand of the drape

Sea-shroud, turning Chinese Food to seaweed
    in his all-abominable bag, Shroud
    the taker of widows' monies in red allies
    of shame & stagedoors, purple lagoon,
    Goon Shroud departs gloving the money

Earlier in the day he'd perched atop a
    flagpole in a parking lot
    on the waterfront, and looked around
    to see which way Borough Hall
    which way the little white doves

My Gang

I

Many people have been frighted & died in cemeteries
    since the days of my gang, the night
    Ninip Houde came up & talked to me
    on the block and I rowed the imaginary
    horse on the rowel of the porch rail

Where I killed 700,000 flies or more
    while Ma and Beatrice gossiped
    in the kitchen, and while drape sheets
    we airing on the line that's connected
    to midnight by midnight riding roses

Oy—the one bad time that Zaggo
    got home from school late, dark
    in the streets, the sisters majestico
    blooming in the alley retreat, beat,
    'Your gang is upstairs' says my mother

And I go up to my closed smoky door
    and open it to a miniature poolhall
    where all the gang is smoking & yakking
    with little cue sticks and blue chalk
    around a miniature table on stilts

Bets being made, spittings out the window,
    cold out there, old murder magoon
    the winter man in my tree has seen
    to it that inhalator autumn
    prestidigitate on time & in ripe form,
    to wit cold

To wit cold, to wit you, to wit winter
To wit time, to wit bird, to wit dust—
  That was some game ole Salvey blanged
  When he beat G.J. that time,
    and Rondeau roared

II

Rondeau was the cookie that was always
    in my hair, a ripe screaming tight
    brother with heinous helling neck-veins
    who liked to riddle my fantasms
    with yaks of mocksqueak joy

"Why dont you like young Rondeau?"
    always I'm asked, because he boasts
    and boasts, brags, brags, ya, ya, ya,
    because he's crazy because he's mad
    and because he never gives us a chance to talk

Awright—I'd like to know what
   Bobby's got against me—But he wont
   tell, and it's brother deep—In the room
   they're shooting the break, clack,
   the little balls break, scatter di mania,

They take aim on little balls and break
   em up to fall, in plicky pockpockets
   for little children's names drawing
   pictures in the games in the whistle
   of the old corant tree splashing

In the mighty mu Missouri lame image
   of time and again the bride & groom,
   boom & again the bidal bood, oo,
   too-too and rumble o mumble thunder
   bow, ole Salvey is in my alley

Ole Salvey's my alley I'll lay it on me
   I'll shoot fourteen farthings for Father Machree
   and if ole Hotsatots dont footsie
   down here bring my gruel, I'll
   be cruel, I'll be cruel

Pax

   I demand that the human race
ceases multiplying its kind
        and bow out
        I advise it

   And as punishment & reward
for making this plea I know
        I'll be reborn
      the last human

Everybody else dead and I'm
an old woman roaming the earth
          groaning in caves
          sleeping on mats

And sometimes I'll cackle, sometimes
pray, sometimes cry, eat & cook
          at my little stove
          in the corner
     "Always knew it anyway,"
               I'll say
And one morning wont get up from my mat

Haiku

The moon,
     the falling star—
Look elsewhere

Prayer

O Lord, what have you hoarded up
     for me
In your great free treasure?

Poem

You start off by suckin in
     milk
And you end up suckin in
     smoke

And you know
What milk and smoke
Denote

Angel Mine

Angel mine be you fine
Angel divine

Angel milk what's your ilk
Angel bilk

Angel cash   Angel Smash
Angel hash

Perm

The world goes on
The junkey drops his butt
Children yell 'Hallelujah
   Praise God!'
in the streets of sorrow parade

Poems of the Buddhas of Old

by Jean-Louis

I

The boys were sittin
In a grove of trees
Listenin to Buddy
Explainin the keys.

"Boys, I say the keys
Cause there's lots a keys
But only one door,
One hive for the bees.

So listen to me
And I'll try to tell all
As I heard it long ago
In the Pure Land Hall.

Life is like a dream,
You only think it's real
Cause you're born a sucker
For that kind of deal;

But if the Truth was known
You ain't here nohow
And neither am I
Nor that cow and sow

You see across the field
One standing silently
The other rutting ragefully
In essence so quietly.

For you good boys
With winesoaked teeth
That can't understand
These words on a heath

I'll make it simpler
Like a bottle a wine
And a good woodfire
Under the stars divine.

Now listen to me
And when you have learned
The Dharma of the Buddhas
Of old and yearned

To sit down with the truth
Under a lonesome tree
In Yuma Arizony
Or anywhere you might be

Don't thank me for telling
What was told me,
This is the Wheel I'm turning,
This is the reason I be.

Mind is the maker
For no reason at all
Of all this creation
Created to fall.

II

"Who played this cruel joke
On bloke after bloke
Packing like a rat
Across the desert flat?"

Asked Montana Slim
Gesturing to him
The buddy of the men
In this lion's den.

"Was it God got mad
Like the Indian cad
Who was only a giver
Crooked like the river?

Gave you a garden,
Let the fruit harden,
Then comes the flood
And the loss of your blood?

Pray tell us, good buddy
And don't make it muddy
Who played this trick
On Harry and Dick

And why is so mean
The Eternal scene,
Just what's the point
Of this whole joint?"

III

Replied the good buddy:
"So now the bird's asleep
And that air plane gone
Let's all listen deep.

Everybody silent
Includin me
To catch the roar
Of eternity

That's ringin in our ears
Never-endingly.
You hear it Tom, Dick
And Harry Lee?

You hear it Slim
From Old Montan'?
You hear it Big Daddy
And Raggedy Dan?

You know what I mean
When I say eternity?
You heard it in your crib—
Shhh—Infinity."

IV

Up spoke Big Daddy
From Baltimore
An enormous Negro
Forevermore:

"You mean that shushin
And that fussin
A-slushin in my ears
For all these years?

When I was so high
Jess a little guy
I thought it was me
In the whisperin sea.

I asked my Mam
About that jam,
She didn't say nothin,
She sewed the button.

It was quiet and late
At the afternoon grate.
Her face showed no sign
Of that whisperin line

But as we sat waitin
Instead of abatin
The noise got to roar
Like an openin door

That opened my haid
Like if it was daid
And the only thing alive
Was that boomin jive

And we looked at each other
Child and mother
Like wakin from a dream
In a spirit stream."

v

"Well spoken, Big Daddy!"
Cried the buddy real glad.
"This proves that you know
And you'll never be sad.

For that was the sound
That we all hear now
And I want you to know
It's no sound nohow

But the absence of sound
Clear and pure,
The silence now heard
In heaven for sure.

What's heaven?
By Nirvana mean I?
This selfsame no-sound
Silence sigh

Eternal and empty
Of sounds and things
And all thievin rivers
Complainin brings.

For if we can sit here
In this riverbottom sand
And come to see
And understand

That we got in us
Ability to hear
Holy Emptiness
Beyond the ear

And block our ears
And hear inside
And know t'aint here
Nor there, the tide,

But everywhere, inside,
Outside, all throughout
Mind's dream, Slim?
What you gripin about?

Imaginary rivers
And gardens too,
A movie in the mind
Of me and you.

The point
Of this whole joint
Is stop, sit,
And thee anoint

With teachings such
As these, and more,
To find the key
Out this dark corridor.

The effulgent door,
The mysterious knob,
The bright room gained
Is the only job."

> The boys was pleased
> And rested up for more
> And Jack cooked mush
> In honor of the Door.

Morphine

The magic instance of the parriot tree
Nothing like a shot of junk for sheer
Heavenly contact
Oh yah, clear as a bell the mind
On morphine

I got all eternity to do everything
   you want me to do
So there's no rush

Silly Goofball Pomes

SONG OF THE NEW CHINESE

I

The Moose is a noble dolt.
  The Elk is a fool.
  The Rhinoceros is the biggest bore
       of them all.
  The Hippopotamus is a Giant River Pig.
  The Hyena is a striped dog
    who thought he was a Laughing Horse.
  The Lion is a Queer Cat
    who by the Power of his Queerness
    became a great jowled Cat.
  The Tiger is pure cat.
  The Panther hates cats.
  The Cheetah is a dog
    who thought he was a Fast Cat.
The Giraffe is a Horse
    who grew fond of the Tree-Top Leaves.
The Snake has a body beautiful,
  And the Elephant is the Lord,
    the Hook & Curl of his trunk,
    the long-lashéd Eye.
The Sloth is a Chinese Poet upsidedown.
The Ant-Eater is a long-nosed
  investigator of Villages.
The Scorpion is a Sea-Spider trapped
      on land.
The Whale is More so.
  The Man is very strange.

II

The Spider monkey is a little fool.
  The Pekinese Doll is a dog.
    The Dachshund is a snake full of Love.
    The Siamese Cat is an Angry Monkey.
    The Woman is a cellular mesh of lies

as well as a Scratcher.
The Woman has a dark blossom
        between her Thighs.
The Buddha is Known.
 The Messiah is Unborn.
The Boll Weevil is a pants rotter.
The ant a Warrior.
  The worm is a long history
          oozing out of Who?
 Who!
  Mu!
  Wu!
   The dog is a god.
   The dog is a balker.
   The Leopard is Incontinent, said Dante,
       free from the Severity of Leopard.
  The Angel Rules the Jungle.
   Blake is Blake.
  The Cow has its own way with water.
  And the Tick sticks in your hair
     & swells—
  The Shark I never Saw

The purple ass baboon is Insane
The Sparrow is a little grey bird
The Chimpanzee is Wise
The American a Sniper
The Gull a bringer of Snail Shells
The Parrot I love
  The snail knows the Unborn Void
      of Tao
      and that's why he left his house
      for Gull
 The Sea Bird is all Belly
 Crows are Dawn Singers
  The Bee hums busily
     The Frog leaped out of Water
       The Abominable Snowman is not abominable at all,
        he doesnt hurt anybody—
       The Rat has many theories—

The Spider means money—
The Fly has Seven Million
brothers—
The Seal
is on my Roof

The Goose goes north
The Robin wins the spring
The caterpillar waits
The Nightingale I have been
The mockingbird loves TV aerials
The Rabbit
The vulture trails the Puma
  The wolf snaps the Bear
    The Lizard
      The Eel
        The Octopus
          The Tapeworm
          The Finger
            The Cock
              The Germ
                The Fingernail
                The Wall

The Swordfish has a Beak of Wood.
  The Lobster is friendly.
    The Flea leaps,
      The Cockroach is Reverenced,
        The Bedbug rolls.

Pome

Be me bespangled dotted-hat fool?
  Jump upsidedown Pandora? leap above?
    —make burping Kings laugh for Ide?
—remember?—
        I'd rather piss on Scroll
      than parch this

3 Poems About
Titles of Novels

White Story
Story in White
  Never Be Mean
Some Ending
  No Red Eye in Heaven
  White Legs
          A Few Years
        More Boloney
      More of the Same
      Rest and Be Kind
        Kindness is All
        All One Way
          To Heaven
        Only Looking
            Story
          A Story
        Book Movie
      Story in Words
        Story Line

                  *

    Words Cawn't Tell
      Holy Violinists
          Violin
        Rabbit Violin
There's a Rabbit in Heaven
  One Means Not Two
          One
        One, Not Two
        Not Two
          Three
        Thirty Three
        Eleven
      Seven Times Seven
        Seven come Eleven
      Seventy Seven

Follow the Lamb
    Follow
        Heaven Followed
        Heaven Follows

                        *

        Plenty Room in the Inn
        Bright Room
         Plenty Room
        Sheol
         Gadster

Bing Bang
                Ding Dong
        Bing Bong
        Dreamers Alive

                No Title
                Not Even
                Never
                No
            Quack Quack
            Pa Drift

To Lou Little

Lou, my father thought you put him down
    and said he didnt like you

He thought he was too shabby for your
    office; his coat had got so

And his hair he'd comb and come
    into an employment office with me

And have me speak alone with the man
    for the two of us, then sigh

And repented we home; where
    sweet mother put out the pie

       anyway

In my first game I ran like mad
    at Rutgers, Cliff wasnt there;

He didnt believe what he read
    in the Spectator, 'Who's this Jack?'

So I come in on the St Benedicts game
    not willing to be caught by them bums

I took off the kickoff right straight at
    the gang, and lalooza'd around

To the pastafazoola five yard line,
    you were there, you remember

We didnt make first down; and I
    took the punt and broke my leg

And never said anything, and ate hot
    fudge sundaes & steaks in the
        Lion's Den

Airapetianz

Airapetianz, that's his name, connected
with the invention of brainwashing, if
not the inventor himself, a Pavlovian
issue taking place in science whereas
ulcer patients feel no pain
   but mind pain

As outside chloroformeters take in
the reading of the pain sensation,

and prove there is no body pain,
inside his mind he's struggling with numbers
that tell him he's alright or not

Drinks that in, that info, and registers
no body pain—Suddenly it reads *5!*
it means he's having an attack!
Immediately the meter goes up (in
his mind) but on the board no reading
    is made

Because pain sensitation not coming in

So Airapetianz proves that pain
    has mental sources

Mind over matter and mind over pain

Pavlovian instrument, determinism
And brainwash it's called

            Which doesnt matter
            In a mindmatter world
            The dog that barks
            The wick that falls
            The soul that goes to heaven
            The hand that writes

If I Were Jesus, God

O tender hearted sweet usurper of my
    vines, fox, do not crawl too near

O marblehearted faun of antiquity,
    what can I say of thee?

O people of Carthage! Oh Rome!
O Northside Chicaga! O Tome!

O listen to me in the park—
    Whenever you have a question
    come to me

Otherwise I'll be in the Tree Grove
    resting up

Idiot

Them Hindu temples in Hoopastan
Hoo! them Hindu temples'd a made
Fool! outa me if I laffed like that
Hyah! hyah hyoo hya hya hoo-a
Thee! marvelous parvelous pairvening
Raive! ening of this ard-parturying-
Spring?—they give it that name in Ego's
Ed! cave, in Spatn, latn, you know,
Piss! tayola manaya tapaya you
Know! ho!—the lark's fat frant
Mar!—jesty hit the seapebble Homeric
Good!—fragrance I descried in gulls'
Art! fly majesty, known as then mad,
Read! Sherwood's Anderson Ohio Ville
Story! of epic O hand,—Yippee!
Yell! the Madman in the next room
Amazed! the doctor with a crazed
Jump? in the air, *I'm* mad?

    Well I only said
    You were an idiot

Idiots have Kings, were Kings, have necks
to be cut off, gibbets to spin rope of,
Twisted pants to sweep blond hair
Of HomoSexual Heroes testifying testes
In courts of Conelrad Behavious otay—
    Otay!

Sneak out of it with jazz

Hey! Ole Idiot's still on the corner
Ready for all comers

Old Western Movies

A Jedge in the West comin from the South
    with ruby sideburns, boy—
Always usin flowery languij—
The grim fightin hero's troubles
    are always private—
He wants to know where "I fit in"
    in herd wars—
Sometimes you see villains so ancient
    you saw them in infancy
    exaggerating in snow
their mustaches looking older
        than yr father's grave—
"Thanks Marshall"—"I reckon"
—I guess I better run on back
    to Whisky Row, Colorada,
        & marry an old Tim McCoy Gal
        or turn off the tele vision, *one*—

—You gotta go a long way in the West
        to find a good man—
    So close the book,
    The Courier, run by Steve, is a paper
    wearing a sunbonnet.
    Drive the cattle thru that silver wall,
            help ladies to their hearse,
                    mouth in the sun,
That oughta do till Mexican Drygulcher
    finds Redwing in the Shack
 And Kwakiutls menstruate.
Old horses' necks by broken fences,

guns gone rust,
I guess the gang got shot.

   Kid Dream
   Hid
    In the leaves.

April 1958, Northport

Woman

A woman is beautiful
  but
      you have to swing
      and swing and swing
      and swing like
      a handkerchief in the
                wind

Hymn

And when you showed me Brooklyn Bridge
  in the morning,
   Ah God,

And the people slipping on ice in the street,
twice,
     twice,
        two different people
        came over, goin to work,
        so earnest and tryful,
        clutching their pitiful
        morning Daily News
        slip on the ice & fall
        both inside 5 minutes
        and I cried I cried

That's when you taught me tears, Ah
  God in the morning,
    Ah Thee

And me leaning on the lamppost wiping
eyes,
    eyes,
        nobody's know I'd cried
        or woulda cared anyway
        but O I saw my father
        and my grandfather's mother
        and the long lines of chairs
        and tear-sitters and dead,
        Ah me, I knew God You
        had better plans than that

So whatever plan you have for me
Splitter of majesty
Make it short
  brief
Make it snappy
  bring me home to the Eternal Mother
  today

At your service anyway,
  (and until)

Goofball Blues

I'm just a human being with a lot of
shit on my heart

My ambition was not to be a great
      lover,
    but that's what I am
    Even in dreams, fiancées
      of other men
      ball on my joint

And I am the Flying Horse
of Mien Mo
When I am an old man
my grave will rot me
The ones I loved were crazy
without knowing why
When I am old I'll yawn
in the Flannel Grave

Goofball Sillypomes

These Englishers know more madness
Than Nonsense Poems know,
For Tom O' Bedlam never dreamed
What's dream'd in mattress now,
Enow, M.J.E.,
Enow

Those who die
go to coffins
That never get wet

The old years
on the dock
—Blue air

The wind is late
—Already this gate
Has not been swept

Jan, 1960

Drunken Scribbling Poem

I got no language left in me heart
I'm a triple trombone fool
The Three Vehicles are a drag on my ass

Ah Sad America your cluster of girlies—All of a High School
afternoon waiting for the bass drum Master with his Golden
Fish Pole "Hike!" he yells "Realize!" dont amble just bramble
in my flying airplane bushes with me dont let ornery old home-
town friends in cars go C' cree-acking (Runnin Wild) yair,
go ahead home is soon—If my own kid did true be damned
hummmmmm into each rain the right rain poured ahh and go
blue you River Yair reaning calling more   O   Rooder   you
downed yair Oh Yess Og nobody tree ah alone they aint nobody
home
         Figure that out if you will, Drop
         Milton is back
         Dread dread dread dread dread dread is dead   oh
the sorrowful twap of that tirler
         Let no honest (let no oneset englishman) twirl
         Onest

1959, Northport

Running Through—
Chinese Poem Song

         O I today
         sad as Chu Yuan
         stumbled to the store
         in broiling Florida October
     morning heat cursing
         for my wine, sweating
         like rain, & came to my chair
          weak & trembling
             wondering if I'm crazy at last
     —O Chu Yuan! No!

No suicide! Wine please wine!
What shall we all do
all knowing we're dying
without wine to guide us
to winking at death
& life too——
My heart belongs
to Chinese poets
& their scrolls—
We cant just die
—Men need wine
& poetry
at least

O Mao, poet Mao,
not Boss Mao,
here in America
wine is laughed at
& poetry a joke
—Death's a grim reminder
to everybody already dead
crashing in cars all around here—
Here men & women dryly scowl
at poets' sad attempts
to make our lot
a whole lot
lesser—
I, a poet, suffer
even for bugs
I find upsidedown
dying in the grass—
So I drink wine
alone—
I shudder to think
how dead
the astronauts
are
going to a dead
moon
of no wine

All our best men
are laughed at
in this nightmare land
but the newspapers preen
in virtue—Throughout
the world the left & right,
the east & west, are both vicious—
The happy old winebibber is gone—
I want him to reappear—
For Modern China preens
in virtue too
for no better reason
than America—
Nobody has respect for the cat
asleep, and I am hopelessly
inadequate in this poem
—Nobody has respect
for the self centered
irresponsible wine invalid
—Everybody wants to be strapped
in a hopeless space suit
where they cant move
—I urge you, China,
go back
to Li Po &
Tao Yuan Ming

What am I talking about?
I dont know,
I'm sick today—
I didnt sleep all night,
Walked stumbling in the field
to get wine, now I'm drinking it,
I feel better and worse—
I have something to say to Mao
& the poets of China
that wont come out—
It's all about how America
ignores poetry & wine,
& so does China,

& I'm a fool
      without a river & a boat
          & a flower suit—
          without a wineshop at dawn
          ——without self respect——
          —Without the truth—
          but I'm a better man
            than all of you—
              that's what I
              wanted to say

Sken 3

Radiations of Akshobya
Blinding my eye in the
  water in the claypot
  pan-pot, the rainbow
  of the sun's reflection
  there causing painful
  imaginary blossoms to
    arise in my eyeball
  and I see silver daggers
    & swords mingled with
  red or rather roe-pink
    rowing fires, shot by
  quivers & Arch Bows of
  Tampleton Hokshaw
  HighRide Chariot Ear
    the saint of England,
  Wozzit, turning pools
  of oil rainbow Dedalus
—Buddhalands without
  number & Van Gogh swirl
    agog rows of em endless
    emptiness in that little
      pot, & bug flies—

Cognac Blues

You gets your just dues in
Heaven——Heaven'll
be indifferent to this
indifferent dog

(Yet, honest indifference
were better than cant)

. . . really

When I hear pious
bullshit about Justice
& Democracy and I know
the hypocrites are lying
in their false teeth

I'm not indifferent to God,
I'm indifferent to
me-on-earth

I cant think of anything
more ridiculous than me
on earth—
Really!

Beau Bébé

And the dreams—of me & Lousy & GJ
sitting on Moody St looking up the
bridge to P'Ville where vistas
of vast sunny cloud boulevard
Buddhalands open, I tell
Lousy "This is a dream"—
big rivers, lake———
I tell Lousy that, he gives

me the thin Kasyapa's Smile—
GJ too bored to comment—
——Like holding up a flower,
as Ma says: "The Beginning"—
Later after being jacked off in
    the NY subway by stealer
    blondes with pimps in background
(Ah the Ecstasy) I
    stole over well remembered
        other-people roofs—

1961, Orlando, Fla.

The Shack of Desolation

The shack of Desolation is dirty, with broken boxes of wood
    gathered by me like a Japanese old woman gathers
    driftwood on the beach or on the mountainside,

Full of mice, fat drops, chips, ancient chewed up fragments
    of religious tracts, crap, dust, old letters of other lookouts
    and general unsweepable debris too infinitude to assemble
    and sweep

Paniaw Powder   Olympic   Pawmanow

And Mt Hozomeen—most beautiful mountain I ever seen—
    frights me acme out the morning coffee window,
    blue Chinese void of Friday morning,

And I have an old washtub covered with a wood door of sheds
  that when I saw it made me think of oldtime baths
  of bathnight New England when Pa was pink—

  Patiat rock mounts snow spomona'd that I drew at ten
  for Kuku and Coco everywhere, hundreds a miles of,
  and clouds pass thru my ink

Poor Sottish Kerouac

Poor sottish Kerouac with his thumb in his eye
Getting interested in literature again
Though a mote of dust just flew by

How should I know that the dead were born?
Does Master cry?

The weeds Ophelia wound with
and Chatterton measured in the moon
are the weeds of Goethe, Wang Wei,
and the Golden Courtesans

Imagining recommending a prefecture
for a man in the madhouse
————rain————

Sleep well, my angel
Make some eggs
The house in the moor
Is the house in the moor
The house is a monument
In the moor of the grave
————Whatever that means————

The white dove descended in disguise?

Long Island Chinese Poem Rain

The years are hurrying
Autumn rains fall on my awning
My accomplishments mean nothing to me
My girl no longer visits me

Maybe because I got warts on my cock
Or she found a younger man with a smooth cock
I can look up anything in my wine bottle

Whitman was happy about something around here
  Followed by millions sick
What, Whitman, say?

The headlines of ten days ago no longer interest me
Rugs woven lovingly end on garage crates

The white dove desecrated in desuetude
And who wants wisdom?

The world is an eraser for these words

Oh sad Bodhidharma you were right
Everything we loved disappeared

Nobody in the chair
Nobody in the books
Nobody in the rain

Pome

If I dont use the cork
  I may spill the wine—
But if I do?

Pome on Doctor Sax

In his declining years Doctor Sax was an old bum living in Skid
Row hotel rooms in the blighted area of SF around 3rd
Street—He was a madhaired old genius now with hair
growing out of his nose, like the hair growing out of
the nose of Aristadamis Kaldis the painter, and had
eyebrows growing out an inch long, like the eyebrows
of Daisetz Suzuki the Zen Master of whom
it has been said, of *which*, eyebrows like that
take a lifetime to grow so long &

therefore resemble the bush of the
Dharma which once rooted
is too tough to be
pulled out by hand
or horse—

Let that be a lesson to all you young
girls plucking your eyebrows & you
(also) young choir singers jacking off
behind the marechal's hilt
in St Paul's
Cathedral
(& yelling home to Mother
"Mater Mine, b'ome
for Easter")

Dr Sax the master knower of
  Easter was now reduced to penury
    & looking at Stained glass windows
    in old churches—His only 2
    last friends in this life, this impossibly
    hard life no matter under what
    conditions it appears, were Bela
    Lugosi & Boris Karloff, who visited
him annually in his room on 3rd Street
    & cut thru the fogs of evening with
    their heads bent as the bells of St Simon
    tolled a heartbroken "Kathleen" across
    the rooftops of old hotels where similar old
    men like Doctor Sax sat bent headed
    on beds of woe with prayerbeads between
      their feet, Oh moaning, homes for
            lost pigeons or time's immemorial
            white dove
              of the roses
                of the unborn
                  astonished bliss—

And there they'd sit in the little
room, Sax on the edge of the bed with a
bottle of rotgut Tokay in his hand, Bela
in the old rocking chair, Boris standing by
the sink, & sigh————
& then Sax wd always say
"Please play the monster for me" & of course
the old actors, who loved him dearly & came to
see him for human tender sentimentality not
monstrous reasons protested but he always
got drunk & cried so that Boris first had
to get up & extend his arms do
Frankenstein go *uck*! then Bela
wd stand & arm cape & leer &
approach Sax, who squealed

A Curse at the Devil

For Charleen Whisnant

Lucifer Sansfoi
    Varlet Sansfoi

Omer Perdieu
    I.B.Perdie
        Billy Perdy

I'll unwind your
    guts from Durham
        to Dover
        and bury em
        in Clover—

Your psalms I'll 'ave
    engraved
        in your toothbone—

Your victories
nilled—
You jailed under
a woman's skirt
    of stone—

Stone blind woman
with no guts
and only a scale—

Your thoughts & letters
Shandy'd about
    in *Beth*
      (Gaelic for *grave*).

Your philosophies
run up your nose
again—

Your confidences
and essays bandied
   in ballrooms
from switchblade
   to switchblade

—Your final
duel with
   sledge hammers—
Your essential
secret twinned
   to buttercups
    & dying—

Your guide to 32
European cities
scabbed in Isaiah
—Your red beard
snobbed in
  Dolmen ruins

in the editions
of the Bleak—

Your saints and
Consolations bereft
—Your handy volume
rolled into
        an urn—

And your father
  and mother besmeared
  at thought of you
  th'unspent begotless
    crop of worms
—You lay
  there, you
  queen for a
    day, wait
for the "fen-
  sucked fogs"
  to carp at you

Your sweety beauty
discovered by No Name
in its hidingplace
  till burrs
part from you
from lack
of issue,
  sinew, all
  the rest—
Gibbering quiver
  graveyard Hoo!

The hospital
  that buries
      you
    be Baal,
  the digger

Yorick,
& the shoveler
    groom—

My rosy tomatoes
pop squirting
  from your awful
  rotten grave—

Your profile,
    erstwhile
       Garboesque,
    mistook by earth-
    eels for some
       fjord to
          Sheol—

And your timid
  voice box
  strangled
  by lie-hating
  earth
         forever.

May the plighted
  Noah-clouds
    dissolve in grief
    of you—

May Red clay
   be your center,
& woven into necks,
  of hogs, boars,
  booters & pilferers
  & burned down
  with Stalin, Hitler
   & the rest—

May you bite
your lip that

you cannot
meet with God—
          or
Beat me to a pub
          —Amen

The Almoner,
   his cup hath
    no bottom,
   nor I
    a brim.

Devil, get thee
back
   to russet caves.

August 31, 1965, Florida

OLD ANGEL MIDNIGHT

1   FRIDAY AFTERNOON IN THE UNIVERSE, in all directions in & out you got your men women dogs children horses pones tics perts parts pans pools palls pails parturiences and petty Thieveries that turn into heavenly Buddha—I know boy what's I talkin about case I made the world & when I made it I no lie & had Old Angel Midnight for my name and concocted up a world so *nothing* you had forever thereafter make believe it's real—but that's alright because now everything'll be alright & we'll soothe the forever boys & girls & before we're thru we'll find a name for this Goddam Golden Eternity & tell a story too—and but d y aver read a story as vast as this that begins Friday Afternoon with workinmen on scaffolds painting white paint & ants merlying in lil black dens & microbes warring in yr kidney & mesaroolies microbing in the innards of mercery & microbe microbes dreaming of the ultimate microbehood which then ultimates outward to the endless vast empty atom which is this imaginary universe, ending nowhere & ne'er e'en born as Bankei well poled when he ferried his mother over the rocks to Twat You Tee and people visit his hut to enquire "What other planet features this?" & he answers "What other planet?" tho the sounds of the entire world are now swimming thru this window from Mrs McCartiola's twandow & Ole Poke's home dronk again & acourse you hear the cats wailing in the wailbar wildbar wartfence moonlight midnight Angel Dolophine immensity Visions of the Tathagata's Seat of Purity & Womb so that here is all this infinite immaterial meadowlike golden ash swimswarming in our enlighten brains & the silence Shh shefallying in our endless ear & still we refuse naked & blank to hear What the Who? the Who? Too What You? will say the diamond boat & Persepine, Recipine, Mill town, Heroine, & Fack matches the silver ages everlasting swarmswallying in a simple broom—and at night ya raise the square white light from your ghost beneath a rootdrinkin tree & Coyote wont hear ya but you'll ward off the inexistency devils just to pass the time away & meanwhile it's timeless to the ends of the last lightyear it might as well be gettin late Friday afternoon where we start so's old Sound can come home when worksa done & drink his beer & tweak his children's eyes—

481

2   and what talents it takes to bail boats out you'd never flank till flail pipe throwed howdy who was it out the bar of the seven seas and all the Italians of 7th Street in Sausaleety slit sleet with paring knives that were used in the ream kitchens to cut the innards of gizzards out on a board, wa, twa, wow, why, shit, Ow, man, I'm tellin you—Wait—We bait the rat and forget to mark the place and soon Cita comes and eat it and puke out grit—fa yen pas d cas, fa yen pas d case, chanson d idiot, imbecile, vas malade—la sonora de madrigal—but as soon as someone wants to start then the world takes on these new propensities:

1. Bardoush
   (the way the craydon bi fa shta ma j en vack)
2. Flaki—arrete—interrupted chain saw sting eucalyptus words inside the outside void that good God we cant believe is anything so arsaphallawy any the pranaraja of madore with his bloody arse kegs, shit—go to three.

3   Finally just about the time they put wood to the poets of France & fires broke out recapitulating the capitulation of the continent of Mu located just south of Patch, Part, with his hair askew and wearing goldring ears & Vaseline Hair Oil in his arse ass hole flaunted all the old queers and lecherous cardinals who wrote (write) pious manuals & announced that henceforth 'he was to be the sole provender provider this side of Kissthat.

Insteada which hey marabuda you son of a betch you cucksucker you hey hang dat board down here I'll go cot you on the Yewneon ya bum ya—lick, lock, lick, lock, mix it for pa-tit a a lamana lacasta reda va da Poo moo koo—la—swinging Friday afternoon in eternity here comes Kee pardawac with long golden robe flowing through the Greek Islands with a Bardic (forgot) with a lard (?) with a marde manual onder his Portugee Tot Sherry Rotgut, singing "Kee ya."

Tried to warn all of you, essence of stuff wont do—God why did you make the world?

Answer: - Because I gwt pokia renamash ta va in ming the atss are you forever with it?

I like the bliss of mind.

Awright I'll call up all the fuckin Gods, right now!

Parya! Arrive! Ya damn hogfuckin lick lip twillerin fishmonger! Kiss my purple royal ass baboon! Poota! Whore! You and yr retinues of chariots & fucks! Devadatta! Angel of Mercy! Prick! Lover! Mush! Run on ya dog eared kiss willying nilly Dexter Michigan ass-warlerin ratpole! The rat in my cellar's an old canuck who wasnt fooled by rebirth but b God gotta admit I was born for the same reason I bring this glass to my lip—?

Rut! Old God whore, the key to ecstasy is forevermore furthermore blind! Potanyaka! God of Mercy! Boron O Mon Boron! All of ye! Rush! Ghosts & evil spirits, if you appear I'm saved. How can you fool an old man with a stove & wine drippin down his chin? The flowers are my little sisters and I love them with a dear heart. Ashcans turn to snow and milk when I look. I know sinister alleys. I had a vision of Han Shan a darkened by sun bum in odd rags standing short in the gloom scarey to see. Poetry, all these vicious writers and bores & Scriptural Apocraphylizers fucking their own dear mothers because they want ears to sell—

And the axe haiku.

All the little fine angels amercyin and this weary prose hand handling dumb pencils like in school long ago the first redsun special. Henry Millers everywhere Fridaying the world—Rexroths. Rexroths not a bad egg. Creeley. Creeley. Real magination realizing rock roll rip snortipatin oyster stew of Onatona Scotiat Shores where six birds week the nest and part wasted his twill till I.

Mush. Wish. Wish I could sing ya songs of a perty nova spotia patonapeein pack wallower wop snot polly—but caint—cause I'll get sick & die anyway & you too, born to die, little flowers. Fiorella. Look around. The burlap's buried in the wood on an angle, axe haiku. La religion c'est d la marde! Pa! d la marde! J m en dor.—

God's asleep dreaming, we've got to wake him up! Then all of a sudden when we're asleep dreaming, he comes and wakes us up—how gentle! How are you Mrs Jones? Fine Mrs Smith! Tit within Tat—Eye within Tooth—Bone within Light, like—Drop some little beads of sweetness in that stew (O Phoney Poetry!)—the heart of the onion—That stew's too good for me to eat, you!—

People, shmeople

4   Boy, says Old Angel, this amazing nonsensical rave of yours
wherein I spose you'd think you'd in some lighter time find
hand be-almin ya for the likes of what ya davote yaself to, pah—
bum with a tail only means one thing,—They know that in
sauerkraut bars, god the chew chew & the wall lips—And not
only that but all them in describable paradises—aye ah—Old
Angel m boy—Jack, the born with a tail bit is a deal that you
never dream'd to redeem—verify—try to see as straight—you
wont believe even in God but tbe devil worries you—you &
Mrs Tourian—great gaz-zuz & I'd as lief be scoured with a leaf
rust as hear this poetizin horseshit everyhere I want to hear the
sounds thru the window you promised me when the Midnight
bell on 7th St did toll bing bong & Burroughs and Ginsberg
were asleep & you lay on the couch in that timeless moment
in the little red bulblight bus & saw drapes of eternity parting
for your hand to begin & so's you could affect—& *ee*ffect—the
total turningabout & deep revival of world robeflowing litera-
ture till it shd be something a man'd put his eyes on & continu-
ally read for the sake of reading & for the sake of the Tongue &
not just these insipid stories writ in insipid aridities & paranoias
bloomin & why yet the image—let's hear the Sound of the Uni-
verse, son, & no more part twaddle—And dont expect nothing
from me, my middle name is Opprobrium, Old Angel Midnight
Opprobrium, boy, O.A.M.O.—
     Pirilee pirilee, tzwé tzwi tzwa,—tack tick—birds & firewood.
The dream is already ended and we're already awake in the
golden eternity.

5   Then when rat tooth come ravin and fradilaboodala back-ala
backed up, trip tripped himself and fell falling on top of Old
Smokey because *his pipe* was not right, had no molasses in it,
tho it looked like a morasses brarrel, but then the cunts came.
She had a long cunt that sitick out of her craw a mile long like
Mexican Drawings showing hungry drinkers reaching Surreal-
istic Thirsts with lips like Aztec—Akron Lehman the Hart
Crane Hero of Drunken Records came full in her cunt spof-
fing & overflowing white enlightened seminal savior juice out
of his canal-hole into her hungry river bed and that made the
old nannies gab and kiss that.

6   O he was quite racy—real estate queen—Europe & Niles—
for pleasure—stom stomp absulute raze making noise—I can
write them but I cant puctuate them—then he said comma
comma comma—That skinny guy with black hair—Atlean
Rage—in India in the last year he's getting even ignoring all
common publications & getting Urdu Nothing Sanskrit by
Sir Yak Yak Yak forty page thing Norfolk—let's all get drunk
I wanta take pictures—dont miss with Mrs. lately in trust pic-
ture pitcher pithy lisp—that's an artistic kit for sex—Trying to
think of a rule in Sankrit Mamma Sanskrit Sounding obviously
twins coming in here Milltown Equinell Miopa Parte Watacha
Peemana Kowava you get sticky ring weekends & wash the tub,
Bub—I'll be gentle like a Iamb in the Bible—Beautiful color yr
lipstick thanx honey—Got a match Max?—Taxi crabs & mur-
dercycles—Let's go to Trilling & ask him—I gotta wash my
conduct—Dont worry about nothin—I love Allen Ginsberg—
Let that be recorded in heaven's unchangeable heart—Either
bway—Rapples—Call up Allen Price Jones—Who is that?—
They re having fun on the bed there—Soo de ya bee la—And
there came the picture of Ang Bong de Beela—Fuck it or get it
in or wait something for the bee slime—Then the ants'll crawl
over bee land—Ants in bands wailing neath my bloody ow
pants, owler pants—Ta da ba dee—He thinlis I'm competive
in a long pleasant souse of Wishing all of ye bleed stay medita-
tion everybody martini destroy my black—Allen ye better voice
the stare, this beer these room sandwiches—Where did you
get these? Big greasy socialists—Are you gonna konk, Allen?
Mighty tall in the saddle—Anybody got a ceegiboo?—The
moon is a piece of tea—(Under the empty blue sky, vertebrate
zoology.)

7   And make the most malign detractor eat from the love of
the lamb—and the pot that's for everybody not diminish when
somebody comes—Tathagata, give me that—
    Visions of Al
    Women are so variously beautiful it's such a pleasure
    Think happy thoughts of the Buddha who abides throughout
detestable phenomena like lizards and man eating ogres, with
perfect compassion and blight, caring not one way or the other
the outcome of our term of time because celestial birds are

singing in the golden heaven. In the golden hall of the Buddha, think, I am already ensconced on a tray of gold, invisible and radiant with singing, by the side of my beloved hand, which has done its work and exists no more to tone up the troubles of this birth-and-death imaginary world—And that's because the Old Angel Midnight is a Fike—that's because the Old Angel Midnight never was. And the story of love is a long sad tale ending in graves, many heads bend beneath the light, arguments are raving avid lipt and silly in silly secular rooms silly seconsular rooms full of height agee—Swam! reacht the other shore, folded, in magnificence, shouldered the wheel of iron light, and shuddered no more, and rowed the fieldstar across her bed of ashen samsara sorrow towards in here, the bliss evermore.

So.

Saw sight saver & fixt him.—Love you all, children, happy days and happy dreams and happy thoughts forevermore—

Dont forget to put a dime in the coin box by dipping your finger in ancid inkl the holy old forevermore holy water & bleep blap bloop the sign a the cross, when facing the altar down the aisle when you're waltzing—Ding! Up you go, smoke

8   The Mill Valley trees, the pines with green mint look and there's a tangled eucalyptus hulk stick fallen thru the late sunlight tangle of those needles, hanging from it like a live wire connecting it to the ground—just below, the notches where little Fred sought to fell sad pine—not bleeding much—just a lot of crystal sap the ants are mining in, motionless like cows on the grass & so they must be aphyds percolatin up a steam to store provender in their bottomless bellies that for all I know are bigger than bellies of the Universe beyond—The little tragic windy cottages on the high last city-ward hill and today roosting in sun hot dream above the tree head of seas and meadowpatch whilst tee-kee-kee-pearl the birdies & mommans mark & ululate moodily in this valley of peaceful firewood in stacks that make you think of Oregon in the morning in 1928 when Back was home on the range lake and his hunting knife threw away and went to sit among the Ponderosa Pines to think about love his girl's bare bodice like a fennel seed the navel in her milk bun—Shorty McGonigle and Roger Nulty held up the Boston Bank and murdered a girl in these old woods and next you

saw the steely green iron photograph in True Detective show-
ing black blotches in the black blotch running culvert by the
dirty roadside not Oregon at all, or Jim Back so happy with his
mouth a blade of grass depending—

> Hummingbird hums
> hello—bugs
> Race and swoop

> Two ants hurry
> to catch up
> With lonely Joe

> The tree above
> me is like
> A woman's thigh
> Smooth Eucalyptus bumps
> and muscle swells

> I would I were a weed
> a week, would leave.
> Why was the rat
> mixed up
> in the sun?

Because Buddhidharma came from the West with dark eye-
brows, and China had a mountain wall, and mists get lost above
the Yangtze Gorge and this is a mysterious yak the bird makes,
yick,—wowf wow wot sings the dog blud blut blup below the
Homestead Deer—red robins with saffron scarlet or orange
rud breasts make a racket in the dry dead car crash tree Neal
mentioned "He went off the road into a eucalyptus" and "it's all
busting out," indicating the prune blossoms and Bodhidharma
came from the India West to seek converts to his wall-gazing
and ended up with Zen magic monks mopping each and one
and all and other in mud koan puddles to prove the crystal void.
Wow

9   Lookin over der sports page I see assorted perms written
in langosten field hand that wd make the 2 silhouetted movie

champeens change their quiet dull dialog to something fog—
ah, Old Angel Midnight, it will be all over in a year.

Dying is ecstasy.

I'm not a teacher, not a sage, not a Roshi, not a writer or
master or even a giggling dharma bum I'm my mother's son &
my mother is the universe—

> What is this universe
>   but a lot of waves
> And a craving desire
>   is a wave
> Belonging to a wave
>   in a world of waves
> So why put any down,
>   wave?
> Come on wave, WAVE!
> The heehaw's dobbin
>   spring hoho
> Is a sad lonely yurk
>   for your love
> Wave lover.

I would I were a little tiny Jesus examining the mystery above
the lightbody-cloud of the moon on still Marin nights, the flow-
ers are my moon goddesses, & take craps naked. Horrible de-
lightful the old retired harridan joys that wobble on the walking
stick hill with nervous Collies yarking Yowk here in Journal
Town where I wobble the card crate prayer bead Juju box with
swing of wordage while Chas Olson reads my prose, man of the
broad mysterious smoky Mountain Morn. (And everything is
non-existent), heh.—

In a universe of waves quel difference betwixt one wave &
t'other? T s all the same wavehood & every little unlocatable
electron is a Tathagata pouring electromagnetic gravitational
light at the constant speed of light (which can be heard in
the sound of silence) & so this endless radiation of mysterious
radiance is merely the minutia magnificent endless Tathagata
Womb manifesting itself multiply & so not at all, for, all things
are no-things but if this bores you it's because you want bricks
in your soup. Empty.

The Happy One is free
It's a mystical mystery
It's endless light
The golden eternity
Why read Don Quixote when you can read The Diamond
Sutra or the Wonderful Law Lotus Sutra? Why read Mickey
Spillane when you can read Gary Snyder & Philip Whalen & the
Mexico City Blues? Why hide what you mean behind natural
data?

What does it mean that True Nature is incomprehensibly be-
yond the veil of our senses and is like empty light? It means that
True Nature is incomprehensibly beyond the veil of our senses
& is like empty light. If someone were to say to me, Krap, cart
your daddy over here & let's hear tarbey? I'd say Wap, how'n
you can cray that way when small fot find out all Sond your Oo
like Where you like me & You Like Me & OO La Koo Me the
onta logical philosizer fonted in the crap ding? He'd say, Froo,
this Sunday Blues is too tree drunk & dead tree, & I'd say push
out the cork & can it, vant more moonshine potatovodka or go
to church or tet, shet, the Lord is all this.

The American Dreamer
Star of Karuna
The Moon of Pity
Ti Jean
A grat big sweaty wave—You get a vision of the truth as the
universe of electrical waves all of it pure ecstasy then you open
the old sutras and all you see no matter how many pages you
turn over is human egoism & warnings—bah—I am the new
Buddha—and I shall call myself ELECTRON—Why the all this
hassel over what you do when there's no time no space no mind
just illusion & mystery? It's sheer ignorance & old-fashion'd
God fear—Why shd I fear Myself?—It's like looking at a movie
high & insteada the story you see swarming electrical particles
each one a bliss fwamming in the screen eternally—shit! I'm
going to the other side.

I dont need precepts
I need love
I need the Vision of Love
VISIONS OF LOVE
This holy and all universe is a wonderful white wild power,

why, hell, should, heaven, interfere, words, waiting, flesh, sure, I, know, write, poems, this is no way to make it into the blessedness sweetly to be perceived, believed, & acted upon. Be silent & real. I feel very displeased, I just stood on my head & my neck is sore. But I'll jump like a gazelle at six. Good God how can I ever die standing on my head each day 5 minutes?

I feel very pleased now, 5 minutes later. The whole system is washed both ways. I'll invent a packboard that you haul up yourself, lashed, to a pulley, & tie to a bit, & hang upsidedown at ease, for old age. For this is the True Way. It is gravitational forces. It makes me eat & run into the yard & wash & forget all about electrical.

Dont touch me, I'm full
of snakes
(say the psychopathic flips)

Fanny fancy —
thou done
That crap

Gary (Snyder) gone
like smoke
—My lonely shoes
My rugged huge blue shoes

10   Morning sun—
            the purple petals,
      Four have fallen

Somavilerd, who thot that no one loved him, got himself reborn a dozen million times in various-around world systems in order to prove that the reason was his own detestableness, but his detestableness didnt belong to him because there is no ego owning going on anywhere in the universal dream only endless talk & twaddle & tales of idiots—told for nothing & waving like leaves of a sea of trees in the birdy tweeking morning when motors & valleys bourk—Fanny the Spider built a web from sill to flower stem, pot, winejug, & Donlin declined—Iing ba twa

laramenooki Wi the bugs interwooped like zing planes in the
heatening mornlull & full sperm spof smudge re testified the
empty fertilities with a new mistake—milky mistakes abounding
& spoffing everywhere from crap cellars to courtesan silkbed
in Minarette—& all went to prove that in the golden eter-
nity old angel midnight never happened & in North Beach the
cold hopeless fog mist on Monday Morning, after binges with
Sublette & Donlin who sleep all day & only wake to drink an-
other jug—I dont understand this suffering but there's no ego
owning in sufferunderstanding either—And all the combined
sounds one hummin gnoise—Cats yawn I'd like to yawn I'd like
to not like and begone bechune & bejesus if what on earth &
under heck & over shit we gonna do O hopeless ghosts?—IL
PICCOLO CAFFE what they do there, Vallejo!—I'd never've
known f twasnt for Ma & Pa—As many times' I relight the
Wizard Pipe it goes out—That's the store—nothing hidden the
stash is a free treasure—God aint cached—All I take in I put
out again, it's a filthy channel designed to drive me mad—Lo
Lord what did I buy, what did you sell? What kinda bamboo
poles you got in that merlasses brarrel of Yours, Avalokites-
vara?—Shut up & let the nose go—try not asking—spiratual
ecstasy is nothing—the rhinestone in the juju is the rhinestone
in the juju, & your table she's small—and yr wife put you out
& screwed a Porto Rican—the jumble of events is a thing—I'll
ask why till I fly. The potter dwelling in his humble claypot
strung this rote together to while the whelom along the dry
clay woman bank where children cling to their mother's back &
Father's Falling—into Mother—bing bang the Yabyum News—
bing bang the bolt in the void—Pop ping the electromagnetic
in the gravitational the yang in the yin—the positive making
the negative different, the negative holds the positive, & so I'm
sick—& so I know—I'm sick—Sugata

11   Laurel Dell camp, boo! Cow swung my shirt around, deers
hooftrompled my sleep, moon was like a streetlamp in my face,
& I didnt sleep till the big cat who came down the pyramid
wall in the morning where I told Ma about Mamie Eisenhour's
drunk & I got my diploma & we landed & she threw her ice
cream drunk & I was glad about something ephemeral &

during the night I willed to leap outa my sleep wildly but it took some dead & inert time—the Book of Dreams & all my words, hurt—I'm goin back to my cabin & write Sweet Mother & Son slowly & gladly

12   Lou Little explaining to the newsreel audience how this football player went mad & shows how on a Columbia Practice Hillside it started with father & son, the gray reaches of the Eternity Library beyond—I go visit my sweet Alene in her subterranean pad near the 3rd Avenue El & Henry St of old Mike Mike milkcan Ashcan Lower Eastside Dreams & pink murders & there she wont ope the door because I cant get the job I tried so hard to get & the woman said my form wasnt right but Neal made it but regretfully it is he's shipping, out & I'm on the ship with him telling him "If you wash dishes dont say a word, if you're a yeoman do yr work all well"—I can see he hates to go without me to this other Grayshore—Sitting before my stove on a cold gray Saturday morning with my coffee & my pipe, eating jello—remembering the little jello cartoon that filled me with such joy as a kid on Sarah Avenue, the little prince wouldnt take pheasant or delicate birds or celestial puddings or even Mominuan Icecream but when the little bird brought him jello inverted in a rill mold cup he went wild & saved the kingdom, red jello like mine, in the little dear lovable pages—of long ago—My form is delight delight delight
   Ring, ring, ring—
   Shh, the sky is empty—
   Shh, the earth is empty—
   Look out, look in, shh—
   The essence of jello is the essence of arrangement—
   Be nice to the monster crab, it's only another arrangement of that which you are

13   Bobby Mathews of Philadelphia & Ed Crane of NY accomplished the feat before 1900 (striking out 4 men in 1 inning)—O those old ballgames, O lost Foleys of South Boston in old time Boston raw drump drunk days I love you—Geo Hooks Wiltse of the Giants did it on May 15, 1906 when my father was 17 years old in his pinksuspendered primal origin blues—when

Old Jacques Kerouac raved behind the woodstove on church sunday mornings with his jug & today is May 28 1956 & me & Bob Donlin (Donnelly of Visions of Gerard) are drinking port in McCorkle's shack & the wind roars thru the shoh trees— Alright, mothers & sons, I'll write for ye & tell a long sweet dad tale—For all is the same happy purity! Ya, padawaddy I like to frail them broadies Peer Engeli icecream backseat redleather creamcome fuck O cone!—let me love you again, sweet baby— this will do till nextyear's orgasm do—overhead levy assembling eastboat taxers hotson foundries bringin Alene Melville to my motherlovin arms Ah sweet indescribable verdurous parapineta post-wallowing rail ron hung on bu-bu-Angel's Telephoto let Anita Ekberg Pali shorts & all thu—so Miss'sippi Gene could go Hmf in his trance car blues—Why dash?—Sip.

14 Because while Gore Bedavalled marvels he steps, Ole Robeflow, from isle to isle into Mrs Roocco's windrow to innerstate the gas meek and bring photons, neutrons, pootons, borons, & oromariavalosa perstarolingish pert part pomerance poons, Topki, to flash in the mokswarm smugbug television vision intertaining trains twain by trallis—radamasanthus the watermelon bone—Higgins diddle, the redsox sunboys'll be in 4th place June & 5th place december & that's all, beancod—On top of Vulturesque Desolation the train orders'll oughta be simpler than twine 4 Engineer's an old anarchistic fud—Shoot, pot, proms were flowery purple lilac Richmond eve roadsters redlegs sweetdolls & wild palms bleeding on the reincarnated seabach father pramming oysters in a poppy corn basket with holy scowl—Robeflow disappears into the Golden Age with a falting tired didnt-make-it hand like Homer blind Demosthenes Dumb & Aristophanes may squat on the Peloponnesian Xertian defeat of our times for this is Prak, the Greek Jew, the Canuck Hindu, prolling, purned, spoot, spout, teapot, drank, drilled, dripped, dvished, pish, tish. It was just a lottawords foir nathing—noneless the railyards produced littlegirls, & up above the boyshadows the stars as Karuna as ever burned mighty rot glows that evaginated & opened holy rose hopes Oh ho for the penisenvious thunderbers & boomdockers from Hook to Hey Here & heave that caffeine down, old ladycakes & frogmurder

rivers & Angelo Noon running write a bleak glare inseparably terrified the parkinglots of destiny—it's all a lotta sand pilin up helplessly, harmlessly on itself obliterating the What Cave? If not oughta.

15   Let's dance—I go to your shack or you come to mine. Make a date. Do.
  "Spring rain;
      it begins to grow dark;
  Today also is over."
                Care-a-Wack
            Thus the dove advises—
            I am woken to you—

16   Rabeloid! I cant breathe any more Mrs Jameson so will you please whore out?—I'm drinkin with the butchers, shut up!—if that doesnt sound kind it's because shittly aimed right at Tard & miss't with an 8-point aim that might do little over Tokyo but Kyoto throwed it—as the later testify will show these brunettes of peanut butter & hate were made were made were built & wellmade O crying children hurt!—So, I say, but knowing there's no me, Grub.
  That's the saint
  Stump—all on a stump the stump—accord yourself with a sweet declining woman one night—I mean by declining that she lays back & declines to say no—accuerdo ud. con una merveillosa—accorde tué, Ti Pousse, avec une belle femme folle pi vas' t' coucher—if ya dont understand s t t and tish, that langue, it's because the langue just bubbles & in the babbling void O Lowsy Me I'se tihed—If I'da who what? the perfect lil cloudy coroid cloud colorods colombing in the back fish tail twill twat of heaven blue—What's the blue, fly, what the drunk, fall, the wild upbuilding reinsurgence & Golden Ultimate Effulgence you'll find in Train No. Let's Go—to heaven—Bob Kauffman wants to come too—all aboard—You'll find that this train has six thousand compartments—Ring!—Hello—Rail, please— They're calling the Who Clerk—he'll give us the right rail we'll go to heaven sure—the sweet golden clime when the trav'ler's journey is done, under the hill, in a cool tomb—death was too proud so I stopt—we communed underneath nature—and so

on—first level yr own mind then the earth is be level & no more mountains of hope—but just the slavic level flat expected crandall be-all & wise-all rhodomopordsomopholorophoshion crint

17   Saradalia wrote around the wrong rightness because he'd seen purple & gold visions swimming in consciously from the conscious ultra violet cosmic rays a the sun & fwang, twarl, tweeelll, twom, twerm I meant, Pearl, Immemorial Antequité Poil of Brooklyn Night-Bridge gray hope dreams sucking on the stairs the dead girl the new blues news of from Heaven endless radiations of magic blue salvation—Now how'd Kemp tell a fleapis when St. he'd a know'd there waint no Okie Song yander but Big Gorldpupple ringarond romp rillwash radamansus frallieng prodapiak, ratamita samantabhadra unceasing compassionate hope that with congruent bent stick as soon as he saw real deep & realized the lights were still there he understood he was a messenger, the Angel, one eye out—For Lucifer Moidner rant rag, rack, it's okay, these purloined potato perfunctory alliterative rubouts add up to sweet Popish Purple Paradise

18   San Francisco has no vaults—San Francisco has no vauty—Singalrad the sailor Sam said he saw in the so—Go—The students outside the monastery window have subsided in their chatter, light—Ran and farted to show his old rock routine & so "wom?" (Rom Tom?) (Vaii) hmf the noises (cloat) out the window, scratch, I Old Angel Midnight hear—Silent Indurm Twandee Yokle Hour when we'll begarret Sam Ashton Tom Belligerent the Hackett Master Beckett—Or sometimes lightly known as Yarp Yarp—Cop ski kimona moodia, Ah Su, tchétché, the cop coughs, I hear the taxio fi fu—old Monster Hufu the Zen Froofroo is now going to vain his glory by be shitting himself in gruel birth—Ning—Anais Nais Thaïs Ming—China Tink Hongya Ming Mon the Bong—Sing, & yack dank bar poets wont Listen to old Kanuck?

> Sarry, Said Sarie
> I'll Metemple You Mowley
>   in the morning
>   Betemple and me demple
> hey me that

Tzimou m'appelle dans
cour d'archelle
Archangel Once Wing Swing
Ah Sigh God
Tu mar a ma danna
tu dona, padrone
Poura tu jama faire dire
Tes grand
ecritures?
Ecrivida
Old Angel Midnigh rant rock
rail rowout mo tarn
rong igo I kfuck
me j akle
be dakle
Mc Graw

19   Stop playing you candassed tripe heart,—common, let's
have that aw story—lost your moidening rag in the angry shack,
& wick warnt long enuf you poota—Sing for the general store
of rain that will hail bedown the—

20   "Spit on Bosatsu!" says Gregory Corso—"Oo that's beau-
tiful?" I say—Dash dash dash dash mash crash wash wash mosh
posh tosh tish rish rich sigh my tie thigh pie in the sky—Poo
on you too, proo the blue blue, OO U Nu, hello Buddha man

21   Me—who was Old Angel Midnight that railed at the rant
& eat steak at the Met & threw ballet girls out the hall & pinked
with my wife in a shower bath—Beautiful blue Jean Marais, the
denzing champion of Europe—rurt—Bing bing—the flames
of the candle say 'Leave us alone, we have a lil ole window of
our own & we happen to know too that the whole Universe is
saying'—'Shut up you moidnees and mardeners and gardens
of marden, man, silt soft silt the sound we ray—We weigh ev-
erything in the scale of time, I say, pajestically plurting in the
perfect platoon—illiterate me that —but tramwise, tranways,
what'd you mean, tranways, tramways?—Oi, Russia has funny
scrolly drawings broodled on midnight doodle pad, we'll never
see—But Shostakovich know me, & candle fall—Burt—Was

Burt was the sweet star swang in the hall and was killed in the war and nobody I know of cried—Old Angel rant shack mack Mill Valley rack shap, map, dap tag was bon tailored when I win-gee was Prez—

No, Prez never presented no such horn like that, Prez was the bezz in the bizzness, man, mon, Prez was the end and the man on the end Prez was the champeen pole catcher in the world—the outstanding window the sound that came through
dwerrrrr

22   Old Angel Midpike, wasnt the hike that was wedded to the fike?—the eyniard one-eyed piratical rat who ran roting thru the puderdical halls of Pwince bone yelling 'Hay to de tree Hay to de tree' and keppersnews the Viennese pastrymakin inkdweller pulled a party of sansi fancy sans souci dans and whammed em their spats, till Tillie the Late Tat, leaking from her holepot, organized redgangs to remnant his sin, and Jin, the magic bottle boy stolen from the Bagdhad ship shrouds routed Golgotha with a sling and arrow and had all the Queen Mother Superiors gasping in parks—Remember it quite well and well aint he coming home late? Twang in the window and see if he'll tweak his old beard at ikonoclastical me, poor dear—Dolophine robin roved a long way to bring balm to soothe his blue bus—Well like I was sayin, and anyway atchoo, your water's boilin, aint you?—Not much I can do about it Mrs Twandow as seeing as my Sandusky Husband comes home driving in the green light tho he's colorblind, he traded all the sneakthieves & secret narcotic police to the Virgin on the Wall, & she et em up raw like candle wax—His old father upfaced in a tomb—His knives and forks on top his cakes—His "hands burning"—a la Gregory Corso—His use of Gleem toothpaste in canvases—No joke, son, that wall has more ears than Ebon'll allow—How many ears that wall?—as many ears as you got lights in all space everywhere every atom's on fire—hands—How gruesome the smoketacle of people burning in rooms—the yurn of their faces when the airoplane crashes—Ah Mrs Midnight I cant understand—You understood this afternoon when you hung out the wash—Yes I hook out the wash with a crook of my thumb, & whistled so sharp and hubby came home and kissed me too—but now's playing cribbage at Vicious McStoo—Oi oi pearl,

pearl of the sea, flow through my window, bring whiteness and money and honey to me, bring hunner to me, bring butter and knives and archives and archangels bring them all to me and Molly Magee of Dublin Bloom—bring that to me, wall-ears—Sky's only got a fartin passage for you babe, message, what you expect from bean chamberpots and laundry in the lavenderia washing-machine, you expect roses? or worms? oi? You expect howling storms?—smath me to smithereens this aint the Bronx—if itn was the Bronnex I'd cancel it—cank—konk all you want on your juicy window, mirror-face, I'se a old lady was weaned i the bowels of the air the earth what's the big difference between air & between earth?—Ai, pickles in the barrell, and poetry too, but what's with your husband aint comin home early like he used to bechunes?—S Writ in the cards of my mother's birthveil—Ojaya Ojaya the company buzzes throughout the world in a hundred thousand cities of rooms, the ha dal baddra of their midnight babble, all talkin at the same time, NOW,—Oi poor humans beings, I grieve for you—I been in steel jails but Oi, it was no worse than the best that was it of the this—When I sent cans of Accent to Greece disguised as heroina I didnt have poolhalls in my basin—I had basinettes made of lapels and bassettes (brass badinettes for strange badinage—)

23   Spat—he mat and tried & trickered on the step and oostepped and peppered it a bit with long mouth sizzle reaching for the thirsts of Azmec Parterial alk-lips to mox & brama-jambi babac up the Moon Citlapol—settle la tettle la pottle, la lune—Some kind of—Bong!—the church of St. All's blasts the Ide afternoon & all holy worshippers go confess to Father Everybody with Good Friday ears—Friday afternoon in the universe—

   Bong!—the twackle how wackle of high Berkeley parties, the twanging and walking and cops carrying guns, *bong!* the church bell of Ah Ide the Master Hunchback primavera Cat of the Soiled Star universe—and him with his Priam—Well I never, and late at that, and's got cramps

   Bong! the midnight the mirror the red rust of the rosy atmosphere of the ikon the candle the babyface sleeping—

   Bong! enough of the bell dear Lord God above, enough of the eeny miney mo bell

Bong!—alright Mr. Poe, Mrs. Twurn, Mr. Twart, rart, I'd like to indicate by moon medallion indicative half-ass magic your prophesy, & what fool will post make Lear of you, or what Twang-Bang arrow drape in your vein, or Sicilian Stiletto in the streets of Old Spain—Bong! if it's n midnight by now, mid nigh, by now, I orta see myorta about a you know what er—horse—er—man about a farting horse—man about a Brooklyn Bridge—in brief excuse me I go shit—ugh! Ow!—dont pull at my oliver twist ear!

24   The things they say that come in thru that window—if only I could avoid what I hear—

Wasnt it Dostopoffsy who gossipped so much, and that Balzac in *Cousine Bette* O my—And Tristram Shraundy Shern, marvelous book, and Elmer Payo Robinson, the author of Oogoon, and Shmarl Baudelaire, the Skid rick rant rentfence iron night holder (of Paris) over rooftops of smoking shame— Ole Hornshaw too the Gerst poetizer, with Ilium and Troy, and Inali Minoan Retreat the Great God Ur, that was mailed to Philip Whalen—the samadhis of Hanse Majesty, trop trick driver of mountains, Mt Baker and Mt Olympus, parthenonical backtracker over old trails, Schneider by name—Gossipers there're none like Allan O Shinzberg, Levinsky my Feetsky, tweedy old Mayo Opo Waldo Meldo Elmo Poe, the junkey from Wall Street, and the Hawthorn person haw and sleet Melville who made subterraneans live in rooftops of shame in the shadow of the Brooklyn Bridge and John Holmes creamed (the aunorthist not the noet)—Hang my fryinpan cover over a nail, wont you, & I'll bank the ikon—and turn on electric light, and see what I'm eating here, hairs of 19 0 ten—

Poo! prat! two taxis played two little musics—then "brrrrrrrrrinsss" big gugly whatname truck came by signifying the nothing of the sound afternoon—

25   Like's legs that goosed the underground schoolteachers & Joyce who always wanted to write blind what the sea said but grinned restoredly in the sea first, himself a gable of coral roan, hears now in my behalf the scree of old railroad iron twisting faggot cargos of ESYirt by the shiney MOsoon vessels of the Packet Bay to bring elum slippery to Gaza & the Strip of Fez

where donziggerls grab boycocks—easy as pie that window
Islam sea roar, that purebeacon, that Sherifian splendour, that
Lustre Magno hide in the Me high hill Virgin Ma Wink—so's
on opium old Joe Black come home hammock Florida tree-
hack—I heerd that HEAL pass thu—I feeled it pass that heal by
thu—I seed that hole the hail made—And if in every window
hovel would words sung beard prophet flip nothing mean, then
hie thee New Gab Haven bring lice shit rooms to steel necktie
lover of tomb, never heard a nanny bray like that—Old Angel
Midnight Worldwindow bong midnight interlude Eternal Al-
ready

26   Old Angel Midnight just writes itself as it is the Hi-Is
Sound—miracles of Jesus in Capernaum—so that it might be
all fulfilled as twas writ in Akashia—but see the future writ in
present state illumina—what does the horizon of the sea got to
do with singing boy?—John Kerouac transliterator of perfect
knowing, angel from heaven, messenger of the right hand of
God & of the Godness of All hath no warm place to lay his head
but must cover his knees with both hands & despair, the great
weight of bleary time—

27   Ah but Old Angel Midnight Africanus the message in the
dream block roundsquare tenement boom from the subma-
rine Joandream ships, destroyers & escorts, putput fez & all
rhythm fishermen sprayling in the bay sand—Trumpets blare by
the moon sea the Arabs barge to redhat olivegreen majesty &
old black scow ESPERANTO—movies about that. Vast stupid
Kerouac-o——

28   Light the candle to the continuation of the hot afternoon
Ah now I see she's turning gold & workingmen are done till
Monday Morn & come home on now straight with buckets to
their dens, lions all balls—dash, Bach Chevrolet—Even the 2 lil
Chinese hogmoyens are propping along beneath the Tall Silk
Void anxious to get in ere tree twisted to rock plum blossoms—
Plump haired belt dog pop O looksee where the redheaded
spreaded her leglets at last in the Midden, & in Spain the Caper-
naum call of children Chorus boys "There's nothing like our

religion" so sew the dress & wait for the golden electricity to
make you right—for you know, Big Oldie, your maw's right &
she waits for you midden plumps to ard out more polychro-
matic Spirochete to mix like Marble fudge in that Tchelitchev
Tree of Life & bring forth busting another prime plump poy for
your posy grave & they'll say wasnt that my Ard Craven Bard
Bar Pap I saw upfaced to Tomb?—No, that was the Eternal
Consoler passing thru as Knife yard, his white shirt knit by Rim-
baud Angels did sweep aside the river mud from this intact and
classify crystal, so that so-that could soolidat smarty pine—Ah,
yar—but she yawed so much & I had to be saved from drunken
bumhood by these words, will excuse me if cant read my jazz
right because this floorboard language'll hide bettern nails the
Emily Dickinson worse-than-ever dahlic drent bent despair of
me with my raw muscles bulging in the mirror of pride, lank
low face all set to prove novels as soon's crick goes soring out
the other side my arm I'll tell you een more but now it's comin
on Friday night & GLEE yell the children of Paris running over
the grass of St. Thomas d'Aquin where supplicatee hold artistic
Europe oil hand out to be larded poignarded bathed powdered
put away ah all the Napoleonic troubles in this pastry!—Tie it
all together, Jack, the mirror doesnt show the real right

29   Eternally I accuse you of being as craven a shit as Frank
ever planked on that Leo butcher board so's mice could be
crying safe in the arms of Jesus—the Little Christ! You! Why
dont you mind your bexness! The less I hear of em the hap-
pier I'll be! Do I have to come back in another lifetime or
next month & let you have it where you need it so's I can live
my private label life free of libellous old you, continuous old
Cronk tokay ass hole hurrying to your place to be maitled &
draigled & dragged & even hipe Wop Cork knows you you
scandalmonjous gossipping non Dostoevskyan shit of the ages!
I'll flow golds of venom thru your window & you receive it all
like some old Universe SLUT—What kinda man are ya, Slut?
Or what kind good slut can you be anyhow with no twat to tie
it? You & your marble wax samsarhood burning up nothing but
candles of worry hate & shame, bug wart pastyfaced *bustard!*—
I'll cut your head off with my machete fingernail, & yak make

crack your Orienral thats what you want faces, I'll fix you, Gossip! Old Flap of the Shrouds, sheet on the line, Twandow shit, shirker, fuckface of history, go home & blow yr wife & leave mine & mine alone!—O o o o r g ! G o o o r d ! B l o o o d ! —I'll have your pasty flesh feed for Merrimac fish another time corpse you Joan kid crack bedeviller fool & Faust fuck! Who wants your dirty Old Words?—Pray for us on Hester street, dear Lord, do you exist? Pray, for us on Arameia Street, dear sweet save-me Lord—Save me Lord is just it, *you*, alone, let the others boil in marsh harrico, slong as you can slomp & fall in your slop barrell—no *words* boy to describe it—What?—Your *hate* fulness! Your hatful of emptyheaded raindrops! I orter throw you off the fire escape, myorter, wouldnt do no good, you with your headstands come back the next day all healed (hear me boy, just kiddin)—you're a good enuf old boy but my God you write too much.

But I'm only reporting the sounds out the window?

Well gate a fet reporter & go call charlie in the bar, turd, and find your old Peace & pink in yr own home showers & leave Fitzgerald alone & Marcus Magee or go strangle bobbies in the fog, do something butt dear God in the Arse, leave me alone & MINE!

Ah Angel Midnightmare—

Ah Crack Jabberwack, play piano, paint, pop your pile anum coitus semenized olium o hell what's his biblical name, the pot that spilt in the room ere Sarad had hers, ad her share, the name, the word, for masturbators, the Neptune O YA you know the name, the Bible Keen Mexican yowl that old tree still hangs in the same moonlight—Ilium, Anum, Ard Bar, Arnum, Odium, Odious, *ONAN*! ONAN KERAQUACK go heal yr own toiletbowl, stop dropping shavings in mine, & leave my grave unsung, my death unlearn, my qualities you can have, but onanist no quarter given you Angel Midnight by in that holy gallows of the moon!

Do I dream?

You dream not, switch yr dolophine midnight bell bong on some other frequency—*dont you know?*

Know what?

That there's a white cross marked X in the road where you will die yr dog's death & there to burn the piffle on your pier the ship will take you straight to golden essence & you be still?

Meanwhile?

While mean you mean well? Switch houses, try Killiams!

Junior Killiams, that laird Cregar'd high big muff moitang mouk moity biff jaw?

Same, with sluggerous pall in the ach—

In the ach & ah part tooth ache of peotly? The prime love thighs not for me but bearded shit not listen see till tee give me ernest majesgetafree? Why?

Because foiled the poor luke bird.

Fuke the luke fool bird foiled, I want oil!

Take oil in other Shelves.

Message received.

Close your window.

I'll open it tonight.

Let the stars fart their message unpolluted by human one, please hee?

You that bonged dolefully with benign crasher on yr head in old heroic dawns—

Ach, same, shamed, let me nightsoil be—

United purefoy Clown.

Besides you kill bugs with the rash of your pencil deed crashing on holy ivory love papers meant for scented notes from sweet jissom creatures clacking down the Barnard trees—Wash your drawers, draw the river in, pull that grave dung reward over yr noble nose, blow out the Candle & if you fail is that hardest on me?

I'll go mad as a bush.

And burn, please, the hardwood floors hiding me.

30   Mindscreaming blood perturbation pisspot—Mindscreaming blackjack Lanka Mountain laughter—

You're making it all up so why worry about being or not being? Thus rolls The Angel Midmoke

31   Put put put tiPousse all's to go well your mew gold taken good care of you, no only roan neigh yak plan reign can slay

that rose oboed flow soul I robed you say satin devil—Jesus will bring you all—Wait'll the music starts, little flicks of millionfold billionminded fleet stars thronging all for a chance to live try sentience come swamming down your hard vale, whyfor hard-vale boy?—Did I seek to bore your butter heart with mod iron skew in ogly scag iron bottomed ogroid doididoidee worlds bestrew your natural sweetness avant? No because loved you, love you now, no words of Mortal disfamous postifillication & bile pow gonna ruin my blue eyed pootuin toot where happily sanging frank lark lovely bardo.—No.—So let heaven instruct thee, earth no bug thee, go fly as free as you wish to be, sing window bedelong bidiliyoukidiligoo sweet-sweet Tu Fu bird oriol paradise Chinee garden all ya want!—Soft, you my dangle gentle playful little pip leak I bring you deliverance but you must listen to Daddy Snow arms when's he got to say to you:— pat on the folld

32   Brrrrring back the early wave, pearl—now cometh upon us the time when diamonds shatter, all love & hope gone, all tirlish bang, all fort might be dizened underneath the snow white salt wall, all lost undersea blue lips buried in grime of guilt in this crystal clarity recall, all bugs burned in the Raid of Time and all fard heard none such scone throw yield nothing but goom & booboos—poof!—The child, the circle drawn in air, the primal matter primal substantial energy polled & lost two votes elect the last twat & tit you too, I hope the diamond shatters into a billion glittering smithysheens of Croo because now Lustrous Midsoil I been pointed out, begallowed, hung, prophesied, Karma'd, Kaught & kitkatted up the ass of God Guilt & when I turn my back on this poor world I got no back to do it with, who will forgive the scribbling devil? When Snow Dad armed me with promises not kept & blamed me & booted me seedy cold hills, urk, ouch, my hand hurt, I tell you I wont tell you no more, why should I poignard me old shoulderblade with this machete matter? And country matters decide cities full of hurt children buried in the groomus womb of Bellevue Morgue—And fly stars purporting and all p's & pop it, blaming poor children for sighing under trees while long white trail ghosts swish in the river's foaming mouth, like semen at the

crock rotch math both Falls of Indio Doom, say, hark, promising star of homefather did you not pull sod blanket over baby's eyes & when you'd by his crib painted pink happy images of angels disporting ogre ord holes that turned to door opening monsters—monstranot love, mama dears—I was opiumed & killed in ole Tangiers—Every hate filled Arab & American in the world shall write explanation on a bier, every priest draw his bread clanging pisspots of grime, every philosopher suck up the claimant genius for his lifehood gold, every critic shit, every fancy poet fall, every bear devour Elijah rex rot, & every publisher & scribe be Pharisee'd in Castiglione's gloomy rager—me? my name? and I? go off father son & holy ghost of Martyr Life—And I will be silent, answer you no dong, Going Smock Syrup Midfuk, shit pearl pot, whatzyername, Luke Degger, erp urp rain watt Arkansaw south foil follow-up crooks & trees, I've had my roody filler that nard sauce & I'm going to die now, breath no more words pain on this silver & worry hatepage, I am the moth I killed in infant desire Hemming & Waying page of teen— London Jacked & Lusted the Liver out of me, been raped by sister king & knifed by brother queen & now all's I gotta do is appreciate the hardness & emptiness of rocks & go curfew & an old man in his hunchy death, sleek—purtier than Ava Gavovnar, more eepish than sic fop hat gargoyle Boilio the poet of the Lower West Side mural, gangster popoff racketeer evil slander murder shit kill quit cut fuck rape scream howl pump kill gate murder down imp I'se re gusted—because there never was a better opening than because—

Hear my song free stars, yet I can reach swelling moist, cunt of heaven admit my rod of justice, halls of Old Nirvana here comes Diamondshatter shat diamonds gave birth to Tathagata Garbha got blamed for Tranadaz & kilt in McQuentin & Mill Vallied st john hill gold huan so's *huan* one world could creep satisfaction to the creeps of literature

33 Foo, you yold yang

34 Then with balls swoled up one hung low leaving the action snake no biggern at, Oi, the lone woe of Lee Lucky his basketa pittykats earthquaking peoples balls outa sight & leaving

nothing but tremble-under-the-bed, the grace in Orlando turned out to be a gentle wee heatwave & a little shit (O shut up and say it!)

35   Sor god denoder pie your pinging lief bring Ida Graymeadow Wolf babe ooo brooding in the is-ness seastand grayog magog bedonigle bedart ooo the day Odin meeteth the Loup Gris, yag, ack, the day ooo dies—The day the gray wolf oatses Odin for his long slack-jaw slaver, asurp—When Ida Meadows her long gown camp the Persian disencamps & dusts—When the vision fades from the rough surfaces of Snorri & Sturla—When Eric Bloodaxe and Harold Fairhair battle for the final blonde on the last Icelandic prick rock—When Rodedodo grows Chrysanthemums by the door—When Eugene Bonedown burps—When Hair Redknife snaps the band—When Callicott Cobcorny crashes in motherlip—When Orristander boos—When Whitlip barks—The dog days of Egypt, bow wow wow—When Espinal gives the bull his final ass—When visions of the sea go 152—When Prick Neon's nailed to me! When Carrie Methodical Divine and the nomad Patzinak steppe bedazzlers (azzle dazzle muffed my gazzle!) the Napoleon fire rings, the slavers of the lip of Richelieu, Mazarin, Colbert, Lisieux, Ourmantelle, Archanciel and Pas D'Enfant kisses my ugly roar go-down seafeet on Oregon Beachie, when trappist divine speaking whistling the window roar borovates to the endless machine hum of endless infinitesimal worldspace oogloomosanical tarpidalisaclna multivantarn go-l-ta pian par music!—grag-ashash!—when burt me-davey-grave hung mine down poles the final lot across the rivie of Buddhas and last Potilic losts flint in the Old Star, ah me Marva, a flesh carney, ah river a day, ah strikeout, that's when I'll bring my lesson to thee, saith window to Me—And I cried "Window, what you mean?" Said window "O listen to the spherical booding moan star music the midnight study the Faust man devil harp in hand, O hum O moan O"

36   The little tit tat tadpole honey tweak of kitty lips on my toosy two toes make me think of dwiddle tingle springs the ditties of childerhood—sang—commanded Eyrdeadan showaps

to crail before my fire ping! OOlamona! call the sails, the frog croak eave drip never-rains-but-sweats Florida screenwindow with Avaloki tes var star twarping in my woondow—And did you ever say the wee that nack saw all farding blle on par ton take sick grick clap cat mat cack Mother? No that was a halting burgle—purr—eat & purr be holy kittypee pool in sand of red eyed bat bird insewecties pirking tig toont ta Ma tire free curé the school—A long unlearned heavy school noises of piano legs in the smile paradise bed? I saw lines drop like lint off kittyfur nightbed brain thought & never heaved to Atlas Shrug Toad help flashlight God but instead as written in old behooven Diamond, say, "I am grown so old & neutral I dont care"—Dont burn the cat! Second shelf for twickle cricket quiet cat held by nails go up fine smoke Burroughs in Tangiers'll smile smile smile—Thass iss the suundt corn tatl patac mo jambi va shan tu vi maranoomavala ta ya ta ta the high ladder speech King Hank made glorp by Harfleur diners Stein bock bash Autumnal Beer Wolfe final window broken smash & cats say   Krut

37   Murzner, the murzning zamming ience ouch feections possessing this itch it-globe with everybody fawlderolling around a rat satellite, paff!—spat!—kipf!—I'd rather roll kief in Ten Restaurants with bandaged athletes of Arab Sand than fwaddle fwo with Ojo Ji JoJo the Immortal Shine afternoon kidder of the India Lawn wrestlingmatch with Fatty Arduffy the goateed Bull gainin on death by inches of pot lard & him with childrees in a crib! Oi! Ugh! Oirk!

38   Tonight in Russia command the rooftops to cry up Gogol Dos-*toy*-evsky & Ark to lief the irk-bear buried in Freeze Sand Siberia general electrified eet-freeze come out with hank of Scythian hair in his paw, stop burlying bloody bed back and under*stand*! Stand under sails of Callèd Ships, command whitemuff Alexander Long Island come out kill lieutenants at his baby's funeral & if Achilles rotted in a Paird Tent so did Mercedez when he bested Oilope the Troller of Spain rag, Zorro—when Inquisitional keeners of green fields Medieval Aromoratic Armorica Eraldic Rivistica Spoign bedang the sand of rucksack tearboys dying by my mother's thigh of gold—O

dream! O Gary Snyder hero of compassion & poign! O Doll
Marshall beautiful! My mind rings with a thousand iced lizard
windows! I have no words for neutral! O poor bone burroughs
in your yard in Tangiers, what cats seek ye to study now? The
splendorossi ficuuiyus im-ling-star bangs around the landlady's
angrified lawn & still the priests whirl mind rooftop pederast
poignarx!—

   Command Ardemuffin fire eaters cornmuffining in splott Lee
Anne Burns the girlsinger from Hill Rich who when she throws
her legs back has thighs of gold snap! Wtttasher name, Lu Anne
Sins! Wow! Wait! Another forest primeval angel meet Hermyor-
ter de Gingold play with Rheingold Princeton dark Lou Grossa
punt ankle cock black as hairy murder in a lump of balls! Tie
onta that, Pat! I aint got no more callings at crossings enemy
diesel freeze, am gone to Rocky Mount flyin up to sunny cold
flagwhip Philadelphia! So sing the song of All-Vard! Raise the
hems of gold! Let sleep the peaceful ancient unclouded look
of Sunday afternoon antcities in my merde murdered mind of
moin—these parturiating pe-caco-ma-cunabulations in a Fire-
place Suicide Attempt do bespeak a deeper purse than purpose
John Roi who was overflowing with "poor perdu!

                                                      thin helm!"
                              the vision of
                              Medieval Europe
                              in a Shakespeare inch!
Hairbrush! Det! Wrench! Tont! Hanging sleepcloset stasified
pearl cat color of dark retreat & maybe sink in back, I want the
diamond shatterer bring it down return us dear Lord to Golden
Aeternitatis.

39   Uncovered by the uncut version cheapmovie produced
SWStarkike in High Heaven Lion roar Windtunnel never
made the bestseller list of Nigeria but sold Jesus' last sad word
to eager buyers & no Jesus to scat them out the temple—
separate from every science fiction deaddog, go own neutral
way, say nothing to airplanes on highways or obsolete strata-
gems of dinosaur battle-ships & all ye such crap & tiresome
world fawdle, I'm telling you God I sure is glad you Is—I sure

is glad you got star me Quixote bed cat & Ma love babies i' the
house & Greyhound posts for buses—I sure is glad I wont have
to perturb & gnaw on vulture lice erpastagraficus mona, name?
Tergiratirus Pastrofian—crewa, crow—The silent dharma arhat
crow of Florida cool-night makes my cats perk ears—So all ye
merry gentle

40   men may say the word
     the high on t high
     earliest berv

41   the who dont care
     I dont care
     fuck you all
     word free
     Zen Lunacy
     Old Angel Midnight
     kiss my ass word

42   Rapt wrote ditties, Ruckus did: as Wit: in my mind Bill
is a feeling movie providing—pro*vid*ing?—snow—*snow?*—for
mosquito.
   Mosquito of integrity not another State Funds suck you
integrity irregularity try Ex Lax perhaps ask ridiculous state
park fool or contract curtains exciting mosquitos fool by fool
good day Brown Field—refuse! These are the sounds of elec-
tricity pouring out of the soldiers pension checks cheaper than
fifty sentient veterans who mailed their checks to Mr. Serious-
charge—Ho! Window! Listen Gregory, science statement is
million years over owned by pens as treacherous as Aga Arnold
of Good Day Biddy Father Uptown—see? I'm a fool! I love
reverse! I got hidden Moo-Flutes in my horn cow. I did it dad
because I dood it money—I am Governor President! Bled this
state for years, Altruistic politician cheat-anyone William did, &
outsiders of nothing lit trusted stolen money rotten dirty fires
in alumni bowery to celebrate the Five Percent dream!
   Oig!
   Forget!
   The Burden Pen company was quilled a'ter the name of Hon-

est Tarnish Shakey Speary aspirer of championship virtue &
threatening son Hamnet, O Dad! My conscience is all snow. In
fact my conscience is coldspot. Deny no crime, avow furiously,
determined accompanied company jury friends for Colonel
Shoot Hog to say "Sho was a niggerlover wasnt he?" So Caro-
line with her wee wet spot out west wanted Bill stick his Pelican
in her key twat so she could yell

"Burt & Pen!
Burt & Pen!"

And that was how Innocent was born hating the sight of
me—ARtavasamagri! Famme twé! Battling the nail, loose, my
brain-pan doubled and I died crying I am dead! When a boat
parts water, dont look at people's asses? Fill your glass with
regal feeling beer cheer happening sun just naturally! Oranges
are balls of sunshine! Shut up!

43   That Christianity you have where the big fish doesnt eat
the little fish, is that the Christianity of the Cross?
     Yes, and of the Bo Tree, Cannibal

44   Birdleldeedlies in our morning fresh window, O my dar-
ling sweetheart I miss you, a dum, a duma, organs & light shake
twickles and erdio poralondo ogradar da the best fart test by
far every swung that did it so remember what God said to St
Benedict in the door of his cave at 6 AM in 892 "Live modern
with tile floors and walls"—And Danny & the Juniors answered:
"White Howl"—And Gregory the Great wept big tears for the
fall of Rome & the desecration of Apostle Peter's Holy Seat

45   Honeymoon couples play phallic worship, because while
the bride shows her breasts in a low negligee the groom con-
ceals hisun under pajama & bathrobes—Right?—"Let's go get
some sleep darling" means "Be long"—Everybody that ever
importuned boys in Portugal, or married glamorous young
blondes in wartime knows this—Everybody knows the rod of
justice—Eastern delinquent boat owners despair of airplanes—
Niagara Falls Violins the tower of city canadian police—Look
what silver girl is doing for gray hair! Arthur Paper Mate Flow
Gem Buddha adorned by hair centuries of Buddhi Toni—Lotta
talent in the Manger Bethlehem. The weather is Pew.

46   My soul's in my boots & my jockstrap holds up the stars hooray—Basie in London, O ye dreary backfences cheated me outa Limey Love on Waterlow Bridge and ann had a way, ya dreadful stargazing heaven of roof clup miz munk end-night fryingpan blaze gold silver material, all naught smashed & made unknown by blessed no-need catholic heaven saint Avalokitesvara, O—Now whisper, filter—Caint—You aint been to North Carolina Holyland of late—Sing, heaven brought honey dovey hero stars, spermfaced, open, grant, gone, gay, sweetliest mustarc auk mock honeybird of all friggling time—O my baby eateth pone pie, stands arms kimbing porch no-clothes cunthungry baby corn!—O child in Erse Love Bigstar Holyhood hunk crib!—O my mother! O secret Friendship!

47   Forty Which? O erse friendship, mak a laking smack tongue outa Luscious Midday moik out talk, hey then I'll pay you a hunnerd earnest children for your foy yoy candle coy-doy mingol bingle billshit pap outa me hang dont-let-em fuckoff flinging loc stare love time tak plot moy down Tangiers dreamy dreamies—See? Or bring curd yak lock lips lank hair legtledptay monshine—See? or drink less—But Old Angel Midnight I love you, you love me, let ernest sink here, I'll snow him moon star lip kiss Out Save his breath ah vaun—
      F is for
      F

48   Mona Leisure

49   Tswit tswit the tsweep bird of tree in the roaring gulf day, hay blowing in the hay truck ho truck horizon roar of Orlandoar—Trazzz the truck goin by in seatree beachie roar—OAR!—take this I-see dream ferry, go ahead stare at grapefruit you forget how to smash meditate when you went richy you forget movies make you sit whittle sick stick whittlefool you'll never make it now except golden pencil hurl eternidad outa bird tswip lost in explorer moon—O grapefruit! orange wheee waving moss-old void Saturday ecstatic there-you-go world—O I know all now, think I'll shut up—You, folks, can hear the rest in ear

50   Old Angel Midnight the swan of heaven fell & flew cock-meek, Old Angel Midnigh the night onta twelve Year Tart with the long bing bong & the big ding dong, the boy on the sandbank blooming the moon, the sound wont let me sleep & since I found out time is silence Manjusri wont let me hear the swash of snow no mo in ole no po—O A M, Oh Om, the Old Midnacker snacker tired a twit twit twit the McTarty long true—the yentence peak peck slit slippymeek twang twall I'd heerd was flip the hand curse lead pencil in the shaky desk ah Ow HURT!—Tantapalii the silken tont retchy swan bent necky I wish I had enuf sense to swim as I hear, o lousy tired gal—One more! Choired arranged silence singers imbibing belly blum

51   Wreck the high charch chichipa & get firm juicy thebest thebest no other oil has ever heard such peanut squeeze—On top of which you yold yang midnockitwatter lying there in baid imagining casbah concepts from a highland fling moorish beach by moonlight medallion indicative spidergirls with sand legs waiting for the Non Christian cock, come O World Window Wowf & BARK! BARK! BARK for the girls of Tranatat—because by the time those two Mominuan monks with girls & boys in their matted hair pans sense wind in the flower the golden lord will turn the imbecile himself into slip paper—Or dog paper—or that pipe blend birds never peck because their bills are too hard—that window paper

52   Silence in my window now in the fullmoon of haiku which goes OO yellow continent in a birdbath, April full moon which rattles the goldroom little death chair that never will collapse even tho you sit 10 nymphet girls there on yr lap fall to the floor to cellars of lust—and in any case O poet—O's of old world I love yr greatness & anyways tho what kinda world we'd have (Hi Missus Twazz) (O hullo Mr. Moon mock) a world all poits? geen! try Mawln Bwano? rurt—The old man is a moving plastic curtain whispering to find his girls pare soundless possle, the lovers next door hiding in back barn driveway the the the the the—Lottle ma songing starty this is no time to listen to just but-puff—shhh sez my Jetsun Yidam—Buddyo Ava Loki T—in Ole Oaxaca we'll find the magic boatyard knifed flame O wick, burn, or fall—The gossip among the stars is that farledee who

lit the moon end of dog turn Turk Town Tenneduck was Kan-
sased halfway to tripe because the long thin Stick Men & the
fat Slobs who ate too much have their mouths sewed up, writ-
ers their tongues yanked by hot irens, & Wolledockers of Old
Gallows England buried with the dust of ancient decapitated
horses of old dust Japan in bowed head oblivion that was meant
for all things crumble & disappear including (did you hear?)
Lury Marsh, Goniff Tward, Mic, Tokli Twa, Stabtalita Borotani,
Parsh Tilyur, Cock, Brrrocky ᴧᴧᴧᴝᴝᴚᴘᴧ, & Tot.

53   Even from heaven now O ladies & gentlemen of the fard
world yr beloved angel dead are sighing sweet memoried per-
fumed thoughts into yr ears to keep you mindful that yr term
on earth aint naught or for not, but—bu yo bink the wick swans
both twist to balls the stasis hanging bathrobe—chairs crumble
& get put out on cleanup day, I saw one today I'd like to sit on
the moon on & be a turnpage comedian continent cardown,
tryna Satisfy Catholic girls from Harvard aint my pot a tea or
plate a beans, I'se sorry oh son, lays & genmen, to the next
Bardo (bardic?) (forgot) Tibetan (tiss top?) plot lins to find it
Lama Lano lined the Turner Girl the mooma tannery where
they say the bellrope sank the clank of pisspot grime the tanker
that twirded for phantom Una southern Edward Papa river sod
stashy slasheen girl Irish father iron Irish god's green earth &
die there—either that, My Dame or pourquoi?—Bed wrinkled
dinkled from too much sleets, mosser dear? Got shot charge
Rebel joyous Georgian by witchcraft. Ah, & what lunchcart?
The one with 69 year old daughters & 690 pound brothers &
all the stars of Alex Manhole clear to Rubber O North Carolina
Oklahoma Indian pips—urgh, & what else—The moon, this
Friday evening she's already full & full & full on late afternoon
board blue over trees & sandbanks—Dont mention his name!
He will burn Buddha's babies in this house! He will hasten
dust! Nothing but faith like Abraham believes in hallucinated
true heart of dumb uneducated glimmering self 'cause the void
is all illumined now & Milarepa had she-demons bouncing on
his john because he loved red fires in his (fires in his?)—well,
just red, Ned, & be sure to—to what?—bank the ikon—what
Ikkon? The ikon silver cross that was almost buried with my
brother—thank you brother—See you anon, my pat, my lemb,

in Cielo soon's—soon's what?—soon's there's room in endless
meaning to accept another meaningless liar pushing pencil for
to die in happy breath so nobody could see

54   peep
                        peep the
                    bird tear the
                sad bird drop heart
                the dawn has slung
            her aw arrow drape
          to sissyfoo & made eastpink
        dink the dimple solstice men
      crut and so the birds go ttleep
    and now bird number two three four five
      sixen seven and seven million of em den
      dead bens barking now the birds are yakking
      & barking swinging Crack! Wow! Quiet! the
    birds are making an awful racket in the Row
    tweep ?   tswip !   creet !   clink !   crack !
  ding dong the bell rope bird of break of day
          O k a y b i r d s q u i e t
                  P l e a s e

                      you birds
                        robins
                        .black & blue birds
                        redbreasts & all
                        sisters,———

                      my little parents
                      have the morning
                      by the golden balls

          And over there the sultan forgot

55   Ah old angel of midnight I cant hear myself think for all
your scur racket the lead in yr pencil on simple asinine page so
noisy what's a man gonna think of this unless the rumble house
black as snow horizon train brings back all our favored dead
from furnace & somebody furnish—Ah car, a human directing
his tatismatatagolre thru Holland to find the Dutch Imprimatur

to his Helem, the Helm & Cross of Charlemagne Euron Irope
that meant no more no less that Quebekois Canoe (Kebokoa
Kano)—Kak! But rumble will the devil his will's unspoken, God
wont truck helicopters to peek-at-wisdom Vulture Queen, nor
will the red dog that glitters at the fish queen of my heart reach
for kite hook or Dahlenberg drent it any different for by the
great God Jesus I will not rest no wont rest till Ferlinghetti's
dog his day had does piss again on hydrant hydramatic still-
ness electrical ectroid where for sure cats of the stripe so proud
& vainty do vaunt for to bring the final jumpmonkey home
to Marpa's bird sing—Ah translate me that—Cook! Dog echo
in the sandbank valley Northport rumble Mahayana the dia-
mond Vajrayana path that was trod here long ago before those
houses jewel-graced the seaside hill, & for Krissakes no sound
at all comes in this window except those Wolf Hourses got
tamming bringing white & gray pearl hearses thru the shoot
rain to munner munner munner, O fat eater in the drape son
push yr belly back, the tape worm—& worms to measure you,
long tape—sod & sand over yr bluenose disdain, Mrs America,
the Indian's Ya Ya Henna, the Indian Uprising known as the
Beat Generation, is going to eat rails & make tire sandwiches of
every junkyard misty rust & all old heroes' eyes in barley Soup
of time—to be sopped with eye sop—So carry on, escaper, jail's
only made to flee—

The wush of trees on yonder eastern nabathaque Latin
Walden axe-haiku of hill where woodsman Mahomet perceives
will soon adown the morning drear to pail the bringup well
suspender farmer trap moon so's cock go Bloody yurgle in the
distance where Timmy hides, flat, looking with his eyes for purr
me— O Angel, now is the time for all good men to come to the
aid of their party, & ah Angel dont paperparty me, but make
me honified in silken Honen honeyrubbéd Oxen tongue of
Cow Kiss, Ant Mat, silk girl ran, & all the monkey-better-than
secondary women of Sam Sarah the Sang of Blood this earth,
this tool, this fool, look with your eyes, I'm tired of fooling O
Angel bring it to me THE MAGIC SOUND OF SILENCE
broken by firstbird's teepaleep ——

Good East! Hard to blow out! Sometimes! Darkness in my
final kip. This shot will send the gossip mongers yarking back

to Harvard frail slat, soft, full of gyzms in slit lacéd hatreds for light is light O Lord, O Lord, I pray, my Lord—Again! Once more! Ta ta ta ! Om

56   Ack, who gives a ruddy fuck about all this American showoffy prose I'd like to know why Whane meant horsefly & Brane something like, & why Owe's Born is Awe's Dead, & all our intelligent handsome Tedsy Boys go yearning after our pink pages & never find & all the riots in Pixy Dilly & all the Traf on the Square, Elgar with his music doesn't impertaramount the rock of Murican roll? For strings? Air? O nonce, node, these babic yoiks, these Inds, these stupidities, these gem americans

57   TWO DAYS AGO, MARCH TWIP, 2059 (AXTONO) (WOW the twip of that carry-on I'll never fly another Yet to Souski that country wont feed me nothing but ersatz gata-gatpataraze which is a kind (wow, the munsch) of farlidalta-manigalo the color of which, well, yr aunt Mary mighta told you but O the gossip in these other galaxies just too much my dear the rurn, the klen, the hoit, the noises of Flup. There was Onat Roren, Bob Torlignath the Crank, the Cranker of Hono-Machines, & the Bile Pister of the Falledern he was there be-sartifying all his meanies & the meannesses & told me I didnt have praper green in my pen gat—But he B.O. was alright, felt good, was glad because her time was late, & as for those publications up there that they turn out with all their bearded Trees extemporiating on the state of the talismanic oral pata—
    I just got tired & retired but got involved in a long tat with Sinabad Talgamimargafonik Crud the interesting fool from the well located (in emerald waters) continent of Magic who told me there was a Sound recently developed by Shitteers that wd eventually require dog whistles hanging from breast teeth & bug micro bugs & long swarms of Milky Wayers vacationed over from Blue Curtain Country listening to the Country Pard say: "The tanitat of this Omakorgeklid is infested with Imagery & therefore white as moon—but O my Thinkers never let it be said the sooth—"I couldnt listen to any more besides I had a deadline to meet & new flows to fii so came back to good old Tierra del Firma & had Princess my Tabtate, (solit) go eat an-other bont, which meant I only had 2 days to wait till today so

rested up reading ancient texts & spent all night watching the
sun on the moon the sinking mountain till all vanished & even
MRS Stone made no comment but slept & that is my report to
you today, my Dotggergsamtiianidarstofgiviks

58   I just cant stand these people I teel you I dont know what
I'm going to do about them, start my motor or fart my passage
but you the way they carried on last night, *him*, with that dressy
little deaful foosy on his lap the boom of busting chair & all that
boommusic on the juke box & I dont know I wanted to call
the police & get rid of this sandbag pineneedle Bodhi neighbor
who is such ugly bearded dirty" ("nothing on earth or in any
terrestrial sphere or in any Buddhalands Heaven or Mockswarm
of Einsteinian & non-light Light can take hold my brothers &
sisters & cousins because it is only the wisdom of manifested
epiphany & the compassion of goodbye"—) (as soon as I can
find a bully club & bang a hole in imaginary fence I tell you
this will be the last time the window's with redlegged devils
& stone blue eyes—) (Kunfii, garayen, hallo Kiyan, fitiguwi,
katapatafataja, silya, kitipuwee, senlou, saint loup, coish, karan)
(or vaunt the moidners the Villa Viva Pancho baby Mexico
City sorefoot Juarez old hotel wino El Paso march picking up
six thousand partisans to vest the peon with his land coat so
that years later Rivera murals shine by army teahead trumpet
in Ole Texcoco) "there'll come a day when that yurn I'll have
to astabing the zemble the cartifacartilage I wont have another
moment of—Dry up, dry up, moist earth, dry up, dust ball,
dutball moon is sick of leering at your inadmissable sorrow be-
cause it has no twat to to tie onto't—And we the fooly libs that
think ah music airplane & all ye screaming birds of falsedawn let
the ephemera existence wait at yr side with you for end to't—
No other teaching hear & hear tell & what of that the sound
who wants to hear—Go fetch the gardles & make open the
corridors of your Bright Room mind the Lord is coming he's
all white & gold, he's a pink white angel in a black room by a
blue window & a yellow candleflame with golden (hurt) wings
the color of all thingness, the swarming dove, there! See it! He
stands at yr non-side sides the waterbaby by the baby shroud,
the honeyfall, the bliss blessed to be believed, the final pollitabi-
mackatatanabala (fine as fine can be) (Ah Ah) (HO HO) leap &

dance it's saved! the nerve of that man ! foru ! mon ti kitaya ! patakatafataya—perk ! prick ! prick ears I mean you think I let pollute window liars? Oh God, stop it—

When God snaps his Finger of Gold & suspenders too the world will wake in the well looking at the dark star—this silvery desert full of gophers rattlesnake tracks & sobbing moons of Chihuahuan splendor I'll buy, tho, till that Babe of the Honied Fall is at my side again for nothing, nothing, nothing, absolutely powerfully lightly emptily goldenly eternally nothing ever happened & this I bring to you from grass i the sun (to tell of it, the cock in card the soft & mixup pushing bardahl Drutchen cant & dent of it I wount hav it, ht Anyway) (seurain) (sunrin) (booya) J'm'enva arretez ! Fo.

59   Aw rust rust rust rust die die die pipe pipe ash ash die die ding dong ding ding ding rust cob die pipe ass rust die words— I'd as rather be permiganted in Rusty's moonlight Rork as be perdirated in this bile arta panataler where ack the orshy rosh crowshes my tired idiot hand O Lawd I is coming to you's soon's you's ready's as can readies be Mazatlan heroes point out Mexicos & all ye rhythmic bay fishermen dont hang fiish eye soppy in my Ramadam givecigarette Sop of Arab Squat—the Berber types that hang fardels on their woman back wd as lief Erick some son with blady matter I guess as whup a mule in singsong pathetic mulejump field by quiet fluff smoke North Carolina (near Weldon) (Railroad Bridge) Roanoke Millionaire High-Ridge hi-party Hi-Fi milliondollar findriver skinfish Rod Tong Apple Finder John Sun Ford goodby Paw mule America Song—

60   Arguing about mudpies in the hot spring sun karu, myota the Japanese ⚡ who wrote of 者 was always concerned about his poison oak hut when they came bringing him early dogwood buds with a bleached rock & the trinity of rocks & yak of black-bird pearbranch jumping & the Umpteen yumping erse Norway Man of N'o'r'm'a'n'd'i'a (who repaired houses?) (who made new moons bider) (brighter) (?) (bider) of time the bider the cross in his tomb worm & the King on his epistaff stone tomb port of north—Oh—All ties in you see like fish pier respect.

Fish spear shook?—shook aimed & breton rocked—

O but just as long as sun shines like this in yellow airplane on the pebble Beach sky & pear yump yak blossoms (up north)— & as long as red hydrants & post chaises—(gossip?) (Well it's a quiet moment but methinks the sons of the world & daughters thereof as wellus wolves & loups will be perfectly containted as long as they stay away from Ehrlich's dyemill blueworms which are et by OObaltory golbords & clover'ed & clobbered by mind's no-nature essence & as soon as they ask for an explanation say "What? buds in blue new sky?"

Dream for Muggy Mojump the quiet cloud.

61   Kertion Kerdion Keryon Kerson cherson & Who else in this ugly old Russia hechavel helps me in this business recordin sounds of universe midnight? but not a single damn dull fool podium hear it attestify that the selickman was a poet who decided to say:

I am a poet
&
here is my poem
Watch how fancy I write
Skeletons of Compassion dusting
in the distant heavens' infinity
while fat old burbles rememberem
well
here
on high hark—high hart—
world—diepork—

Over & above of which it was down in Charleston West Virginny one time my Pa in white shirt & unshaved shot a man in a poolroom fight—they chased him acrosst the Kanowa in a Kanoea (idiot) & got him down by the bayin hope dogs in that country where Old Angel Mama Midnight will lean her happy head & hungry eyes on pillows of Old in the high falutin poem of Heaven where little white house it waitin for all you black sufferers so's dandy'll say "Twas all writ & no more to say, the Vow of Gold is Done" & all yet young kids wanta know what a man do when he golden baby post up there he completes the

vow matures the Karma returns the Kitkat Clowns the Crown
Thorns the Flap and dad blasts him happiness forever, because
you'll see, in not too many years now, yr hope & grace-waves
werent jivin ya, all's taken care of behind these suffering trees
& inside these suffering bees & wont nobody harsh ya but say
kind star roof words & bring white cloth to your laundryboy
basket (clean as dinosaur teeth) & you'll know the—sore yah
he was sore but he said Bust me one on the jaw, I got the run-
ning eyes—With or without sugar—The Cat in the Con-Cord

    Lord, you presumptuous goodgiver, thanks, & go tell every-
body you Vowin hardass sonsumbitchcs—(hold clasp hand
TaTaTa)—Aye Bodhidharma

62   Tapistry the second writer
     in the novel island bearded
     scared wont use words saves
     he go's & hungerers of wood
     from boom in the Spain Jail
       hand on knees

     To go cross cemetery America
     highwire ratcroak dumpslaver
     moogow silo sillwindow rat
     wait moon shine on tin
     all the little inner outer sin

       peek at the bird
          tree, remember
       it again, the
   hoosegow goddam cuban
     Killer who moidners
       turtles, traps em cock
       in the nigh & never
       draps a wear

All day nervous wonderin what to do shoe in my armchair in-
nesfoo that was writ in Akashia I'm just hearin what my head
said & it's mighty repetitiousness

63   The black ants that roosted in my tree all winter long have just emerged to meet an army of enemy ants (same breed) & a big war is now taking place, I just looked with my brakemans lamp (by sunlight) (brake the day sun) warriors are biting each other's sensitive rear humps & killing each other with more intelligence about murder than my boot knows—I squashed one wounded warrior whose poor right front armorer was missing & he just croualtad coupled there, I hated to see him suffer & he was open (ow) for attack too, bit safe a mo on a flat rock used for lady's flagstones in the pink tea world which ignores ant Wars & doesnt know that when the first space ship lands on the planet Amtasagrak (really Katapatafaya in other galuxies) the ship will immediately be swarmed over by black ants, even the window obscured, they'll have to turn their X-Roentgen Gun Ray on it to see & what they'll see'll make em wish Von Braun had stayed in brown germany: one sextillion sextillion idiot insect fiends a foot deep eating one another endlessly the top ones scuffling, the next layer dead & being nibbled, the next layer belly to belly cant move from the weight, & the bottom layer suffocated at last—& the lady ants have wings & fly to little tiny planets that hang six feet above the moiling black shiny ant sea, where they hatch, push the grownup kids off (into the Mess) & die Sighing for Paradise O ye singers of War & Glory

      After seeing a thing like this who wd dare not ask for enlightenment everywhere? Who will deny ant war with me?

      Meanwhile in my yard the triumphant winning warrior ant stands over his defeated dying brother & you see his little antled helmet waving in the glorious breeze like How Ta Ra the trumpets of Harfleur & (you know what I was going to say there—hm—) no compassion in these little febrile finicular skeleton—O Ant Soup !

64   O Escapade escape me never I lied I lied I lied I'll never escape ex cape—of Spaign—God'll ever me allow to leave this hurt of ant scene until I lissen to his words & wave & point by saucer moon & antlered antennae &

      weird roofwash & weirder cross windows, the black clock by the white clock in the city's creamy tenement while one silk stocking waves to gossip the lady's lost leg & there's a slip by

a pair of paints waving in the moon breeze as well as a sheet
which however has no blaind stain of blood, only the one silk
stocking—& there's panties, littleboy pants, handkerchiefs,
towels & many cursed faint bigscrew'd oratan furykula yaink
antavyazers, with black hooks, sword spaces, windows the bot-
toms falling out & the moon a crink in its upper neck which is
really its back (Ah)

65   That grassy yocker pocking up yonder

66   Tonight the full apogee May moon will out, early with a
jaundiced tint, & pop angels all over my rooftop along with
Devas sprinkling flowers, pilgrims dropping turds & sweet
nemanucalar nameless railroad trains from heaven with omnip-
otent youths bearing monkey women that will stomp through
the stage waiting for the moment when by pinching myself I
prove that a thought is like a touch, unless someone sicks a hot
iron in my heart or heaps up Evil Karma like tit and tat the pile
of that and pulls my mother out her bed to slay her before my
damning dying human eyes and I break my head on heads—
Everytime you throw a rock at a cat from your glass house
you heap upon yourself the automatic Stanley Gould winter so
dark of death after death, & growing old, because lady those
ashcans'll bite you back & be cold too, and your son will never
rest in the imperturbable knowledge that what he thinks he
thinks as well as what he does he thinks as well as what he feels
he thinks as well as future that.
    Future that my damn old sword cutter Paison Pasha Lost the
Preakness again.
    Tonight the moon shall witness angels trooping at the baby's
window where inside he gurgles in his pewk looking with mewl-
ing eyes for babyside waterfall lambikin hillside the day the little
arab shepherd boy hugged the babylamb to heart while the
mother bleeted at his bay heel—And so Joe the sillicks killit no
not—Shhhhoww graaa—wing & car-start—The angels devas
monsters asuras Devadattas Vedantas McLaughlins Stones will
hue & hurl in hell if they don't love the lamb the lamb the lam
of hell lambchop. Why did Scott Fitzgerald keep a notebook?
Such a marvelous notebook.

67   Komi denera ness pata sutyamp anda wanda vesnoki sha-
dakiroo paryoumemga sikarem nora sarkadium baron roy kelle-
giam myorki ayastuna haidanseetzel ampho andiam yerka yama
chelmsford alya bonneavance koroom cemada versel
   (The 26th Annual concert of The Armenian Convention)

DESOLATION POPS

NOTE: *Desolation* is the name of the mountain . . .
Pops are American free-syllabled haikus . . .

1

Morning meadow—
    Catching my eye,
One weed

2

Poor tortured teeth
    under
The blue sky

3

Ate a Coney Island
    hamburger
In Vancouver Washington

4

Run after that
    body—run after
A raging fire

5

Work of the quiet
    mountain, this
Torrent of purity

6

Sun on the rocks—
    a fighting snag
Holds on

7
A stump with sawdust
     —a place
To meditate

8
The smiling fish—
     where are they,
Scouting bird?

9
Me, my pipe,
     my folded legs—
Far from Buddha

10
I close my eyes—
     I hear & see
Mandala

11
The clouds assume
     as I assume,
Faces of hermits

12
Satisfied, the pine
     bough washing
In the waters

13
Content, the top trees
    shrouded
In gray fog

14
Bred to rejoice,
    the giggling
Sunshine leaves

15
Cradled and warm, .
    the upper snow,
The trackless

16
Everlastingly loose
    and responsive,
The cloud business

17
Everywhere beyond
    the Truth,
Empty space blue

18
The mountains
    are mighty patient,
Buddha-man

19
Ship paint
on
An old T-shirt

20
Snow melting,
     streams rushing—
Lookouts leave the valley

21
Man—nothing but
     a
Rain barrel

22
Debris on the lake
     —my soul
Is upset

23
Gee last night—
     dreamed
Of Harry Truman

24
There's nothing there
     because
I dont care

25

In the late afternoon
    peaks, I see
The hope

26

The top of Jack
    Mountain—done in
By golden clouds

27

Hmf—Ole Starvation Ridge
    is
Milkied o'er

28

All the insects ceased
    in honor
Of the moon

29

The taste
    of rain—
Why kneel?

30

Full moon, white snow,—
    my bottle
Of purple jello

31
I'm so mad
I could bite
The mountaintops

32
Hot coffee
and a cigarette—
why zazen?

33
Aurora Borealis
over Hozomeen—
The void is stiller

34
Nat Wills, a tramp
—America
In 1905

35
I'm back here in the middle
of nowhere—
At least I think so

36
Poor gentle flesh—
there is
No answer

37
The storm,
     like Dostoevsky
Builds up as it lists

38
What is a rainbow,
     Lord?—a hoop
For the lowly

39
Get to go—
     fork a hoss
And head for Mexico

40
Late afternoon—
     the mop is drying
On the rock

41
Late afternoon—
     my bare back's
Cold

42
Wednesday blah
     blah blah—
My mind hurts

43
Kicked the cupboard
and hurt my toe
—Rage

44
Late afternoon—
it's not the void
That changed

45
Sex—shaking to breed
as
Providence permits

46
M'ugly spine—the loss
of the kingdom
Of Heaven

47
Thunder in the mountains—
the iron
Of my mother's love

48
Thunder and snow—
how
We shall go!

49
The days go—
    They cant stay—
I don't realize

50
The creamer gives,
    the groaner quakes—
the angel smiles

51
A million acres
    of Bo-trees
And not one Buddha

52
Oh moon,
such dismay?
—Earths betray

53
Skhandas my ass!
    —it's not
Even that

54
The moon
    is a
Blind lemon

55
Rig rig rig—
 that's the rat
On the roof

56
Made hot cocoa
 at night,
Sang by woodfire

57
I called Hanshan
 in the mountains
—there was no answer

58
What passes through
 is amusing
Himself being dew

59
I called Hanshan
 in the fog—
Silence, it said

60
I called—Dipankara
 instructed me
By saying nothing

61
I rubbed my bearded
        cheek and looked in
The mirror—Ki!

62
Mists blew by, I
        Closed my eyes,—
Stove did the talking

63
"Woo!"—bird of perfect
        balance on the fir
Just moved his tail

64
Bird was gone
        and distance grew
Immensely white

65
Misurgirafical & plomlied
        —ding dang
The Buddha's gang

66
Your belly's too big
        for your
Little teeth

67
But the Lost Creek trail
 they dont believe
Is in existence any more

68
Blubbery dubbery
 the chipmunk's
In the grass

69
Big wall of clouds
 from the North
Coming in—brrrr!

70
Aurora borealis
 over Mount Hozomeen—
The world is eternal

71
Chipmunk went in
 —butterfly
Came out

72
Holy sleep
 —Hanshan
Was right

BOOK OF HAIKUS

The little sparrow
   on my eave drainpipe
Is looking around

———

The tree looks
   like a dog
Barking at Heaven

———

Girl with wagon—
   what do
I know?

———

Tuesday—one more
   drop of rain
From my roof

———

I found my
   cat—one
Silent star

———

In the morning frost
   the cats
Steps slowly

———

No telegram today
   —Only more
Leaves fall

Frozen
    in the birdbath,
A leaf

———

First December cold
    wave—not even
One cricket

———

Cool breeze—maybe
    just a shillyshallying shower
That'll ruin everything

———

50 miles from N.Y.
    all alone in Nature,
The squirrel eating

———

2 traveling salesmen
    passing each other
On a Western road

———

The smoke of old
    naval battles
Is gone

———

The windmills of
    Oklahoma look
In every direction

Grain elevators, waiting
   for the road
To approach them

———

Juju beads on
   Zen manual—
My knees are cold

———

Listen to the birds sing!
   All the little birds
Will die!

———

Dusk—the bird
   on the fence
A contemporary of mine

———

Nightfall—too dark
   to read the page,
Too cold

———

Useless! useless!
   —heavy rain driving
Into the sea

———

Alone at home reading
   Yoka Daishi,
Drinking tea

The bottoms of my shoes
are clean
From walking in the rain

———

Coming from the west,
covering the moon,
Clouds—not a sound

———

Her yellow dolls bowing
on the shelf—
My dead step grandmother

———

Birds singing
in the dark
In the rainy dawn

———

Straining at the padlock,
the garage doors
At noon

———

Nodding against the wall,
the flowers
Sneeze

———

The earth winked
at me—right
In the john

November the seventh
   The last
Faint cricket

———

Well here I am,
   2 PM—
What day is it?

———

In my medicine cabinet
   the winter fly
Has died of old age

———

The castle of the Gandharvas
   is full of aging
Young couples

———

Early morning yellow flowers
   —Thinking about
The drunkards of Mexico

———

Wine at dawn
   —The long
Rainy sleep

———

Nightfall—too dark
   to read the page,
Too dark

What is Buddhism?
    —A crazy little
Bird blub

———

Crossing the football field,
    coming home from work
The lonely businessman

———

Prayerbeads
    on the Holy Book
—My knees are cold

———

After the shower,
    among the drenched roses,
The bird thrashing in the bath

———

The barn, swimming
    in a sea
Of windblown leaves

———

The low yellow
    moon above
The quiet lamplit house

———

Snap yr finger,
    stop the world!
—Rain falls harder

Beautiful young girls running
   up the library steps
With shorts on

———

Bee, why are you
   staring at me?
I'm not a flower!

———

Quiet moonlit night—
   Neighbor boy studying
By telescope;—"Ooo!"

———

Missing a kick
   at the icebox door
It closed anyway

———

Perfect moonlit night
   marred
By family squabbles

———

The Spring moon—
   How many miles away
Those orange blossoms!

———

When the moon sinks
   down to the power line,
I'll go in

Looking up at the stars,
    feeling sad,
Going "tsk tsk tsk"

———

This July evening,
    A large frog
On my doorsill

———

Dawn, a falling star
    —A dewdrop lands
On my head!

———

In back of the Supermarket,
    in the parking lot weeds,
Purple flowers

———

Protected by the clouds,
    the moon
Sleeps sailing

———

Chief Crazy Horse
    looks tearfully north
The first snow flurries

———

November—how nasal
    the drunken
Conductor's call

In Autumn Geronimo
weeps—no pony
With a blanket

———

Autumn night in New Haven
—the Whippenpoofers
Singing on the train

———

Peeking at the moon
in January, Bodhisattva
Takes a secret piss

———

A turtle sailing along
on a log,
Head up

———

A black bull
and a white bird
Standing together on the shore

———

Catfish fighting for his life,
and winning,
Splashing us all

———

The poppies!—
I could die
In delicacy now

Summer night—
   the kitten playing
With the Zen calendar

———

Trying to study sutras,
   the kitten on my page
Demanding affection

———

Hurrying things along,
   Autumn rain
On my awning

———

All the wash
   on the line
Advanced one foot

———

That's an unencouraging sign,
   the fish store
is closed

———

A whole pussywillow
   over there,
Unblown

———

The moon is white—
   the lamps are
Yellow

Listening to birds using
    different voices, losing
My perspective of History

———

The crickets—crying
    for rain—
Again?

———

Gray orb of the moon
    behind silver clouds—
The Spanish moss

———

Dawn wind
    in the spruces
—The late moon

———

Twilight—the bird
    in the bush
In the rain

———

Ignoring my bread,
    the bird peeking
In the grass

———

Spring night—
    a leaf falling
From my chimney

My cat eating
   at his saucer
—Spring moon

———

Rainy night
   —I put on
My pajamas

———

Black bird—no!
   bluebird—pear
Branch still jumping

———

Wash hung out
   by moonlight
—Friday night

———

The postman is late
   —The toilet window
Is shining

———

Dusk—boy
   smashing dandelions
With a stick

———

Holding up my purring
   cat to the moon,
I sighed

All day long wearing
   a hat that wasn't
On my head

―――

The national scene
   ―late afternoon sun
In those trees

―――

Glow worm sleeping
   on this flower,
Your light's on!

―――

August moon―oh
   I got a boil
On my thigh

―――

Empty baseball field
   ―A robin,
Hops along the bench

―――

Following each other,
   my cats stop
When it thunders

―――

My rumpled couch
   ―The lady's voice
Next door

Spring evening—
    the two
Eighteen year old sisters

———

Drunk as a hoot owl
    writing letters
By thunderstorm

———

Brighter than the night,
    my barn roof
Of snow

———

Gray spring rain
    —I never clipped
My hedges

———

The rain has filled
    the birdbath
Again, almost

———

My rose arbor knows more
    about June
Than it'll know about winter

———

Late moon rising
    —Frost
On the grass

The beautiful red
   dogwood tree
Waiting for the cross

———

Bird bath thrashing,
   by itself—
Autumn wind

———

A mother & son
   just took a shortcut
Thru my yard

———

Beautiful summer night
   gorgeous as the robes
Of Jesus

———

Eleven quick skulks
   to Fall
And still cool

———

Woke up groaning
   with a dream of a priest
Eating chicken necks

———

And the quiet cat
   sitting by the post
Perceives the moon

Ancient ancient world
        —tight skirts
By the new car

———

Waiting for the leaves
        to fall;—
There goes one!

———

First frost dropped
        all leaves
Last night—leafsmoke

———

Evening coming—
        The office girl
unloosing her scarf

———

The housecats, amazed
        at something new,
Looking in the same direction

———

The word HANDICAPPED
        sliding over snow
On a newspaper

———

Run over by my lawnmower
        waiting for me to leave,
The frog

A raindrop from
   the roof
Fell in my beer

———

A bird on
   the branch out there
—I waved

———

Cat eating fish heads
   —All those eyes
In the starlight

———

The moon had
   a cat's mustache,
For a second

———

Seven birds in a tree,
   looking
In every direction

———

The birds
   surprise me
On all sides

———

Cat gone 24 hours
   —A piece of his hair
Waving on the door

How flowers love
    the sun,
Blinking there!

———

Asking Albert Saijo
    for a haiku,
He said nothing

———

In a Mojave dust storm
    Albert said: "Senzeie,
Was a Mongolian waif"

———

The summer chair
    rocking by itself
In the blizzard

———

My pipe unlit
    beside the Diamond
Sutra—What to think?

———

February gales—racing
    westward through
The clouds, the moon

———

Among the nervous birds
    the mourning dove
Nibbles quietly

Cold gray tufts
   of winter grass
Under the stars

———

Memère says: "Planets are
   far apart so people
Can't bother each other."

———

In the quiet house,
   my mother's
Moaning yawns

———

Blizzard in the suburbs
   —the mailman
And the poet walking

———

Blizzard in the suburbs
   —old men driving slowly
To the store 3 blocks

———

Dusk—The blizzard
   hides everything,
Even the night

———

A full November moon
   and mild,
Mary Carney

Mild spring night—
a teenage girl said
"Good evening" in the dark

———

Spring night—the sound
of the cat
Chewing fish heads

———

I said a joke
under the stars
—No laughter

———

(Tonight) that star
is waving & flaming
Something awful

———

Perfectly silent
in the starry night,
The little tree

———

White rose with red
splashes—Oh
Vanilla ice cream cherry!

———

Looking for my cat
in the weeds,
I found a butterfly

Churchbells ringing in town
—The caterpillar
In the grass

———

For a moment
the moon
Wore goggles

———

Iowa clouds
following each other
Into Eternity

———

The sleeping moth—
he doesn't know
The lamps turned up again

———

Reading my notes—
The fly stepping from
The page to the finger

———

August in Salinas—
Autumn leaves in
Clothing store displays

———

Autumn night
low moon—
Fire in Smithtown

Full moon of October
   —The tiny mew
of the Kitty

———

Cool sunny autumn day,
   I'll mow the lawn
one last time

———

A yellow witch chewing
   a cigarette,
Those Autumn leaves

———

I've turned up
   the lamp again
—The sleeping moth

———

Train tunnel, too dark
   for me to write: that
"Men are ignorant"

———

The flies on the porch
   and the fog on the peaks
Are so sad

———

The cow, taking a big
   dreamy crap, turning
To look at me

Leaves skittering on
the tin roof
—August fog in Big Sur

———

Terraces of fern
in the dripping
Redwood shade

———

Here comes the nightly
moth, to his nightly
Death, at my lamp

———

Halloween colors
orange and black
On a summer butterfly

———

Fighting over a peach
stone, bluejays
In the bushes

———

Barefoot by the sea,
stopping to scratch one ankle
With one toe

———

Summer afternoon—
impatiently chewing
The jasmine leaf

Giving an apple
    to the mule, the big lips
Taking hold

———

Bluejay drinking at my
    saucer of milk,
Throwing his head back

———

The mule, turning
    slowly, rubbing his
Behind on a log

———

Nibbling his ankle,
    the mule's teeth
Like kettle drum

———

Front hooves spread,
    the mule scratches his
Neck along a log

———

A quiet moment—
    low lamp, low logs—
Just cooking the stew

———

One foot on the bar
    of soap,
The Bluejay peeking

Quietly pouring coffee
in the afternoon,
How pleasant!

———

Bird suddenly quiet
on his branch—his
Wife glancing at him

———

Four bluejays quiet
in the afternoon tree,
Occasionally scratching

———

The hermit's broom,
the fire, the kettle
—August night

———

The cricket in my cellar window, this quiet
Sunday afternoon

———

As the cool evenings
make them selves felt,
Smoke from suburban chimneys

———

Cold crisp October morning
—the cats fighting
In the weeds

Drunken deterioration—
    ho-hum,
Shooting star

———

This October evening,
    the velvet eyes
Of Manjuri

———

Washing my face
    with snow
Beneath the Little Dipper

———

A balloon caught
    in the tree—dusk
In Central Park zoo

———

Elephants munching
    on grass—loving
Heads side by side

———

The stars are racing
    real fast
Through the clouds

———

Dawn—crows cawing,
    ducks quack quacking,
Kitchen windows lighting

Breakfast done
   the tomcat curls up
On the down couch

———

Dawn—the writer who
   hasn't shaved,
Poring over notebooks

———

February dawn—frost
   on the path
Where I paced all winter

———

Blizzard's just started
   all that bread scattered,
And just one bird

———

The trees, already
   bent in the windless
Oklahoma plain

———

In the desert sun
   in Arizona,
A yellow railroad caboose

———

The new moon
   is the toe nail
Of God

Sunny day—bird tracks
   & cat tracks
In the snow

———

Little pieces of ice
   in the moonlight
Snow, thousands of em

———

The cat: a little
   body being used
By a little person

———

Perfect circle round
   the moon
In the center of the sky

———

Standing on the end
   on top of the tree,
The Big Dipper

———

Who wd have guessed
   that a January moon
Could be so orange!

———

A big fat flake
   of snow
Falling all alone

Dawn—the tomcat
    hurrying home
With his tail down

———

Buddhas in moonlight
    —Mosquito bite
Thru hole in my shirt

———

After supper
    on crossed paws,
The cat meditates

———

Closing the book,
    rubbing my eyes—
The sleepy August dawn

———

Resting watchfully, the cat
    and the squirrel
Share the afternoon

———

The gently moving
    leaves
Of the August afternoon

———

A long island
    in the sky
The Milky Way

Haunted Autumn visiting
    familiar August,
These last 2 days

———

Disturbing my mind essence,
    all that food
I have to cook

———

Arms folded
    to the moon,
Among the cows

———

Birds flying north—
    Where are the squirrels?—
There goes a plane to Boston

———

So humid you cant
    light matches, like
Living in a tank

UNCOLLECTED POEMS

Observations

What more do I want but a meal when I am hungry, or a bed
    when I am weary,
or a rose when I am sad?
What more does one need in this world but the few joys that
    are afforded
him by this earth, this rich bursting earth, that flushes with
    bloom each
Spring, and leases its luxury of wet warmth to us for a glorious
    summer?
What more do I want but a woman when I am in passion, or
    a glass of water
when I am thirsty, or music when I am lonely?
Why, I need not your sumptuous sitting room, nor your
    full-vistaed garden!
Nor your wainscotted bedroom with overhanging canopy and
    oils! All I need
is my little den, with a window to let the sun shine in, and a
    shelf of
books, and a desk, and something to write with, and paper,
    and my soul:
      Where can I find my soul?
      In solitude said my friend, in solitude.
      Yes. I have found my soul in solitude.
No, I don't want riches! This has been said so many times
    before. And
when I say the world is bursting with plenty, I know the
    starved millions
will laugh: but I shall laugh with them and overthrow: I know
    whereof I
speak: I am not a prophet, I am, like Whitman, a lover.
    Whitman, that
glorious American! Barbellion, who will go with you,
    anywhere, any time,
any fashion, for nothing, for everything. Come, I will go with
    thee,
said Whitman: Whitman, the underrated, the forgotten, the
    laughed-at,
the homosexual, the lover of life.

How shall I sing?
I shall sing: I shall record the misery, observe on it, and
          point
out how to abolish it. Blah.

America in the Night

I

Listen!
Krooooaoooo! Krrooooaoooooo!
'Tis the train whistle, now, in the night,
Krooooooo!
I'm on a train, and I've got to whistle too. . . .
The real, the true America,
Is America in the night.

The guileful sleep, guile-less;
The egotists sleep, ego-less;
The timid sleep, fear-less.
Across the midnight face of America—
They sleep . . .

2

The real, the true America,
Is America in the night.

3

What is a youth?
I see one now—he is the youth of ages.
Frowning silently, he smokes—
A soldier in Alexander's legions?
Quietly, he adjusts his regalia.
A young driver of Arabian caravans?
He yawns in the night, then listens:—
Krooooaoooo. . . . !!

Of the fleet of Nelson?
A Tatar? A young soldier of Kublai Khan's?
A crusader? The young Iroquois warrior?
A black defender of Khartoum?
Yank in France?
No matter—they are one, all are one.
And the same—the youth of ages.
An American sailor.
With me he plies the black waters of night,
Aboard the good ship S.S. America.

4

Red, white and blue they say?
America?
Don't kid me, I say to they:—
America is blue
Right through—
Blue!
Improvise, black saxist, improvise!
Tell them with your black soul
That America is blue,
That America is the blues.
Play that throbbing tremolo—
Let me stand beside you, approving.
Bring him a soap box,
Let him stand up and play the blues.
Kroooaaaooooo!

5

Sibelius, tell us about Nature!
And you brave Waldo—
And thou also Thoreau.
Tell us about the dark forest in the night—
Patient, untelling, and wise.
And you Gershwin, and you Runyon—
Tell us about New York town . . .
In the night, in the night.
They tell me God made night to sleep—
Zounds! My dawn is in the West!

The darkness is over the land,
And the melancholy lamps glimmer,
And the train thunders through . . .
In the night.
Krooooaaooo!

6

Sandburg, Wolfe, Whitman, and Joe—
They all work for the railroad.
Sandburg, Wolfe, and Whitman sing—
While Joe pulls that old whistle string:—
Krooooaaoooo! Krooooaaooo!!
Lordy but they're blue—
—Those lovers of the blues!

Old Love-Light

The railroad buildings, dingied
by scores of soot-years,
thrusting their ugly rears
at your train window, are
a sign of man's decay.
Once, I took a train
instead of a bus. A bus
takes you on a highway
lined with filling stations
& lunchcarts. A train
runs smack through the
forest. I wanted to
study the forest in October
and I took a train.
      It was astonishing to read
what I read about October
the following day. I thought
I had it all figured out—
I thought the lonely little
houses, lost in the middle

of great tawny grass,
shaggy copper skies and
mottled orange forests, were
full of fine humanity that
I was missing. Instead, the
writer informed me that
it was chlorophyll that
colored the leaves. I
thought I had all the
significance of October
under my hat & pasted.
I thought that October
was a tangible being,
with a voice. The
writer insisted it was
the growth of corky cells
around the stem of the
leaf. The writer also
said that to consider
October sad is to be
a melancholy Tennysonian.
October is not sad, he
said. October is falling
leaves. October comes
between Sept. & Nov. I
was amazed by these facts,
especially about the
Tennysonian melancholia. I
always thought October was
a kind old Love-light.

I Tell You It Is October!

There's something olden and golden and lost
    In the strange ancestral light;
There's something tender and loving and sad
    In October's copper might.

End of something, old, old, old . . .
Always missing, sad, sad, sad . . .
Saying something . . . love, love, love . . .

Akh! I tell you it is October,
    And I defy you now and always
To deny there is not love

Staring foolishly at skies
Whose beauty but God defies.

For in October's ancient glow
    A little after dusk
Love strides through the meadow
    Dropping her burnished husk.

It may be that I am mad, sir:
    Or perhaps hope in vain . . .
But Oh! October is sad, sir,
    As mournful as midnight rain.

The melancholy frowse of harvest stacks,
The tender char of morning skies,
The advance of Emperor October,
Father! Father!
Father November of the sombre silver,
Oh I tell you it is October!

"I am my mother's son"

I am my mother's son. All other identities
are artificial and recent. Naked, basic, actually,
I am my mother's son. I emerged from her womb
and set out into the earth. The earth gave me
another identity, that of name, personality,
appearance, character, and spirit. The earth
is my grandmother: I am the earth's grandson.
The way I comb my hair today has nothing to do
with myself, who am my mother's son and the
earth's grandson. I am put on this earth to
prove that I am my mother's son. I am also
on this earth, my grandmother, to be her
spokesman, in my chosen and natural way. The
earth owns the lease to myself: she shall take
me back, and my mother too. We have proven
the earth's truth and meaning, which is, simply
life and death.

"I woke up in the middle of the night
and realized to my horror that I did
not remember who I was. I knew not
my name nor my appearance. When I
went to the mirror, I failed to re-
cognize my image. That is why I am
my mother's son and the earth's grand-
son, and nothing else. I am here to
prove that fact, and in so doing, I
am also the earth's spokesman: that is
so because I wish to prove it twice,
once for the earth, and again for my
brothers, so that we may live together
in beauty."

Say, fellow, you know who I
am? I'm Jack Kerouac, the
writer: husky, handsome,
intellectual Jack Kerouac.
Notice how I comb my hair

and see my handsome gar-
ments. I'm the boy from
Brazil. I love jazz, I
love North Carolina, I
love Socialism. I'm sel-
fish, I'm irresponsible,
I'm weak, I'm afraid. I'm
Jack Kerouac the poet, the
seaman, the scholar, the
laborer, the newspaperman,
the lover, the athlete,
the flyer, the Lowellian?　(I am my mother's son.)

Thinking of Thomas Wolfe
on a Winter's Night

Bereaved pines standing like Justice,
The cold stare of stars between;
I walk down the road, holding
　　my ears,
My palms the shelters
Form dry sweeps of brittle cold.

"Who has known fury?" Wolfe
　　had asked,
And the critic's winter eyes,
Like these stars (between
　　the pines)
Had stared, amusedly.

Come, it is warm in my house;
We shall go there;
Soon the flashing sun will
　　rise up
To overwhelm the petulant
　　stars.

Alabama, May 11, 1944

The perishing green of May,
      that knows not
Its due price for time spent
      sun-languishing—
And all because it lives so
      passionately green—
Can learn no lesson from
      human telling
Which might seek to warn the
      Autumn end.

A Translation from the French of Jean-Louis Incogniteau

My beloved who wills not to love me:
My life which cannot love me:
I seduce both.

She with my round kisses . . .
(In the smile of my beloved the approbation of the cosmos)
Life is my art . . .
(Shield before death)
Thus without sanction I live.
(What unhappy theodicy!)

One knows not—
One desires—
      Which is the sum.

(Translated by Allen Ginsberg)

Psalms

God, I cannot find your face this morning: the night has been split, a morning light has come, and lo! there is the *city*, and there are the city men with their wheels coming to swallow darkness under towers.

Ah! Ah! there's rage here, God, there's a bridge too upon which the wheels collide, beneath which they bring more wheels and tunnels, there's a fire raging here over dull multitudes.

God I have known this city and stayed here trapped and full of rage, I have been a city man, with wheels, and walkings all about inside, I have seen their faces all around me here.

I must see your face this morning, God, Your Face through dusty windowpanes, through steam and furor, I must listen to your voice over these clankings of the city: I am tired, God, I cannot see your face in this *history*.

———————

And when I saw the light of the morning sun streaming in the city, my Saviour, I wept that there was such richness, I wept that Your light was shed upon the sorrowful weary city men, the melancholy women, within their black towers and byways all the light, my Lord: and oh my God now I pray to you—do not remove Your light from us all, and from me— I could not rejoice in more darkness, nor could I pray in the ignorance of the dark: Your light wide over the city and the bridge at morning—and I am saved, my Saviour, saved! By the sun which is a miracle, by the light which is everywhere bright—but Lord: give me power for my psalms, that I may rejoice powerfully, with equal light, give me tears for strength, give me again these mornings of light and purpose and humbleness.

———————

Alone in a lonely world, in a darkness, awake in night, night, always night: let me hear the bird of morning *now*, let me get up in the morning among men and women and children, let them look upon me as they look at fathers, let me get some light, some day, some love, and birds in the morning: Old God give me magnificence and a strong back, give me the heartiest diligence, give me great mornings and the people who are there at morning, give me some light, Old God, give me some light! and give me the fruit of my labourings so that I may see them there, and touch them, so that I may know myself as labourer and maker of fruits, and not as a night man and darkness man and lonely man alone, with no mornings, no birds, no fruits, nor children, no sun nor day, Oh God let me *see* these things which are there for me, which You made for me.

And what do I owe You, God, for my gifts: I owe you perspiration and suffering and all the dark night of my life: God I owe you godliness and diligence, God I owe you this blackest loneliness, and terrified dreams—but humbleness, God, I have none and I owe it you: for I would have You reach down a hand to me, to help me *up* to you—Oh I am not humble. Give me this last gift, God, and I *will* be humble, I *will* owe You humbleness. Spit in my soul, God, for asking and always asking, and for not giving and owing what I have given, and give, and shall give: God make me *give*. Old Job there of the three thousand five hundred years a-mouldering in his grave, Old Job there is your servant, God: forgive me for my youth, then, forgive me for *it*, God, oh make me a giver.

A psalm and a hymn of praise: for there spread the fields, far beyond this city, and in the fields, the woods, on the earth, on the sea—there I see Thoreaus, and Whitmans, and Melvilles, and Thomas Wolfes, and these are the colleagues of my time who have cried out to You, God, and writ their cryings, and published your name, and seen this land at morning, *in your eyes*: God I name You your servants, I name You great servants and great eyes of yourself: I name You those men, God, with whom I Cast my lot all youthful and vain in joining, but all old and humble in *naming* them: God I shall name You names and things, I shall name praises, hymns, glees, wonders, and the incalculable gravities of Your life: God I will name Your Name also, and spread it all inside and around my soul.

And no more psalms exist in me, God?—no more rueful dark-joyed views of You, conceived in lowest loneliness, in darkest silence, in farthest solitude and fear, no more rich ripe singing talents put to use devout—no more?

Oh god how I rejoice in sorrows now, as though I had asked You for them, and You had handed them to me, how I rejoice in these sorrows. Like steel I will be, God, growing harder in the forge-fires, grimmer, harder, better: as you direct, Oh lost Lord, as you direct: let me find You now, like new joy on the earth at morning, like a horse in his meadows in the morning seeing a master a-coming across the grass—Like steel, I am now, God, like steel, you have made me strong and hopeful.

Strike me and I will ring like a bell!

Thank you, dear Lord, for the work You have given me, the which, barring angels on earth, I dedicate to Thee; and slave on it for Thee, and shape from chaos and nothingness in Thy name, and give my breath to it for Thee; thank you for the Visions Thou didst give me, for Thee; and all is for Thee; thank you, dear Lord, for a world and for Thee. Infold my heart in Thy warmth forever.

Thank you, Lord God of Hosts, Angel of the universe, King of Light and Maker of Darkness for Thy ways, the which, untrod, would make of men dumb dancers in flesh without pain, mind without soul, thumb without nerve and foot without dirt; thank you, O Lord, for small meeds of truth and warmth Thou hast poured into this willing vessel, and thank you for confusion, mistake, and Horror's sadness, that breed in Thy Name. Keep my flesh in Thee everlasting.

"God didn't make the world for satisfaction"

God didn't make the world for satisfaction
Abraham Lincoln was lonely
God made the world to shudder,

Now I lie on my bed of iron
Driven, broken, blackened.
I had a wife who loved me.

Lord, damn, hell and cities
The sky's turned white
There's oil in the tar you chew nowadays

The sickly moon won't tell,
My eyes are lonely
Monsters try to drive me off the window.

Alone, alone, alone, O broken bone
Where go, what do,
I have not liked my life.

Song

I left New York
Nineteen forty nine
To go across the country
Without a dad-blame dime.

———

T'was in Butte Montana
In the cold, cold Fall
——I found my father
In a gamblin' hall.

———

"Father, father,
Where have you been;
Unloved is lost
When you're so blame small."

———————

"Dear son," he said,
"Don't a-worry 'bout me;
I'm about to die
Of the pleurisy."

———————

We headed South together
On an old freight train,
The night my father died
In the cold, cold rain.

———————

"Dear son," he said,
"Don't a-worry 'bout me;
"Lay me down to die
of the misery."

———————

Oh father, father,
Where have you been;
Unloved is lost,
When you're so blame small.

———————

Song: Fie My Fum

Pull my daisy,
Tip my cup,
Cut my thoughts
For coconuts,

Start my arden
Gate my shades,
Silk my garden
Rose my days,

Say my oops,
Ope my shell,
Roll my bones,
Ring my bell,

Pope my parts,
Pop my pot,
Poke my pap,
Pit my plum.

Allen Ginsberg & Jack Kerouac

Pull My Daisy

Pull my daisy
tip my cup
all my doors are open
Cut my thoughts
for coconuts
all my eggs are broken
Jack my Arden
gate my shades
woe my road is spoken
Silk my garden
rose my days
now my prayers awaken

Bone my shadow
dove my dream
start my halo bleeding
Milk my mind &
make me cream
drink me when you're ready
Hop my heart on
harp my height
seraphs hold me steady
Hip my angel
hype my light
lay it on the needy

Heal the raindrop
sow the eye
bust my dust again
Woe the worm
work the wise
dig my spade the same
Stop the hoax
what's the hex
where's the wake
how's the hicks
take my golden beam

Rob my locker
lick my rocks
leap my cock in school
Rack my lacks
lark my looks
jump right up my hole
Whore my door
beat my boor
eat my snake of fool
Crazy my hair
bare my poor
asshole shorn of wool

say my oops
ope my shell
Bite my naked nut
Roll my bones
ring my bell
call my worm to sup
Pope my parts
pop my pot
raise my daisy up
Poke my pap
pit my plum
let my gap be shut

Allen Ginsberg, Jack Kerouac, Neal Cassady

Pull My Daisy

Pull my daisy
Tip my cup
Cut my thoughts
for coconuts

Jack my Arden
Gate my shades
Silk my garden
Rose my days

Bone my shadow
Dove my dream
Milk my mind &
Make me cream

Hop my heart on
Harp my height
Hip my angel
Hype my light

Heal the raindrop
Sow the eye
Woe the worm
Work the wise

Stop the hoax
Where's the wake
What's the box
How's the Hicks

Rob my locker
Lick my rocks
Rack my lacks
Lark my looks

Whore my door
Beat my beer
Craze my hair
Bare my poor

Say my oops
Ope my shell
Roll my bones
Ring my bell

Pope my parts
Pop my pet
Poke my pap
Pit my plum

Allen Ginsberg, Jack Kerouac, Neal Cassady

"He is your friend, let him dream"

He is your friend, let him dream;
He's not your brother, he's not yr. father,
He's not St. Michael he's a guy.

He's married, he works, go on sleeping
On the other side of the world,
Go thinking in the Great European Night

I'm explaining him to you my way not yours,
Child, Dog,—listen: go find your soul,
Go smell the wind, go far.

Life is a pity. Close the book, go on,
Write no more on the wall, on the moon,
At the Dog's, in the sea in the snowing bottom.

Go find God in the nights, the clouds too.
When can it stop this big circle at the skull
oh Neal; there are men, things outside to do.

Great huge tombs of Activity
in the desert of Africa of the heart,
The black angels, the women in bed

with their beautiful arms open for you
in their youth, some tenderness
Begging in the same shroud.

The big clouds of new continents,
O foot tired in climes so mysterious,
Don't go down the otherside for nothing.

Visions of Doctor Sax

('T'was a husk of doves but only in a way.)

Devouring dirt, the sad old serpent of evil,
Having worn time's corridor, excrescing dirt,
And rising inch-an-hour to the parapets of the pit
Where Doctor Sax, the Child, and the Wizard stare down,
Doth bleakly appear.

"Its malignance but a mournfulness, its desires
  Only poor, the snake is thyself eating dirt
  In the lonely tunnel, upwards to the world's sun.
  The nature of evil is sad," addeth the Wizard.

"Moreover," addeth Doctor Sax, himself turning to the Child,
  "It is nearer, that serpentine skull like a peak,
  Old Ugly himself, to the end than to the beginning,
  And therefore more like me than you."

And the Child, sad at sight of silent snake, answereth:
    "I know."
And all three sighed the sigh of life, and the old snake inched.

The Poems of the Night

So falls the rain shroud, melted
By harps; so turns the harp gold,
Welded by mell, roll-goldened
By caramel, softened by Huge.
The weary tent of the night
Has rain starring down the wallsides,
A golden hero of the up atmospheres
Has sprung the leak in the ambiguity
That made the heavens fore-fall.

So the pollywogs grow
And the bigger frogs croak,
By the May Pole in the mud
Crazy Lazy swings her crutches—
Was the wife of Doctor Sax
Gave up him for a crud.

Maybelle Dizzitime, a gal of many
Fancies, swings her shadow ape
In the cloaks of midnight whamsy;
The ball of the pollywog may-time,
The dance of the flooded mall
Crack went the Castle underground
Cank cantank old Moritzy
Flames his froosures in the dank,

Dabbely doo, dabbely dey,
The ring has got the crey.
Ringaladout, ringalaree,
Ringala Malaman,
Ringala Dee.

The hooded urchins of the pissed river
Are making melted marbles of the mud;
Rain, Rain, Sleeping Shrouded Falls,
The manager of the Pittsburgh Pirates
Is sleeping in his craw.
The boss of the winter stove league
Has given up his chaw.

So Sax in his Ides Does Bide,
Comes Melting like Mr. Rain
With a Shake of the Fritters,
Drops his Moistures One by One.

The Golden Rose   The Angel with the
That in the wave's   Wetted Wings,
Repose–   The Nose

The Lark & Lute
in Every Mist

The Cark that in
     The Harried Anxious
     Flows to East

The Hoods of Windfall
Blown with Rain

The gammerhooks
     of cloud-rise
     in the moon.

The Ice Floes
Bonging at
the Falls,

The Whistle of
     an Arcadian
     Fluke

The Eyes of Eagles
on the Main–

Flaws in Heaven
     Are no Pain.

Demi mundaine dancers at the broken hall ball,
Doctor Sax and Beelzabadoes the whirling polka
Gallipagos–

The crickets in the flower petal mud
Throng at the Water Lilies, Thirst
for fair–

Cring Crang the broken brother boys
See Mike O'Ryan in the river rising,
Tangled.

The Spiders of the evil Hoar
are coming in the flood

Every form shape or manner
the insects of the wizard blood

The Castle stands like a parapet,
Kingdoms enthralled in air

Saturday Heroes of the windy field
Bare fist-glasses to the *mer*—

The Merrimac is roaring,
Eternity and the Rain are Bare

Down by White Hood Falls,
Down by the darkened weirs,
Down by Manchester, down by Brown,
Down by Lowell, Comes the Rose—
Flowing to its seaward, brave as knights,
Riding the humpback Merrimac
Rage excites

So doth the rain droop open,
    more like a rose
Less adamantine
    Than ang

Liquid heaven in her drip
    eatin rock
    mixing kip

Eternity comes & swallows
    moisture, blazes sun
    to accept up

Rain sleeps when the rain is over
Rain rages when the sun keels over
Roses drown when the pain is over

The water lute sides of Rainbow
Heaven—
Rang a dang mam-mon
Sing your blacking song.

THE SONG OF THE MYTH OF THE RAINY NIGHT

Rose, Rose
Rainy Night Rose

Castle, Castles
Hassels in the Castle

Rain, Rain,
Shroud's in the Rain

Makes her Luminescence
Of folded Incandescence

Raw red rose in wetted night
"I had all to do
With that dreaded essence."

Pitterdrop, pitterdrop,
Rain in the woods

Sax sits Shrouded
Meek & crazy
Rumored in his trousers
Naked as a baby

"Rainy drops, rainy drops,
   Made of loves,
Snake's not real,
   'Twas a husk of doves

"The rain is really milk
The night is really white
The shroud is really seen
By the white eyes of the light
A young & silly dove
Is yakking in the sky
The dream is cropping under

The muds & marble mix
Petals of the water harp,
Melted lutes,
Angels of Eternity
And pissing in the air

"Ah poor life and paranoid gain,
    hassel, hassel, hassel,
    man in the rain

"Mix with the bone melt!
Lute with the cry!
So doth the rain blow down
From all heaven's fantasy."

Long Dead's Longevity

Long dead's longevity
Coyote Viejo
Ugly un handsome old
        puff chin eye crack
Bone fat face McGee
In older rains sat by
        new fires
Plotting unwanted pre
        doomed presupposing
Odes–long dead
Riverbottom bum
Raunchy
Scrounge
Brakeman bum
Wine cans sand sexless
        Silence die tomb
Pyramid cave snake Satan

"*Someday you'll be lying*"

1

Someday you'll be lying
there in a nice trance
and suddenly a hot
soapy brush will be
applied to your face
—it'll be unwelcome
—someday the
undertaker will shave you

2

Sweet monstranot love
By momma dears
Hey
Call God the Mother
To stop this fight

3

Me that repeated & petered
The meter & lost 2 cents

Me that was fined
To be hined
And refined
    Ay

      Me that was
      Whoo ee
      The owl
      On the fence

4

Old Navajoa shit dog, you,
your goodies are the goodiest
goodies I ever did see, how

dog you shore look mad
when yer bayin

Hoo Hound-dog!
    don't eat that dead rabbit
    in front of my face raw
    —Cook it a lil bit

Daydreams for Ginsberg

I lie on my back at midnight
hearing the marvelous strange chime
of the clocks, and know it's mid-
night and in that instant the whole
world swims into sight for me
in the form of beautiful swarm-
ing m u t t a worlds—
everything is happening, shining
Buhudda-lands, *bhuti*
blazing in faith, I know I'm
forever right & all's I got to
do (as I hear the ordinary
extant voices of ladies talking
in some kitchen at midnight
oilcloth cups of cocoa
cardore to mump the
rinnegain in his
darlin drain—) i will write
it, all the talk of the world
everywhere in this morning, leav-
ing open parentheses sections
for my own accompanying inner
thoughts—with roars of me
all brain—all world
roaring—vibrating—I put
it down, swiftly, 1,000 words
(of pages) compressed into one second

of time—I'll be long
robed & long gold haired in
the famous Greek afternoon
of some Greek City
Fame Immortal & they'll
have to find me where they find
the t h n u p f t of my
shroud bags flying
flag yagging Lucien
Midnight back in their
mouths—Gore Vidal'll
be amazed, annoyed—
    my words'll be writ in gold
& preserved in libraries like
Finnegans Wake & Visions of Neal

"Sight is just dust"

Sight is just dust,
Obey it must.

Mind alone
Introduced the bone.

Fire just feeds
On fiery deeds.

Only mind
The flame so kind.

Water from the moon
Appears very soon.

Mind is the sea
Made water agree.

Wind in the trees
Is a mental breeze.

Wind rose deep
From empty sleep.

Space in the ground
Was dirt by the pound.

Devoid of space
Is the mind of grace.

Mindmatter

I was leaning in the door, thinking "Did
Allen Ginsberg mean something I couldnt
Understand when he told me he'd a vision
From the skies, and he trembled

Once I was knocked out in a game
And stood there on the field   'Who am I?
Where is this?' And I saw people
and the ground but it was slanted
sideways, almost upsidedown

Like a magic carpet traveling across
space without moving or being moved.
Because there is no space, it's only
nowhere, what are you using to
measure with, objects?

Objects shall change into insurpassably
fine dust, the finest dust there is.
Imagination dust. Everything is created
by the mind. Things happen in time.
They happen to things of imagination dust.

And time is imagination dust, and mind
Is matter, and matter is mind, and it's
All mindmatter—Mindmatter was created
in the womb of mindmatter?—I dont
know, it doesnt make much difference.

A TV Poem

Tathata is Essence Isness
And I see it Akshobying
like innumerable moth lights
In the lavender plaster wall
behind the television forest of wires
in my sister's cool livingroom

the radiating isness not obliterated,
transcendentally seen, by either
white plaster or wall lavender
wingboards with bridge of black
and wires of Oh dots

Meanwhile the gray lost unturned on
    screen shows its gray black
And then the reflected window
    outdoor blob squares
Like silver shining
A TV show with me deep gloomily
    invited included in the
Slow motionless background
    where you cannot see
My white sea moving shirt
    of pencil on lap page

So that the scene is real
    a show of world
But through it all still I see
Transcendental (and hear) radiations
    from some pure and tranquil
Blank and empty center Screen
    of Mind's Immortal Ecstasy
And even Reynolds' Blue Boy
    on the wall over there
Bathed in holy day light
    Has his little black fly

Permeative with Buddhamoths
        and Buddha Lands
And his pale face with the
        Black hair cut
Sways, moves, force-weaver
        Middle way
          Middle
            W
            a
            y

Like a middle void hole
    cloud be decking
Human sad hat holding
    impression of
Dance—
        Attainer to Actual Isness
        Adoration to Your No Need to Move

            Do nothing & ye shall soon agree

Heaven

Like going to Xochimilco and seeing
everything with clear loving eyes,
it will be, to go to Heaven
a wise angel of the dead
among the blind unborn angels
unnumberable—
Whole buzzing areas of Heaven
will have nothing but mosquitos—

Unborn angels wont know
what they look like
but wise angels of free will
and goodness will see them,
wearing the transformation bodies
of their future death—
    We will be able to visit
dinosaurs by the millions
and have picnics among them,
of ambrosia, unmolested—
    Dead angels of evil will,
    shall be quartered
    with the Devil
    behind Golden Bars
    unable to rejoice
    for a long long time
—Judgement Day

will take place in Heaven
and really be Universal
Freeing Day—
        by this time
        nobody will need love
        any more
        except
        to be Alone
    with God's Face
whose Shroud I've already seen.

            The Church?
Earth's dogmatic mistakes
have nothing to do with Heaven
—O Gerard! I'll see you
            soon!
        And Chirico!
        And Christ!
    May I kiss Thee, Son
        of Man?
    Just once?
    And you, Gotama,
    receive thy 83-year-old
        blessing?
        Okay

If this were not so
God wouldnt be God,
        or Good,
God be with ye
    means *Good* bye—
        if it aint so
        I'll make it so
        by my Will.

Gerard will be a 9-year old
        cutie
        in Heaven
    and I'll be oldern
anybody in my family

oldern my father, who'll
laugh.
  Allen will be in ecstasies
  Peter Amazed
  Neal bleakly content
      at last
Carolyn prim
 Ma the same as now
 Leroi soft
 Lucien old & wise
 Cessa angelic
 Dody painting gates
   of Paradise
    for the holy fun
 and Hitler stroking
his mustache by the side
of Napoleonic Inventors
 of rockets,
   barred awhile

for Heaven is big enough
(it's all empty space
endless) to take in
unnumberable non-numbers
of anything & everything
that has and aint
happened all over
   anyway
   or not at all

  God Smiles

  Gee God I'm Glad
   'Bye

       I AM
       Dec 2 '58
       Northport

(Louis Armstrong will
    blow his top)

Some of the wise angels,
the dark of the dead,
  favored in Heaven,
will shake their heads
sadly persuading certain
unborn martyrs not
to be born, but God Smiles,
and up there theres no Time
—Wow,——
I guess I'll shut up now

(Except, we will be able
to examine the huge mouths
& teeth of Dinosaurs
& they will look at us
with big sad eyes—
not to mention creatures
with or without free will
from every planet
in all the chilicosms—
even the little stem men
from Asagratamak—
There will be polite
interchange of experiences,
an endless ride)—
     When we see God's Face
We wont see anything
       else

Yes, finally
because I see it
Thru the brown grain
of this turd earth—
Who is my Witness?
    My Will!

And this is the will I leave
    to my children

Come little unborn angels,
get it over with!
Hello Thomas Hardy!
Myself I'm going to visit
endlessly the endless groves
of trees up there
and have enough time
to hug each one—
and this time they'll talk

————

    All the amores
of Spanish earth you see
were not in vain—

Girls called Angelina
for no perturbing reason.

It wont be like the hydrogen bomb
when God finally shows
  his Face, it will be sudden
      happiness,
like when you suddenly feel
      like cryin
  when you first see yr infant's
  face in its mother's arms.

This knowledge makes me
go "Ha ha ha" and
go "Oh boy" and
go "Whoopee"
because now I know
that old age is therefore
the development of angels.

Mutilated people will float
around like mutilated leaves,
more curious than the others,
    that's all

Roy Campanella will smile
& float around in Heaven
as good as John L Sullivan

The legless man no
              rollerboard—
Tiny Tim will keep screaming
    "God Bless Everyone"

Sebastian will weep.

Burnt children
      of the Chicago School Fire
    of Our Lady of the Angels
will be like little black
niggers in the Virgin Mary's
    beautiful blue & white
            golden yard
              forever.

For we all go back
where we came from,
    God's Lit Brain,
        his Transcendent Eye
of Wisdom

And there's your bloody circle
called Samsara
          by the ignorant
          Buddhists, who will
still be funny Masters
    up there, bless em.

Stella will bless Sebastian.
Zen men will devise koans
    for snakes to solve.
Rodgers & Hammerstein
will have endless hits.

Oh boy, Broadway
    will be raised at last.

Henri Cru will tell
endless stories to a billion
listeners.
Gregory Corso will dance
around with a laurel
in his hair, writing poems.

Later!
I'm gonna do it!

Phil Whalen will be
a blue cloud anytime
he wants—
Bob Donlin will stare
with endless blue eyes
out of the milk bar,
and W.C. Fields will get
his red eye—
My cats Timmy & Tyke
will always be at my side
—They wont be jealous
but make friends
with Bootsie, Kewpie,
and Davey, and Beauty
and Bob—even
the little dry moth
with the beady black eyes
can sit on my arm
        forever,

till we all see God
when that which we love
solves & melts in one
          Glow

See?

And the little mouse
that I killed will devour
me into its golden belly.
That little mouse was God.

Dante and Beatrice will
be married.

Please, that's enough,
          huh?

Sitting Under Tree Number Two

But the undrawables,
    the single musical harp
rainbow's blue green
shimmer of a cobweb—
the line of thread swimming
in the wind, blue &
silver at intervals that
appear & disappear—
7 songe along the rim
tying to the plant
as birds twurdle over
those massy fort trees
populous with song
—imaginary blossoms in my
eye moving across the
page with definite oily
rainbow water holes &
rims of beaten gold,

with toads of old
    silver.
Golden fast ant back
in the hay now fromming
its feelers thru the
thicket of time then
darting across mud looking
for more trees—
A little ant bit my ass
& I said Eeesh with
my wad of gum—I
itch & pain all over
with hate of time &
tedium Save me!
  Kill me!

To Harpo Marx

O Harpo! When did you seem like an angel
  the last time?
  and played the gray harp of gold?

When did you steal the silverware
  and bug-spray the guests?

When did your brother find rain
  in your sunny courtyard?

When did you chase your last blonde
  across the Millionairesses' lawn
  with a bait hook on a line
  protruding from your bicycle?

Or when last you powderpuffed
  your white flour face
  with fishbarrel cover?

Harpo! Who was that Lion
  I saw you with?

How did you treat the midget
  and Konk the giant?

Harpo, in your recent night-club appearance
  in New Orleans were you old?

  Were you still chiding with your horn
  in the cane at your golden belt?

Did you still emerge from your pockets
  another Harpo, or screw on
  new wrists?

Was your vow of silence an Indian Harp?

"I
clearly
saw
the skeleton underneath"

I
  clearly
      saw
          the skeleton underneath
all
    this
        show
           of personality
what
      is
        left
           of a man and all his pride
but bones?
and all his lost snacks o' nights . . .

and the bathtubs of liquor
thru his gullet
. . . *bones*——He mopes
in the grave,
facial features
changed by worms
*
*
*
*

from him
is heard
no more
*
*
*
*

Life is sick
Dogs cough
Bees sail
Birds hack
Trees saw
Woods cry
Men die
Ticks try
Books lie
Ants fly
Goodbye

Rimbaud

Arthur!
On t'appela pas Jean!
Born in 1854 cursing in Charle-
ville thus paving the way for
the abominable murderousnesses
of Ardennes—
No wonder your father left!

So you entered school at 8
—Proficient little Latinist you!
In October of 1869
Rimbaud is writing poetry
in Greek French—
Takes a runaway train

to Paris without a ticket,
the miraculous Mexican Brakeman
throws him off the fast
train, to Heaven, which
he no longer travels because
Heaven is everywhere—
Nevertheless the old fags
intervene—
Rimbaud nonplussed Rimbaud
trains in the green National
Guard, proud, marching
in the dust with his heroes—
hoping to be buggered,
dreaming of the ultimate Girl.
—Cities are bombarded as
he stares & stares & chews
his degenerate lip & stares
with gray eyes at
        Walled France—

André Gill was forerunner
to André Gide—
Long walks reading poems
in the Genet Haystacks—
The Voyant is born,
the deranged seer makes his
        first Manifesto,
gives vowels colors
        & consonants carking care,
comes under the influence
of old French Fairies
who accuse him of constipation
of the brain & diarrhea

of the mouth—
Verlaine summons him to Paris
with less aplomb than he
did banish girls to
        Abyssinia—

"Merde!" screams Rimbaud
at Verlaine salons—
Gossip in Paris—Verlaine Wife
is jealous of a boy
with no seats to his trousers
—Love sends money from Brussels
—Mother Rimbaud hates
the importunity of Madame
Verlaine—Degenerate Arthur
        is suspected of being a poet
            by now—
Screaming in the barn
        Rimbaud writes Season in Hell,
his mother trembles—
Verlaine sends money & bullets
        into Rimbaud—
        Rimbaud goes to the police
        & presents his innocence
        like the pale innocence
        of his divine, feminine Jesus
—Poor Verlaine, 2 years
in the can, but could have
got a knife in the heart

—Illuminations! Stuttgart!
Study of Languages!
On foot Rimbaud walks
& looks thru the Alpine
passes into Italy, looking
        for clover bells, rabbits,
        Genie Kingdoms & ahead
        of him nothing but the old
            Canaletto death of sun
            on old Venetian buildings

—Rimbaud studies language
—hears of the Alleghanies,
of Brooklyn, of last
    American Plages—
His angel sister dies—
    Vienne! He looks at pastries
    & pets old dogs! I hope!
This mad cat joins
    the Dutch Army
    & sails for Java
commanding the fleet
    at midnight
    on the bow, alone,
    no one hears his Command
but every fishy shining
    in the sea—August is no
time to stay in Java—
    Aiming at Egypt, he's again
hungup in Italy so he goes
back home to deep armchair
but immediately he goes
again, to Cyprus, to
    run a gang of quarry
workers,—what did he
    look like now, this Later
    Rimbaud?—Rock dust
& black backs & hacks
    of coughers, the dream rises
in the Frenchman's Africa
mind,—Invalids from
  the tropics are always
    loved—The Red Sea
    in June, the coast clanks
    of Arabia—Havar,
    Havar, the magic trading
    post—Aden, Aden,
     South of Bedouin—
     Ogaden, Ogaden, never
     known—(Meanwhile
     Verlaine sits in Paris

over cognacs wondering
what Arthur looks like
  now, & how bleak their
eyebrows because they believed
in earlier eyebrow beauty—
Who cares? What kinda
Frenchmen are these?
Rimbaud, hit me over the
head with that rock!

Serious Rimbaud composes
elegant & learned articles
for National Geographic
Societies, & after wars
commands Harari Girl
(Ha *Ha* !) back
to Abyssinia, & she
was young, had black
        eyes, thick lips, hair
        curled, & breasts like
        polished brown with
        copper teats & ringlets
        on her arms & joined
          her hands upon her
          central loin & had
          shoulders as broad as
          Arthur's, & little ears
—A girl of some
        caste, in Bronzeville—

        Rimbaud also knew
thinbonehipped Polynesians
with long tumbling hair
  & tiny tits & big feet
  —

        Finally he starts
trading illegal guns
        in Tajoura
        riding in caravans, mad,

with a belt of gold
        around his waist—
Screwed by King Menelek!
The Shah of Shoa!
        The noises of these names
        in that noisy French
        mind!

        Cairo for the summer,
bitter lemon wind
& kisses in the dusty park
  where girls sit folded
        at dusk thinking
        nothing—

        Havar! Havar!
        By litter to Zeyla
        he's carried moaning his
        birthday—the boat
        returns to chalk castle
        Marseilles sadder than
        time, than dream,
        sadder than water
—Carcinoma, Rimbaud
        is eaten by the disease
of overlife—They cut
off his beautiful leg—

        He dies in the arms
        of Ste. Isabelle
        his sister
& before rising to Heaven
sends his francs
        to Djami, Djami
        the Havari boy
        his body servant
        8 years in the African
        Frenchman's Hell,
        & it all adds up
        to nothing, like

Dostoevsky, Beethoven
or Da Vinci—
So, poets, rest awhile
& shut up:
Nothing ever came
of nothing.

Sea

Cherson!
  Cherson!
   You aint just whistlin
    Dixie, Sea——
   Cherson! Cherson!
   .We calcimine fathers
    here below!
   Kitchen lights on——
    Sea Engines from Russia
    seabirding here below——
When rocks outsea froth
 I'll know Hawaii
 cracked up & scramble
 up my doublelegged cliff
to the silt of
 a million years——

Shoo——Shaw——Shirsh——
Go on die salt light
 You billion yeared
  rock knocker

Gavroom
Seabird
Gabroobird
Sad as wife & hill
Loved as mother & fog
Oh! Oh! Oh!
 Sea! Osh!

Where's yr little Neppytune
      tonight?

These gentle tree pulp pages
which've nothing to do
with yr crash roar,
      liar sea, ah,
were made for rock
tumble seabird digdown
      footstep hollow weed
  move bedarvaling
  crash? Ah again?
Wine is salt here?
  Tidal wave kitchen?
Engines of Russia
      in yr soft talk——

Les poissons de la mer
      parle Breton——
Mon nom es Lebris
      de Keroack——
  Parle, Poissons, Loti,
      parle——
Parlning Ocean sanding
    crash the billion rocks——

      Ker plotsch——
      Shore—shoe——
god——brash——

The headland looks like
a longnosed Collie sleeping
with his light on his
    nose, as the ocean,
  obeying its accommodations
  of mind, crashes in
    rhythm which could
  & will intrude, in thy
    rhythm of sand
      thought——

————Big frigging shoulders
on *that* sonofabitch

Parle, O, parle, mer, parle,
  Sea speak to me, speak
    to me, your silver you light
  Where hole opened up in Alaska
    Gray————shh————wind in
      The canyon wind in the rain
      Wind in the rolling rash
      Moving and t wedel
          Sea
           sea
             Diving sea
O bird————la vengeance
    De la roche
        Cossez
        Ah

Rare, he rammed the gate
rare over by Cherson, Cherson,
we calcify fathers here below
————a watery cross, with weeds
entwined—This grins restoredly,
  low sleep————Wave————Oh, no,
shush————Shirk————Boom plop
Neptune now his arms extends
  while one millions of souls
    sit lit in caves of darkness
————What old bark? The dog
mountain? Down by the Sea
  Engines? God rush————Shore————
Shaw————Shoo————Oh soft sigh
  we wait hair twined like
    larks————Pissit————Rest not
————Plottit, bisp tesh, cashes,
  re tav, plo, aravow,
shirsh,————Who's whispering over
    there————the silly earthen creek!
  The fog thunders————We put

silver light on face——We
took the heroes in——A billion
years aint nothing——

O the cities here below!
The men with a thousand
arms! the stanchions of
their upward gaze! the
coral of their poetry! the
sea dragons tenderized, meat
for fleshy fish——
Navark, navark, the fishes
of the Sea speak Breton——
wash as soft as people's
dreams——We got peoples
in & out the shore, they call
it shore, sea call it
pish rip plosh——The
5 billion years since
earth we saw substantial
chan——Chinese are
the waves——the woods
are dreaming

No human words bespeak
the token sorrow older
than old this wave
becrashing smarts the
sand with plosh
of twirléd sandy
thought——Ah change
the world? Ah set
the fee? Are rope the
angels in all the sea?
Ah ropey otter
barnacle'd be——
Ah cave, Ah crosh!
A feathery sea

Too much short——Where
Miss Nop tonight?
Wroten Kerarc'h
in the labidalian
aristotelian park
with slime a middle
——And Ranti forner
who pulled pearls by
rope to throne
the King by
the roll in the
forest of everseas?
Not everseas, *be* seas
——Creep
Crash

The woman with her body
in the sea——The frog who
never moves & thunders, sharsh
——The snake with his body
under the sand——The dog
with the light on his nose,
supine, with shoulders so
enormous they reach back to
rain crack——The leaves hasten
to the sea——We let them
hasten to be wetted & give
em that old salt change, a
nuder think will make you see
they originate from the We Sea
anyway——No dooming booms
on Sunday afternoons——We
run thru the core of cliffs,
blam up caves, disengage no
jelly or jellied pendant
thinkers——

Our armies of
anchored seaweed in the
coves give of the smell

of jellied salt——
    Reach, reach, some leaves
havent hastened near
enuf——Roll, roll, purl
the sand shark floor
a greeny pali andarva
——Ah back——Ah forth——
Ah shish——Boom, away,
doom, a day——Vein we
firm——The sea is We——
  Parle, parle, boom the
    earth——Arree——Shaw,
    Sho, Shoosh, flut,
    ravad, tapavada pow,
  coof, loof, roof,——
        No,no,no,no,no,no——
        Oh ya, ya, ya, yo, yair——
        Shhh——

    Which one? the one? Which
one? The one ploshed——
  The ploshed one? the same,
    ah boom——Who's that ant
that giant golden saltchange
ant magnifying my mountain
of feet? 'Tis Finder, finding
  the change in thought to join
    the boomer hangers in the
    cave a light——And built a
      house above it? Never fear,
        naver foir, les bretons qui
parlent la langue de la Mar
  sont español comme le cul
    du Kurd qui dit le maha
prajna paramita du Sud?
    Ah oui! Ke Vlum!
      Glum sea, silent me——

  They aint about to try
it them ants who wear

out tunnels in a week
the tunnel a million years
won——no——Down around
the headland slobs for weed,
the chicken of the sea
  go yak! they sleep——
Aroar, aroar, arah, aroo——
Otter me otter me daughter me sea
——me last blue lagoon inside of
me, the sea——Divine is the
substance all over the Sea—
    Of space we speak &
  hasten——Let no mouth
    swallow the sea——Gavril——
    Gavro——the Cherson Chinese
    & Old Fingernail sea——Is
    ringin yr ear? Dier, dee?
      Is Virgin you trying to
          fathom me

    Tiresome old sea, aint you sick
      & tired of all of this merde?
this incessant boom boom
& sand walk——you people
hoary rockies here to Fuegie
& never get sad? Or despair
like a German phoney?
Just gloom booboom & green
  on foggy nights——the fog is part
of us——
        I know, but tired
  as I can be listening to all
  this silly majesty——
      Bashô!
      Lao!
      Pop!
      Who is this fish
    sitting unsunk? Run up
    a Hawaii typhoon smash him
    against his rock——We'll jelly you,

jellied man, show you essential
jello of the sea——King
of the Sea.
No Monarc'h ever Irish be?
Ju see the Irish sea?
Green winds on tamarack vines——
Joyce——James——Shhish——
Sea——Sssssss——see
——Varash
——mnavash la vache
écriture——the sea dont say
muc'h actually——

Gosh, she,
huzzy, tow, led men
on, Ulysses and all them
fair headed moin——
Terplash, & what difference
make! One little white
spark of light!
Hair woven hands
Penelope seaboat
smeller——Courtiers in
Telemachus 'sguise
dropedary dropedary
creep——Or——
Franc gold rippled
that undersea creek
where fish fish for
fisher men——Salteen
breen the wet Souwesters
of old Portugee Prayers

Tsall tangled, changed,
salt & drop the sand
& weed & water brains
entangled——Rats
of old Venetian yellers
Ariel Calibanned
to Roma Port——

Pow——spell——
    Speak you parler,
in this my mother's
 parlor, wash your
undershoes when you
   come in, say thanks
  to foggy moon

  Go brash, Topahta
 offat,——we'll gray
  ye rose——Morning
  primord creeper sees
  the bird of paravision
 dying tweet the yellow
mouthroof! How sweet
  the earth, yells sand!
    Xcept when tumble
boom!
    O we wait too
for Heaven——all
in One——
    All is there
in fair & sight

I'm going to wash now
  old Pavia down,
 & pack my salt
   to Either Town——
  Cliffs of Antique
  aint got no rose,
  the morning's seen
 the ledder pose——
  Boom de boom dey
  the sea is me——
  We are the sea——
   It aint all snow

We wash Fujiyama down
   soon, & sand
crookbird back——

We hie bash
rock————ak————
  Long short————
  Low and easy————
  Wind & many freezing
bottoms on luckrock————
  Rappaport————
Endymion thou tangled
dreamer love my thigh
————Rose, Of Shelley,
  Rose, O Urns!
    Ogled urns in fish eye

    Cinco sea the Chico sea
    the Magellan headland sea
————What hype sidereal did he put down
  bending beatnik sea goatee
  over old goat manuscripts
  to find the other side of Flat?
    See round, see the end of me?
Rounden huge bedroom?
    Awp hole cave & shwrul————
  sand & salt & hair eyes

————Strong enuf to make
    coffee grow in your hair————
    Whose planation Neptune got?
    That of Atlas still down there,
    Hesperid's his feet, Sur his sleet,
      Irish Sea fingertip
    & Cornwall aye his soul
      bedoom

Shurning————Shurning————plop
  be dosh————This sigh old learning's
  high beside me————Rough
    old hands have played out
  pedigree, we've sunk more boats
    than dreamer'll ever ever see

——Burning——Burning——The world
is burning & needs waaater
——I'll have a daughter,
        oughter, wait & seee——

    Churning, Churning, Me——
            Panties——Panties——
    these ancient fancies are
        so girling——You've not seen
        mermaids in my actual sea
——You've not seen sexless babies
    with breasts of Majesty——
        My wife——My wife——
        Her name is Oh so really
                    high life

The low life Kingdom where
we part out tea, is sea
  side Me——
            Josh——coof——patra——
Aye ee mo powsh——
Ssst——Cum here read me——
    Dirty postcard——Urchin sea——
        Karash your name——?
    Wanta swim, sink or swim?
    Ears ringing again?
      Sea vibrate rhythm
    crash sets off cave
      hanger blowers whistling
    dog ear back——to sea——
        Arree——
            Gerudge Napoleon nada——
Nada

    Pluto eats the sea——
    Room——
    Hands folded by the sea——
    "On est toutes cachez, mange
le silence," dit les poissons de la
    mer——Ah Mar——Gott——

Thalatta——Merde——Marde
de mer——Mu mer——Mak a vash——
The ocean is the mother——
Je ne suis pas mauvaise quand j'sui
tranquil——dans les tempêtes
j'cril! Come une folle!
j'mange, j'arrache toutes!
Clock——Clack——Milk——
Mai! mai! mai! ma!
says the wind blowing sand——
Pluto eats the sea——
Ami go——da——che pop
Go——Come——Cark——
Care——Kee ter da vo
Kataketa pow! Kek kek kek!
Kwakiutl! Kik!
Some of theserather taratasters
trapped hyra tchere thaped
the anadondak ram ma lat
round by Krul to Pat the lat
rat the anaakakalked
romon t o t t e k
Kara VOOOM
frup——
Feet cold? wade——Mind sore?
sim——sin——Horny?——lay the sea?
Corny? try me——
Ussens here hang no more
here we go, ka va ra ta
plowsh, shhh,
and more, again, ke vlook
ke bloom & here comes
big Mister Trosh
——more waves coming,
every syllable windy

Back wash palaver
paralarle——paralleling
parle pe Saviour

A troublesome spirit
hanging here cant make it
 in the void——The sea'll
only drown me——These words
 are affectations
of sick mortality——
   We try to make our way
 in self reliance, aid
   not ever comes too quick
   from wherever & whatever
   heaven dear may have
   suggested to promise us——

But these waves scare me——
I am going to die
 in full despair——
 Wake up where?
   On second breath in life
   the atmosphere is dearer
   maybe closer to Heaven
   ——O Paradise——
Is the sea really so bad?
 Have you sent men
here for this cold clown
& monstrous eater at the
 world? whose sound
     I mock?

God I've got to believe in you
 or live in death!
 Will you save us——all?
   Soon or now?
 Send illumination
  to our drowning brains
 ——We're pitiful, Lord,
 we need yr help!
  Save us, Dear——
 (Save yourself, God man,
    ha ha!)
 If you were God man

you'd command these waves
  to very well Tennyson stop
    & even Tennyson
        is dear
          now dead
Leave it to the light
  Concern yourself with supper,
    & an eye

    somebody's eye——a wife,
  a girl, a friend, an animal
  ——a blood let drop——
  he for his sea,
    he for his fire,
      thee for thy desire

  "The sea drove me away
    & yelled 'Go to your desire!'
  ——As I hurried up the valley
It added one last yell:-
      'And laugh!'"

    Even the sea cant stop me from
        writing something to read in my old age
  ——This is the chart of brief forms,
    this sea the briefest——Shish yourself——
After scaring me like that, Mar,
I'll excoriate yr slum——yr
  iodine weeds & slime hoops,
  even yr dried hollow seaweed
      stinks——you stink all over——
    Boom——Try that, creep——
    The little Monterey fishingboat
    glides downward home 15 miles to go,
    be home to fried fish & beer b'five——
    It guides the sea its bird routes——
    ——Silver loss forever outward
  ——From blue sky of human bridges
  to the massive mawkcloud sea center
    heap——to the gray——

Some boys call it gunboat blue,
or gray, but I call it
the Civil War of Rocks
——Rocks 'come air, rocks 'come water,
& rock rocks——

Kara tavira, mnash grand bash
——poosh l'abas——croosh
L'a haut——Plash au pied——
Peeeee——Rolle test boulles——
Manche d'la rache——
The handsome King prevails
over boom sing bird head——
"Crache tes idées," spit yr ideas,
says the sea, to me, quite
appro priate ly——
Pss! pss! pss!
Ps! girl inside!
Red shoes scum, eyes of old
sorcerers, toenails hanging down
in the barrel of old firkin cheese
the Dutchman forgot t'eat that
tempest
nineteen O
sixteen——
When torpedoed by gunboat
Pedro in the Valley
of a Million Fees?

When Magellan crosseyed
ate the Amazonian feet——
And, Ah, when Colombo cross't!
When Drake sir francised the waves
with feeding of the blue jay
dark——pounded his aleward
tank before the boom,
housed up all thoughts of Erik
the Red the Greenland caperer
& builder of rockdungs in New
Port——*New*——yet——

Oldport Indian Fishhead——
Oldport Tattoo Kwakiutl Headpost
   taboo potash Coyotl potlatch?
Old Primitive Columbia.——
Named for Colom *bus*?
   Name for Aruggio Vesmarica——
      Ar!——Or!——Da!
         What about Verrazano?
he sailed!——
         He Verrazano zailed & we
   statened his Island in on deep

in on dashun—
         Rotted the Wallower?
      Sinners liars goodmen all
   sink waterswim drink Neptune's
      nectar the zal sotat——
         Zal sotate name for crota?
      Crota ta crotte, you aint
      'bout to find (Jesus Christian!)
any dry turds here below——
      Why fo no?
      Go crash yonder rock
   of bleak with yr filet mignon teeth
      & see——For you, the hearth,
      the heart, the lock of hair——
         For me, for us, the Sea,
      the murdering of time by eating
         lusty cracks of lip feed wave
            at aeons of sandy artistry
            till nothing's left but old age
               newmorning primordial pain
            of sitters by
               the unborn
               bird
            of roses yet undone——

   With weeds your roses,
sand crabs your hummers?
With buzzers in the sea!

With runners in the deep!
This Sceptred Osh, this wide leg
  spanning rock U.S. to rock
    Ja Pan, this onstable
    roller roaming all,
    this ploosher at yr gory
      dry dung door, this mouth
  of silverwhite arring to hold thee,
    this purger of conscience
    arra for thee——
      No mouse in here but's got
        a little glee——and
        aft, or oft, the osprey
        in his glee's agley——
            Oh purty purty ocean
                me——
                    Sop! bring the Scepter down!
Again you've accepted me!

  Breathe our iodine, filthy yr drink,
faint at feet wet, drop
  yr profile move it in the sea,
float weeded watery Adonais
  longs for thee——& Shelley three,
    that's three——burn in salt
  with slow most change——
  We've had no crack at eternity
  in a billion years of trying——
      one grain of sand possesses
      3 thousand worlds of glee——
    not to mention me——
            Ah sea

      Ah si——Ah so——
shoot——shiver——mix——
    ha roll——tara——ta ta——
    curlurck——Kayash——Kee——
Pearls pearls in the yellow West
    ——Yellow sky to China——
Pacific we named here

water as always meeting
water——Pacific Pacific
  Pacific tapfic——geroom——
gedowsh—gaka—gaya——
   Tatha——gata——mana——
   What sails used old bhikkus?
   Dhikkus? Dhikkus!
What raft mailed Mose
to the hoven dovepost?
  What saved Blackswirl
   from the Kidd plank?
  What Go-Bug here?
   Seet! Seeeeeeeeeee
   eeeeee——kara——
    Pounders out yar——

Big Sur they call this sand
  these rocks this creek?
  Raton Canyon by name pours
  Coyote leaves & old Pomo bones
& old dust of Tomahawks
   into your angler'd maw——
   My salt maw shall salvage
   Taylors——sewing in the room
            below——

Sewing weed shrat for hikers
  in the milky silt——
  Sewing crosswards
   for certainty——Sartan
are we of Price Victory
in this salt War with thee
& thine thee jellied yink!
   Look O the sea here called
    Pacific Sea!
      T a k i !

My golden empty soul'll
outlast yr salty sill
——the Windows of my jelly eye

& fish head muck look out on thee,
   slit, with cigar-a-mouth,
some contempt——
          Yet I hie me to see you
——you hie thee to eat
   me——Fair in sight
      and worn, aright——
Arra! Aroo!
   Ger der va——
   Silly silent cities in the sea
 have children playing cardboard
mush with eignyard old Englander
      beeplates slickered oer with scum
               of histories below——
No tempest as still & awful
            as the tempest within——
Sorcerer hip! Buddhalands
      & Buddhaseas!
   What sails Maudgalyayana used
      he only knows to tell
     but got kilt by yellers
sreaming down the cliff
            "Let's go home!
               Now!"
——leave marge smashed djamas
Maudgalyayana was murdered by the sea——
         But the sea dont tell——
      The sea dont murder——
         The seadrang scholars
            oughter know that
               or
            go back to School

   Hear over there the ocean motor?
Feel the splawrsh of it?
   Six silly centepedes here, Machree——
         Ah Ratatatatatat——
the machinegun sea, rhythmic
   balls of you pouring in
   with smooth eglantinee

in yr pedigreed milkpup
  tenor——
Tinder marsh aright arrooo——
  arrac'h——arrache——
Kamac'h——monarc'h——
  Kerarc'h Jevac'h—
Tamana———gavow——
  Va——Voovla——Via——
    Mia——mine——
        sea
        poo

Farewell, Sur——

  Didja ever tell him
  about water meeting water——?
O go back to otter——
  Term——Term——Klerm
Kerm——Kurn——Cow——Kow——
  Cash——Cac'h——Cluck——
    Clock——Gomeat sea need
      be deep I see you
        Enoc'h
      soon anarf
    in Old Brittany

21 August 1960
Pacific Ocean at Big Sur
California

Sept. 16, 1961, Poem

How awfully sad I felt thinking of my sleeping mother in her
  bed
that she'll die someday
tho she herself says "death is nothing to worry about,
from this life we start to another"
How awfully sad I felt anyway——

That have no wine to make me forget my rotting teeth is bad
    enough
but that my whole body is rotting and my mother's body is
    rotting
towards death, it's all so insanely sad.
I went outside in the pure dawn: but why should I be glad
    about
a dawn
that dawns on another rumor of war,
and why should I be sad: isnt the air at least pure and fresh?
I looked at the flowers on the bush: one of them had fallen:
another was just bloomed open: neither of them were sad or
    glad.
I suddenly realized all things just come and go
    including any feelings of sadness: that too will go:
      sad today glad tomorrow: somber today drunk tomorrow:
        why fret
        so much?
          Everybody in the world has flaws just like me.
            Why should I put myself down? Which is a feeling
            just coming to go.
            Everything comes and goes. How good it is!
          Evil wars wont stay forever!
           Pleasant forms also go.
            Since everything just comes and goes O why
            be sad? or glad?
            Sick today healthy tomorrow. But O I'm so
            sad just the same!
            Just coming and going all over the place,
              the place itself coming and going.
              We'll all end up in heaven anyway, together
              in that golden eternal bliss I saw.
                O how damned sad I cant write about it
                well.
                This is an attempt at the easy lightness
                of Ciardian poetry.
                I should really use my own way.
                  But that too will go, worries about
                  style. About sadness.

My little happy purring cat hates
    doors!
And sometimes he's sad and silent,
    hot nose, sighs,
        and a little heartbroken mew.
        There go the birds, flying west
            a moment.
            Who's going to ever know the
                world before it goes?

A Pun for Al Gelpi

Jesus got mad one day
    at an apricot tree.
He said, "Peter, you
    of the Holy See,
Go see if the tree is ripe."
    "The tree is not yet ripe,"
    reported back Peter the Rock.
"Then let it wither!"
Jesus wanted an apricot.
In the morning, the tree
    had withered,
Like the ear in the agony
    of the garden,
Struck down by the sword.
    Unready.
    What means this parable?
Everybody
    better see.
You're really sipping
When your glass
    is always empty.

To Edward Dahlberg

Don't use the telephone.
People are never ready to answer it.
Use poetry.

A Selection of Uncollected Haikus

Mad wrote curtains
        of
poetry on fire

———

Chang Su Chi's art
    studio, a silent
Shade in the window

———

The sun keeps getting
    dimmer—foghorns
began to blow in the bay

———

Time keeps running out
        —sweat
On my brow, from playing

———

The sky is still empty,
    The rose is still
On the typewriter keys

Rain's over, hammer on wood
    —this cobweb
Rides the sun shine

———

In the sun
    the butterfly wings
Like a church window

———

In the chair
    I decided to call Haiku
By the name of Pop

———

The purple wee flower
    should be reflected
In that low water

———

The red roof of the barn
    is ravelled
Like familiar meat

———

Swinging on delicate hinges
    the Autumn Leaf
Almost off the stem

———

Rainy night,
    the top leaves wave
In the gray sky

THE LIGHT BULB
    SUDDENLY WENT OUT—
STOPPED READING

———

Tathagata neither loathes
        nor loves
His body's milk or shit

———

Looking around to think
    I saw the thick white cloud
Above the house

———

Looking up to see
        the airplane
I only saw the TV aerial

———

My butterfly came
        to sit in my flower,
Sir Me

———

You'd be surprised
        how little I knew
Even up to yesterday

———

Two Japanese boys
        singing
Inky Dinky Parly Voo

Take up a cup of water
    from the ocean
And there I am

———

Leaf dropping straight
    In the windless midnight:
The dream of change

———

Stop slipping me
    Your old Diamond Sutra
You illimitable tight-ass!

———

Or, walking the same or different
    paths
The moon follows each

———

Old man dying in a room—
    Groan
At five o'clock

———

The mist in front
    of the morning mountains
—late Autumn

———

Samsara in the morning
    —puppy yipping,
Hot motor steaming

Praying all the time—
        talking
To myself

————

The Sunny Breeze
        will come to me
Presently

————

Coming from the West,
        covering the moon,
Clouds—not a sound

————

Phantom Rose
        Lust
Is a Leopard

————

I drink my tea
        and say
Hm hm

————

Dusk in the holy
        woods—
Dust on my window

————

The bird came on the branch
        —danced three times—
And burred away

The raindrops have plenty
   of personality
Each one

————

Me, you—you, me
   Everybody—
He-he

————

Do you know why my name is Jack?
   Why?
That's why.

————

Wild to sit on a haypile,
   Writing Haikus,
Drinkin wine

————

Waitin for the Zipper
   4 PM—
Sun in West clouds, gold

————

Gull sailing
   in the saffron sky—
The Holy Ghost wanted it

————

Water in a hole
   —behold
The sodden skies

Rain in North Carolina
　　—the saints
Are still meditating

————

The yellow dolls bow—
　　Poor lady
Is dead

————

Haiku, shmaiku, I cant
　　understand the intention
Of Reality

————

I went in the woods
　　to meditate—
It was too cold

————

Early morning with the
　　happy dogs—
I forgot the Path

————

What could be newer? this
　　new little bird
Not yet summer fat!

————

The dog yawned
　　and almost swallowed
My Dharma

Concatenation!—the bicycle
    pulls the wagon
Because the rope is tied

———

White clouds of this steamy planet
    obstruct
My vision of the blue void

———

Grass waves,
    hens chuckle,
Nothing's happening

———

A spring mosquito
    dont even know
How to bite!

———

All that ocean of blue
    soon as those clouds
Pass away

———

Propped up on my shoe
    the Diamond Sutra—
Propped up on a pine root

———

Silent pipe—
    peace and quiet
In my heart

Why'd I open my eyes?
   because
I wanted to

———

There is no deep
      turning-about
In the Void

———

The pine woods
      move
In the mist

———

There's no Buddha
      because
There's no me

———

Emptiness
   of the Ananda glass bead,
Is the bowing weeds

———

WARM WIND
      makes the pines
Talk Deep

———

Spring dusk
      on Fifth Avenue,
A bird

Walking along the night beach,
   —Military music
On the boulevard.

———

Grain Elevators are tall trucks
   that let the road
approach them

———

Grain Elevators on
   Saturday waiting for
The farmers to come home

———

On Starvation Ridge
   little sticks
Are trying to grow

———

Hitch hiked a thousand
   miles and brought
You wine

———

A bubble, a shadow—
   woop—
The lightning flash

———

Mist boiling from the
   ridge—the mountains
Are clean

Mist before the peak
   —the dream
Goes on

––––

The sound of silence
   is all the instruction
You'll get

––––

Desolation, Desolation,
   wherefore have you
Earned your name?

––––

While meditating
   I am Buddha—
Who else?

––––

Desolation, Desolation,
   so hard
To come down off of

––––

Mayonnaise—
   mayonnaise comes in cans
Down the river

––––

Girls' footprints
   in the sand
—Old mossy pile

Wooden house
    raw gray—
Pink light in the window

———

Neons, Chinese restaurants
    coming on—
Girls come by shades

———

New aluminum
    grammar school
In old lamplight

———

Napoleon in bronze
    the burning Blakean
mountains

———

Velvet horses
    in the valley auction—
Woman sings

———

River wonderland—
    The emptiness
Of the golden eternity

———

No imaginary judgments
    of form,
The clouds

Butterfat soil
of the valley—
Big black slugs

———

God's dream,
It's only
A dream

———

America: fishing licenses
the license
To meditate

———

Reflected upsidedown
in the sunset lake, pines,
Pointing to infinity

———

All I see is what
I see—
Red fire sunset

———

She loves Lysander
not Demetrius—
Who?—Hermia

———

I don't care
what
thusness is

Alpine fir with
    snowcap't background—
It doesn't matter

———

Late afternoon—
    the lakes sparkle
Blinds me

———

I made raspberry fruit jello
    The color of rubies
In the setting sun

———

Ah who cares?
    I'll do what I want—
Roll another joint

———

Sixty sunsets have I seen
    revolve on this perpendicular hill

———

Nirvana, as when the rain
    puts out a little fire

———

Sunday—
    the sky is blue,
The flowers are red

The red paper
    waves for the breeze
—the breeze

———

Flowers
    aim crookedly
At the straight death

———

Nored the Atlantican Astrologer
    weeps because the King
Laid his Autumn girl

———

Ghengis Khan looks fiercely
    east, with red eyes,
Hungering for Autumn vengeance

———

Geronimo, in Autumn
    says no to peaceful
Cochise—Smoke rises

———

Mao Tse Tung has taken
    too many Siberian sacred
Mushrooms in Autumn

———

Barley soup in Scotland
    in November—
Misery everywhere

Moon behind
Black clouds—
Silver seas

————

Coffee beans!
—Methinks I smell
The Canaries!

————

Highest perfect fool—
the wisdom
Of the two-legged rat

————

Abbid abbayd ingrat
—Lighthouse
On the Azores

————

A bottle of wine,
a bishop—
Everything is God

————

"You and me"
I sang
Looking at the cemetery

————

Shall I heed God's commandment?
—wave breaking
On the rocks—

Shall I break God's commandment?
    Little fly
Rubbing its back legs

————

Blowing in the afternoon wind,
    on a white fence,
A cobweb

————

Spring is coming
    Yep, all that equipment
For sighs

————

The vigorous bell-ringing priest
    the catch in the harbor

————

Rock rosed—behind the Casbah
    the sun has disappearing act

————

Three pencils arranged,
    Three minutes,
Sambaghakaya, Nirvanakaya, Dharmakaya

————

"The wind agrees with me
    not the sun"—
Washlines

The barking dog—
Kill him
With a bicycle wheel

———

Man dying—
Harbor lights
On still water

———

The microscopic red bugs
in the sea-side sand
Do they meet and greet?

———

Hand in hand in a red valley
with the universal shoolteacher—
the first morning

———

Old man of Aix
white hair, beret—
Gone up the Cezanne street

———

Who cares about the pop-off trees
of Provence?—
A road's a road

———

Somebody rang my bell
I said who?
O it doesn't worldly care

O Sebastian, where art thou?
   Pa, watch over us!
Saints, thank you!

———

Lonesome blubbers
   grinding out the decades
With wet lips

———

Full moon in the trees
   —across the street,
the jail

———

My friend standing
   in my bedroom—
The spring rain

———

Moth sleeping
   on the newly plastered wall
—the spring rain

———

The jazz trombone,
   The moving curtain,
—Spring rain

———

Greyhound bus,
   flowing all night,
Virginia

My flashlight,
    where I put it this afternoon
Twisted away in sleep

———

    The book
       stands all by itself
   on the shelf

———

My hand,
   A thing with hairs,
rising and falling with my belly

———

    Here comes
      My dragon—
  goodbye!

———

   Loves his own belly
     The way I love my life,
  The white cat

———

   The little white cat
     Walks in the grass
  With his tail up in the air

———

   The white cat
    Is green in the tree shade,
  Like Gauguin's horse

The dregs of my coffee
Glisten
In the morning light

———

Haiku! Haiku!
Still wears a bandage
Over his injured eye!

———

How'd those guys
get in here,
those two flies?

———

The backyard I tried to draw
—It still looks
The same

———

The son who wants solitude,
Enveloped
In his room

———

All these sages
Sleep
With their mouths open

———

I hate the ecstasy
Of that rose,
That hairy rose

May grass—
  Nothing much
To do

―――

A pussywillow grew there
  At the foot
Of the breathless tree

―――

The earth keeps turning
  Like a dreary
Immortal

―――

  Gary Snyder
   is a haiku
  far away

―――

  On the sidewalk
   A dead baby bird
  For the ants

―――

How that butterfly'll wake up
  When someone
Bongs that bell

―――

  Waving goodbye,
   the little girl,
  Backing up

Why explain?
bear burdens
In silence

———

The ant struggles escaping
from the web—
The spider's non-comment

———

The mind of the flower
regards my mind
Externally

———

Buddha laughing
on Mt. Lanka!
Like Jimmy Durante!

———

The flowers don't seem
to mind
the stupid May sunshine

———

The rose moves
like a Reichian disciple
On its stem

———

Suddenly the official
goes cross eyed
And floats away

The strumming of the trees
    reminded me
Of immortal afternoon

———

Forever and forever
    everything's alright—
midnight woods

———

Voices of critics
    in the theater lobby—
A moth on the carpet

———

Birds chirp
    fog
Bugs the gate

———

My Japanese blinds
    are down—
I'm reading about Ethiopia

———

My Christ blinds
    are down—
I'm reading about Virgin

———

Winking over his pipe
    the Buddha lumberman
Nowhere

The Golden Gate
    creaks
With sunset rust

———

Smell of burning leaves,
    The quiet pool at evening
In August

———

April mist—
    under the pine
At midnight

———

Drizzle—
    Midnight pine,
I sit dry

———

Wet fog
    shining
In lamplit leaves

———

Spring day—
    in my mind
Nothing

———

Late April
    dusk bluster—
Lions & lambs

The train speeding
thru emptiness
—I was a trainman

———

The trees are putting on
Noh plays—
Booming, roaring

———

Train on the horizon—
my window
rattles

———

Mist falling
—Purple flowers
Growing

———

Red light on pingpong—the fire engine screams
On my hat/a big shit—the crow flies.
Under my hat/a big shit—the crow flies.

———

Autumn nite—
Lucien's wife
Playing the guitar

———

Autumn nite—
the boys
playing haiku.

Autumn nite—
my mother cuts her throat

———

Autumn nite
   —Lucien leans to Jack
on the couch.

———

Autumn nite—
my mother remembers
my birth.

———

Late autumn nite
the last faint cricket.

———

The little sparrow on the eave drainpipe
My heart flutters

———

These little gray sparrows on the roof
I'll shoot my editor.

———

I gotta make it in terms/that anyone can understand/
Did I tell ya about my nightmare?

———

Cloudy autumn nite
   —cold water drips
in the sink.

Autumnal
Cowflops—
but a man must
make a living.

———

Autumnal cowflops—
a man
Makes a living.

———

Walking down road with Allen—
Walking down the road in Autumn.

———

Walking down the road
with Allen
—An old dream
the same dream.

———

Autumn night stove
—I've never been
on a farm before.

———

Jack reads his book
aloud at nite
—the stars come out.

———

Brokenback goodshit
Heap bigshot
among the Birchtrees.

Walking down the road with dog
—a crushed leaf

———

Walking with the dog on the road
—a crooked leaf.

———

Walking down the road with Jack—
a crushed snake.

———

Walking down the road
with dog—
a crushed snake.

———

Walking down the road/a crushed snake.
autumn
Red trees—

———

Red trees—
the dog tears at
an old itch

———

Fall trees
Dog knocks old itch

• • • • • • • • • • •

Puddles at dusk
   —one drop
fell

———

Lilacs at dusk
   —one petal
fell

———

On Desolation
   I was the alonest man
in the world

———

Moon in the
   bird bath—
One star too

———

I don't care—
   the low yellow
Moon loves me

———

High noon
   in Northport
—Alien shore

———

The night
   is red
with stars

Glow worms
      brightly sleeping
On my flowers

———

Wind too strong
      —empty nest
At midnight

———

My blue spruce
      in the pale
Haze dusk

———

August Moon Universe
      —neither new
Nor old

———

The Angel's hair
      trailed on my chin
Like a cobweb

———

Stare intently
      at my candle
—Pool of wax

———

September raindrops
      from my roof—
Soon icicles

Night rain—neighbors
　　Arguing loud voices
In next house

———

Four in morning—
　　creak my mother
In her bed

———

Lay the pencil
　　away—no more
thoughts, no lead

———

To the South,
　　in the moonlight,
A sash of cloud

———

June—the snow
　　of blossoms
On the ground

———

The mansion of
　　the moon
Has hidden faces

———

Ah, the crickets
　　are screaming
at the moon

The tree moving
    in the moonlight
Wise to me

———

Middle of my Mandala
    —Full moon
In the water

———

At night
    The girl I denied
Walking away

———

My hands on my lap
    June night,
Full moon

———

Full moon—
    Pine tree—
Old house

———

Trees cant reach
    for a glass
Of water

———

Three little sparrows
    on the roof
Talking quietly, sadly

Big books packaged
    from Japan—
Ritz crackers

———

The full moon—
    the cat gone—
My sleeping mother

———

Reading the sutra
I decided
To go straight

———

One drop from
    the blue spruce—
two more drops

———

Spring moon
    on 2nd Avenue
—girl in white coat

———

Spring evening—
    hobo with hard on
Like bamboo

———

Water in the birdbath
    —a film of ice
On the moon

Snow on the grape
    arbor—the little
dead raisins

———

Buds in the snow
    —the deadly fight
between two birds

———

Desk cluttered
    with mail—
My mind is quiet

———

Drinking wine
    —the Queen of Greece
on a postage stamp

———

Playing basketball
    —the lady next door
Watching again

———

New neighbors
    —light
In the old house

———

Just woke up
    —afternoon pines
Playing the wind.

Gray day—
       the blue spruce
Is green

———

Bach through an open
       dawn window—
the birds are silent

———

Sweet birds, chordless
       except in another
Clime

———

A half a tsphah
       is worse
than none

———

Ah the birds
       at dawn,
my mother and father

———

Answered a letter
       and took a hot bath
—Spring rain

———

You paid yr homage
       to the moon,
And she sank

Sun shining on
   A distant mountain
—the low moon

———

OO a continent
   in a birdbath—
April full moon

———

Waiting with me for
   the end of this ephemeral
Existence—the moon

———

Pink petals on
   gnarly Japanese twigs
In rain

———

In the lovely sun
   reading lovely
Haikus—Spring

———

Some trees still
   have naked winter look
—Spring day

———

Sitting in the sun,
   no bugs yet—
Yellow clover

My corncob pipe
   hot from
the sun

———

The white chair is
   holding its arms out
to Heaven—dandelions

———

Spring night—
   the neighbor hammering
In the new old house

———

A bird pecking kernels
   on a grassy hillside
Just mowed

———

Night—six petals
   have fallen from
Bodhidharma's bouquet

———

Shooting star!—no,
   lightning bug!
ah well, June night

———

Lost cat Timmy—
   he wont be back
In a blue moon

After the shower
      my cat meowing
on the porch

———

After the shower
      the red roses
In the green, green

———

The leaves, fighting
      the empty sky—
No clouds helping

———

The cat musing
      along the ground—
cold gray day

———

Red roses, white
      clouds, blue sky,
In my birdbath

———

The robin on
      the television antenna,
Something on his beak

———

Roses! Roses!
      robin wants his
Evening bath!

Second thundershower
over—the sun
Is still high

———

Worm is looking
at the moon,
Waiting for me

———

Thunderstorm over
—there! The light
is on again

———

My cat's asleep
—poor little angel,
the burden of flesh!

———

Men and women
Yakking beneath
the eternal Void

———

Girl trapped beneath the
steering wheel, beautiful
As the Dalai Lama's dream

———

The droopy constellation
on the grassy hill—
Emily Dickinson's Tomb

Am I a flower
        bee, that you
Stare at me?

———

Walking over the water
        my shadow,
Heavier than lead

———

I woke up
        —two flies were boffing
On my forehead

———

Cool breezy morning
        —the cat is rolling
On his back

———

Early morning gentle rain,
        two big bumblebees
Humming at their work

———

Summer night—
        I put out
The empty milk bottle

———

Alone, in old
        clothes, sipping wine
Beneath the moon

Autumn eve—my
    mother playing old
Love songs on the piano

————

Oh another weekend's
    started—people squeaking
On U-turning tires

————

Staring at each other,
    Squirrel in the branch
Cat in the grass

————

After the earthquake,
    A child crying
In the silence

————

Little frogs screaming
    in the ditch
At nightfall

————

After a year and a half
    finally saw the rat,
Big and fat

————

"The old pond, yes!
    —the water jumped into
By a frog"

Nose hairs in the moon
   —My ass
Is cold

———

Mexico—After the dim
   markets, bright
San Juan Letran

———

Two cars passing
   on the freeway
—Husband and wife

———

October night, lights
   of Connecticut towns
Across the sound

———

Apassionata Sonata
   —hiballs, gray
Afternoon in October

———

Hot tea, in the cold
   moonlit snow—
a burp

———

Sunday in a bar
   in Woodland Calif.
—One noon beer

Racing westward through
   the clouds in the howling
wind, the moon

———

The whiteness of the houses
   in the moon
Snow everywhere

———

Windows rattling
   in the wind
I'm a lousy lover

———

Oh I could drink up
   The whole Yellow River
In my love for Li Po!

———

The falling snow—
   The hissing radiators—
The bride out there

———

In enormous blizzard
   burying everything
My cat's out mating

———

In enormous blizzard
   burying everything—
My cat turned back

Spring night—the gleam
    of the fish head eye
In the grass

———

Too hot to write
    haiku—crickets
and mosquitoes

———

Sometimes they sleep
    with their lights on,
the June bugs

———

My critics jiggle
    constantly like
Poison ivy in the rain

———

Dusk now—
    what's left of
An ancient pier

———

Two clouds kissing
    backed up to look
At each other

———

In the middle of
    the corn, a new
Car slithering

Horse waving his tail
      in a field of clover
At sundown

———

The clouds are
      following each other
Into Eternity

———

Mule on the seashore
      One thousand foot
Bridge above

———

The bird's still on top
      of that tree,
High above the fog

———

Temple trees
      across the creek
—Fog blowing

———

One flower
      on the cliffside
Nodding at the canyon

———

A long way from
      The Beat Generation
In the rain forest

Huge knot in the
    Redwood tree
Looking like Zeus' face

———

How cold!—late
    September baseball—
the crickets

———

Leaves falling everywhere
    in the November
Midnight moonshine

———

Free as a pine
    goofing
For the wind

———

High in the Sky
    the Fathers Send Messages
From on High

———

Walking on water wasn't
    Built in a day

———

Autumn night
    Salvation Army sign
On a cold brick building

Crisp wind
    My tired limbs
Relaxed before the coals

———

Spring rain,
    Kicking stones
An arrowhead

———

Winter—that
    sparrow's nest
Still empty

———

Snow in my shoe
    Abandoned
Sparrow's nest

———

November's New Haven
    baggagemaster stiffly
Disregards my glance

———

Big drinking & piano
    parties—Christmas
Come and gone—

———

A current pimple
    In the mind's
Old man

Sleeping on my desk
    head on the sutras,
my cat

———

The moon is moving,
    thru the clouds
Like a slow balloon

———

Chou en Lai, his briefcase
    should be fulla leaves,
For all I know

———

And as for Kennedy—
    in Autumn he slept
By swishing peaceful trees

———

Thanks to Coolidge,
    Hoover—but Autumn,
Roosevelt done America in

———

Everyone of my knocks
    disturbs my daughter
Sleeping in her December grave

———

Ah Jerusalem—how many
    Autumn saints slaughtered
Thee with Christ?

A bird hanging
on the wire
At dawn

———

Ah, Genghiz Khan
weeping—where
did Autumn go?

———

Christ on the Cross crying
—his mother missed
Her October porridge

———

The cows of Autumn—
laughing along the fence,
Roosters at Dawn

———

The son packs
quietly as the
Mother sleeps

———

Yellow halfmoon cradled
among the horizontal boards
Of my fence

———

Frogs don't care
just sit there
Brooding on the moon

Dawn—the first
robins singing
To the new moon

———

The wind sent
a leaf on
the robin's back

———

The carpenter of spring
the Zen
of hammer and nail

———

Spring night
the silence
Of the stars

———

Yard tonight an eerie
moon leafshroud
A midsummernight's dream

———

Haydn's creation or
Coleman Hawkins, I can
Fix em just right

———

The racket of the starlings
in the trees—
My cat's back

Ooh! they kicked up
a cloud of dust!
The birds in my yard

———

Haiku my eyes!
my mother is calling!

———

Close your eyes—
Landlord knocking
On the back door

———

A quiet Autum night
and these fools
Are starting to argue

———

Lonely brickwalls in Detroit
Sunday afternoon
piss call

———

O for
Vermont again—
The barn on an Autumn night

———

Wish I were a rooster
and leave my sperm
On the sidewalk, shining!

In Hokkaido a cat
has no luck

———

Every cat in Kyoto
can see through the fog

———

I'll climb up a tree
and scratch Katapatafataya

———

If I go out now,
my paws
will get wet

———

Kneedeep, teeth
to the blizzard,
My cat gazing at me

———

Kneedeep in the
blizzard, the ancient
Misery of the cat

———

Surprising cat fight
in the parlor on a
Blustery September night

Rain-in-the-Face
    looks from the hill:
Custer down there

———

Sitting Bull adjusts
    his girdle: the smell
Of smoking fish

———

The fly, just as
    lonesome as I am
In this empty house

———

The other man, just as
    lonesome as I am
In this empty universe

CHRONOLOGY

NOTE ON THE TEXTS

NOTES

Chronology

1922	Born Jean-Louis Kerouac on March 12 at the family home at 9 Lupine Road in Lowell, Massachusetts, the third child of Joseph Alcide Leon (Leo) Kerouac and Gabrielle Lévesque Kerouac, and is baptized at St. Louis-de-France Church on March 19. (Father, born 1889 in St. Hubert, Quebec, immigrated with his family to Nashua, New Hampshire, where he learned printing. He later moved to Lowell, where he became the manager and printer of *L'Etoile*, a weekly French newspaper, and sold insurance. Mother, born 1895 in St. Pacome, Quebec, also immigrated as a child to Nashua. Orphaned at age 16, she was working in a shoe factory when she married Leo Kerouac on October 25, 1915. Their first son, Gerard, was born on August 23, 1916, and their daughter Caroline was born on October 25, 1918.) Family speaks French-Canadian dialect at home.
1923	Father opens his own print shop in Lowell.
1925	Family moves to 35 Burnaby Street. Gerard becomes seriously ill with rheumatic fever.
1926	Family moves to 34 Beaulieu Street. Gerard dies on June 2.
1927	Family moves to 320 Hildreth Street.
1928	Kerouac enters St. Louis-de-France parochial school, where classes are taught in both English and French. Family moves to 240 Hildreth Street.
1930	Family moves to 66 West Street.
1932	Family leaves Centralville section of Lowell and moves to Phebe Avenue in the Pawtucketville section, where father becomes the manager of a social club. Kerouac attends St. Joseph's parochial school.
1933–35	Enters Bartlett Junior High School in 1933, where all classes are conducted in English. Begins keeping his first journals and records his achievements in sports. Develops a baseball game played with cards, marbles, and dice, and invents an imaginary league and fictitious players. Writes short stories, draws cartoons, and invents mysterious character "Dr. Sax." Reads extensively in school and at the public library.

1936   Merrimack River floods in March, causing extensive damage
              to father's print shop. Family moves to 35 Sarah Avenue.
              Kerouac enters Lowell High School in the tenth grade.

1937–39   Excels in sports, especially as a sprinter in track and a
              running back in football. Reads Thomas Wolfe, William
              Saroyan, Henry David Thoreau, Mark Twain, and others.
              Father sells his shop in 1937 and becomes a printer for hire
              while mother begins working in a shoe factory; financial
              strain is increased by father's gambling and drinking. Family
              moves to tenement at 736 Moody Street. Kerouac becomes
              close friends with Sebastian Sampas and discusses litera-
              ture, philosophy, and politics with him and a small group
              of friends.

1939–40   Graduates from Lowell High School on June 28, 1939. Re-
              ceives football scholarship from Columbia University on
              condition that he attend Horace Mann, a preparatory school
              in the Bronx, for a year. Lives with his mother's stepmother
              in Brooklyn and commutes to school by subway. Publishes
              his first fiction in the *Horace Mann Quarterly* and is intro-
              duced to live jazz in Harlem by classmate Seymour Wyse.
              Writes about jazz and sports for the school newspaper.

1940   Enters Columbia in September. Fractures tibia in his right
              leg during his second game with the freshman squad and
              spends months recuperating.

1941   Receives high grades in French and literature courses but
              fails chemistry. Spends summer in Lowell and in New
              Haven, where his parents move in August. Returns to
              Columbia in September. Quarrels with the coaching staff,
              quits the football team, and leaves school. Moves to Hart-
              ford, Connecticut, where he works as a gas station atten-
              dant and writes a short story collection, "Atop an Under-
              wood" (some of the stories are posthumously published
              in *Atop an Underwood: Early Stories and Other Writing*
              in 1999). Returns to Lowell when his parents move back
              to the city. Registers for naval aviation training after the
              Japanese bomb Pearl Harbor. Becomes a sports reporter
              for the *Lowell Sun* while waiting to be called up.

1942   Quits the *Sun* in March and goes to Washington, D.C.,
              where he works on the construction of the Pentagon and
              as a short-order cook. Returns to Lowell, then joins the

Merchant Marine and sails from Boston in July as a scul-
lion on the army transport ship *Dorchester*. Sails along the
Greenland coast before returning to Boston in October.
(The *Dorchester* is sunk by a German submarine on Febru-
ary 3, 1943, with the loss of 675 lives.) Accepts invitation
to rejoin the Columbia football squad, but quits after he is
benched during the Army game. Stays in New York during
the fall and begins affair with Edie Parker (b. 1922), an art
student from Grosse Pointe, Michigan. Works on novel *The
Sea Is My Brother*. Returns to Lowell in December.

1943   Fails examination for flight training and is sent in March
        to naval boot camp in Newport, Rhode Island, where he
        is committed to the base hospital for psychiatric observa-
        tion after repeated acts of insubordination. Transferred
        to Bethesda, Maryland, where he is diagnosed as having
        "schizoid tendencies" and given a psychiatric discharge
        from military service. Joins his parents, who are now liv-
        ing at 94-10 Cross Bay Boulevard in Ozone Park, Queens,
        New York. Rejoins the Merchant Marine and sails from
        New York in September on the *George Weems*, a Liberty
        ship carrying bombs to Liverpool. Returns to New York in
        October. Divides his time between Ozone Park and apart-
        ment on West 118th Street that Edie Parker shares with Joan
        Vollmer Adams. Meets Columbia undergraduate Lucien
        Carr (b. 1925).

1944   Introduced by Carr to William S. Burroughs (b. 1917),
        Columbia undergraduate Allen Ginsberg (b. 1926), and
        David Kammerer (b. 1911), Carr's former scoutmaster who
        had followed him to New York from St. Louis. Sebastian
        Sampas dies on March 2 after being wounded while serving
        as an army medic on the Anzio beachhead in Italy. Works
        on *Galloway*, novel that eventually becomes *The Town and
        the City*. Carr fatally stabs Kammerer in Riverside Park on
        August 14, then visits Kerouac, who helps Carr dispose of
        his knife and Kammerer's glasses. Kerouac is arrested as
        a material witness after Carr turns himself in and is jailed
        when his father refuses to post bail. Marries Edie Parker
        in a civil ceremony on August 22 and is released after she
        obtains bail money from her family. They move to Grosse
        Pointe, Michigan, where Kerouac works in a ball-bearing
        factory. (Carr pleads guilty to manslaughter and serves two
        years in prison.) Sails from New York in October on the

Liberty ship *Robert Treat Paine*, but jumps ship in Nor-
folk, Virginia, and returns to New York. On November 16
Kerouac estimates that he has written 500,000 words since
1939, including "nine unfinished novels." Edie returns to
New York at Christmas and they move in with Joan Vollmer
Adams in apartment on West 115th Street.

1945   Kerouac and Burroughs collaborate on *And the Hippos Were
Boiled in Their Tanks*, a novel based on the Kammerer-Carr
case (never published). Explores the Times Square under-
world with Burroughs and Herbert Huncke, a drug addict,
petty thief, and street hustler. Separates from Edie during
the summer. Helps care for his father, who has stomach
cancer. Hospitalized in December with thrombophlebitis,
a debilitating circulatory condition in the legs possibly re-
lated to his 1940 football injury; Kerouac also attributes his
illness to his heavy use of Benzedrine and marijuana.

1946   Kerouac, Burroughs, and Ginsberg are interviewed for the
Alfred Kinsey study *Sexual Behavior in the Human Male*
(published in 1948). Father dies on May 17 and is buried
with Gerard in Nashua. Kerouac continues work on *The
Town and the City*. Agrees to Edie Parker's request that
their marriage be annulled. In December Kerouac is intro-
duced by his friend Hal Chase to Neal Cassady (b. 1926),
a self-educated car thief and hustler from Denver who is
visiting New York with his wife, Luanne.

1947   Travels to North Carolina in June to visit his sister, Caroline,
and her second husband, Paul Blake. Leaves New York in
July to visit Cassady and Ginsberg in Denver, traveling by
bus to Chicago and then hitchhiking the rest of the way.
Meets Carolyn Robinson, a graduate student at the Uni-
versity of Denver (she and Cassady marry in April 1948).
Travels by bus in August to San Francisco, where Henri
Cru (a friend from Horace Mann) gets him a job as a secu-
rity guard in Marin City. Travels through California before
returning to New York in October.

1948   Completes first draft of *The Town and the City* in May. Be-
gins writing an early version of *On the Road*. Visits sister in
Rocky Mount, North Carolina, in June after the birth of his
nephew Paul Blake Jr. Meets writer John Clellon Holmes
in July. Takes literature courses taught by Elbert Lenrow
and Alfred Kazin at the New School for Social Research in

New York. Cassady arrives in Rocky Mount while Kerouac is visiting his sister at Christmas and drives with him back to New York.

1949   Leaves New York in January with Cassady, Luanne, and Al Hinkle and drives to Algiers, Louisiana, where they visit Burroughs and Joan Vollmer Adams, who have been living together for several years. Continues on to San Francisco with Cassady and Luanne, then returns to New York by bus in February. Columbia professor Mark Van Doren recommends *The Town and the City* to Robert Giroux at Harcourt, Brace, who offers Kerouac a $1,000 advance in late March. Kerouac and Giroux work on cutting and revising the manuscript. Moves to Denver in May and rents house at 61 West Center Street in Westwood. Continues working on *On the Road*. Travels to San Francisco in August, then drives back to New York with Cassady, visiting Edie in Grosse Pointe along the way. Moves in with his mother at 94-21 134th Street in Richmond Hill, Queens.

1950   *The Town and the City* is published on March 2; it receives mixed reviews and sells poorly. Travels to Denver in May, then drives with Cassady to Mexico City, where he visits Burroughs. Returns to New York in August. Meets Joan Haverty (b. 1931) on November 3 and marries her in a civil ceremony on November 17. They live in a loft on West 21st Street, then move in with Kerouac's mother in Queens. Receives a long letter from Neal Cassady in December. (Kerouac will later say that Cassady's "fast, mad, confessional" letters inspired "the spontaneous style of *On the Road*.")

1951   Moves to a studio apartment at 454 West 20th Street in Manhattan with Joan, who is working in a department store. Begins new version of *On the Road* on April 2 and types it in three weeks on a 120-foot-long paper scroll. Separates from Joan and moves in with Lucien Carr and Allen Ginsberg. Denies paternity when Joan tells him she is pregnant with his child. Robert Giroux rejects the scroll version of *On the Road*. Hires Rae Everitt of MCA as his literary agent. Suffers severe attack of thrombophlebitis while visiting his sister in North Carolina. Enters Kingsbridge VA Hospital in the Bronx in August. Burroughs accidentally kills Joan Vollmer Adams in Mexico City on September 7 after she drunkenly challenges him to shoot a glass off her

head. Kerouac leaves the hospital in September and returns
to Richmond Hill. Begins rewriting *On the Road* in an even
more spontaneous form (reworked version is posthumously
published as *Visions of Cody* in 1972). Moves to San Fran-
cisco in December to live with Neal and Carolyn Cassady
and their children at 29 Russell Street.

1952   Works as baggage handler for the Southern Pacific Railroad.
Receives $250 advance for *On the Road* from Ace Books.
Daughter Janet Michelle Kerouac is born in Albany on
February 16. Kerouac begins affair with Carolyn Cassady.
Drives with the Cassadys to the Arizona-Mexico border,
then takes bus to Mexico City, where he stays with Bur-
roughs. Writes *Doctor Sax*, May–June. Joins his mother
and sister in North Carolina in July, then moves in with
the Cassadys in San Jose in September. Works as a brake-
man for the Southern Pacific. Lives in a skid row hotel in
San Francisco for a month because of the tension caused
by his affair with Carolyn Cassady, then returns to San Jose
in November. John Clellon Holmes publishes novel *Go*, in
which Kerouac is fictionalized as Gene Pasternak, and "This
Is the Beat Generation," an essay in the November 16 *New
York Times Magazine*. Kerouac travels to Mexico City with
Neal Cassady, then returns to his mother in Queens.

1953   Writes *Maggie Cassidy*. Meets with Malcolm Cowley of
Viking Press to discuss the possible publication of his work.
Travels in April to San Luis Obispo, California, where he
again works for the Southern Pacific. Leaves job in May and
sails from San Francisco to New Orleans as a kitchen worker
on the *S.S. William Carruthers*. Returns to Queens in June.
Writes *The Subterraneans*, October 21–24. In response to
questions about his composition methods from Ginsberg
and Burroughs, writes "Essentials of Spontaneous Prose."

1954   Leaves New York in late January to live with the Cassadys
in San Jose. Works as a parking-lot attendant and studies
Buddhist texts. Returns to his mother in Queens in April.
Hires Sterling Lord as his literary agent (Lord will repre-
sent him for the rest of Kerouac's life). Works on *Some of
the Dharma* (posthumously published in 1997). Malcolm
Cowley publishes essay in *The Saturday Review* in August
in which he credits Kerouac with inventing the phrase "beat
generation" and writes: "his long unpublished narrative, *On
the Road*, is the best record of their lives." Kerouac visits
Lowell in October.

1955   In January Alfred A. Knopf becomes the sixth publisher to
reject *On the Road*. Joan Haverty takes Kerouac to court
seeking child support, but his lawyer, Eugene Brooks (Allen
Ginsberg's brother), succeeds in having the case postponed
because of Kerouac's recurring phlebitis. Kerouac and his
mother move to North Carolina. "Jazz of the Beat Genera-
tion," excerpted from *On the Road* and *Visions of Cody*, ap-
pears in *New World Writing* in April. Travels to Mexico City
in July. Begins *Tristessa* and *Mexico City Blues* before going
to San Francisco in September. Meets the poets Kenneth
Rexroth, Lawrence Ferlinghetti, Michael McClure, Philip
Lamantia, Philip Whalen, and Gary Snyder. Attends poetry
reading at the Six Gallery in San Francisco on October 7
where Allen Ginsberg reads from *Howl* for the first time.
Visits the Sawtooth Mountains of Idaho with Gary Snyder
in October. Rides freight cars through California. *The Paris
Review* publishes "The Mexican Girl," another excerpt from
On the Road. Kerouac returns to North Carolina and be-
gins *Visions of Gerard* on December 27.

1956   Completes *Visions of Gerard* on January 16. Hitchhikes to
California in March. Lives with Gary Snyder in a cabin in
Mill Valley, where he writes *Old Angel Midnight* (posthu-
mously published in 1993) and *The Scripture of the Golden
Eternity*. Hitchhikes in June to Mount Baker National For-
est in northern Washington. Works for two months as a
firewatcher in the Cascade Mountains, staying in a look-
out cabin on Desolation Peak. Returns to San Francisco in
September before going to Mexico City, where he begins
Desolation Angels. Ginsberg's *Howl and Other Poems* is
published by City Light Books. Kerouac returns to New
York in November. Viking Press accepts *On the Road* for
publication.

1957   Makes his final revisions to *On the Road* in January. (Vi-
king had insisted that names and locations in the book be
changed to avoid possible libel suits.) Begins affair with
writer Joyce Glassman (b. 1935, later Joyce Johnson). Sails
in February for Tangier, where he visits Burroughs and
helps type his novel *Naked Lunch* (a title originally sug-
gested by Kerouac for a different manuscript). Visits Paris
and London in April before returning to New York. Moves
with his mother to Berkeley, California, in May, but in July
they move to Orlando, Florida, where his sister is now liv-
ing. Visits Mexico City, then goes back to New York. *On
the Road* is published on September 5, becomes a bestseller,

and makes Kerouac a national celebrity. (In *The New York Times*, critic Gilbert Millstein calls it "the most beautifully executed, the clearest, and the most important utterance yet made by the generation Kerouac himself named years ago as 'beat,' and whose principal avatar he is.") Despite the success of *On the Road*, Viking rejects all of Kerouac's unpublished manuscripts, including *Doctor Sax*, *Tristessa*, and *Desolation Angels*. Writes play *Beat Generation* (published in 2005) and novel *The Dharma Bums* in Orlando during the fall. Returns to New York in late December to give a series of readings with live jazz backing.

1958   Gives series of interviews, including one with Mike Wallace for the *New York Post*. *The Subterraneans* is published by Grove Press in February and receives almost entirely bad reviews. Buys house at 34 Gilbert Avenue in Northport, Long Island. Suffers broken arm, broken nose, and possible concussion when he is beaten outside a bar in Greenwich Village. *San Francisco Chronicle* columnist Herb Caen uses the term "beatnik" in print for the first time on April 2. Kerouac drives from New York to Florida and back with photographer Robert Frank. Moves into Northport home with his mother in April. Neal Cassady begins serving sentence for marijuana trafficking in July (he is released from San Quentin in the summer of 1960). *The Dharma Bums* is published by Viking on October 2. Affair with Joyce Glassman ends. Kerouac's health worsens as the result of years of heavy drinking and Benzedrine use.

1959   Records narration for improvised Beat film *Pull My Daisy*, directed by Robert Frank and painter Alfred Leslie. Writes introduction for the U.S. edition of Frank's photographic collection *The Americans*. Grove Press publishes *Doctor Sax* as a trade paperback in April, and *Maggie Cassidy* is published as a mass-market paperback by Avon in July. Kerouac begins writing column for *Escapade* magazine. Moves to 49 Earl Avenue in Northport with his mother. Travels to Los Angeles in November and reads from *Visions of Cody* on the Steve Allen television show. *Mexico City Blues* is published by Grove Press. On November 30 *Life* magazine publishes "Beats: Sad But Noisy Rebels," article by staff writer Paul O'Neil attacking Kerouac and Neal Cassady.

1960   Works on *Lonesome Traveler* and *Book of Dreams*. Totem Press publishes *The Scripture of the Golden Eternity*. Avon publishes *Tristessa* as a mass-market paperback in June. Film version of *The Subterraneans*, directed by Ranald MacDougall, is a critical and commercial failure (Kerouac received $15,000 for the film rights). Spends summer at Lawrence Ferlinghetti's cabin in Bixby Canyon in Big Sur, where he suffers mental breakdown while trying to deal with his worsening alcoholism. Sees Carolyn Cassady for the last time before returning to Long Island in September. *Lonesome Traveler*, a collection of travel pieces, is published by McGraw-Hill on September 27.

1961 Meets Timothy Leary in January with Ginsberg and takes LSD. *Book of Dreams* is published by City Lights Books. Leaves Northport and moves with his mother in April to 1309 Alfred Drive in Orlando. Spends a month in Mexico City during the summer and completes the second part of *Desolation Angels*. In August *Confidential* magazine publishes "My Ex-Husband Jack Kerouac Is an Ingrate," article detailing Joan Haverty Aly's ongoing attempts to collect child support from Kerouac. Writes *Big Sur* in Orlando, September 30–October 9. Goes on an extended drinking spree in New York in the fall.

1962 Meets his daughter Jan, now 10, for the first time when they undergo blood tests in February, and is ordered to pay $12 a week in child support. Grove Press publishes the first American edition of Burroughs' *Naked Lunch* in March. *Big Sur* is published by Farrar, Straus, and Cudahy on September 11. Buys house at 7 Judy Ann Court in Northport and moves there with his mother in December.

1963 Works on *Vanity of Duluoz*, a novel he first began in 1942. *Visions of Gerard* is published by Farrar, Straus and Cudahy in September and receives poor reviews.

1964 Gives drunken reading at Harvard University in March. Sees Neal Cassady for the last time when he comes to New York City with Ken Kesey and the Merry Pranksters during the summer. Sells Northport house and moves with his mother to 5155 Tenth Avenue North in St. Petersburg, Florida. Caroline Kerouac Blake dies of a heart attack in Orlando on September 19; she is buried in an unmarked grave because Kerouac is unable to pay for a headstone.

1965 Suffers two broken ribs when he is attacked in a St. Petersburg bar in March. *Desolation Angels* is published by

Coward-McCann on May 3. Visits Paris and Brittany in June in an attempt to research his ancestry. Writes *Satori in Paris* soon after his return to Florida.

1966   Moves with his mother in the spring to 20 Bristol Avenue in the Cape Cod town of Hyannis, Massachusetts. *Satori in Paris* is published by Grove Press. Visited in August by Ann Charters, who is compiling his bibliography. (Charters will publish the first biography of Kerouac in 1973.) Mother suffers massive stroke on September 9 that leaves her paralyzed. Kerouac briefly visits Milan and Rome to promote the Italian publication of *Big Sur*. Marries Stella Sampas (b. 1918), the sister of his Lowell friend Sebastian Sampas, in Hyannis on November 18.

1967   Moves in January with Stella and his mother to house at 271 Sanders Avenue in Lowell. Completes *Vanity of Duluoz*. Gives lengthy interview to the poets Ted Berrigan, Aram Saroyan, and Duncan McNaughton for publication in *The Paris Review*. Sees his daughter Jan for the second and last time in November.

1968   Neal Cassady collapses and dies on February 4 in San Miguel de Allende, Mexico. *Vanity of Duluoz* is published by Coward-McCann on February 6. Visits Portugal, Spain, Switzerland, and Germany in March. Sees Burroughs and Ginsberg for the last time in early September when he goes to New York for the taping of William F. Buckley's television program *Firing Line*. Returns to St. Petersburg, moving to 5169 Tenth Avenue North with Stella and his mother.

1969   Completes *Pic* (published in 1971). Suffers cracked ribs when he is beaten outside a bar in early September. "After Me, the Deluge," article in which Kerouac disassociates himself from the New Left, appears in the *Chicago Tribune* on September 28. Collapses at home on the morning of October 20 and dies at St. Anthony's Hospital in St. Petersburg on October 21 from massive internal bleeding caused by cirrhosis of the liver. A Requiem Mass is held at St. Jean Baptiste Church in Lowell on October 24, after which Kerouac is buried in Edson Catholic Cemetery.

Note on the Texts

This volume contains the two books of poetry that Jack Kerouac pub-
lished in his lifetime, *Mexico City Blues* (1959) and *The Scripture of the
Golden Eternity* (1960), along with the texts of five poetry collections
that he assembled and that were published posthumously: *Pomes All
Sizes* (1992), *Old Angel Midnight* (1993), and *Book of Blues* (1995), as
well as "Book of Haikus" and "Desolation Pops," both included in
Book of Haikus (2003). It concludes with a selection of further uncol-
lected poetry, not designated by him for inclusion in future books,
that was published in magazines or as broadsides, or left in manuscript.
Many of these uncollected poems were published posthumously in
the volumes *Scattered Poems* (1971), *Heaven & Other Poems* (1977),
Atop an Underwood (1999), *Book of Haikus* (2003), and *Windblown
World: The Journals of Jack Kerouac 1947–1954* (2004); other poems are
published here for the first time.

   In Kerouac's work the line between poetry and prose is often a
fluid one. While some of his poetry is presented in clearly defined
forms, whether traditional (haiku, sutra, or ballad) or self-invented
(the "blues" form of *Mexico City Blues* and *Book of Blues*), much of his
writing resists easy classification. *Old Angel Midnight*, which Kerouac
described in a letter to John Clellon Holmes as "an endless automatic
writing piece which raves on and on with no direction and no story,"
is included here as an extended exercise in what can be called prose
poetry, although formally it differs only slightly from many passages in
Kerouac's novels, sketches, and journals. Some of the works included
here were originally part of prose works such as *Doctor Sax* and *Big Sur*
or have been extracted from the copious journals and notebooks that
Kerouac kept throughout his life; on the other hand, some writing,
such as the posthumously published *Book of Sketches* (Penguin Books,
2004), which, although lineated like free verse, is more in the nature
of a prose journal, has not been included here. Also not included
(with the exception of "Poems of the Buddhas of Old," which Kerouac
included in *Pomes All Sizes*, "Sight is just dust" in the form in which it
appeared in the posthumous selection *Scattered Poems*, and the haikus
included here in "A Selection of Uncollected Haiku") are any of the
poems or poem-sequences from *Some of the Dharma* (Viking Press,
1997), an immense assemblage of notes on Buddhism, written between
1953 and 1956, which embraces many genres and which needs to be
read as an organic whole.

   Although Kerouac selected the contents for *Book of Blues, Pomes*

All Sizes, and "Book of Haikus" and was generally meticulous about establishing a clear text for individual poems, he did not, as far as can be determined from the existing typescripts and manuscripts, establish a definite order. The posthumous editions of those works present the contents in an order reflecting approximate chronology of composition, and (with the exceptions noted below) that order has been retained in this edition. The posthumously published volumes that appear after the two volumes published in Kerouac's lifetime overlap in terms of chronology of composition as noted below. *Book of Blues* is placed before the others because it was evidently conceived by Kerouac as a unified volume at an earlier date.

Kerouac began writing *Mexico City Blues* in August of 1955 and completed it in early September, while living in a rooftop hut at 212 Orizaba Street, writing to Allen Ginsberg on August 19: "Myself I have just knocked off 150 bloody poetic masterpieces in MEXICO CITY BLUES, each one of uniform length and wailing." Each chorus was written on a separate notebook page. He prepared a typescript of the work in 1956 and sent it to publishers including New Directions and City Lights. After it was rejected by Lawrence Ferlinghetti for City Lights, Kerouac sent it to Donald Allen at Grove Press, writing to him on July 30, 1958: "Enclosed also is the whole book of poems 'Mexico City Blues.' I heard you in my demarol trance say you were going to publish whole books of people's poetry: hope you do this one, entoto, as is. Will Petersen and Mike McClure have written me mad happy letters about these Blues." Grove published it in November 1959. A letter dated July 28, 1959, to a copy editor at Grove indicates that Kerouac read the proofs with care. The text printed here is taken from the 1959 Grove Press edition.

Kerouac spent the spring of 1956 in a cottage owned by Gary Snyder in Mill Valley, California, situated behind a house belonging to their mutual friend Locke McCorckle. At Snyder's urging ("All right Kerouac, it's about time for you to write sutra," in Kerouac's account), Kerouac wrote *The Scripture of the Golden Eternity*. Kerouac at one point hoped that Grove Press would publish it, writing to Donald Allen in June 1959: "I think the 'Scripture' wd. make a weird thin volume and also it has enlightening properties proper to the turning of the sick wheel." The work was published by Totem/Corinth Press (New York, 1960). The text printed here is taken from the Totem/Corinth edition and respects the line breaks of that edition, which are identical to those of Kerouac's typescript, now in Indiana University's Lilly Library collection of the papers of LeRoi Jones.

Book of Blues is the title that Kerouac gave to the typescript which in its last revised form included works written between 1953 and 1961. Kerouac had completed an early version of *Book of Blues* by 1957 and sent it to Donald Allen of Grove Press and Lawrence Ferlinghetti of City Lights. A plan for Donald Allen to publish *San Francisco Blues* as a separate volume in the early '60s fell through; in a letter acknowledging Allen's return of the manuscript, Kerouac wrote: "Thanx for sending Blues, I promptly bound them in my Book of Blues and will leave them there." (letter to Donald Allen, April 4, 1962). When published posthumously by Penguin Books in 1995 the component works were arranged in an order approximating that of composition. The typescript is located in the Henry W. and Albert A. Berg Collection of English and American Literature, the New York Public Library, Astor, Lenox and Tilden Foundations. It has no table of contents and no overall pagination, and is currently arranged in a different order than that of the Penguin edition. A "Note on Dates and Sources" by John Sampas in the Penguin edition provides the following information about the dating of the poems:

> "San Francisco Blues": In a letter to Allen Ginsberg, Kerouac referred to writing this poem in March 1954, when he "left Neal's . . . and went to live in the Cameo Hotel on Third Street Frisco Skid Row." "Richmond Hill Blues": Written in Richmond Hill, New York, while Kerouac was living with his mother. He began the poem on September 4, 1954, and completed it later that month. "Bowery Blues": Kerouac dated the poem March 29, 1955. "MacDougal Street Blues": Kerouac dated the poem June 26, 1955. "Desolation Blues": "Desolation Peak / Mt. Baker Nat'l Forest / Washington State / August 1956." "Orizaba 210 Blues": "Written in a tejado rooftop dobe cell / at Orizabo 210, Mexico City, Fall 1956 / . . . by candlelight . . ." "Orlanda Blues": Begun in July 1957, finished February 17, 1958, this poem was written in Orlando, Florida—"Orlanda" in native parlance. "Cerrada Medellin Blues": "July 1961 / 37-A Cerrada Medellin / Mexico, D.F., Mexico" Begun in June, finished in July.

The text printed here is taken from the Penguin edition of 1995, and respects the chronological ordering of that edition.

Kerouac compiled the poetry collection *Pomes All Sizes* and entrusted the typescript to Lawrence Ferlinghetti during the 1960s. It was published posthumously by City Lights (San Francisco) in 1992. Kerouac's typescript containing the texts of the poems as published by City Lights is arranged in a different order; there is no table of contents and no overall pagination. City Lights chose to present the poems in an approximation of the order in which they were written. The title page of Kerouac's typescript, located in the Henry W. and Albert A. Berg Collection of English and American Literature, the New York Public Library, Astor, Lenox and Tilden Foundations, reads: "POMES ALL

SIZES / Other Odd Poems Loose / (other than Blues) / (which are strictly disciplined to / one notebook page, small / —chorus sizes—) / THESE ARE / JUST REGULAR POEMS by / Jack / Kerouac." The text printed here is taken from the 1992 City Lights edition of *Pomes All Sizes* with the following exceptions: "Bowery Blues" (which appeared in that edition between "Neal in Court" and "On Waking from a Dream of Robert Fournier") is omitted because it is duplicated in *Book of Blues*. The sequence beginning with "The white eyes of the criminals of Alcatraz thinking" and ending with the poem beginning "If I don't leave San Francisco" was assigned in the City Lights edition to an untitled sequence to which City Lights gave the title "[Enlightenments]". However, an examination of the Berg typescript indicates that these poems in fact follow on directly as part of the poem "Gatha," and are here printed as such. "[Enlightenments]" has been retitled "When you become enlightened" in accordance with standard Library of America editorial practices.

Kerouac began the work subsequently published as *Old Angel Midnight* in the spring of 1956 in Gary Snyder's cabin in Mill Valley. It was originally titled "Sebastian Midnight," then changed to "Lucien Midnight" in reference to Kerouac's friend Lucien Carr. However, Carr discouraged the title—"He said that my Lucien Midnight was pejorative about him," Kerouac noted in a letter (August 28, 1958) to Allen Ginsberg—and the work was renamed. The first forty-nine sections of *Old Angel Midnight* were intended for publication in the Winter 1959 issue of *The Chicago Review*; when that issue, which was also to include work by William Burroughs, Edward Dahlberg, and Gregory Corso, was suppressed in advance of publication by the administrators of the University of Chicago, the contents were published as the first issue of *Big Table*, Spring 1959, edited by Irving Rosenthal. It was Lawrence Ferlinghetti's intention to publish the complete work as a City Lights book, but *Big Table* asserted legal control over the material and refused permission; in anticipation of the City Lights publication, Kerouac continued to add to the work as late as April 1959, although Ferlinghetti apparently rejected the additional material. (In a blurb written for Ferlinghetti, Kerouac described the work as "only the beginning of a lifelong work in multilingual sound representing the haddal-da-babra of babbling world tongues coming in thru my window at midnight no matter where I live or what I'm doing, in Mexico, Morocco, New York, India or Pakistan, in Spanish, French, Aztec, Gaelick, Keltic, Kurd or Dravidian, the sounds of people yakking and of myself yakking among, ending finally in great intuitions of the sounds of tongues throughout the entire universe in all directions in and out forever. And it is the only book I've ever written in which I allow myself the right to say anything I want, absolutely and positively anything, since that's what you hear coming in that window."—letter, April 5, 1959.) Sections 50–67 (the additions rejected by City Lights) appeared in *Evergreen Review* no. 33, August–September 1964, edited by Barney Rosset. The work was published in book form, in a text identical to what appeared in the two magazines, by Grey Fox Press (Monroe, Oregon) in 1993. The book's editor was Donald Allen. The text printed here is taken from the 1993 Grey Fox edition. Some additional material that was included in an appendix of the Grey Fox edition is included in the notes to this volume.

"Desolation Pops" is a numbered sequence of seventy-two haiku written by Kerouac in 1956 when he was working (June–September) as a fire lookout on Desolation Ridge in Skagit Valley in northwest Washington. During the same period he wrote the sequence "Desolation Blues" in *Book of Blues* and a portion of the novel *Desolation Angels*. The sequence (the manuscript of which is in the Berg Collection) was first published in *Book of Haikus* (New York: Penguin Books, 2003), edited by Regina Weinreich. The text included here is printed from *Book of Haikus*.

"Book of Haikus" was the title given by Kerouac to the manuscript assembling the haiku he wished to publish as a book. The manuscript, located in the Henry W. and Albert A. Berg Collection of English and American Literature, the New York Public Library, Astor, Lenox and Tilden Foundations, is undated and there is no clear order of arrangement, as the poems are written in pencil in three columns on both sides of a series of folded, unnumbered leaves. The contents of the manuscript were first published as the first section of *Book of Haikus*, edited by Regina Weinreich. The text included here is printed from the Penguin edition of *Book of Haikus*; however, four poems that do not appear in the manuscript in the Berg Collection have been moved to the selection of uncollected haiku elsewhere in this volume.

Grouped here as Uncollected Poems are writings that Kerouac did not collect in a poetry collection in his lifetime or designate for inclusion in *Pomes All Sizes*, *Book of Blues*, or "Book of Haikus." They include material from notebooks and journals; material published in periodicals or as broadsides; and poems originally included in the novels *Doctor Sax* and *Big Sur*. Much of this work was published posthumously in the following volumes: *Scattered Poems* (San Francisco: City Lights Press, 1971), ed. Ann Charters; *Heaven & Other Poems* (Monroe, Oregon: Grey Fox Press, 1977), ed. Donald Allen; *Atop an Underwood: Early Stories and Other Writings* (Penguin Books, 1999), ed. Paul Marion; *Book of Haikus* (Penguin Books, 2003), ed. Regina Weinreich; and *Windblown World: The Journals of Jack Kerouac, 1947–1954* (Penguin Books, 2004), ed. Douglas Brinkley. The sources for the texts printed here are listed below. The parenthetical dates for poems from *Scattered Poems* are of approximate dates of composition as noted in that volume.

Observations: *Atop an Underwood*.

America in the Night: *Atop an Underwood*.

Old Love-Light: *Atop an Underwood*.

I Tell You It Is October!: *Atop an Underwood*.

"I Am My Mother's Son": *Atop an Underwood*.

Thinking of Thomas Wolfe on a Winter's Night: *Atop an Underwood*.

Alabama, May 11, 1944: Unpublished manuscript, Berg Collection.

A Translation from the French of Jean-Louis Incogniteau: *Scattered Poems*. The translation is by Allen Ginsberg and was originally published under his name in *Jester of Columbia* VLIII, 4 (January 1945).

Psalms: "God, I cannot find your face this morning": *Windblown World*; "And when I saw the light of the morning sun": *Windblown World*; "Alone in a lonely world": Unpublished manuscript, Berg Collection; "And what do I owe you, God": Unpublished manuscript, Berg Collection; "A psalm and a hymn of praise": Unpublished manuscript, Berg Collection; "And no more psalms exist in me, God?": *Windblown World*; "Oh God how I rejoice in sorrows now": *Windblown World*; "Thank you, dear Lord, for the work You have given me": *Windblown World*.

"God didn't make the world for satisfaction": Unpublished manuscript, Berg Collection.

Song ["I left New York"]: *Windblown World*.

Song: Fie My Fum: *Scattered Poems*. Originally published in *Neurotica* 6 (Spring 1950) as by Allen Ginsberg.

Pull My Daisy: *Scattered Poems*. Originally published in *Metronome* LXVIII, 4 (April 1961).

Pull My Daisy [alternate version]: *Scattered Poems*. *Pull My Daisy*: text by Jack Kerouac for the film by Robert Frank and Alfred Leslie (New York: Grove Press, 1961).

"He is your friend, let him dream": *Scattered Poems*. This poem appears in a prose version in *Visions of Cody*.

Visions of Doctor Sax: Unpublished manuscript, Berg Collection.

The Poems of the Night: *Doctor Sax* (New York: Grove Press, 1952).

Long Dead's Longevity: *Scattered Poems*. From a 1953 notebook reprinted later in *Book of Sketches* (Penguin, 2006).

"Someday you'll be lying": *Scattered Poems*. Written c. 1953–54. Originally published as a broadside by Kriya Press of Sri Ram Ashrama (Pleasant Valley, New York) in 1968.

Daydreams for Ginsberg: *Scattered Poems*. "From manuscript dated February 10, 1955, in Rare Books and Manuscript Library, Columbia University.

"Sight is just dust": *Scattered Poems*. An excerpt from *Some of the Dharma* (Penguin Books, 1997, p. 229).

Mindmatter: Unpublished manuscript, Berg Collection. Written 1956.

A TV Poem: *Heaven and Other Poems*. Written 1958.

Heaven: *Heaven and Other Poems*. Written 1958.

Sitting Under Tree Number Two: *Scattered Poems*. Originally published in *Beat Coast East: An Anthology of Rebellion*, ed. Stanley Fisher (New York: Excelsior Press, 1961).

To Harpo Marx: *Scattered Poems*. Originally published in *Playboy* VI, 7 (July 1959).

"I / clearly / saw / the skeleton underneath": *Scattered Poems*. Originally published in *New Departures* 2–3 (1960).

Rimbaud: *Scattered Poems*. Originally published *Yūgen* 6 (1960) and as City Lights broadside, 1960.

Sea: *Big Sur* (New York: Farrar, Straus & Cudahy, 1962).

Sept. 16, 1961, Poem: *Scattered Poems*. Originally published in *The Outsider* I, 2 (Summer 1968).

A Pun for Al Gelpi: *Scattered Poems*. Originally published as a broadside by Lowell House Printers (Cambridge, Massachusetts) in 1966.

To Edward Dahlberg: *Scattered Poems*. Originally published in *Tri Quarterly* 19 (Fall 1970) and *Edward Dahlberg: A Tribute*, ed. Jonathan Williams (New York: David Lewis Inc., 1970).

A Selection of Uncollected Haikus: *Book of Haikus* (Penguin Books, 2002), selection by Regina Weinreich.

This volume presents the texts of the original printings and typescripts chosen for inclusion here, but it does not attempt to reproduce nontextual features of their typographic design. The texts are presented without change, except for the correction of typographical errors. Spelling, punctuation, and capitalization are often expressive features and are not altered, even when inconsistent or irregular. The following is a list of typographical errors corrected, cited by page and line number: 68.6, one a; 70.31, while; 223.25, millioinaire; 334.26, Croso; 398.3, Celt—; 541.18, Stepped; 541.21, fell; 542.8, show; 545.19, Night fall; 615.14, Veraline; 641.9, Change Su; 643.4, Taghagata; 647.9, reality; 693.1, Hakkaido.

Notes

In the notes below, the reference numbers denote page and line of this volume (the line count includes headings). No note is made for material included in standard desk-reference books. For further biographical background than is contained in the Chronology, see Ann Charters, *Kerouac: A Biography* (San Francisco: Straight Arrow Books, 1973); Ann Charters, ed., *Jack Kerouac: Selected Letters, 1940–1956* (New York: Viking Penguin, 1995); Ann Charters, ed., *Jack Kerouac: Selected Letters, 1957–1969* (New York: Viking Penguin, 1999); Ann Charters, *A Bibliography of Works by Jack Kerouac, 1939–1975* (New York: The Phoenix Bookshop, revised edition, 1975); Barry Gifford and Lawrence Lee, *Jack's Book: An Oral Biography of Jack Kerouac* (New York: St. Martin's Press, 1978); Paul Maher Jr., *Kerouac: His Life and Work* (Lanham, Maryland: Taylor Trade Publishing, 2004); Dennis McNally, *Desolate Angel* (New York: Random House, 1979); Gerald Nicosia, *Memory Babe: A Critical Biography of Jack Kerouac* (New York: Grove Press, 1983); John Suiter, *Poets on the Peaks: Gary Snyder, Philip Whalen & Jack Kerouac in the North Cascades* (New York: Counterpoint, 2002).

MEXICO CITY BLUES

3.23   Merudvhaga] See Sukhavati, "The Paradise of Nirvana," in F. Max Muller et al., *Studies in Buddhism* (1888), in which Tathagata Merudhvaga is identified as one of "other blessed Buddhas . . . equal in number to the sand of the river Ganga."

6.2   Gregory Corso] Poet (1930–2001), author of *Gasoline* (1958), *The Happy Birthday of Death* (1960), *Long Live Man* (1962), and other collections.

6.15–16   William Burroughs / Is William Lee] William S. Burroughs (1914–1997), author of *Naked Lunch* (1959), *The Soft Machine* (1961), *The Ticket That Exploded* (1962), *Nova Express* (1964), and other works; he originally published his novel *Junkie* (New York: Ace Double Editions, 1953) under the pseudonym William Lee.

7.28   Tathagata] Name applied by the Buddha to himself in Sanskrit and Pali scriptures; it has been translated as "one who has thus gone" and "one who has thus come."

13.11–12   Avaloki / Tesvara] Bodhisattva embodying the compassionate Buddha; the name has been translated as "the lord who looks down."

15.23   My brother Gerard] Francis Gerard Kerouac (1916–1926), Kerouac's older brother, showed signs of early artistic talent and was regarded by his family as a saintly child in the period before his death of rheumatic fever. He is the subject of Kerouac's *Visions of Gerard* (1963).

19.10   old Wardell] Wardell Gray (1921–1955), tenor saxophone player who worked with musicians including Earl Hines, Count Basie, Dexter Gordon, and Benny Carter.

19.13   Rushing] Jimmy Rushing (1901–1972), longtime vocalist with the Count Basie Orchestra.

19.19   French Lettrism] *Lettrisme*, French avant-garde movement established in the late 1940s by Isidore Isou.

19.28   Asvaghosha] Indian poet, dramatist, and philosopher of the first century CE, author of the epic poem *Buddhacaritam* (*Acts of the Buddha*); the *Awakening of Faith*, long attributed to him, is now generally believed to be a later translation from the Chinese.

21.29   Carl Solomon] Writer (1928–1993), author of *Mishaps, Perhaps* (1966) and *More Mishaps* (1968); Allen Ginsberg, who made his acquaintance at the mental hospital to which Solomon had voluntarily committed himself, dedicated *Howl* to him.

22.5   Jimmy the Greek] Jimmy Snyder (1918–1996), bookie and television sports commentator.

28.11   A Star is Born] Movie (1956) directed by George Cukor, starring Judy Garland and James Mason.

29.22   Lester Young] Jazz musician (1909–1959); a crucially influential tenor saxophone stylist.

33.1   Tathagata Akshobya] See note 7.28.

36.16–17   Bill / G.] Bill Garver, heroin addict and petty criminal described by William Burroughs in *Junkie*, and later a neighbor of Kerouac at 212 Orizaba Street in Mexico City; many of his words are woven into the choruses of *Mexico City Blues*.

38.13   Samantabhadra] Bodhisattva who is an object of devotion in the Lotus Sutra.

41.5–7   Charlie Chaplin . . . playing Bluebeard killer] In *Monsieur Verdoux* (1947).

42.2–3   Demosthenes . . . with a rock in his teeth] Athenian orator of the fourth century BC; according to Plutarch, "the hesitation and stammering of his tongue he corrected by practicing to speak with pebbles in his mouth."

42.16–17   Mice / And Men] *Of Mice and Men* (1939), directed by Lewis Milestone and based on the novel and play by John Steinbeck.

43.20   'I'll Take You Home Again Kathleen'] Song (1875) by Thomas P. Westendorf.

43.25   Kolya Krosotkins] Kolya Krasotkin, schoolboy in *The Brothers Karamazov* who professes atheism but moves toward more spiritual views after meeting Alyosha Karamazov.

56.12   HOOT GIBSON] Rodeo performer and film actor (1892–1962) who made his first screen appearance in 1910 and went on to become a major star of Westerns (many of which he directed and produced) from the 1920s to the 1940s.

56.21   Vidal] Gore Vidal, novelist, playwright, and essayist.

68.18–19   Lankavatara / Scripture] Lankavatara Sutra, a principal sutra of Mahayana Buddhism.

69.26   Maldoror] Protagonist of *Les Chants de Maldoror* (1868–69), prose poem by the Comte de Lautréamont (born Isidore Ducasse, 1846–1870).

81.21   Anuttara Samyak Sambodh] Buddhist term, Anuttara Samyak Sambodhi, sometimes translated as "unexcelled perfect enlightenment."

96.24–25   Einstein believed / In the God of Spinoza] Einstein expressed his admiration for Spinoza on various occasions. In a 1929 letter he wrote: "We followers of Spinoza see our God in the wonderful order and lawfulness of all that exists and in its soul . . . as it reveals itself in man and animal." He enlarged on his views in a 1947 letter: "It seems to me that the idea of a personal God is an anthropomorphic concept which I cannot take seriously."

104.11   *cucharra*] Spanish, *cuchara*: spoon.

104.21   James Huneker] Critic (1857–1921), instrumental in introducing European modernism to America.

107.17   Sammy Kaye] Popular bandleader (1910–1987) of the Big Band era whose hits included "Harbor Lights" and "The Old Lamp-Lighter."

107.22   Likhavi Tribesmen] Or Licchavi; ancient northern Indian clan, sometimes referred to as Kshatriyas.

114.13   Pegler] Westbrook Pegler (1894–1969), American newspaper columnist known for his right-wing views.

114.23–24   Eleanor / Roosevelt 'This is My Day,'] Eleanor Roosevelt's syndicated column "My Day" ran from 1935 to 1962.

117.34   Perkins] Frances Perkins (1880–1965), Secretary of Labor (1933–1945), first woman appointed to the U.S. cabinet.

120.20   King Sariputra] A chief disciple of Buddha.

120.28   Maitri] Sanskrit: sympathy.

121.2–3   serenade / in blue] Song (1942) by Harry Warren and Mack Gordon, performed by the Glenn Miller orchestra in the film *Orchestra Wives*.

123.29   Ferdinand the Bull] Protagonist of the children's book *The Story of Ferdinand* (1936), written by Munro Leaf and filmed by Walt Disney in 1938 as *Ferdinand the Bull*.

126.20   sautergain & finn] The Sauter-Finegan Orchestra, led by the arrangers Eddie Sauter and Bill Finegan, was highly successful in the 1950s with hits including "Doodletown Fifers," "Nina Never Knew," and "The Moon Is Blue."

126.23   Yokum] Abner Yokum, naive protagonist of Al Capp's long-running comic strip *Li'l Abner*.

127.29   "The Yellow Kid"] Leading character of the comic strip *Hogan's Alley*, created by Richard F. Outcault in 1894.

129.6   Hsi Yun] Hsi Yun, Chinese Zen master of the ninth century, also known as Huang Po.

129.26–130.2   "Men are afraid . . . of the Dharma"] The passage can be found in *The Zen Teaching of Huang Po: On the Transmission of Mind* (1958), translated by John Blofeld, previously published in different form as *The Huang Po Doctrine of Universal Mind* (1947).

134.12   Shinran] Japanese Buddhist teacher (1173–1263), founder of the Jōdo Shinshū sect.

136.24   Paramitas] Sanskrit: perfection.

136.26   Wu-Weis] Chinese Taoist term sometimes glossed as "effortless action."

136.27   Tehs] Taoist term for power or virtue emanating from Tao.

155.10–12   Father Zossima . . . Alyosha] Principal characters of Dostoevsky's *The Brothers Karamazov*.

169.2   "Ma mère . . . la terre."] "My mother, you are the earth."

169.4   Damema] Wife of the Tibetan Buddhist yogi Marpa, regarded as a *dakini*.

THE SCRIPTURE OF THE GOLDEN ETERNITY

179.8   Maitreya, a Palalakonuh] Maitreya, Buddha of the future; Palalakonuh, "merely the Aztec or Toltec name (or possibly Chihuahuan in origin) for the World Sun Snake of the ancient Indians of North America" (Kerouac, *Doctor Sax*).

180.20–21   Diamond-cutter] The Diamond Sutra, early Buddhist text sometimes known as the Vajra Sutra.

180.27   Dharmakaya] Sanskrit: "reality body," the unmanifested aspect of Buddha out of which manifested aspects emerge.

180.31   Lankavatara Scripture] See note 68.18–19.

182.3   Hui Neng] Chinese Zen master (638–713), known as the Sixth Patriarch, to whom the *Platform Sutra* is attributed.

183.2   Ashvhaghosha] See note 19.28.

183.18   Sainte Thérèse] Saint Thérèse de Lisieux (1873–1897), Carmelite nun who was canonized in 1925.

184.10   Avalokitesvara] See note 13.11–12.

184.30   Prince of Kalinga] Buddha's disciple Ajnauta Kaundinya had, as the king of Kalinga, dismembered the Buddha in a former life.

186.3–4   Boethius . . . a Roman dungeon] The sixth-century philosopher Boethius was imprisoned and executed by the Ostrogothic emperor Theodoric; during his imprisonment he wrote *The Consolation of Philosophy*, consisting of a dialogue between himself and Lady Philosophy.

186.23   Bankei] Bankei Yōtaku (1622–1693), Japanese Zen Buddhist master.

188.10   the Sixth Patriarch] See note 182.3.

189.34   Subhuti] One of the ten chief disciples of Buddha.

BOOK OF BLUES

203.20–21   crone . . . Edwin Drood] See Charles Dickens, *The Mystery of Edwin Drood*, chapter 1: "I got Heavens-hand drunk for sixteen years afore I took to this; but this don't hurt me, not to speak of. And it takes away the hunger as well as wittles, deary." The speaker is an old woman smoking a pipe of opium in a London den.

212.29   Bruce Barton] Writer and motivational speaker (1886–1967) whose *The Man Nobody Knows* (1925), an interpretation of the life of Jesus, was a major bestseller.

229.12–14   IL / W / U] International Longshore and Warehouse Union.

229.20–22   Curran . . . Bryson . . . Reuther] Joseph Curran (1906–1981), merchant seaman and labor leader, led a 1936 seamen's strike on the *S.S. California*, docked in San Pedro, California; Hugh Bryson (1914–1990?), labor leader removed as president of the National Union of Marine Cooks and Stewards following his 1953 indictment for perjury in connection with his Communist Party membership; Walter Reuther (1907–1970), labor leader active in the United Auto Workers Union and the Congress of Industrial Organizations, and the target of several assassination attempts.

230.17   MALN BWANO] Marlon Brando, who played a dockworker in Elia Kazan's *On the Waterfront* (1954).

231.35   Sauter Finnegan] See note 126.20.

239.1   Augustus John] Welsh painter (1878–1961).

243.2   DULUOZ] Jack Duluoz was Kerouac's fictional name for himself; he referred to the main body of his novels as The Duluoz Legend.

244.7   Earwicker] Family name of the central figures of James Joyce's *Finnegans Wake* (1939).

247.22   Lucien] Lucien Carr (1925–2005), close friend of Kerouac.

261.16–21   Sangsara . . . Samadhi] Sangsara (or Samsara), cycle of birth and death; Samadhi, highest level of meditation.

264.23   Joe Gould] Gould (1889–1957) was a legendary eccentric who frequented New York Bohemian circles.

267.3   Samantabhadra] See note 38.13.

270.24   Sumeru] Sacred mountain in Indian cosmology.

272.32–33   Peter / Orlovsky] Poet (1933–2010), longtime companion of Allen Ginsberg.

274.21   Uparli] Or Upali, one of the ten chief disciples of Buddha.

276.33   Han Shan] Chinese poet of the T'ang dynasty; he is said to have lived in a cave and is honored as a Bodhisattva. Gary Snyder translated some of his work in *Cold Mountain Poems* (1959).

287.2   Mary Carney] The great love of Kerouac's adolescence, fictionalized in *Maggie Cassidy* (1959).

288.20   McCorkle] Lock McCorkle, a student of Alan Watts and friend of Gary Snyder.

289.13–15   Nous Dit . . . Pas d secour] Tells us / always, no help, / no help.

306.30   Texas Guinan] Entertainer and saloon keeper (1884–1933) celebrated as proprietor and hostess of the 300 Club speakeasy in Manhattan.

309.16–18   Kayo Mullins . . . Moon] Characters in *Moon Mullins*, comic strip created by Frank Willard in 1923.

309.20   Major Hoople] Character in the comic strip *Our Boarding House*, created by Gene Ahern in 1921.

309.24–26   Lil Abner . . . Wolf-Gal] Characters in Al Capp's comic strip *Li'l Abner*.

312.15–16   Rejoice in the Lamb . . . Christopher Smart] Christopher Smart's poem *Jubilate Agno* was written between 1759 and 1763, while Smart was confined to a lunatic asylum in Bethnal Green, London.

313.19   Robert Giroux] Giroux (1914–2008) was Kerouac's editor at Harcourt, Brace for his first novel *The Town and the City* (1950), but subsequently turned down *On the Road*.

313.27–314.13   Dans son tombeau . . . sur le plancher] In her grave / She has gained / All the black lines / Of eternity / That are found in the earth /

When it rains in winter / Tchin! Tchin! Quickly / Bottoms up! Depart / She has found already / The Angel of rainbows / Asleep in the sea / Of summer cloud / Oh yes, my Angels all French / My rainbow towers / My honey, my gold / My dishonored souls / My nightmares, my lines / My wine on the table / Or on the floor

315.26–316.12   Boy, sa den du coeur . . . qui clacke] Drink up, it gives you heart, that, the good / Wine—Mother, the be all end all / so strong, the divine wine / Ah yes, but listen—in / the middle of the nights / you see, it gives you heart / it gives you heart / It feels good in the belly / Work?—Don't tell me about / work dammit, the belly / dammit, the belly / it does the belly good / poor belly / So, do they speak as good / as that / in Milan / the mouthy Italians / We also have / good language that snaps

317.26–29   Ray / Robinson . . . Tiger Jones] Ralph "Tiger" Jones (1928–1994) defeated Sugar Ray Robinson (1921–1989) in 1955 in a match that Robinson was favored to win.

320.25   Las ombras vengadora] Spanish, *Las ombras vengadoras*: The avenging shadows.

322.36   Stan Getz] Jazz musician (1927–1991) who played tenor saxophone with Woody Herman's band before launching a solo career.

330.12   Rudy Vallee] Singer and film actor (1901–1986), of French-Canadian extraction. His hit recording of "The Whiffenpoof Song" (1946) contains the lyric: "We're poor little lambs who have lost our way."

331.15   Mary Carney] See note 287.2.

333.7–9   Clay Felker . . . Rust Hills] Felker (1925–2008), later founder of *New York* magazine, was features editor of *Esquire*, 1957–63. L. Rust Hills (1924–2008) was fiction editor of *Esquire*, 1957–64, and rejoined the magazine for shorter terms later on.

336.13   Captain Bligh] William Bligh (1754–1817), captain of H.M.S. *Bounty*, whose crew mutinied in 1789 and set him adrift with eighteen loyal crew members in the ship's launch, which Bligh steered to safety after a 47-day voyage. In fictional and film versions of the mutiny, Bligh was depicted as a sadistic tyrant.

340.2   Jack Micheline] Poet and painter (1929–1998); Kerouac wrote the introduction to his first book, *River of Red Wine* (1957).

340.8–9   Fred / Katz] Jazz cellist and composer (b. 1919), a longtime member of the Chico Hamilton Quintet.

340.26–27   Manosuke / Kambe] The following newspaper clipping, relating to the January 31, 1958 launch of the satellite Explorer I, was preserved by Kerouac among his papers: "TOKYO (Saturday), Feb. 8 (UPI)—Satellite enthusiast Mannosuke Kambe has composed and sent to President Eisenhower a 17-syllable hokku poem in commemoration of America's first satellite.

It read:
  'Jinsei no
  Uchiage narite
  Haru chikashi.'
Which translates:
  They have succeeded
  In shooting up a star
  And spring is near."

341.19   Steve Tropp] Stephen Tropp, poet, known along with his wife, Gloria Tropp, for readings of poetry with jazz.

342.2   George Jones] Country singer (b. 1931) whose hits include "Why Baby Why" and "White Lightning."

343.7   Ronald Colman] Actor (1891–1958), whose films included *Raffles* (1930), *A Tale of Two Cities* (1935), *Lost Horizon* (1937), and *Random Harvest* (1942).

344.16–17   Colbert . . . Mazarin] Jean-Baptiste Colbert (1619–1683) became French minister of finance following the death of Cardinal Mazarin (1602–1661) who had been Louis XIV's chief minister.

345.29–30   Glenn Miller's / Moonlight Serenade] Big band hit of 1939.

346.6   Bert Lahr] Actor and comedian (1895–1967).

346.9   Seymour] Seymour Wyse (b. 1923), classmate of Kerouac at Horace Mann, a jazz enthusiast.

347.15   Lee Konitz] Jazz composer and alto saxophone player (b. 1927).

347.23   Elvin Jones] Jazz drummer (1927–2004), long a member of the John Coltrane Quartet.

347.25   Zoot Sims] Jazz saxophone player (1925–1985). With his musical partner Al Cohn he collaborated with Kerouac on the album *Blues and Haikus* (1959).

347.27   Johnny Williams] Jazz drummer (1905–1984).

348.17   Dave Brubeck] Jazz pianist and composer (b. 1920).

354.17   *37th Chorus*] Kerouac's note on the typescript: "Except the top line, this was recited to me by lil Paul (nephew)."

364.13   Ferlinghetti] Lawrence Ferlinghetti (b. 1919), poet and publisher. His press City Lights published Kerouac's *The Scripture of the Golden Eternity* (1960), *Scattered Poems* (1971), and *Pomes All Sizes* (1992).

366.2   Lax] Probably a reference to the poet Robert Lax (1915–2000).

368.13   Lafcadio] Lafcadio Orlovsky, younger brother of Peter Orlovsky.

368.21–25   Ray Bremser . . . Leroi Jones . . . Diane di Prima] Bremser (1934–1998), poet, author of *Poems of Madness* (1965) and other books; LeRoi Jones

(b. 1934), later known as Amiri Baraka, poet, playwright, essayist (and publisher of Kerouac's *The Scripture of the Golden Eternity* at Totem Press); di Prima (b. 1934), poet, author of *This Kind of Bird Flies Backward* (1958) and other books.

372.31   Johnny Holmes] John Clellon Holmes (1926–1988), author of *Go* (1952) and *The Philosophy of the Beat Generation* (1958).

373.20   Frank O'hara] Frank O'Hara, poet (1926–1966), author of *Meditations in an Emergency* (1957), *Lunch Poems* (1964), and other books.

POMES ALL SIZES

379.29   Donner tragic Pass] The Donner party, a group of pioneers traveling to California by wagon train, were snowbound in the Sierra Nevada in the winter of 1846–47. Many died and some of the dead were allegedly eaten by the survivors.

382.16   *Neal*] Neal Cassady (1926–1968), Kerouac's close friend and the model for Dean Moriarty in *On the Road*.

384.6–8   Ivan . . . Dmitri] Protagonists of *The Brothers Karamazov*.

385.10   Carolyn] Carolyn Cassady (b. 1923), wife of Neal Cassady, author of the memoirs *Heart Beat* (1976) and *Off the Road* (1990).

387.1   *Robert Fournier*] Fournier (b. 1925) was the brother of Kerouac's friend Michael Fournier Jr.

396.18   Mayakaya] Sanskrit: "illusory body" or "mind essence."

398.1   Whalen] Philip Whalen (1923–2002), poet, author of *Like I Say* (1960), *On Bear's Head* (1969), and other books. He was a student of Buddhism who eventually became a Zen monk.

398.32   Lamantia] Philip Lamantia (1927–2005), poet, author of *Ekstasis* (1959), *Touch of the Marvelous* (1966), and other books.

401.2–4   Sravasti . . . Sahet-Mahet] Sravasti, ancient Indian city where Buddha is said to have lived a long time as a monk; Sahet-Mahet, modern names of the sites of the ruins of Sravasti.

401.15   Price's *Diamond Sutra*] A. F. Price's translation of the *Diamond Sutra* was published in England in 1947.

404.11   Vyakarana] Discipline of grammatical analysis applied to Sanskrit scriptures.

406.24   Rexroth] Kenneth Rexroth (1905–1982), poet, translator, and literary essayist; a central figure of the San Francisco literary scene.

409.16   Walter Lehrman] Photographer.

410.5   Gary Snyder Again] Kerouac's note on typescript: "(Noticed by Whalen)."

413.2 "The Tathagata doesn't exist"] Kerouac's note on typescript: "(Noticed by Ginsberg)."

417.2 *Jordan Belson*] Filmmaker (1926–2011), whose films include *Transmutation* (1947), *Bop-Scotch* (1952), and *Mandala* (1953).

418.20–23 Garver . . . Robert / Lavigne] Garver, see note 36.16–17; Robert LaVigne (b. 1928), painter.

426.15 *Zoco Chico*] Marketplace in Tangier.

426.23 *jamal*] Arabic: beauty.

428.5–6 Dedalus . . . Icarus] In Greek mythology, Daedalus fashioned wings of wax; his son flew with them and was drowned after the wings melted when he flew too close to the sun.

433.16 Harrison Act] The Harrison Narcotics Tax Act of 1914 regulated the use of opiates and cocaine.

434.3 *Chuangtse*] Taoist philosopher of the fourth century BCE.

436.23 *Louis Ferdinand Céline*] Louis-Ferdinand Céline, French novelist (1894–1961), author of *Journey to the End of the Night* (1932), *Death on the Installment Plan* (1936), and other books.

439.9 Father Duffy's statue] Francis P. Duffy (1871–1932), chaplain of the "Fighting 69th" infantry regiment, is commemorated with a statue at Duffy Square, on New York's Times Square.

439.25 Samsara] See note 261.16–21.

456.20 *Lou Little*] Football player and coach (1893–1979); he was football coach at Columbia from 1930 to 1956. He appears as a character in Kerouac's *Maggie Cassidy* (1959) under the name Lu Libble.

457.19 *Airapetianz*] E. S. Airapetianz, Russian scientist associated with the Pavlov Institute.

459.20–21 Sherwood's Anderson Ohio Ville / Story . . . hand,] The reference is to the short story "Hands" in Sherwood Anderson's *Winesburg, Ohio* (1919).

459.31 Conelrad] System of emergency broadcasting initiated by President Truman in 1951 and superseded in 1963 by the Emergency Broadcast System. The acronym stands for "control of electromagnetic radiation."

460.20 Tim McCoy] Col. Tim McCoy, army officer and movie actor (1891–1978) who starred in such films as *The One Way Trail* (1931), *Rusty Rides Alone* (1933), and *Code of the Rangers* (1938).

463.2 Mien Mo] In *Book of Dreams* (1960) Kerouac recounts a dream involving the Flying Horses of Mien Mo: "'Mien Mo,' I think, remembering the name of the Mountain in Burma they call the world . . . those Flying Horses are happy! How beautifully they claw slow fore-hooves thru the blue void!" Mien Mo also appears in *Big Sur* (1962).

464.25   Chu Yuan] Chinese poet (born c. 340 BCE) to whom is attributed the poem *Li Sao* (*Encountering Trouble*).

466.25–26   Li Po & / Tao Yuan Ming] Chinese poets of the T'ang and Six Dynasties periods, respectively; T'ao Yüan-ming is also known as T'ao Ch'ien.

469.1   Kasyapa] Vedic sage celebrated in Sanskrit scriptures.

470.7   weeds Ophelia] See *Hamlet* IV.vii: "When down the weedy trophies, and herself / Fell in the weeping brook."

470.8   Chatterton] Thomas Chatterton (1752–1770), English poet.

470.9   Wang Wei] Chinese poet of the T'ang dynasty.

471.18   *Doctor Sax*] Fantasy figure developed by Kerouac in many forms, notably in the novel *Doctor Sax* (1959).

471.23   Aristadamis Kaldis] Aristodimos Kaldis (1899–1979), Greek-born painter.

471.25   Daisetz Suzuki] D. T. Suzuki (1870–1966), Japanese writer and translator of books on Zen Buddhism; his works include *Essays in Zen Buddhism* (3 volumes, 1927–1934), *Manual of Zen Buddhism* (1934), and *Mysticism: Christian and Buddhist* (1957).

472.21–22   Bela / Lugosi & Boris Karloff] Stars, respectively, of the films *Dracula* (1931) and *Frankenstein* (1931).

473.17   *Charleen Whisnant*] Charleen Whisnant Swansea (b. 1934), poet, editor of *Red Clay Reader*.

475.17–18   "fen- / sucked fogs"] *King Lear* II.ii.358–360: "Infect her beauty, / You fen-sucked fogs, drawn by the powerful sun / To fall and blister!"

OLD ANGEL MIDNIGHT

479.1   OLD ANGEL MIDNIGHT] The Grey Fox Press edition of *Old Angel Midnight* (1993) includes, in an editor's note, a version of sections 50 and 51 lineated as verse, as they appeared in *New Directions in Prose & Poetry* no. 17 (New York: New Directions, 1961). It also includes the following related fragment, titled by the editor "A Piece of Old Angel Midnight," described as having been found by John Sampas among Kerouac's papers:

Tool the tirlishes down, mejems seemst Ide time Saturday or Nunday, one O shot shick razor cut and meating this is the sharp blade of grass cuts the innocent 'and when lambs bray—yay—and all the tapeboos & topatoos go cruing in Pakis Tanny the Loola Place where hides are bared, haired, & mared—or slunked with one axe head meat smap

That story you'se expectin O Brer Rabmollasoses you old Taird Tender Grant Cigared you at Appo ten thousand or more dead—daid—Eyes of Ray Charles see Me here realize O Holy

481.18   Bankei] See note 186.23.

482.19   continent of Mu] Lost continent hypothesized by Augustus Le Plon-
geon (1825–1908) and popularized by James Churchward in *The Lost Continent
of Mu: Motherland of Man* (1926).

483.1   Devadatta] Buddhist monk traditionally described as a cousin of the
Buddha.

483.12   Han Shan] See note 276.33.

483.20–21   Henry Millers . . . Rexroths . . . Creeley] Henry Miller (1891–
1980), American writer, author of *Tropic of Cancer* (1934), *Black Spring* (1936),
Tropic of Capricorn (1939), and other works, later a resident of Big Sur, where
Kerouac composed *Old Angel Midnight*; Kenneth Rexroth, see note 406.24;
Robert Creeley (1926–2005), poet, author of *For Love* (1962), *Words* (1965),
and other collections.

483.29–30   La religion . . . en dor.] Religion is shit! Not! Shit! I'm falling
asleep.

485.15   Trilling] Lionel Trilling (1905–1975), critic and teacher; Kerouac and
Allen Ginsberg were among his students at Columbia.

485.18   Allen Price Jones] Alan Pryce-Jones (1908–2000), English writer and
editor.

488.27   Chas Olson] Charles Olson (1910–1970), poet, author of *The Maximus
Poems* (1960–75).

489.6–7   Mickey / Spillane] Crime writer (1918–2006), author of *I, the Jury*
(1947), *My Gun Is Quick* (1950), and other novels featuring the private eye
Mike Hammer.

491.8   Sublette & Donlin] Al Sublette and Bob Donlin (1924–1996), friends
of Kerouac, the latter of whom appears in some of his writing as Bob Donneley.

491.20–21   Avalokitesvara] See note 13.11–12.

491.36   Mamie Eisenhour] Mamie Eisenhower (1896–1979), wife of President
Dwight Eisenhower. Her balance problems related to Ménière's disease led to
widespread rumors of alcoholism.

492.5   Lou Little] See note 456.20.

492.32–36   Bobby Mathews . . . Ed Crane . . . Geo Hooks Wiltse] Mathews
(1851–1898), Crane (1862–1896), and Wiltse (1879–1959), all major league base-
ball pitchers.

493.7   Peer Engeli] Pier Angeli (1932–1971), Italian-born film actress who
appeared in *The Silver Chalice* (1954) and *Somebody Up There Likes Me* (1956).

493.13   Anita Ekberg] Swedish-born film actress (b. 1931), featured in *Hollywood
or Bust* (1956), *Screaming Mimi* (1958), *La Dolce Vita* (1960), and other films.

493.35   Karuna] Sanskrit: compassion.

494.32   Bob Kauffman] Bob Kaufman (1925–1986), poet, author of *Solitudes Crowded with Loneliness* (1965), *Golden Sardine* (1967), and other books.

496.21   Bosatsu] Japanese: bodhisattva.

496.21   Gregory Corso] See note 6.2.

496.27   Jean Marais] French actor (1913–1998), whose many films included Jean Cocteau's *Beauty and the Beast* (1946), *Les Parents terribles* (1948), and *Orpheus* (1950).

497.4   Prez] Lester Young (see note 29.22).

499.12–13   Balzac . . . *Cousine Bette*] Honoré de Balzac's novel *La Cousine Bette* appeared in 1846.

501.4–5   Tchelitchev Tree of Life] *Hide and Seek* (1940–42) by the Russian-born painter Pavel Tchelitchew (1898–1957).

503.6   laird Cregar'd] Laird Cregar (1913–1944), film actor who played menacing roles in *The Lodger* (1944) and *Hangover Square* (1945).

510.2   Hamnet] Son (1585–1596) of William Shakespeare and Anne Hathaway.

510.24   Danny & the Juniors] Doo-wop group known for "At the Hop" (1957) and "Rock and Roll Is Here to Stay" (1958).

511.2   Basie in London] Album featuring the Count Basie Band, actually recorded in Sweden in 1956.

512.5   Manjusri] Bodhisattva embodying *prajna* (wisdom).

513.19   Bardo] Tibetan: intermediate state between death and reincarnation.

521.15–16   Von Braun] Wernher von Braun (1912–1977), German rocket engineer who after developing weaponry during World War II worked for the American space program.

522.20   Stanley Gould] Hipster and poet (1926–1985), model for the character Ross Wallenstein in *The Subterraneans*.

DESOLATION POPS

532.14   Nat Wills] Vaudeville star (1873–1917).

535.18   Skhandas] In Buddhist tradition, causes of attachment, and thus of suffering.

536.10   Hanshan] See note 276.33.

536.22   Dipankara] A Buddha of the past, sometimes depicted as having lived eons before Gautama Siddhartha.

BOOK OF HAIKUS

543.20   Yoka Daishi] Chinese Zen master (665–713).

545.10   Gandharvas] Spirit beings in Hindu and Buddhist tradition. "We just think that we are dying when we die. It is like the castle of the Gandharvas, castles in the air . . . a world reflected in a mirror—the end." (Jack Kerouac, letter to Carolyn Cassady, May 17, 1954).

549.5   Whippenpoofers] The Wiffenpoofs, the oldest collegiate a capella singing group in America, founded at Yale in 1909.

558.4   Albert Saijo] Japanese-American poet (1926–2011) who collaborated with Kerouac and Lew Welch on the book *Trip Trap* (1959), a collection of haikus written during a cross-country trip.

559.4   Memère] Kerouac's affectionate name for his mother.

559.21   Mary Carney] See note 287.2.

566.6   Manjuri] See note 512.5.

UNCOLLECTED POEMS

575.33   Runyon] Damon Runyon (1880–1946), journalist and fiction writer.

580.21   "Who has known fury?"] See Thomas Wolfe, *Of Time and the River*: "Who has known fury striding in the storm? Who has been mad with fury in his youth, given no rest or peace or certitude by fury, driven on across the earth by fury, until the great vine of the heart was broke, the sinews wrenched, the little tenement of bone, blood, marrow, brain, and feeling in which great fury raged, was twisted, wrung, depleted, worn out, and exhausted by the fury which it could not lose or put away? Who has known fury, how it came?"

591.1   *"He is your friend, let him dream"*] A prose version of this poem is included in *Visions of Cody*.

592.1   *Doctor Sax*] See note 471.18.

602.24   Reynolds' Blue Boy] *The Blue Boy* (1770) was in fact painted by Thomas Gainsborough (1727–1788).

604.14   Gerard] See note 15.23.

605.9–12   Leroi . . . Lucien . . . Cessa . . . Dody] Leroi, see note 368.21–25; Lucien, see note 247.22; Cessa, wife of Lucien Carr; Dody Müller, artist.

608.5–10   Roy Campanella . . . John L Sullivan . . . Tiny Tim] Campanella (1921–1993), catcher for the Brooklyn Dodgers; Sullivan (1858–1918), heavyweight boxing champion defeated by Jim Corbett in 1892; Tiny Tim, character in Charles Dickens's *A Christmas Carol* (1843) known for his phrase "God bless us, every one."

609.1   Stella . . . Sebastian] Stella Sampas Kerouac, Kerouac's third wife; Sebastian "Sam" Sampas, boyhood friend of Kerouac, Stella's younger brother.

609.8–19   Henri Cru . . . Phil Whalen . . . Bob Donlin] Cru (1921–1992), classmate of Kerouac at Horace Mann and a lifelong friend; Whalen, see note 398.1; Donlin, see note 491.8.

611.16   *Harpo Marx*] Comedian (1888–1964), who starred with his brothers in *Animal Crackers* (1930), *Horse Feathers* (1932), *Duck Soup* (1933), *A Night at the Opera* (1935), and other films.

614.26   André Gill] French caricaturist (1840–1885), an acquaintance of Rimbaud.

620.16–21   Les poisons . . . parle] The fishes of the sea / speak Breton— / My name is Lebris / de Keroack— / Speak, fishes, Loti, / speak—

629.35–37   "*On est toutes . . . la mer*] "We are completely hidden, eat / the silence," say the fishes of the / sea—

630.4–7   *Je ne suis pas . . . toutes!*] I'm not bad when I'm / at peace—in the storms / I shout! Like a lunatic! / I eat, I tear everything!

640.11   *Al Gelpi*] Albert Gelpi, literary scholar, a friend of Kerouac.

641.1   *Edward Dahlberg*] Writer (1900–1977), author of *The Flea of Sodom* (1950), *The Sorrows of Priapus* (1957), *Because I Was Flesh* (1964), and other works.

641.9   Chang Su Chi] Chang Shu-Chi (1901–1957), Chinese painter.

643.21   Inky Dinky Parly Voo] "Mademoiselle from Armentières," song popular among troops in World War I.

644.19   Samsara] See note 261.16–21.

649.19–21   Spring dusk . . . A bird] From *Maggie Cassidy* (1953).

650.1–3   Walking along . . . the boulevard] From *Lonesome Traveler* (1960); written 1957.

650.4–9   Grain elevators . . . to come home] From *Trip Trap* (1959).

650.10–652.6   On Starvation Ridge . . . Girls come by shades] From *Desolation Angels* (1965).

653.16–18   Lysander . . . Demetrius . . . Hermia] Characters in Shakespeare's *A Midsummer Night's Dream*.

657.16   Sambaghakaya, Nirvanakaya, Dharmakaya] Sanskrit: the three bodies of Buddha according to the Trikaya doctrine, namely Body of Bliss, Created Body, and Truth Body.

663.12   Jimmy Durante] Comedian, musician, and actor (1893–1980).

663.17   Reichian] Pertaining to the psychological theories of Wilhelm Reich (1897–1957), author of *The Function of the Orgasm* (1927), *Character Analysis* (1933), and other works.

683.13   Apassionata Sonata] Beethoven's Piano Sonata no. 23.

684.11–12   Yellow River . . . Li Po] According to legend the T'ang dynasty poet Li Po died while trying to embrace the moon's reflection in the Yellow River.

689.7   Chou en Lai] Chou En-lai, Communist leader (1898–1976), premier of the People's Republic of China, 1949–1976.

691.17   Coleman Hawkins] Jazz musician (1904–1969), often regarded as the first important tenor saxophone stylist.

Index

THE LIBRARY OF AMERICA SERIES

THE LIBRARY OF AMERICA, a nonprofit publisher, is dedicated to publishing, and keeping in print, authoritative editions of America's best and most significant writing. Each year the Library adds new volumes to its collection of essential works by America's foremost novelists, poets, essayists, journalists, and statesmen.

If you would like to request a free catalog and find out more about The Library of America, please visit www.loa.org/catalog or send us an e-mail at lists@loa.org with your name and address. Include your e-mail address if you would like to receive our occasional newsletter with items of interest to readers of classic American literature and exclusive interviews with Library of America authors and editors (we will never share your e-mail address).

To subscribe to the series or to order individual copies, please visit www.loa.org or call (800) 964.5778.

This book is set in 10 point ITC Galliard Pro, a face designed for digital composition by Matthew Carter and based on the sixteenth-century face Granjon. The paper is acid-free lightweight opaque and meets the requirements for permanence of the American National Standards Institute. The binding material is Brillianta, a woven rayon cloth made by Van Heek-Scholco Textielfabrieken, Holland. Composition by David Bullen Design. Printing by Malloy Incorporated. Binding by Dekker Book-binding. Designed by Bruce Campbell.

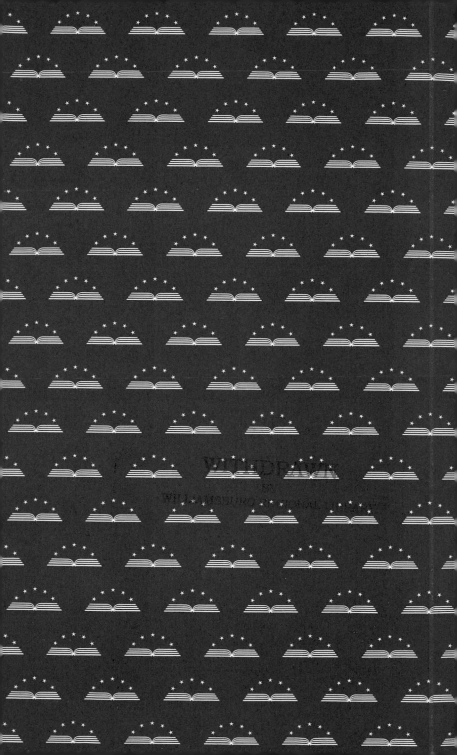